AFGHANISTAN

AFGHANISTAN

GRAVEYARD OF EMPIRES:
A NEW HISTORY *of the* BORDERLANDS

DAVID ISBY

PEGASUS BOOKS
NEW YORK

To the memory of Mohammed Malik Mehrodin,
who, in Kabul on 3 November 2008, while unarmed,
prevented the kidnapping by terrorists of a foreign aid worker.

AFGHANISTAN

Pegasus Books LLC
80 Broad Street, 5th Floor
New York, NY 10004

Copyright © 2010 by David Isby

First Pegasus Books edition January 2010

Revised edition June 2011
Interior design by Maria Fernandez

Library of Congress Cataloging-in-Publication Data is available.

ISBN: 978-1-60598-189-5

10 9 8 7 6 5 4 3 2 1

Printed in the United States of America
Distributed by W. W. Norton & Company

"Afghanistan has been known over the years as the graveyard of empires. We cannot take that history lightly."

—GEN David H. Petraeus, USA, 2009

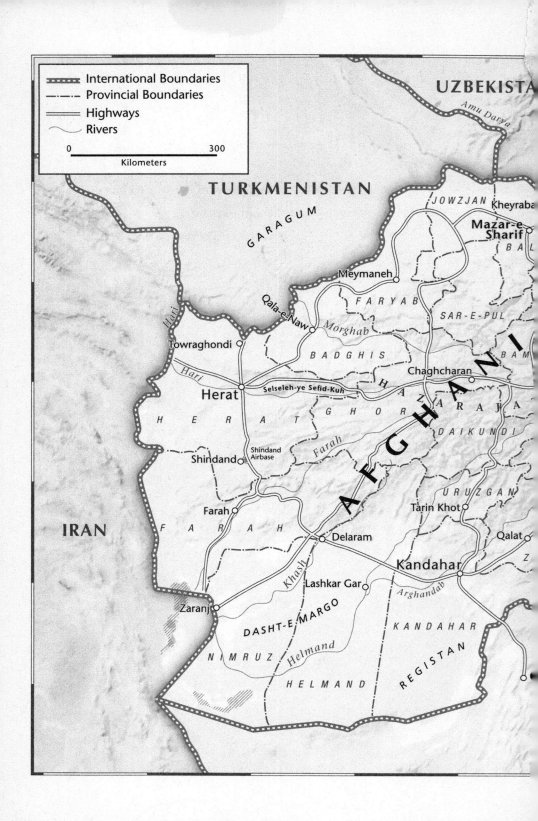

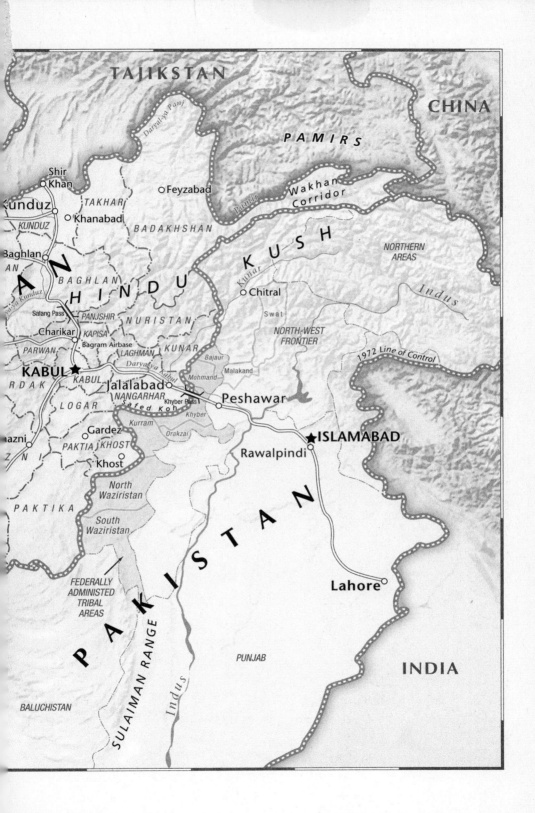

CONTENTS

GLOSSARY
xi

CHRONOLOGY
xvii

PROLOGUE
OUT OF THE VORTEX
1

PART ONE
LANDS IN THE VORTEX
19

CHAPTER ONE
AFGHANISTAN: A COUNTRY DEFINED BY CONFLICTS
21

CHAPTER TWO
DWELLERS IN THE VORTEX
61

CHAPTER THREE
PAKISTAN IN THE VORTEX
89

PART TWO
THREATS FROM THE VORTEX
105

CHAPTER FOUR
TRANSNATIONAL TERRORISM
107

CHAPTER FIVE
AFGHAN INSURGENTS
130

CHAPTER SIX
AFGHAN NARCOTICS
170

CHAPTER SEVEN
AFGHANISTAN'S INTERNAL CONFLICTS
187

CHAPTER EIGHT
PAKISTAN'S INSURGENCY
244

———

PART THREE
WINNING THE CONFLICTS
289

CHAPTER NINE
COUNTERING AFGHANISTAN'S INSURGENCY
291

CHAPTER TEN
AID AND DEVELOPMENT
333

CHAPTER ELEVEN
CONCLUSION: THE FUTURE
368

———

AFTERWORD
399

ACKNOWLEDGMENTS
401

SOURCES
405

INDEX
437

GLOSSARY

AB: Airbase.

Al Qaeda: Literally "the base," transnational Islamic terrorist organization associated with Osama bin Laden.

Alim: (plural, ulema) Islamic clergy.

ANA: Afghan National Army.

AMF: Afghan Military Force (now disbanded).

Amir: Leader.

ANP: Afghan National Police.

ANP: Awami National Party, Pakistan; primarily Pushtun members, dates to pre-partition nationalism. Winner of 2008 election in NWFP.

ANSF: Afghan National Security Forces (including ANA and ANP).

AP: Associated Press.

Barevli: School of Islamic practice originating in the subcontinent. Influenced by Sufic and traditional practices.

Baluchi: Ethnolinguistic group, native to Pakistan, Afghanistan, and Iran. Sunni Muslim, in Pakistan their tribal system remains strong under the leadership of hereditary sardars.

BG: Brigadier General.

Bonn conference/process: Transition to constitutional rule in Afghanistan, 2001–05. Process started with a conference at the Petersburgerhof resort near Bonn, Germany, in 2001 and included the Emergency Loya Jirga, Constitutional Loya Jirga, the 2004 presidential and 2005 parliamentary elections.

CF: Canadian Forces.

CN: Counter narcotics.

COL/Col.: Colonel (US Army/other).

Constitutional Loya Jirga: Meeting of 502 delegates that drafted the current Afghan constitution, meeting in Kabul December 2003 to January 2004. The draft constitution was not voted on but was adopted by consensus.

Darbar: Ritualized assembly by a leadership figure to receive pledges of loyalty and provide benefits to clients.

Deobandi: School of Islam established in India following 1857 and the rise of British rule. Deobandi practices aimed to return to Islamic roots and away from influences from the subcontinent and Sufic practices. Influenced by but distinct from Wahabism.

Durand Line: Current border between Afghanistan and Pakistan, which largely follows the line established by an 1893 treaty, surveyed under orders of Sir Mortimer Durand. No Afghan government has ever accepted the permanence of the Durand line, while all British and Pakistani ones have.

Durrani: The main Pushtun tribal grouping of southern Afghanistan. Except for 1930 and 1978–2001, all Afghan heads of state have been Durrani.

Falah-e-Insaniat: Successor group to Lashkar-e-Taiba, Pakistani group, name changed following 2008 Mumbai terrorist attack.

FATA: Federally Administered Tribal Areas. Seven agencies administered by the Pakistani federal government. All separate the Durand Line from NWFP. From south to north, consists of: South Waziristan, North Waziristan, Kurram, Orakzai, Khyber, Mohmand, and Bajaur.

Fatwa: Muslim religious edict, issued by an alim, having the force of law.

FCR: Frontier Crimes Regulations, with British colonial (1901) origins that apply in the FATA rather than the laws of Pakistan.

Frontier Corps: Pakistani paramilitary formations, established by the British, of Pushtuns recruited to serve in the FATA and nearby areas. Under the Ministry of the Interior. Commanded by seconded army officers. Pushtuns do not serve in their home areas. The main uniformed force in the FATA.

Frontier Constabulary: Pakistani national police formation.

FR: Frontier region. One of six regions in the NWFP with special (FATA-like) legal status.

GEN: General (US Army).

Ghilzay: A major Pushtun tribal grouping of south-central and eastern Afghanistan. Sometimes seen as rivals to the Durrani for power.

GIRoA: Government of Islamic Republic of Afghanistan (post-2001).

Golden Age: Normally used, with or without irony (depending on politics), to describe the later years of the reign of the former King Zahir, 1949–73, notable for experiments with democracy, increased centralization of power, and ultimately setting the stage for the conflicts of 1978–2001.

Governance: How communities regulate themselves to preserve social order and maintain security; different from government, ruling by state authority over the population.

Harakat-ul-Mujahideen: Party formed for cross-border insurgency from Pakistan into Kashmir. Recruited from Afghan and Pakistani Pushtuns.

Haram: Unclean for Muslims.

Hawala: Afghan money transfer system with international links; hundi is Pakistani equivalent.

Hazara Jat: Land of the Hazaras, region in central Afghanistan cutting across several provinces.

Hoqooq: Local traditional dispute resolution body, especially dealing with land and water disputes.

HiH: Hezb-e-Islami party of Gulbuddin Hekmatyar, one of the Peshawar seven 1978–02, waged civil war against ISA 1992–96, joined insurgents post-2001.

HuT: Hezb-ut-Tahrir. Transnational Muslim group advocating a worldwide Khalifait, explicitly eschewing violence.

IEA: Islamic Emirate of Afghanistan (Taliban regime 1996–2001).

IRA: Islamic Republic of Afghanistan (post-2001).

ISI: Inter Service Intelligence directorate (Pakistan). Primarily the military's "directed telescope" inside Pakistan, it has, as a secondary mission, planned and executed Pakistan's Afghanistan policies since the 1970s, often to the exclusion of other governmental institutions.

JIA: Jamiat-e-Islami-Afghanistan. Islamist political party with roots in Kabul pre-1978. Leader Dr. Burnhaddin Rabbani. Members included Ahmad Shah Massoud and Ismail Khan. Largely Dari-speaking. One of the Peshawar Seven parties 1978–92. Participated in ISA government 1992–1996.

JI: Jamaat-e-Islami. Oldest Pakistani religious party. Supporter of Afghan Taliban, HiH and Hezb-ul-Mujahideen, Jamaat-e-Islami Kashmir, and terrorist organizations. Opposed to JIA, sees US as leading an anti-Pakistan alliance.

Jihad: Holy war. In Islam, can be internal (in the soul of the believer) or external (against an outside force).

Jirga: Afghan meeting for collective decision-making or dispute resolution, similar to *shura* but less likely to be a standing body.

JeM: Jaish-e-Muhammad. Formed to take part in cross-border insurgency in Kashmir, recruited mainly in Punjab. Successor to Harakat-ul-Mujahideen.

JUI: Jamiat-ul-Ulema-e-Islam. Pakistan religious party, ally of HiH pre-1996 (part of MMA). Runs the largest network of Deobandi-influenced madrassas in Pakistan.

Kandak: Battalion in ANA.

khan: Term of respect, especially for a patron but also for anyone in secular authority.

LeT: Lashkar-e-Taiba, formed to take part in Kashmir insurgency, involved in 2008 Mumbai terrorist attack, declared a terrorist organization by UN.

Lok Sabha: Lower house of the Indian parliament, subjected to a high-profile terrorist attack in 2001 by Lashkar-e-Taiba.

LTG: Lieutenant General.

Madrassa: Muslim religious school. Maderi is plural, although madrassas is colloquial English usage. May be free-standing or associated with a mosque (*deeni maderi*).

Majlis-e-shura: Requirement for an Islamic government to have consultation, or a body set up to provide such consultation.

Malik: Pushtun tribal figure that provides interface with the government. In Pushtun, appointed by the government, became a hereditary position in some tribes.

Maulavi: Alim associated with a madrassa, often *deeni maderi* associated with a mosque.

MG: Major General.

MMA: Muttahida Majlis-e-Amal. Popularly known as the "Mullah and Musharraf alliance," a coalition of Pakistani religious political parties that, after the 2002 elections, formed governments in NWFP and Baluchistan.

IEA: Islamic Emirate of Afghanistan (Taliban).

IRoA: Islamic Republic of Afghanistan (post–2001).

ISA: Islamic State of Afghanistan (Northern Alliance supported, 1992–2001).

LTG: Lieutenant General.

NDS: National Directorate of Security (post-2001 Afghanistan intelligence service), the Amaniyat (literally, security). Also abbreviated NSD.

Northern Alliance: Pro-ISA, anti-HiH and Taliban coalition 1992–2001 mainly of Tajik, Hazara, and Uzbek groups which included substantial Pushtun allies in the form of Dr. Abdurrab Rasul Sayyaf Ittehad-e-Islami (one of the Peshawar Seven) and the Nangarhar shura of Haji Qadir (previously part of HiK) plus a number of Pushtun leaders that were opposed to the Taliban, including Hamid Karzai, who became president of Afghanistan. Ahmad Shah Massoud was the major figure associated with the Northern Alliance.

NSP: National Solidarity Program.

NWFP: North West Frontier Province. One of the four original provinces of Pakistan, renamed Khyber Pakhtunkhwa in 2010.

Orientalism: Projecting a self-made and culturally biased understanding of a foreign culture, regardless of fact.

PATA: Provincially Administered Tribal Areas in NWFP. Laws of Pakistan normally apply, with modifications, in these areas. Swat is a PATA.

Peshawar: Capital and largest city of NWFP, on traditional trade routes from the subcontinent to Afghanistan through the Khyber Pass. Headquarters of the Sunni Afghan resistance parties in 1978–92.

Peshawar Seven: The seven Sunni Afghan resistance parties supported by Pakistan during the 1978–92 conflict with headquarters in Peshawar. All except JIA were led by and predominantly composed of ethnic Pushtuns.

PIB: Pakistan Intelligence Bureau. Pakistan's civilian-based intelligence agency (CIA equivalent). Secondary to ISI under military governments, has been emphasized by some elected governments but has never been allowed to control Afghanistan policy.

Pir: Saint in human form, holy man. Important in traditional Afghan Islam as a focus of devotion. Can be hereditary. Considered unIslamic by Deobandi and especially Wahabi influenced Islam.

PRC: People's Republic of China.

Purdah: Literally "veil," the practice of female separation from non-family members in the private sphere of life.

Qawm (also quam): Afghan affinity group, a building block of Afghan society. Based on blood ties, ethnicity, locality, religious practice, or other bonds.

Qazi: Alim learned in Sharia law.

Salafi: Fundamentalist Islamic movement that aims to recreate the practices of the first generation of Muslim believers.

Sardar: Hereditary Baluch tribal leader, having much stronger and more unitary authority than a Pushtun tribal chief.

Sayid: Descendant of the Prophet Mohammed.

Sipah-e-Sahaba: Pakistani terrorist group with roots in violence against Shia landlords in south Punjab. Participated in conflicts in Kashmir, Afghanistan (where they committed atrocities against Afghan Shias), and the FATA.

Sharia: The body of Islamic religious law, Sunni and Shia. The legal framework within which the public and private aspects of life are regulated.

Shomali Plain: Fertile agricultural area to the north of Kabul, subjected to ethnic cleansing and scorched-earth policies by Al Qaeda-inspired Taliban in the late 1990s.

Shura: Body for collective decision-making and dispute resolution. Usually comprised of a number of local elder males with a claim to some legitimate authority.

Shura-e-Nazar: Council of the North, Became part of Northern Alliance, organization founded by Ahmad Shah Massoud in 1980s.

SSG: Special Security Group, Pakistan Army special operations forces.

Sufi (Sufic): The inner, mystical dimension of Islam, applicable to Sunni and Shia Islam. As a mystic in direct personal communion with the infinite, there is tension between the Sufi and the alim, who has an intervening role between the two.

Tablighi Jamaat: Deobandi-influenced Muslim organization, publically eschewing political violence. Believed to operate worldwide and have tens of millions of members.

Takfir: Muslims that are worse than infidels. The Al Qaeda-Taliban definition of these individuals is shared by few genuine theologians, who dispute whether this is a valid categorization.

TNSM: Tehrik-e-Nafaz-e-Shariat-e-Mohammed. Founded by Sufi Mohammed and son-in-law "radio mullah" Fazlullah. Operates in Bajaur, Swat, and NWFP.

Transport Mafia: Colloquial name used to describe many predominantly Pushtun firms that handle Pakistan's inter-city and international truck traffic.

TTP: Tehrik-e-Taliban Pakistan. Coalition of Pakistan Islamic radical insurgent movements, under Behtullah Mehsud.

Wahabi: Islamic movement originating in Saudi Arabia, aiming to implement a "pure" Islam free from local or traditional accretions.

Westphalia: Treaty of 1648 often cited as creating the modern nation-state system.

CHRONOLOGY

1709:	Kandahar revolts under Ghilzay chief Mir Wais Hotaki, secedes from Persian Empire.
1747:	Pushtun chief Ahmad Shah Durrani conquers Kandahar, Ghazni and Kabul, establishes a kingdom and dynasty.
1776:	Capital moves to Kabul from Kandahar.
1839–42:	First Anglo-Afghan War.
1849:	Second Sikh War ends. British annexation of Peshawar and most of what is now NWFP.
1857:	Indian Mutiny. End of HEIC, British imperial rule established in India, replacing Mughal Empire, leads to crisis in Islamic politics in the subcontinent.
1878–80:	Second Anglo-Afghan War. War ends with Afghan acceptance of most terms of the Treaty of Gandamack. Afghanistan gives Britain control of foreign policy in return for support for Kabul government, but retains sovereignty.
1880–1901:	Reign of King Abdur Rahman, "the iron amir" who created the institution of Afghanistan nationhood, consolidating rule from Kabul by force of arms.
1893:	Durand Line created.
1919:	Third Afghanistan War. Kabul tries to raise tribes on British side of the Durand Line.
1919–29:	Reign of King Amanullah in Afghanistan, identified with nationalism, reform, and modernization.
1919:	Amritsar massacre in the Punjab. Start of popular movement for decolonization in the subcontinent.
1921:	Anglo-Afghan Treaty. Afghanistan regains control over foreign affairs from New Delhi.
1926:	Treaty of Neutrality and Friendship with the Soviet Union.
1928–31:	Civil wars in Afghanistan. Following a revolt against the modernizer King Amanullah in 1927, he abdicated in 1929 in favor of his brother Enyatullah. He was succeeded by as king by Habibullah Kalakani (executed 1929) and Mohammed Nadir, who repeals most of Amanullah's reforms (assassinated 1933).

1929:	Tajik leader Habibullah Kalakani (also known as Bacha-e-Saqao) seizes power for nine months.
1933:	Zahir crowned king of Afghanistan, reigns until 1973.
1944–46:	Safi Revolt. Kunar valley ethnically cleansed of Safi Pushtuns.
1947:	Partition of Indian Empire.
1947–49:	First conflict in Kashmir. Pakistan recruits *lashkars* of Pushtuns from both Afghanistan and Pakistan.
1949:	Golden Age starts in Afghanistan, with experimental reform, democratic measures, foreign aid from Soviet Union and US.
1961–63:	Years of deteriorating relationship between Afghanistan and Pakistan. Afghanistan's claims to Pushtunistan lead Pakistan to close the border to trade.
1965:	Indo-Pakistani war. Afghanistan remains neutral.
1970:	First year rains fail in Afghanistan. Leads to widespread crop failures in 1970–73; hardship in rural Afghanistan hurts Kabul's legitimacy.
1971:	Pakistan loses war with India, resulting in secession of East Pakistan as Bangladesh. Afghanistan remains neutral. Pakistan starts looking at countering India through "strategic depth" and Islamic approaches that would provide international strength and threaten India; both affect Afghanistan.
17 July 1973:	King Zahir overthrown in bloodless coup by his cousin, former Prime Minister Prince Mohammed Daoud. End of Golden Age. Afghanistan declared a republic.
July 1975:	"Panjshir revolt" by Pakistan-trained Islamists. Religious leaders also lead uprisings in Badakhshan, Jalalabad, Laghman, and Paktia.
28 April 1978:	Military putsch by Communist Khalqi army officers in Kabul. Daoud and many others in his family and leadership—secular and religious—murdered. People's Democratic Republic of Afghanistan (PDRA) established.
May 1978:	Start of widespread arrests and executions.
Summer 1978:	Start of largest national rising of the twentieth century in Afghanistan.
21 March 1979:	Herat uprising against Soviets leads to increased military intervention, use of firepower.
1979:	Start of external aid, largely routed via Government of Pakistan (especially ISI) for the Afghan resistance. US, China, Saudi Arabia, many other countries supply funding but Pakistan

	insists on a monopoly on resource allocation.
27 December 1979:	Soviet invasion, new Parcham-dominated Afghan government put in place under Babrak Karmal.
1986:	Najibullah (Parcham former secret police chief and ethnic but detribalized Pushtun) put into place as head of pro-Soviet Republic of Afghanistan, replacing Babrak Karmal.
February 1989:	Soviet combat forces withdraw from Afghanistan.
April 1992:	Collapse of Najibullah regime in Kabul, fighting between Afghan groups over city.
August 1992:	Resumed fighting—HiH rocket attacks on Kabul.
5 November 1994:	Taliban occupy Kandahar.
10 May 1996:	Bin Laden arrives in Jalalabad as guest of ISA's Nangarhar Shura, who remember him from the anti-Soviet war.
27 September 1996:	Kabul falls to Taliban.
2000:	ISI dissatisfaction with Taliban, leads to study to plan "Taliban light" as replacement.
21 March 2001:	Destruction of Bamiyan Buddhas by Taliban demonstrates radicalization, Al Qaeda influence.
9 September 2001:	Assassination of Ahmad Shah Massoud by Al Qaeda.
11 September 2001:	Multiple terrorist attacks in US by Al Qaeda.
19 September 2001:	First US intelligence and special operations forces enter Afghanistan.
7 October 2001:	First US airstrikes in Afghanistan.
9 November 2001:	Mazar-e-Sharif entered by ISA forces.
13 November 2001:	Kabul entered by ISA forces, ignoring US appeal to stay out.
14–24 November 2001:	"Airlift of evil," Pakistan permitted to airlift ISI and other forces fighting the ISA from Kunduz before Taliban surrender.
10 December 2001:	Kandahar abandoned by Afghan Taliban; last major city held by them in Afghanistan.
22 December 2001:	Bonn agreement. Hamid Karzai becomes president of Afghan Interim Government, later Transitional government.
23 December 2001:	Terrorist attack on Indian Parliament.
January 2002:	Operation Anaconda. Al Qaeda and Taliban forces retreat from Afghanistan into Pakistan.
20–28 January 2002:	Tokyo Conference.
March 2002:	Initial ISAF deployment to Kabul begins.
21 March 2002:	State schools reopen in Afghanistan on a nationwide basis.

15 April 2002:	Former king Zahir returns to Afghanistan, later appears at Emergency and Constitutional Loya Jirgas, receives title of "Father of the Nation."
June 2002:	Emergency Loya Jirga in Afghanistan; 1,500 delegates selected through indirect UN-supervised elections select head of state (Karzai) and other key officials.
10 October 2002:	Provincial elections in Pakistan. Rise of MMA seen as reaction to defeat of Taliban.
July 2003:	ISAF "NATO-ized," first ground forces commitment in history of alliance.
September 2003:	National Solidarity Program (NSP) established.
November 2003:	US Ambassador Zalmay Khailzad arrives in Kabul.
December 2003 –Janaury 2004:	Constitutional Loya Jirga in Afghanistan. 500 delegates and 50 appointed member debate and approve Afghan constitution. Islamic Republic of Afghanistan established. Hamid Karzai is president of transitional government.
December 2003:	Assassination attempts against Musharraf (two).
11 March 2004:	Madrid train station bombings.
April 2004:	South Waziristan peace accord with insurgents.
9 October 2004:	Presidential elections in Afghanistan. Hamid Karzai elected president of the Islamic Republic of Afghanistan.
February 2005:	Second South Waziristan peace accord.
June 2005:	US Ambassador Zalmay Khailzad departs Kabul.
7 July 2005:	London transport bombings.
18 September 2005:	Parliamentary elections in Afghanistan.
October 2005:	Afghanistan National Development Strategy (ANDS) drafted as roadmap for Afghan and international efforts.
8 October –December 2005:	Earthquake in northern Pakistan and subsequent relief efforts. Pakistan Army relief efforts widely perceived as inadequate.
31 January 2005:	London Conference, initial draft of Afghanistan Compact approved, Initial Afghan National Development Strategy introduced.
7 August 2006:	Transatlantic airline bombing plot by Al Qaeda exposed.
September 2006:	Waziristan Peace accord signed at Miranshah.
April 2007:	Musharraf attempted removal of Chief Justice Iftikhar. Mohammed Chaudry starts crisis.
17 July 2007:	Former King Zahir Shah dies.

29 July 2007:	Lal Masjid incident in Islamabad. Pakistan security forces move against radical mosque associated with insurgents.
9–13 August 2007:	First peace jirga in Kabul with Musharraf and Karzai.
6 October 2007:	Musharraf reelected by national and provincial assemblies, oppositions boycott elections.
3 November 2007:	Musharraf declares state of emergency.
December 2007:	Pakistan Taliban unites under TTP umbrella organization.
27 December 2007:	Assassination of Benazir Bhutto.
18 February 2008:	Election in Pakistan. PPP wins largest share of vote.
12 June 2008:	Paris conference on Afghanistan.
18 August 2008:	Resignation of Pakistan's President Musharraf.
26–27 November 2008:	Mumbai is site of apparent Lashkar-e-Taiba terrorist attack, evidence points to it being launched from Pakistan.
16 February 2009:	NWFP government makes agreement with TNSM giving them effective control of Swat valley.
February 2009:	Pakistan military launches offensive in South Waziristan, withdraws after inflicting heavy casualties on insurgents.
March 2009:	Political crisis in Pakistan as Supreme Court blocks former Prime Minister Nawaz Sharif of the Pakistan Muslim League-Nawaz from holding office. Resolved, followed by return to office of Chief Justice Chaudry.
27 March 2009:	US Obama administration announces strategic review, appointment of Ambassador Richard Holbrooke as special envoy of Afghanistan and Pakistan ("AfPak").
25 April–June 2009:	Pakistan military launches two-division operation to reclaim Swat from TNSM.
5 August 2009:	Death of TTP leader Behtullah Mehsud in US UAV attack.
20 August 2009:	Afghan presidential elections lead to widespread accusations of fraud.
August 2009:	McChrystal report. Assessment of situation in Afghanistan leaked to press, leads to prolonged public consideration of request for more US military personnel to deploy to Afghanistan.
17 October 2009:	Pakistan military launches offensive into South Waziristan.
1 November 2009:	Afghan presidential election runoff prevented by concession of Dr. Abdullah.
25 November 2009:	Pakistan announces it will prosecute seven alleged planners of the Mumbai attack.

1 December 2009:	US presidential address on Afghanistan announces additional troop deployments but concentrates on an exit strategy, with troop withdrawals to begin in 2011.
January 2010:	London Conference. Priority put on negotiation and reconciliation.
February 2010:	Coalition offensive to break insurgent control in Helmand province begins, starting with Marjah district.
7 February 2010:	Mullah Birader, senior Taliban leader, captured by Pakistani authorities. Reportedly released later in 2010.
May 2010:	National Consultative Peace Jirga held in Kabul.
June 2010:	Coalition military operations begin to break insurgent control in western Kandahar province.
6 June 2010:	Interior minister Mohammed Hanif Atmar and NDS head Amrullah Saleh sacked by Karzai.
14 June 2010:	Regional Command-South West split off from Regional Command-South.
23 June 2010:	GEN McChrystal relieved following making statements to the press critical of US civilian leadership. Replaced by GEN Petraeus.
July 2010:	Intense flooding in Pakistan begins - major humanitarian and developmental disaster.
1 August 2010:	Netherlands military forces withdraw from Afghanistan. Police training to be retained. Canadian combat forces to follow by end of 2011.
September 2010:	Increasing UAV strikes and special operations targeting mid-level Afghan insurgent leadership and IED makers.
18 September 2010:	Parliamentary elections in Afghanistan. Security issues prevents voting in many districts in south and east.
1 October 2010:	Government of Pakistan starts temporary halt of all logistics shipments to coalition forces in Afghanistan.
November 2010:	NATO Lisbon summit sets 2014 target for ANSF security take-over.
13 December 2010:	Ambassador Richard Holbrooke dies, replaced by Marc Grossman.
1 May 2011:	Osama Bin Laden, the head of Al Qaeda, was assassinated by U.S. military forces in Abbottabad, Pakistan.

OUT OF THE VORTEX

"The vortex is the point of maximum energy. All experience rushes into this vortex. All the energized past, all the past that is living and worthy to live. All MOMENTUM, which is the past bearing upon us, RACE, RACE-MEMORY, instinct charging the PLACID, NON-ENERGIZED FUTURE. The DESIGN of the future is in the grip of the human vortex. All the past that is vital, all the past that is capable of living into the future, is pregnant in the vortex, NOW!"

—Ezra Pound, "The Turbine,"
BLAST, no. 1, 20 June 1914.

They do not read a lot of Ezra Pound in South Waziristan, the Bajaur Agency of Pakistan, or the Doia Chopan district of Afghanistan's Zabul province. If they did, some of the bearded hard men with their Kalashnikovs, laptop computers, Korans, and limitless faith in their cause would undoubtedly find his description appealing. The capital letters and demands for immediate action to sweep away a bankrupt and immoral status quo fits their mixture of absolutist totalitarian Islam and resentful nationalism, a created past intended to give direction and legitimacy to the desired future.

Where Pound opposed the modern world through poetry and his crankish love of totalitarian ideology, the hard men oppose the post-modern world using explosives, crashing airplanes and bodies everywhere. The hard men are really not about building. They are about destroying, for all their belief that living under Islamic Sharia law in a united worldwide Sunni Khalifait is the path for humanity. The defeat of current elected governments in Afghanistan and Pakistan is a first, necessary, step. The Muslims that hold authority there are tools of an anti-Islamic world order and so are *takfir*, worse than infidels. There will be no place in the future they envision for Muslims who have put worldly power first; even less so for Shias and non-Muslims.

The isolation and underdevelopment of the Vortex that makes up the battlefields of Afghanistan and Pakistan and is trying to engulf the rest of those two struggling countries suits the hard men's purpose. They are not fighting for development, for schools, clinics, and roads; they often destroy these when they have been built by outsiders or their money. Much as they will use, often effectively, modernity's tools, they fundamentally oppose the idea of modernity. Modernity makes women immoral and men lust after money rather than living for honor and Islam, which they consider the proper end of existence. This is a vision of fundamentalists, those who look to return to a mythic Islamic past, not that of Islamists, those that see Islam as a sharp sword to clear away all the traditional and colonial hangovers that keep the Vortex poor and backwards. Most of Afghanistan's Islamists are in Kabul, trying to modernize the country. A few are fighting with the Afghan insurgents despite philosophical differences. That is how the fundamentalist Mullah Omar, leader of the Afghan Taliban, and the Islamist Gulbuddin Hekmatyar, leader of the Hezb-e-Islami (HiH) party, ended up running parallel efforts in the Afghan insurgency, launched from the Pakistan side of the Vortex. They have targeted a government in Kabul that styles itself the Islamic Republic of Afghanistan, contains democrats, conservatives, and Islamists alike, and has a constitution that makes Islamic Sharia the wellhead of Afghanistan's laws.

Islam permeates and directs life, culture—and instinct—to an extent that outsiders find alien. The people of the region, certainly not limited to Pushtuns, know that they and their faith are always going to be there and that Pakistani and Afghan governments and especially infidel foreigners have always proved transient.

Pound's invocation of the importance of race and race-memory would be embraced by many of the Pushtuns living in both Afghanistan and Pakistan. Their oral tradition provides a very real race memory of resistance to outsiders and an embrace of Islam. It is a patriarchal and patrilineal race-memory, which puts aside the unpleasant fact that without the hard work done by women, everyone starves. It seeks an Islamic justification for its folkways and prejudices. What Pound called race-memory is not a crankish theory for the hard men. It is real, as real as tribal lineages, tradition, and laws—transmitted orally rather than what is understood by the readers of treatises—that guide their lives. People there have long memories of the past, which have been received from earlier generations.

Since 2001, Al Qaeda and the sympathizers of radical Islam have succeeded in adding another chapter to this memory, that Islam and their own culture are both under attack by a infidel conspiracy led by the US, and that only the people of the borderlands are uniquely situated to defeat this and wreak a terrible vengeance on those Muslims that would have made common cause with the infidels or have lived in peace next to them.

The hard men of the Vortex share Pound's vision—insert the obligatory references to Islam and it could be used by them—as well as his predilection for looking for conspiracies that underlie the realities of everyday life. Pound painted a large bull's-eye on the pre-1914 version of the established order of a Western, progressive, increasingly globalized world. The hard men who have never read him are going to have a shot at its present-day counterpart.

The better educated among them—they are by no means all illiterate fanatics—would note Pound's date of publication, a week before the Austro-Hungarian Archduke Franz Ferdinand and his consort made their fatal 1914 visit to Sarajevo that ended in the gunsights of Gavrilo Princip. Princip was part of an organization trained and supported by the intelligence services of a neighboring country (Serbia in his case) and funded by that country's general staff. A youth who resembled today's teenage suicide bombers more than those that send them on their missions, he was inspired by a transnational ideology mixed with nationalism and religion that aimed to shape the future by creating a past in which the only legitimate option was to fight to the death against what was seen as an alien occupying force.

Princip's actions—not a cause but a trigger—brought about the truncated twentieth century (1914–91) of organized violence, ideology as an overweening organizing principle, and man-made mass death, much of it instigated by men who thought like Pound. Today's hard men would like to use the same potent mixture to bring you their version of the twenty-first century. The West's distance from the Vortex, its wealth and power are unlikely to provide adequate defenses. The hard men are fighting with Korans, Kalashnikovs, and computers to change your world and your life. Terrorism organized and inspired by the men in the Vortex has struck at what they consider the "primary enemy" in the US, UK, and Europe. The insurgencies being waged in both Afghanistan and Pakistan have the potential to have widespread impacts if they are successful. The globalized economy has had an impact on people's lives worldwide; globalized terrorism will have no less.

The Vortex's Multiple Conflicts

Welcome to the Vortex. Though it does not have a mailing address or a seat at the United Nations, it is a place as well as a mindset. The Vortex is the borderlands of Afghanistan and Pakistan, divided by the Durand Line, the controversial British-surveyed 1893 division that today serves as the basis for the international border between Afghanistan and Pakistan. It is united by the Pushtun ethnicity of those who live on either side of its heart. But the Vortex affects much more than Pushtuns. It presents an existential threat to these two countries and the regions they border. It took decades to prepare and emerged in its current form from the changes flowing from the 2001 defeat of Al Qaeda and their Taliban allies in Afghanistan by Afghanistan's Northern Alliance, enabled by US and coalition special operations forces, intelligence, and air operations.

The Vortex started on the Pakistani side of the old Frontier, in the Federally Administered Tribal Areas (FATA) and Baluchistan and North West Frontier Provinces (NWFP) (renamed Khyber Pakhtunkhwa in 2010) of Pakistan, along the border with Afghanistan. There, Al Qaeda and the Afghan Taliban were able to find sanctuary, a sympathetic culture, and a Pakistani government that originally moved against only foreign terrorist leaders and plotters, leaving Afghan and Pakistani insurgents alike unmolested. These insurgents' challenge to Western power, worldview, and conventions in the name of both Pushtun ethnicity and global Islam, was able to plug into a pre-existing Taliban culture and create the Vortex, a place where Western and what appear as non-Islamic ways (by a definition that would gain little support from legitimate theologians) were increasingly defined as illegitimate. The Taliban culture has built on the religious and political experience of the Afghan refugee camps, the political and societal frustrations of Pakistan's Pushtuns facing underdevelopment in their home districts and exclusion from state power, and Pushtun nationalism. It espouses violent anti-modern (especially as it relates to liberalism and globalism), anti-US, anti-Western, anti-woman, anti-education, anti-rational (Pound would have loved that), and anti-secular views. It embraces all possible (and impossible) conspiracy theories and international jihad as a concept.

Those who have been nurtured by the Taliban culture in the Vortex have aimed to redefine power and authority on their own terms, first in the FATA—making use of changes in internal authority and breakdown of connections with the central government there—and then to bring it to Afghanistan and the rest of Pakistan. It spread from there, to most of southern and some of eastern Afghanistan and throughout that country wherever there was a receptive ethnic Pushtun population, with roots and branches both running throughout Afghanistan and Pakistan and connecting with transnational Islamic terrorism. By 2008–10, it was spreading farther through those two countries and had the potential to bring non-Pushtuns with grievances into a common struggle. In Afghanistan, few non-Pushtuns have joined with the insurgents. Fear of a resurgent Taliban outweighs the widespread disillusionment with the Afghan government and the foreign presence among Afghan's non-Pushtun groups.

There are multiple threats and conflicts, rather than a unitary Armageddon, emerging from this Vortex. It has assumed an importance comparable to that of the divided states of Germany and Korea in the opening years of the Cold War. In 2008–10, few trends in this region were running the right way. The return to power of civilian rule in Pakistan in 2008 was perhaps the high-water mark of democracy in the region. The failure of civilian rule to address Pakistan's problems has been matched in Afghanistan by the widespread unpopularity of the Karzai government, the continued rise of the culture of corruption, and the widespread perception of fraud in the 2009 presidential election.[1] In a leaked diplomatic cable in October 2008, British ambassador Sir Sherard Cowper-Coles warned that "The current situation (in Afghanistan) is bad, the security situation is getting worse, so is corruption, and the government has lost all trust. The presence of the coalition, in particular, its military presence, is part of the problem, not part of its solution. Foreign forces are the lifeline of a regime that would rapidly collapse without them. As such, they slow down and complicate a possible emergence from the crisis."[2]

Nor were foreigners the only ones concerned. In 2010, polling showed only 28 percent of Afghans thought the country was heading in the right direction, down from 77 percent in 2005; the percentage saying it was headed in the wrong direction has increased from six to 38 percent.[3] The terrorism threat in the Vortex has proven resilient—the absence of a major attack on the "primary enemies" of the US and UK does not mean that the capability has been removed. The insurgencies in Afghanistan and Pakistan have grown and become more effective in almost every measurable way in these years. Opium cultivation, while becoming more concentrated in area, remains intense. While overall poppy production decreased from 2008 to 2010, it continues to contribute to Afghanistan's culture of corruption, leads to crime and instability that in many areas cannot be distinguished from the insurgency, and provides resources for terrorists and insurgents alike. In only a few ways are the US and its coalition partners close to achieving the result they want, and the potential for everything going up in flames in the face of unforeseen events remains very real. But while each of the Vortex's conflicts is distinct and independent, looking at any one alone will miss the essentially regional challenge posed by them.

Terrorism is a worldwide threat. It is linked by a main circuit cable that runs from the Afghan border, through Pakistan's tribal territories, to Karachi, London, and New York. Other links for funding and recruits run to Arabia and the Gulf. Money for terrorism, insurgency, and narcotics flows along with remittances from expatriate workers. A sanctuary on the Pakistani side is now the base for Al Qaeda and many other terrorist organizations and individuals that were in Afghanistan at the time of the 9/11 attacks and largely withdrew intact to Pakistan.[4] In addition to waging terrorist campaigns in both countries, they have explicitly targeted the US and UK, providing inspiration if not hands-on direction to the hands that make the bombs or pull the triggers. Al Qaeda remains committed to achieving an attack that will dwarf that of 9/11.

The Afghan Taliban retreating to Pakistan after their 2001 defeat was able to join forces with a pre-existing Taliban culture that had started to flourish in preceding decades and the support networks that had been built for Pakistani-supported movements in Afghanistan and Kashmir, with the participation of Pakistani intelligence. These networks are shared with transnational terrorists and provide shared access to international funding and support from Pakistan's terrorist groups and religious parties. The post-2001 insurgency in Afghanistan started as a cross-border conflict, though it has since found local supporters inside Pushtun Afghanistan and gained strength from Afghanistan's continuing internal conflicts and foreign presence. The cross-border component of the insurgency remains important. The 434 cross-border attacks in the first six months of 2008 was a 40 percent increase from 269 in the same period in 2007.[5] 2009 saw further increases.

Opium is grown, refined, and transported through the Vortex. Illicit opium is a crop that cannot be grown without insecurity; it needs conflict more than it needs rainfall. Narcotics cultivation and traffic has its roots in the pre-2001 failure of the Afghan state. Successive pre-2001 governments were unwilling or unable to suppress it. The collapse of the economy of rural Afghanistan pre-2001 and limited post-2001 agricultural sector aid provided farmers with few alternatives. Afghanistan has ended up supplying the vast majority of the world's illicit opium.[6] The southern provinces of Afghanistan that are most affected by the insurgency grow the bulk of the opium, but the traffic has an impact even in areas where no poppies grow.

In the Vortex, according to former Afghan finance minister Ashraf

Ghani, "the stakeholders in instability are better organized than stake-holders in stability."[7] Each threat is waging a different but overlapping conflict, and a different set of strategies and tactics is required to defeat them. There are many important discontinuities between effective counter-terrorism and counter-insurgency to make it important to distinguish these two conflicts in Afghanistan. The insurgency is both integral to the terrorist threat to Afghanistan and distinct from it. The defeat of one will not remove the threat from the other. There are significant divergences between the two threats and the conflicts they are waging as well as in the Western response to each threat (for example, ISAF's mandate includes counter-insurgency but not counter-terrorist operations).

Al Qaeda and its allies from their sanctuary in the Vortex aim to overturn a world order that they see as inherently oppressing all Muslims. Insurgents in Afghanistan and Pakistan (Afghan and Pakistani Taliban and their allies) are fighting against governments in Kabul or Islamabad they see as foreign tools and not representing their interests (defined in ethnolinguistic, political, or religious terms). Narcotics growers and traffickers (who need to make money) grow most of their crop in Afghanistan, but much of the refining and value-added is in Pakistan. That they are able to work together despite their differences is a sign of the effectiveness of the networks, originating with Pakistan's Inter Services Intelligence (ISI) and other agencies that bind them, the Al Qaeda-generated offensive in the war of ideas that has allowed them to claim many "hearts and minds," and the failure of their opponents—US, Kabul and Pakistan—to effectively exploit the divisions between them.

Both Afghanistan and Pakistan face internal conflicts. Threats beyond those of terrorism, insurgency, and narcotics have the potential to overturn both states in their current forms. Afghanistan today, in many ways, is a country defined by its conflicts, which are far more extensive than those being waged with weapons. In Pakistan, larger problems have been left unsolved by civilian and military governments alike.

The bearded men with the Kalashnikovs and the laptops in caves are not the only adversaries. Many of the most important adversaries sit in office chairs and wear Western-style business suits or the uniforms of friendly military forces. What makes the threats particularly difficult for the US and the coalition is that not all are from enemies. The US's friends, whether Afghan politicians in Kabul or Pakistani generals in Rawalpindi, are very much part of the reason for the policy failures that made the region a top security concern by 2008–10.

The Pakistani military—an allied force that has been receiving US aid—created the Vortex's infrastructure and support networks to serve Pakistan's strategy starting in the 1970s. The insurgents were supported as part of the conflicts in Afghanistan and Kashmir. The networks originally supporting Afghan resistance groups were expanded to include Punjabi insurgents, and Pakistan's own domestic Islamic radical parties were brought in to the networks to enable these insurgencies and to serve as an internal political balance in favor of the military's role in Pakistan's politics. Other friends that are enabling enemies include the countries in the Middle East where much of the funding for terrorism and insurgency originates, a process much larger than just the network of unofficial moneychanger hawala/hundi transfers that moved the funding for the 9/11 attacks.

What all these diverse conflicts have in common is that they are wars against hope. Before 2001, there was precious little hope in Afghanistan, only civil war, hardship, and repressive Taliban rule. Then, after 9/11, when the US-led coalition intervention enabled Afghanistan's Northern Alliance to defeat the Taliban and their Al Qaeda allies, Afghanistan had hope. It was flooded with hope, had an exportable surplus of hope, hope for peace, for stability, for a better life. The US-led intervention in Afghanistan was identified as bringing this hope and was welcomed by Afghans of all ethnolinguistic groups. By 2008–10, much of this hope had dried up and been turned to dust by Afghanistan's external and internal conflicts, but enough remained to preserve what has changed since 2001. While the foreign military presence had suffered from years of collateral damage and the perception of being part of an international war on Islam that includes the Iraq and Arab-Israeli conflicts, there remains hope that it will at least prevent a return to civil war. Even in Pakistan, there has been hope, especially when the 2008 elections brought an end to military rule, but that hope too has been drying up faced with dysfunctional governance, economic hardship, and insurgency. But, as in Afghanistan, hope remains.

In the US, the UK, and other members of the international coalition, no one wants to see hope fail. But few want to give orders, and fewer still are able to originate and implement effective policies that will prevent a crisis in the near term, because this will mean more casualties, more expense, and more political cost. The hard men know, in their hearts, that in the end the coalition will disengage, that the Afghans trying to rebuild their country will go into exile, and, with the help of their friends in the business suits and the generals' uniforms, they can then go back to their hard business of fighting a civil war in Afghanistan and transforming the country to meet their worldview.

Frontiers and Conflicts

The North West Frontier, where the British Empire came up against Afghanistan until 1947, has become the Vortex, something different, unique, and dangerous. The conflicts emanating from the Vortex include the world's most destructive terrorist leadership, two democratically elected national governments (Afghanistan and Pakistan), power sources ranging from elected legislatures to well-armed warlords, almost all of the world's opium production, and a major commitment by the US and its allies.

Geographically, culturally, and politically, these are the Borderlands. The borders of Afghanistan are more than lines on a map. They are one of the major fault lines between civilizations; a site for both division and interaction. Warrior and trader Pushtun tribes and clans straddle the Afghanistan-Pakistan border: Wazir, Mahsud, Afridi, Shinwari, and Mohmand amongst them.

Frontiers are important for the nation-state. The frontiers of Afghanistan were drawn to make it a buffer state in the competition between the British and Russian empires. Afghanistan was never intended to be cohesive or self-supporting. Frontiers divide, but are also sites of interaction. The Frontier was a geographical and cultural division and, to those that lived there, a political and religious one as well. Afghanistan was outside the ordered world of the imperial inheritance. The inheritance from this past made it possible for Afghanistan's neighbors (and others with strategic interests in the region) to fight out their conflicts with their own money and Afghan lives.

All successful empires know where to draw the line and create a frontier, but frontiers remain zones of interaction as well as exclusion. No one can keep out what happens in the land beyond the frontier. Afghanistan's role as a graveyard of empires is not the result of a particular Afghan pathology or xenophobia, but of the failures of those empires they fought there. The failed empires found themselves unable or unwilling to evolve to meet Afghanistan's fast-emerging and always-mutating challenges. In the end, they took their failure and brought it home.

Force and legitimacy—the tools of the British Empire in 1893—drew the Durand Line that created the Frontier. But the linking factors of Pushtun ethnicity and Islam were never extinguished by the geographic divisions the Frontier represented on the map. Indeed, these divisions were seen at the time, and continue to be seen, largely as illegitimate, in large part because they were not enforceable. Throughout Afghanistan and the Pushtun borderlands of what was to become Pakistan, national power received limited, sometimes nominal, allegiance by secular and religious elites and did not concern the trader or farmer, whose livelihood required travel or trade with neighbors. The Frontier—not limited to what has since become the FATA—began where the British ability to compel compliance ended.

The Frontier demonstrated the inadequacy of the Western reliance on borders and sovereign states to define a world that instead looks to subnational (tribal, ethnolinguistic, or political groups) and supranational (Islam) identification and definitions. The model of the nation-state, which only came to Afghanistan under duress in the late nineteenth century, often fits it poorly despite all the Afghans' pride in it and all they have paid in blood and treasure to own it. The existence of multiple and flexible self-definitions by Afghans and equally diverse sources of authority within Afghanistan are reasons why it is often wrongly alleged that Afghanistan has never been a "proper" nation; for generations before 1978 it had been able to maintain Max Weber's "monopoly on the legitimate use of physical force within a given territory." Order, security, services (to the population, although prior to 2001 this was concerned primarily with elites), and legitimacy (though this was expressed more in support for social and cultural arrangement than the national government) were always part of traditional Afghanistan.

Historically, the Afghan state has appeared to be weak, especially when compared to the centralized systems, intended to maintain state control and with the military as their highest priority, of its neighbors in Pakistan and Iran. But Afghan nationalism is not a weak force. Every political group seeks to define itself in Afghan rather than subnational or ethnic-specific terms. The average Afghan, however illiterate and limited in personal horizons, tends to have a sense of an Afghan nationality and aims to live consistent with the tenets of "Afghaniyat," doing things properly the Afghan way.

The Afghan's 1978–1992 struggle against the Soviets and their Afghan supporters and 1992–2001 civil war made the Afghan state fail. Afghanistan has been a battleground for proxy wars and outside military intervention since the 1970s. This, more than any other factor, has led to the continued conflict in Afghanistan since 2001. On the Pakistani side, the insurgency emerging from the Vortex has combined with their pre-existing crisis of governance to threaten the future existence of Pakistan. The crisis of governance in Pakistan—a country where the military controls Afghanistan policy, state school and taxation systems do not function, and ties of blood and family still trump just about everything else in democratic politics—was there before the US intervened in Afghanistan in 2001. Following the 2007 fighting at the Lal Masjid (Red Mosque) in Islamabad and the 2009 insurgent seizure of Swat, even the Pakistani military had to recognize that their internal insurgents were not a force that could be easily controlled.

The Vortex brings together both the potential for a clash of civilizations and conflict within Islam about its future and how it will interact with the rest of the world. Afghanistan is geographically, culturally, and politically outside the Islamic mainstreams of either the Arab world or the subcontinent. Yet it has always had an impact beyond its borders. In the 1920s, Muslim leaders and scholars from the subcontinent advocated that the king of Afghanistan succeed to the Khalifait after the fall of the Ottoman Empire. The traditional role of the Frontier is the seam between civilizations. It is also the source of chastisement to those who do not live by the laws of the Pushtuns that inhabit it, whether they are practicing Muslims, Sikh, British, or others. Add this to the widespread

Afghan belief, especially among Pushtuns, that their faith is both exemplary and unique, providing a light and direction for the rest of Islam. Al Qaeda and a host of Islamic radicals have told them this since 2001, and many believe that this quality makes them a target for evil infidels and their Muslim allies that together are waging a global war on Islam. The Urdu poet Iqbal Lahori saw Afghanistan as the "heart of Asia" and said the entire continent will suffer when the heart is in pain.[8]

The Afghan Taliban had, and apparently retains, ambitions that extend beyond the borders of Afghanistan. This became readily apparent in 1994 (two years before bin Laden returned to Afghanistan from Sudan) when Mullah Omar put on the cloak of the Prophet himself that was revered in a shrine in Kandahar and had himself proclaimed (by fatwa) *Amir-al-Mumineen*—commander of the faithful—a title that embodied a claim for support from devout Muslims everywhere. This meshed well with Al Qaeda's goal of shaping the future of Islam and worldwide networks.

Now that the Frontier has become the Vortex, what may emerge from it has the potential to shape the larger world. The 11 September 2001 attacks on the US were planned and organized in Afghanistan. The global aspirations of the threat, the future of a nuclear-armed Pakistan, and the international effort to support Afghanistan have already made the Vortex of global concern.

Losing the Vortex

The story of the Vortex that I want to tell is primarily about the countries and people that are part of it. Outsiders, especially the US and UK, see the conflict as being about themselves, but it takes nothing away from the bravery of their troops or the devotion of their development workers to remember that the story is about the people of Afghanistan and those parts of Pakistan threatened by insurgencies.

By 2008–10, it was apparent that the battlefield victory of 2001 and the hope it had created in Afghans of all groups was in danger of turning to dust. The continued commitment of the US-led coalition to involvement in Afghanistan remains vital if Afghanistan is to have any chance of avoiding a relapse into civil war. In 2008–10, Afghanistan was dependent on the coalition's support. Yet the coalition's members remain, in the final analysis, limited in their involvement. They always have the option to disengage from Afghanistan, as they did after the Soviet withdrawal in 1989, leaving Afghanistan open to proxy war by its neighbors leading to the bloody and destabilizing conflicts of 1992–2001 and de facto Al Qaeda control. By fall 2010, political support for the war in Afghanistan had dropped to 37 percent in the US. The conflict has less support in the UK, less still in European coalition members. The US commitment in 2008–09 was, in reality, limited by its Iraq involvement.

For Afghanistan and Pakistan, limited liability is not an option. Yet for all the outside participants' limited liability—the Taliban is not going to enter *their* capitals if things go wrong—they still have much at stake in the Vortex. Despite the increased US and coalition presence of 2008–10, it is still Afghanistan's war.

Conflict in Afghanistan is not unwinnable ab initio. Those that have failed in the past—the British after the three Anglo-Afghan Wars, the Soviets in the 1980s, the Pakistanis in the 1990s, and the US and the coalition post-2001—all gained military success and were able to shape, if not control, the government in Kabul. Yet these victors proved unwilling or unable to provide the resources, will, and patience to turn battlefield success into a more comprehensive—even if never complete—victory.

Empires do not last once they lose their sheen of invincibility, their prestige, and, above all, their faith in themselves. It was easy for them to turn away from Afghanistan and consider its land and people outside the frontier. But no great power can fight a small war. Afghanistan's role in the final collapse of the Soviet Union has been described as "the fateful pebble" that caused the stumbling colossus to finally collapse.[9]

Failure in Afghanistan may have contributed to the end of empires, but that says less about what is intrinsic to Afghanistan than it does about the limitations of empires. The Soviets were not the first to fall. The First Anglo-Afghan War (1838–42) started with a spectacular British defeat, however redeemed by subsequent military success, that was one of the many factors that helped bring down the rule over India of Britain's Honorable East India Company. In 1857, all the Indian regiments that had previously been sent to avenge the initial British defeat in Afghanistan either mutinied or were disbanded.[10] The Third Anglo-Afghan War of 1919 contributed to starting the crisis of the Indian Empire that was to bring about the eventual end of the British raj. It is uncertain whether NATO could survive failure in its current mission in Afghanistan.

Afghanistan demonstrated that these outsiders lacked the will, troops, or capability to deal with a problem that seemed peripheral. None of the empires that stumbled over Afghanistan considered it important. It was not the source of revenue, nor of strategic bases and leverage, nor were there constituencies at home insisting Afghanistan be preserved. More importantly, they were unable to use the tools of diplomacy, penetration, or trade and had to rely on foreign troops to create their desired outcome in Afghanistan. Because of this, their wars became costly in terms of money, lives, and especially prestige.

The fact that the US and its coalition partners have demonstrated that the motivation of their post-imperial commitment to Afghanistan is not so that they can control resources or create a buffer, but rather so that they can enable Afghans to rebuild the country so it will not represent a haven for terrorism and a center of instability as it was before 9/11, does not reduce what they have at stake in the conflict. If anything, it increases it.

If the West fails here, the Afghans that had supported, trusted, and worked to rebuild their country along with them will fail, harder and lethally. Success in driving out the outsiders will likely attract resources to fight the government they supported in Kabul from both neighbors fighting proxy wars and Islamic radicals seeking to create a society that fits their doctrines. Coalition disengagement from the conflict in Afghanistan will inspire other hard men elsewhere in the world to look to their Korans and Kalashnikovs to go and make their own version of the future. It will not be the Sunni equivalent of the Iranian revolution, where Sunni-Shia divisions and national borders provided natural firebreaks, but something different and potentially more dangerous. Consider the fact that, by 2008–10, the Taliban movements of both Afghanistan and Pakistan had evolved into political-military movements far different from the one that had emerged, with the encouragement and support of the government in Islamabad, in the borderlands decades before. The emergence of groups such as the "Punjabi Taliban" in Pakistan and the resilience of Al Qaeda suggest that the hard men's cause and their ability to adapt may well continue to have appeal to those in the region and worldwide who oppose a status quo that appears unresponsive and oppressive.

The long record of failures in dealing with Afghanistan must give pause to any Westerner looking at a commitment that includes the use of substantial numbers of troops. But if there is a time certain for disengagement, the supporters of the insurgents and the terrorists will wait until the US and the coalition go home. The security situation of 2008–10 required more foreign troops to prevent a near-term collapse; but these forces, unlike those of past empires, have come not to conquer but rather to prevent a conquest of Afghanistan by terrorists and insurgents.

That, of course, is not how the hard men see it. To them, it is their land and their faith. Foreigners may have something to add as a source for technology and trade, but have nothing to teach about honor or Islam, which is what really matters. To them, these foreigners are no different from conquerors. That is why, in 2005, the Afghan Taliban issued a fatwa (a religious edict) ordering the death of all "infidels" and others supporting the Afghanistan government. Even those aid providers who had worked with the pre-2001 Taliban and tried to distance themselves from coalition military efforts have been portrayed, increasingly, as on the side of darkness with the Zionists and Crusaders. The Taliban had no interest in exempting those non-governmental organizations building things like clinics or schools. Much as these organizations would have liked to have claimed neutrality, to the hard men they are also very much the enemy.[11]

Failure in Afghanistan in the current conflicts would be much like having failed in Germany or Korea in the Cold War. The price for losing the Vortex's conflicts would be paid by the losing "empires": the US, NATO, the UN and international organizations, and the world order as a whole. But the real cost would fall heavily and painfully on those who must live there. If Kabul is *ever* once again in the hands of current Afghan insurgents, their terrorist allies, and their foreign backers, it will not bring peace to Afghanistan. It will mean renewed civil war and misery for the Afghans and a powerful blow to US credibility. Losing in Pakistan is likely to mean continued conflict in Afghanistan. That would be hell indeed for Afghans and Pakistanis. In repeated elections, they have firmly rejected the ways of the Vortex. They have voted for responsible and democratic government, despite the efforts of their own elites to limit and corrupt the process. The hope expressed in those votes, and in the support demonstrated for the new Afghan government and the coalition post-2001, has not yet faded beyond recall. Hope was brought into Afghanistan by the US-led coalition intervention in 2001 and, though much diminished, remains there still. Whether the future of Afghanistan—and Pakistan as well—will reflect this hope or the vision of the hard men remains to be determined.

2008–10 proved to be the most dynamic period in the regions' current conflicts. It started with the US turning its focus away from Iraq and ended with the November 2010 Lisbon summit setting 2014 for the ANSF security takeover. Many divergent or even contradictory policies were considered and implemented in 2008–10, setting the stage for what is planned to be the endgame of foreign military primacy, if not the conflicts. In 2010, central Helmand and Kandahar became ISAF's operational main effort. Some of the security trends, running the wrong way in previous years, were turned around in 2010. In 2010, the insurgents lost the battlefield momentum in much of Afghanistan (except in areas in the north and west where they managed to expand the insurgency). Suicide attacks in Kabul became less frequent. Even Al Qaeda generated propaganda from Pakistan has decreased. Yet insurgents increased the number of attacks country-wide. More districts, mainly in the north and west, were assessed as unsafe for aid workers. International assistance, Afghan governance and the economy continue to lag. No unitary strategy has emerged as the divisions between Washington and Kabul increased. Nor has there been progress in ending insurgent sanctuaries in Pakistan. The 2010 parliamentary elections were marked by less overt corruption than the 2009 presidential election but Pushtun participation was limited by security weakness.

PART ONE
LANDS IN THE VORTEX

CHAPTER ONE

AFGHANISTAN: A COUNTRY DEFINED BY CONFLICTS

"To sum up the character of the Afghans in a few words: their vices are revenge, envy, avarice, rapacity, and obstinacy; on the other hand they are fond of liberty, faithful to their friends, kind to their dependents, hospitable, hardy, frugal, laborious and prudent; and they are less disposed than the nations in their neighborhood to falsehood, intrigue, and deceit."

—Mountstuart Elphinstone,
An Account of the Kingdom of Caubul, 1815

This one-sentence description is of value today, not just sentimental Orientalism. Today, there is still something remaining of the "Old Afghanistan," though nothing has been untouched by the conflicts of 1978–2001. Despite the current impatience of foreigners and Afghans alike, rebuilding will likely be the task of a generation, and whether it will be completed or not depends on the outcome of Afghanistan's conflicts and the commitments of its foreign friends.

Land and People

Afghanistan is a country of enormous complexity. Isolated by its mountainous terrain and limited infrastructure, Afghanistan is rich in culture, has multiple languages and ethnicities, and has a long unique history of

Islamic religious practices and much else. It is harder to generalize about diverse and divided Afghanistan than just about any other country of comparable size and population. Those, usually foreigners, who insist on defining any one fact as "*this* is how it is in Afghanistan," are likely to be misleading themselves. Attempting to understand Afghanistan means realizing the importance of its nuances and context.

Afghanistan is located at the intersection of three critical regions—Iran and the Gulf; central Asia; Pakistan and the subcontinent—and is where global currents meet and interact. China (and the Pacific Rim) even shares a short land border with Afghanistan in the remote northeast Wakhan corridor. Yet Afghanistan is still distinct from all the regions it borders, even though it is influenced by—and has the potential to influence—all of them.

Afghanistan's remote location on the eastern periphery of the Iranian plateau and mountainous terrain has limited control by outsiders.[12] The mountains divide and isolate Afghanistan. The Hindu Kush bisects it. The Safed Koh lines the border with Pakistan. The tallest peaks are those of the Pamirs, in the extended finger of the Wakhan Corridor that stretches to the Chinese border. The territory is generally arid.

A relatively small percentage of the surface area—mainly in river valleys—is suitable for agriculture, which requires irrigation. Afghanistan is vulnerable to multiyear droughts, including a severe one in the early 1970s and another one prior to 2001. Both of these droughts hurt the legitimacy of the then-current governments in Kabul, which demonstrated they could do little to alleviate the hardships of affected Afghans. A drought in 2008 helped worsen a pre-existing food shortage, as Pakistan and Kazakhstan, the region's primary food exporter, had already cut off food sales to Afghanistan to keep their own domestic prices down. The percentage of Afghans telling pollsters they were unable to afford food increased from 54 to 61 percent in 2007–10.[13] This, along with soaring energy costs. created even more hardship and sowed the seeds for more unrest.[14] Afghanistan's politics are shaped by its geography.

Afghanistan's cities—some of great antiquity—provide regional markets. They are linked by trade routes that also stretch back for centuries. Kabul, the capital, with its surrounding area, has been the historic center since the eighteenth century. Afghanistan can be geographically divided into regions around the major cities. The Northwest includes the ancient Silk Route city of Herat and the Hari River. The North, around the city of Mazar-e-Sharif, includes the northern plains. The Northeast stretches from the Shomali plain north of Kabul to distant and mountainous Badakhshan. The central Hazara Jat is effectively surrounded by mountains. In the South, Kandahar is the major city. In the east, Jalalabad and Khost are the major regional centers on trade routes with Pakistan.[15]

Since 2001, no effective Afghan national economy has emerged to tie these seven diverse and disparate regions together. As a landlocked country, the importance of the port of Karachi as Afghanistan's most important link to the world has meant that the relationship with Pakistan is critical to the economy and future of Afghanistan.

The failure to have an effective Afghan national economy post-2001 and the continued economic reliance on Pakistan reflects that the port of Karachi is vital as Afghanistan's link to the outside world. Afghanistan lacks infrastructure and relationships with other countries that would provide an alternative path to markets. Afghanistan has no railroads (though Iran and Uzbekistan have ongoing projects to build spurs of their national systems). The limited road system has, as a result, taken on a great deal of importance. What foreigners call "the ring road" links Afghanistan's major cities and runs to the international borders. It runs south from the old Soviet border at Termez in Uzbekistan, through the Salang Pass tunnel under the Hindu Kush, down to Kabul. From there it follows the path of the traditional trade routes, running south through Ghazni to Kandahar, then west to Herat and north to the border with Turkmenistan. The ring is closed by a secondary stretch linking the western and eastern north-south routes, through Mazar-e-Sharif. There are also paved routes linking Afghanistan's cities with foreign trading partners. The road from Kabul through Jalalabad reaches the Pakistani border at Tor Kham and from there runs through the Khyber Pass to Peshawar, capital of Pakistan's North West Frontier Province (NWFP) and the Grand Trunk Road that leads over the River Indus to the Punjabi cities Rawalpindi and Islamabad, capital of Pakistan. Kandahar is linked by a paved road that crosses the Pakistan border at Spin Boldak, where it runs through the Bolan Pass to Quetta, the capital of Pakistan's Baluchistan province. Another road connects Herat with Iran. The rest of the country relies on secondary roads.

Afghanistan's population has grown to about 30–33 million, from 15–20 million in the 1970s. The high rate of growth has made the demographic "youth bulge" that affects many Middle Eastern countries even more pronounced in Afghanistan, with about 4.5 million young men aged 15–29 and about 6.7 million boys under 15; 45 percent of all males are under 15, two to three times the percentage in developed countries. In the absence of a recent census—the most recent attempt was in 1979, and security concerns have halted post-2001 plans—all population figures, especially those associated with ethnolinguistic groups, remain politically charged estimates.

The population patterns have not recovered from the effects of the conflicts of 1978–2001, which saw Afghans becoming the world's largest refugee population (especially in Pakistan and Iran) and internally displaced many of the more than 75 percent of the population that had lived in rural areas. The numbers of Afghanistan's internal refugees, despite terrible living conditions, led to a considerable increase in urbanization. Even the heavy fighting in Kabul in 1992–96 did not reverse this trend.

Afghanistan's human resources, like its natural ones, remain tremendously underdeveloped. Afghanistan's level of human development is less than any of its neighbors. An estimated two thirds of the population is illiterate. In Pakistan, only the FATA—where male overall literacy is estimated as less than 30 percent and female literacy at fewer than four percent—is worse off than Afghanistan.

The worldwide Afghan diaspora, while highly motivated and devoted to Afghanistan, is relatively small and lacks resources or political influence in the countries they now largely call home. The ties of blood and affection to Afghanistan are limited, in most developed countries, to small communities of exiles and refugees and to that still-smaller group of foreigners that care about or have an interest in its people and future.

Recent UN development indices have shown Afghanistan near the bottom, ranking 174 out of 178 countries in the 2007 Global Human Development Index.[16] The most important activity is agriculture, with the most profitable crop being the illicit cultivation of opium, which has become concentrated in five southern provinces. Specialty agricultural products (raisins and pomegranates), wheat, and other grains are also widely grown. Afghanistan's undeveloped natural resources, including natural gas and copper, may prove valuable in the future, given outside investment and a functioning infrastructure, all now blocked by the conflict and the political weakness in Kabul. US-provided surveys post-2001 have identified what could become valuable industries if a suitable infrastructure is provided. China has started to make investments in natural gas and copper development.

Ethnolinguistic Divisions

While in no significant way homogenous, Afghans nevertheless possess a strong sense of national identity that coexists with correspondingly strong Islamic faith and equally strong overlapping and non-exclusive ethnolinguistic, tribal (especially among Pushtuns of which clan or subclan identification is often strongest), qawm (affinity group), local (e.g., Panjshiris, from the Panjshir valley), and kinship identities. The Western estimates used to produce ethnolinguistic maps and percentages of population associated with each group have to be used with great care.

There is no one consensus among Afghans on what constitute specific ethnic, religious, or racial groups. Afghans all share some aspects of identity with cross-border groups in their neighbors from all three of the adjacent regions: shared language, religion and religious practice, literature, culture, and, in some cases, tribal structure. But the Afghans generally do not perceive themselves as the unredeemed part of a secessionist group. If others from across the border wish to join them, great, but few want to leave. Afghanistan is not the former Yugoslavia.

The Pushtuns (also called Pathan, Pashtun, and Pukhtun) are primarily Sunni (with a few Shia tribes, mainly in Pakistan). Pushtuns are the world's largest tribal grouping, a tribally subdivided, clan-based society. The Pushtuns have been historically the dominant group in Afghanistan. The most credible Western estimates (such as those produced by the UN or the CIA Fact Book) are that Pushtuns currently represent about 38–43 percent of the population of Afghanistan, although some estimates put the percentage up to ten percent greater than these. However, it is an article of faith among the government and elites of Pakistan and Pushtuns around the world that Pushtuns are an absolute majority in Afghanistan.

Afghan Pushtuns are divided into at least four major tribal subgroupings: Durranis, Ghilzays, Ghurghustis, and the Kharoshtis and Eastern Pushtuns. Each of these is divided further into families of tribes and tribes, each tribe divided into khels (clans) and sub-clans. Afghan's Kuchi nomads, a much smaller group, are also ethnic Pushtuns. Pushtuns primarily speak the Pushtu (also called Pashto) language. While there are significant dialect differences between Pushtu-speakers, they all are mutually intelligible. Complicating the ethnic division is the fact that many ethnic Pushtuns are actually primarily Dari-speakers that use Pushtu as a second language.

The Pushtuns have ties running across the Durand Line, which has proven important for the continued conflicts in Afghanistan and Pakistan. Afghanistan's approximately 13.8 million Pushtuns have 26.6 million counterparts in Pakistan, with the heartland in the FATA, North West Frontier Province (NWFP), and Baluchistan, but with substantial populations throughout the country in major cities, especially Karachi. In Pakistan, Pushtuns run the nationwide "transport mafia," "lumber mafia," and other economic activities, making use of their ethnic trading connections.

The largest group of Afghanistan's Persian (Afghan Dari and Iranian Farsi are like British and American English) speakers are Tajiks. Tajiks are defined as Sunni (with some Ismailis), Dari-speaking, and make up an estimated 20 percent of the population. The relatively recent rise of a distinct Tajik ethnic identity shows how these definitions are not fixed in Afghanistan. Many Afghans have said "we only learned we were Tajiks from the BBC." Before that, they were self-defined, perhaps as Heratis, Panjsheris, Badakshis (the natives of Badakhshan province, described by Marco Polo as "Muslim and valiant in war"), or multiple identities.

The Hazara are racially distinct Mongol descendants, predominantly Imami Shia (with a few Sunnis), Dari-speaking, internally divided by tribe and lineage. They make up about eight to ten percent of the population (estimates go to 15–20 percent; their own leaders claim up to 35 percent). Farsiwans are Imami Shia, Farsi (rather than Dari) speaking, closely related to Iranians. Afghanistan's Shia population is estimated at about 16 percent if the urban Qizilbash, Dari-speaking descendants of the Persian Empire's ruling elites that are among Afghanistan's most educated groups, are included. The Aimaqs are less than five percent of the population. They are a Sunni, Dari-speaking, semi-nomadic group, divided into four distinctive clans.

The Uzbeks are the largest group among the speakers of Turkic languages in the north; Sunni, Uzbek-speaking (with Dari as a second language), tribe and clan-based (although this has less military-political meaning than it does for Pushtuns), constituting some 13 percent of Afghanistan's population. In addition to Uzbeks, there are also small populations of Turkmen and Kyrgyz. Unlike the Pushtuns, they have fewer links—economic, political and cultural—with other members of their ethnic groups across national borders in central Asia, a legacy of the decades of the Iron Curtain on Afghanistan's northern border. Many members of these groups, like many Afghan Tajiks, are descended from refugees from Russian or Soviet repression.

Smaller tribes and ethnic and religious groups include Ismaili Shias, called "Seveners," who are primarily Dari-speaking and have their strongest concentration near Pul-e-Khumri on the northern end of the Salang Pass. The Pashai (strongest in Nangarhar and Laghman provinces), Brahui (concentrated in the southern provinces), and Baluchi (in the south, contiguous with their counterparts in Pakistan and Iran) all have their own languages but also speak Pashto as a second language. Other groups include the Nuristanis (whose language is divided into five distinct dialects and use Pashto as a second language) and Gujurs (who speak Dari as a second language). The only non-Muslims are a few hundred Hindus and Sikhs in Kabul, Kandahar, and Jalalabad, remnants of once-thriving trading communities. Afghanistan's Sephardic Jewish communities that, at their height, had their own vigorous culture and traded with others along the Silk Route had been reduced to two aged gentlemen by the time the Taliban were driven from Kabul in 2001.

All in all, there is no agreement as to the number of languages and ethnic affiliations in Afghanistan, even within the seemingly binary division of Pushtun versus non-Pushtun. Despite the lack of agreement as to what constitutes an ethnic group and the lack of a formal census to determine the population's ethnicity, it is apparent that few of Afghanistan's major regions or even its 34 provinces are ethnically homogenous. There is more diversity in Afghanistan than just about any other country of comparable size and population.

Of the major loosely defined geographical regions, the Northwest is populated mainly by Dari speakers but also includes Pushtuns. In the North, Mazar-e-Sharif and the northern plains are the most multi-ethnic area, with communities of Uzbeks and Tajiks being the primary groups alongside substantial Pushtun and Hazara populations. The Northeast is primarily Tajiks but includes a number of smaller groups, such as the Nuristanis. Pushtun minority populations remain in this region. The Hazara Jat is the most cohesive entity, being, as its name implies, the home of the Hazaras. The South and Kandahar is the Pushtun heartland, populated primarily by Durrani and Ghilzay Pushtun tribes. The East is also primarily Pushtun, but is also where that people's tribal fragmentation is most widespread. Kabul, like most of Afghanistan's cities, including Kandahar, was originally Persian-speaking, but for a century attracted emigrants from the countryside even before the 1978–2001 conflicts led to floods of internal refugees. Other regions have their own unique patterns of ethnic divisions. Kunduz, for example, is a Pushtun-majority city in a predominantly Dari-speaking countryside.

It is clear, then, that just as ethnic identification is not fixed, Afghanistan cannot be easily divided into ethnic cantons. Ethnolinguistic maps of Afghanistan are approximations at best and too often misleading. Ethnicity can be fluid, situational, and multilayered. This especially applies to Pushtuns with often-competing loyalties to an overarching Pushtun identity, to tribal groups (e.g., Durrani) and, often most significant, to a specific clan or tribe (e.g., Popalzai, of which President Karzai is also a hereditary chief). Many of the larger groups (especially tribes and clans) share at least a fictive shared descent (usually from a heroic common ancestor). This, along with the patriarchal and patrilineal nature of authority that cuts across most Afghan ethnic groups, makes family lineages important. Among Pushtuns, lineages often determine political alignments and can be a primary cause of infighting.

However, for all these nuances, the divide that is most important for Afghanistan's conflicts is the binary one between Pushtuns and non-Pushtuns, which largely means Persian-speakers. The many other languages including Uzbek, Pashai, Baluchi, Nuristani, and Turkmen do not change the basic bilingual division of Afghanistan. Many small groups, like the Pashai, do not define themselves as a minority. Most small groups are bilingual. The Nuristanis whose homeland is in the most remote part of the Northeast—racially distinct Indo-Europeans converted by the sword to Islam in the nineteenth century—do not share a common language.

While Afghanistan's Persian and Turkic speakers share languages and cultural links with populations outside Afghanistan's borders, these are qualitatively different from the links between Afghanistan and Pakistan's Pushtuns. Pushtun nationalism has a transborder impact far beyond that of other groups. The relationship between Afghanistan and Pakistan has shaped the region for decades, and the impact of the transborder Pushtuns has, in turn, been the critical factor in that relationship.

Since the formation of the proto-Afghanistan state in 1747, the only times when the de facto head of state has not been a Pushtun has been in two periods marked by intensive civil war, 1930 and 1992–96. The ethnolinguistic mobilization of Afghans that has taken place since 1978 means that state power, central power, and rule from Kabul have been increasingly identified with Pushtun power. The belief of many Pushtuns in both Afghanistan and Pakistan that this is the only legitimate possibility for the future of Afghanistan is not accepted by the non-Pushtuns of that country, politically mobilized by decades of conflict and better and more cohesively organized than the tribally divided Pushtuns. While no other group had the numbers of the Pushtun, these have at times been able to use their Dari language and opposition to Pakistan's policies that stressed the importance of Pushtun control of state power in Afghanistan to work together, most notably in the pre-2001 Northern Alliance, which included substantial Pushtun allies in the form of Dr. Abdurrab Rasul Sayyaf Ittehad-i-Islami (one of the Peshawar Seven) and the Nangarhar shura of Haji Qadir (previously part of HiK) plus a number of Pushtun leaders that were opposed to the Taliban, including Hamid Karzai, who became president of Afghanistan.

Faith

Islam is central to the future of Afghanistan. Traditional Afghan Islamic practice is distinct from that of the Arab world, the subcontinent (although this has been the source of most outside influences), and Persia (reflecting the Sunni-Shia divide). Traditional Afghan practice recognized that there is no compulsion in Islam and did not seek to extend its dictates, except by persuasion, beyond the walls of the family compound. Yet this did not prevent Afghanistan's nineteenth-century King Abdur Rahman from converting the polytheistic Kafirs of the northeast to the Muslim Nuristanis by the sword, or conquering alike Shia Hazaras and Sunni Turkic-speakers. While traditional Afghan Islam as a whole has never been fanatic, it has also never been pacific. For example, it reveres the archetype of the ghazi, the raider and warrior, never afraid to strike a blow for Islam and his honor.

Islam has also been the rallying cry that brought together Afghans of different ethnicities and Pushtuns of different tribes to take arms against outsiders. The 1978–92 war against the Soviets and their Afghan supporters was perceived by the majority of Afghans as a jihad, a Muslim holy conflict.[17]

The most significant divisions within the various Sunni populations, not limited to any single ethnolinguistic group, are between the practitioners of traditional Afghan Islam, heavily infused with Sufic practices (many of which have had strong political impacts such as the reverence to pirs, living saints, or the importance of Sufic brotherhoods as solidarity groups). These practices have stressed the importance of jihad but have also been historically resistant to its use to legitimate terrorism. Their opposition are those whose religious practices reflect the critics of Afghan Islam, including Islamists but especially those fundamentalists whose ideology includes elements emanating from the subcontinent (Deobandi) and Arabia (Wahabi or Salafist).

Prior to 1978, there were two primary sources of internal opposition in Afghanistan: Communists (supported by the Soviets) and Islamists (that ended up being supported by Pakistan and money from outside the region). They were both opposed not only to what they saw as Afghanistan's underdevelopment and the practices of rule from Kabul, but also to traditional Afghan Islam. The traditional Afghan Islam, marked by the relative tolerance of the clergy, rooted in their community and qawm rather than responding to a centralized national religious leadership or bureaucracy, was seen as part of the old Afghanistan that Communists and Islamists alike wished to overcome. The religious figures, along with the secular tribal and local leadership, the local khans, provided a set of autonomous checks and balances that neither opposition wished to accept.

For the Communists, there was to be no compromise with the old order. The Islamists, realizing they needed the intensely religious Afghan grassroots on their side, looked to a more gradual strategy of compromise and absorption.

Afghanistan's Communists had been strong opponents of Afghan Islam when the two parties of the People's Democratic Party of Afghanistan (PDPA) emerged in the years before they seized power in the 1978 putsch. When the Communists seized power in the 1978 coup, they turned on the Afghan religious leadership, both because of their atheistic Communist ideology and because religion represented the competition for power and authority in Afghanistan. The Khalqi party, predominantly less-educated Pushtuns from rural backgrounds that resented its strong religious component, saw it as a backward remnant. Khalqis targeted families with hereditary claims to Sufic leadership—critical to religious leadership amongst Pushtuns—for arrest and murder in 1978–79. The more sophisticated urban, Kabuli, Dari-speaking Parcham party, installed in power by the Soviets in December 1979, tended to follow the Soviet central Asia model toward Islam, treating it as something that needed to be engaged with, to be controlled through subsidies and support as well as repression.

Another approach critical of traditional Afghan Islam was that of Afghanistan's Islamists. They were modernizers and, in the years before 1978, were impatient with Afghan religion as, along with the tribal system of the Pushtuns, holding the country back. Afghan Islamists looked to outside voices, especially from the Arab world, which embraced Islam to provide modernity and a shield against Western and Soviet cultural and political imperialism. Afghan Islamists also viewed the rising pre-1978 Communist threat in their own country with great alarm.

Islamism started as the central ideology of pre-1978 opposition parties. The Jamiat-e-Islami Afghanistan (JIA) had its roots in Kabuli intellectuals. Its long-time leader was Dr. Burnhaddin Rabbani, a Cairo-trained theology professor. He retained the leadership of JIA through 1978–92 when it was one of the "Peshawar Seven" of Pakistan-supported Sunni Afghan resistance parties, and was the president of the Islamic State of Afghanistan (ISA) that was formed from the Peshawar seven's leadership in 1992. Though driven from Kabul by the Taliban in 1996, he remained the nominal internationally recognized head of state until after the US-led coalition intervention in 2001. Among the members of JIA were such major Afghan leaders as Ahmad Shah Massoud, one of the foremost resistance leaders against the Soviets who, after fighting through Afghanistan's civil war as the ISA defense minister, was assassinated in northern Afghanistan by Al Qaeda suicide terrorists just before the 9/11 attacks on the US.

A competing source of Afghan Islamism, though one in practice limited to Pushtuns, was the Hezb-e-Islami party. This shared JIA's pre-1978 origins. However, by 1978 it had splintered into two parties, one led by Younis Khalis, a mullah with strong Khogiani Pushtun links from Nangarhar province and the other led by Gulbuddin Hekmatyar, a Pushtun from Kunduz whose one-year attendance at Kabul University had earned him the honorary title of "Engineer." Both of these parties were among the "Peshawar Seven." The Hezb-e-Islami of Hekmatyar (HiH) became the largest single recipient of Pakistan-distributed outside aid to the Afghan resistance in 1978–92 and eventually became Pakistan's "chosen instrument" inside Afghanistan until displaced from this position by the Taliban in 1996. The Hezb-e-Islami of Khalis (HiK) merged into other groups post-1992.

In reality, Afghan Islamist ideology had a limited impact with grassroots Afghanistan. Its leadership figures, with their roots among Afghanistan's elites, found that to have mass appeal, they needed to adapt to more traditional Islamic beliefs and practices and with tribal and other loyalties that the Islamists opposed. Hekmatyar's difficulty in carrying out such adaptation was among the reasons he has remained unpopular in the southern Pushtun heartland, where Sufic-influenced Islam and tribal loyalties remained strong. Despite having strong support from Pakistan, he was unable to gain the degree of support from Afghanistan's Pushtuns that the Taliban had in 1996–2001.

Another source of opposition to traditional Afghan Islam is represented by Islamic fundamentalism. This looks at traditional Afghan practices and Sufic influences as syncretic accretions, with roots in the subcontinent or pre-Muslim society. Fundamentalism influences on Afghan Islam were represented by Deobandi and Wahabi or Salafist approaches, brought in from madrassas abroad and supported with foreign money. Fundamentalists may embrace the tools and technology of modernity; but they are not modernizers, looking instead to achieve the pure Islam of the distant past, with the Shias seen as the most damaging polluters of the pure spring. The Afghan Taliban has been, from their origin, fundamentalists, representing their leaderships' schooling in Deobandi-influenced madrassas in the FATA. This underlay much of their hostility to Islamists in Afghanistan during the 1992–2001 civil war.

In the 1980s and 90s, the critique of Afghan Islamic practice was embodied in the Taliban's Deobandi-based version of a maximalist Islamic ideology that emerged from the refugee camps. It was linked in this with what is termed Wahabism in Afghanistan, a movement that had been imported into Afghanistan to "reform" traditional Afghan Islam—with little success—in the years before 1978. Saudi financial assistance was accompanied with a strong push to spread its intolerant and restrictive Wahabi form of Islam, alien in any case to Afghanistan, with disastrous results. Saudi and Gulf money has subsidized the building and operations of maderi in Pakistan that produced the Taliban and other extremists now threatening the stability of Pakistan. During the 1980s, Wahabism became important, especially in the refugee camps and in madrassa in Pakistan, because of foreign funding. An autonomous Wahabi "kingdom" appeared in the Kunar valley.

Because these influences were strongest in Pakistan and because the

Afghan exile population there was predominantly Pushtun, these outside influences were strongest amongst Pushtuns. Among non-Pushtuns, the Tajiks continued to be closer to traditional practices, despite the Islamist views of many of their political and military leaders. The Shia Hazaras went through a bloody sub-national civil war in the 1980s which saw supporters of Iran's Islamic Revolution trying and failing to seize power in the Hazara Jat, but succeeding in killing or driving into exile many of the Hazara's traditional religious and secular leaders.

Even though the Taliban's ideology was hostile to traditional Afghan Islam, they were able to accommodate many of its grassroots believers in 1992–2001, using shared Pushtun ethnolinguistic links. But, during the Taliban's 1996–2001 rule from Kabul, the increased influence of Al Qaeda and the importance of Arab funding meant that the Taliban paid more attention to the practices of outside supporters and less to that of their Pushtun clients, contributing to the loss of legitimacy the Taliban experienced among many Pushtuns by 2001.

The Afghan Taliban first received Pakistan's backing in 1994 and by 1996 had replaced HiH as Pakistan's chosen instrument in Afghanistan. It was an attempt to continue Pakistan's strategy of aiming at political control in Afghanistan through a new set of clients. President Benazir Bhutto and interior minister Nasrullah Babur were secular nationalists that had no problem with using Islamic fundamentalists as policy tools. Taliban's leadership was drawn from Pushtun ulema (clergy), many with shared backgrounds in the war against the Soviets or in the Deobandi-influenced madrassas of the FATA. This leadership gave the Taliban a capability to mobilize Afghan Pushtuns, reaching across tribal and local lines.

The tension between fundamentalism and traditional Afghan Islam for many years proved a limit on the resurgent Afghan insurgency, but by 2008–10 the Afghan Taliban, well funded and using effective propaganda, had been able to intimidate, infiltrate or bring over many of the Sufic brotherhoods in southern Afghanistan and influence what was being preached in mosques throughout Afghanistan.

Because Afghanistan is decentralized and lacks a tradition of a state-supported unitary national ulema or religious leadership, the nature of Afghan Islam is largely determined at the grassroots level. There is no single question more important for Afghan stability than "to whom do you listen?" at the mosque. Religious authority—either local, reflecting tiers of kinship, tribe, or qawm, or that of more remote figures (especially Sufic leaders) that can have a broader appeal—is important to provide legitimacy for any actions or change, secular or religious. This authority had been in the hands of major figures connected with Sufic orders (such as Pir Sayid Ahmed Gailani and Sayid Sibghatullah Mojadidi, each of whom led one of the seven Peshawar-based Sunni Afghan resistance parties in the 1980s) or their local counterparts, pirs, ulema and sayids. Afghanistan's Shia, especially in the Hazara Jat, have a structure of religious authority separate from Sunni practice, one largely unsupported by pre-2001 Afghan governments. These religious authorities have all been challenged by the emergence of new generations of Afghans (and ulema) that have been affected by Deobandi influences from the subcontinent (the original Taliban leadership were educated in madrassas in Pakistan) and other sources of radical Islam.

The Afghan conflict against the Soviets in 1978–92 was remote to the West. Yet its impact on Afghan life and society cannot be overestimated. To Afghans, it is what the Great War was to Europeans and the Patriotic Fatherland War to the Soviets. Among the many lasting impacts has been the tendency to associate change, reform and modernization with the enemy and what is permanent and resistant—to change as well as conquest—with Islam and Afghanistan.

Islam has increased importance in Afghanistan as both a unifying and a dividing factor. The damage to Afghan society inflicted by the conflicts of 1978–2001, the refugee camps, and the exile experience has led the diverse and divided Afghan people to turn increasingly to Islam (encouraged by the policies of Pakistan and foreign donors from the Islamic world). Today, Islam has a assumed a greater importance in Afghanistan than it did in the years before 1978. Conflict also brought religious radicalization (as well as state failure) to Afghanistan.

This trend towards radicalization has increased the Islamic role in society as well as its political-military impact and has contributed to the greater role of Islam in Afghan life, culture, and politics today compared with "the Golden Age," the generation before the conflicts started in

1978. Purely secular solutions, ones that cannot be legitimated in Islamic as well as Afghan terms, are often ineffective, regarded with hostility or as foreign impositions. But change in Islamic practice is also generally viewed with suspicion, as reflected by the limited acceptance of Wahabi influence despite decades of well-funded efforts from Saudi Arabia and the Gulf to push their practices on Afghans.

The current government in Kabul is formally called the Islamic Republic of Afghanistan. The Taliban regime it displaced was called the Islamic Emirate of Afghanistan. Its 1992–2001 legal predecessor was called the Islamic State of Afghanistan. There is no doubt Afghanistan is Islamic in its nature and government. But its current form differs greatly from what was seen under the Taliban. The current conflicts will determine who will define what is Islamic and therefore what is Afghan.

Legitimacy

Today, Afghanistan has become a nation defined as much by its conflicts as its land, it peoples, and its faith. Conflicts in Afghanistan are fundamentally about legitimacy. Understanding what makes up legitimacy in Afghan terms—who can get, who lacks it—is as vital to understanding the conflicts as are maps to the terrain. A successful regime must be able to legitimate itself in Afghan and Islamic terms. Legitimacy has been the high ground on which the battle for the future of Afghanistan is waged.

"You can't buy Afghans, you can only rent them" is a cynical view of Afghan politics. Yet there are two important qualifications to this: they do not stay rented, and not everyone can rent them. In the 1980s, all the Kremlin's armed forces, gold, and political skills could not create a regime that worked in Afghanistan because of the widely held perception by Afghans of the ab initio illegitimacy of the Soviet presence.

The Soviets could never gain legitimacy. The pre-2001 Taliban was considered legitimate by most of Afghanistan's Pushtuns—plus small numbers from other groups—and saw its legitimacy erode from a broad range of reasons, including their heavy-handed actions regarding Sharia law, gender relations and Islamic practice, their subservience to Al Qaeda, and their unwillingness to embrace the symbolic actions that legitimate Afghan governance and are important in a largely nonliterate society as a demonstration of intent and respect. The result was the collapse of 2001. Only cornered-rat foreigners fought to the end for the Taliban. The majority of their Pushtun supporters cut a deal with the new government in Kabul, whose foreign support seemed then to usher in a new age for Afghanistan. The suspicion of the Taliban and the lasting goodwill toward those that helped remove them have only dissipated slowly with the repeated policy failures since then; polling shows that 87 percent of Afghans thought the ouster of the Taliban was a good thing in 2005, declining to 69 percent in 2009.[18] They switched sides and went with the winners—the US-led coalition and the Afghan Northern Alliance—just as many had switched sides to join with the Taliban during their successes of 1994–96, when opportunistic advances brought them into occupation of Kandahar, Herat, Jalalabad, and eventually Kabul.

The dependence on Afghan perceptions of legitimacy to enlist and motivate supporters is critical to Afghan's conflicts, kinetic and otherwise. The willingness to switch sides is a survival strategy, but it also reflects Afghan attitudes towards legitimacy. The importance of religion in Afghan daily life tends to accord success with the aura of a victory bestowed by the almighty. To try and regain this aura, Al Qaeda and the Afghan insurgents were, in 2008–10, recasting the anti-Soviet jihad in Afghanistan as a conflict in which victory was bestowed for religious fanaticism and piety rather than earned through success and endurance. Similarly, the importance of patronage means that the Afghans will support a winner if it is thought that a larger patron is behind them. Afghans are hardly unique in that they like to follow and respect a winner. In resource-poor Afghanistan, political and military momentum is a powerful force, for there is likely to be little available to counter it. When the situation starts deteriorating in Afghanistan, it can do so with great speed and suddenness and with few stopping points before arriving at the bottom.

Similarly, the US and coalition partners often find it hard to recognize how difficult it is for them to legitimate their presence and interest in Afghanistan and Pakistan in humanitarian and security terms. In Afghanistan, it is hard to accept that a great power can be motivated to act except to further its own immediate advantage; second-order benefits such as preventing the destabilization likely to flow from renewed civil war are not recognized. In Afghanistan and Pakistan, it is common knowledge—among government officials and illiterate farmers alike—that the US presence reflects a covert and subtle strategy rather than a desire to help the Afghans rebuild their country and lives. The US failure to capture Osama bin Laden and Mullah Omar is seen as evidence that they have no desire to do so, but rather are looking for a justification to prolong their presence. The bribes paid to the Taliban in Pakistan to protect the coalition's resupply trucks driving from Karachi to Kabul represent further proof. There is no agreement as to the strategy these policies are serving. Many believe that it is intended to be part of an unending war against Islam or to disarm and dismember Pakistan. Others point to US and western airbases in Afghanistan and central Asia and identify countering influence from Iran, Russia, or China as the real reason for the conflict.

Legitimacy in both Afghan and Islamic terms requires a degree of social justice. The Soviet-backed 1978–92 Afghan regimes were unable to provide it except in a few areas—including much of Kabul—where local alliances, subsidized bread, and make-work jobs could buy stability. That the mujahideen that took Kabul in 1992 failed to bring about the social justice that many of their constituents had actually been fighting for and dissolved in factional fighting enabled the rise of the Taliban.

For many Afghans, social justice is doing the right thing, following the tenets of Afghaniyat or Pushtunwali. In the face of the culture of corruption that has become widespread in 2008–10, there has been widespread nostalgia among Pushtuns for the perceived Islamic rectitude of the pre-2001 Taliban. Mullah Omar's simple lifestyle is often recalled fondly while the more complex reality, such as how the Taliban encouraged opium cultivation and then tried to manipulate the market to maximize its return on this crop of dubious Islamic legitimacy, tends to be forgotten.

An alternative view, also widespread, social justice is seen as equivalent to Sharia law and its administration through a juridical system. This is something the Taliban regime offered when they first came to power and one where its predecessors and successors have often been lacking. A strength of the Taliban in both Afghanistan and Pakistan is its identification with Sharia while both Afghanistan and Pakistan had state justice systems that proved incapable of meeting the needs of the population.

On both sides of the Durand Line—in southern Afghanistan in 1994–96 and in Pakistan post-2001—the rise of the Taliban was enabled because Pushtun secular elites—especially former mujahideen in Afghanistan and maliks in Pakistan—were not seen as delivering social justice. The perception was that many of the leadership figures were self-enriching, extractive, or were on someone's payroll and were, in effect, representing them rather than their fellow tribesmen. Prior to 2001, many of the Taliban leadership and their Arab allies were seen as carrying out similar behavior, and despite their links to religious authority this did not prevent their legitimacy from eroding. In Pakistan, the secular Pushtun tribal leaders were seen as increasingly either self-interested or tools of a distant government (especially the malik system) at the same time as the government was weakening the support structure for them.

Support for Sharia, however, does not necessarily translate into support for the Afghan insurgents or anti-democratic politics. There was widespread resentment, even from many Pushtuns, of the way the Taliban acted to implement Sharia law in 1994–2001. Yet the promise of social justice inherent in the concept of living under Sharia law is still seen favorably by many Afghans. Those that have offered social justice but failed to deliver—the post-1992 mujahideen-based government in Kabul, the pre-2001 Taliban, leaders who appeared more interested in earning money than helping their brethren—lose legitimacy and support.

The failure of the current Afghan government to achieve social justice has made the insurgents' offer to bring back Sharia law appealing to some Afghans. Afghan insurgents have used the appeal of social justice through Sharia to take advantage of the failure of the judicial system. The culture of corruption that has emerged throughout Afghanistan provides a further challenge and has focused resentment on the non-Muslim foreign presence that is widely seen as having created conditions that are the opposite of those inherent in Sharia.

Institutions and Power

Conflicts are about power. This makes the Afghan approach to power important—but not determinative—for understanding the institutions that shape the landscape of peoples and politics alike. Afghanistan has historically been a country where personal links and loyalty, more so than an individual's skills or abilities, determine ultimate success and failure in society. Afghanistan started to move away from the patrimonial model in the nineteenth century when Abdur Rahman started to develop a state, though even the "iron amir" did not aim to centralize all Afghans or create a cohesive national infrastructure.

The institutions of Afghan society are critical to the success or failure of any policy execution. These institutions are all-important for legitimating actions and decision-making undertaken by leadership or elite figures. A wide range of traditional Afghan institutions serve as interfaces between individual Afghans at the grassroots level and the official state. These include tribal, clan, or familial group leaders, especially among the tribally organized Pushtuns and, to a lesser extent, other groups including Uzbeks and Hazaras. Local councils of notables and elders, either ongoing or empaneled for a specific action, are shuras (Persian) and jirgas (Pushtu). While the two have been differentiated in that a shura is made up of elders and meets in response to a specific need, whereas a jirga is more egalitarian and meets on a consistent basis—which is why the Loya Jirga has become a national political structure, whereas the shura has not—in practice there is a wide variety of examples.[19] The hoqooq is a specialist shura dealing with land and water rights, a vital concern in agricultural areas. The possibility of a large-scale assembly for ratifying change is represented by Loya Jirgas and similar assemblies. A darbar, an audience for expression of loyalty and redress of grievances, results when a leadership figure meets the grassroots; it is an important ritual and Afghan leadership figures that fail to carry it out lose legitimacy. Councils of clergy (ulema) have, in recent decades, been increasingly involved in these actions.

A shura or jirga would draw on older, more experienced men, which in tribal areas would often be represented because of their hereditary authority. A shura may be more likely to include—or be dominated by—religious figures or local leaders that have not come out of traditional societal sources of authority. The 1978–2001 conflict saw shuras of guerilla commanders and religious leaders emerging to coordinate operations and fill the vacuum created by the lack of government; these often superseded traditional shuras and jirga. Religious institutions such as the mosque and the madrassa provide moral authority in communities. Funding comes from trusts (*waqf*) and tithes (*zakat*). These have been local institutions, normally without support or hands-on involvement from the central governments. Afghan Islam is by itself not hostile to democracy, with its acceptance of shuras and jirgas (not limited to clergy) for decision-making and dispute resolution.

One of the reasons the political changes instituted in Afghanistan following the fall of the Taliban—although largely implemented by elites and foreigners—have been seen as legitimate, was the use of the Emergency Loya Jirga and the Constitutional Loya Jirga as a visible sign of mass support for consensus building. The Emergency and Constitutional Loya Jirgas proved a good tool to build on the work started in Bonn and partially "demilitarize" Afghan politics, rooted both in the Afghan jirga tradition and the Islamic mandate of majlis-e-shura (requiring that an Islamic government engage in consultation). The use of the Loya Jirga (Great Council) is constitutionally provided for on issues of independence, national sovereignty, and territorial integrity; it can amend the provisions of the constitution and prosecute the president; it is made up of members of parliament and chairs of the provincial and district councils.

In addition to the institution of the president, the Constitution of Afghanistan provides for an upper house of the bicameral parliament consists of the Meshrano Jirga (House of Elders). It has 102 seats, one-third elected from provincial councils for four-year terms, one-third elected from local district councils for three-year terms, and one-third nominated by the president for five-year terms. Because elections for the district councils had not been held at the time of the 2005 parliamentary elections, each provincial council appointed one of its elected members to a seat in the upper house, which meant that a majority of this house is not elected. Half of the presidential nominees have to be women. This house has limited authority but can block legislation.

More power is held by the lower house, the Wolesi Jirga, the House of People, with 249 seats. The was initially directly elected using the non-partisan single non-transferable vote system—which is not constitutionally mandated—for five-year terms in 2005. Members are elected by district. At least 64, two from each province, must be women. The second parliamentary election was held in 2010.

Post-2001, there have been new provincial, district, and village councils established, with foreign assistance. All provincial and district governors and municipal mayors are appointed by the government in Kabul. There were elections for provincial councils in 2005 and September 2009, but planned elections for district and municipal or village councils have not taken place. Elections for district council were scheduled for 2010, but only 35 of 350 coucils were functioning.

The elected provincial councils are without executive powers, largely symbolic aside from participation in development planning. They have no ability to hold Kabul ministries or provincial governors accountable. Donors have been trying to provide the councils with the ability to make a positive contribution to Afghanistan's subnational governance. "If I was a provincial counselor, I'd get fed up with that role" said Jim Drummond, director of the South Asia division of the UK's Department for International Development (DfID).[20]

The provincial and district councils cannot levy taxes and are without real power (with exceptions being noted, such as the Kandahar provincial council where there have been family links between the leadership—it is headed by Walid Karzai, the president's brother—and Kabul). The members of the Ghazni provincial council walked out in March 2009 in protest over their lack of authority.[21] In the cases where they have been able to exercise authority, provincial governors have had to respond to the challenge. Despite the provincial councils' weakness, the September 2009 elections saw widespread allegations of vote-rigging on behalf of council candidates, in many cases reflecting a desire to achieve greater potential access to corruption.

Subnational governance institutions include the Community Development Councils (CDCs) organized under the National Solidarity Program (NSP). These have, in practice, complemented rather than competed with traditional collective decision-making institutions, though this varies greatly throughout Afghanistan. "The NSP for the first time created a space for men and women to decide for themselves and to take an active part in implementing their own decisions," said Eshan Zia, Minister of Rural Rehabilitation and Development.[22]

"The National Solidarity Program initially was hated, now Afghans and the international community love it," is the assessment of former Minister of the Interior Mohammed Hanif Atmar.[23] In the areas where the insurgency has been most intense or where local politics have been especially unresponsive, such as Kandahar, the CDCs have not functioned. This has led to the "suspension of the program in Helmand and Kandahar due to military operations," said Eshan Zia.

In some areas, post-2001 councils or the NSP's CDCs are indistinguishable from their traditional predecessors. Many CDCs are basically reconstituted shuras. In others, the changes—most visibly in the requirement to ensure women's participation—are considerable, and they will deal with issues such as oversight of reconstruction contract awards in a way that was never previously given to local Afghan authority

Afghanistan has had a state justice system since the nineteenth century, but its legitimacy and function were casualties of the 1978–2001 conflicts. The constitution establishes a nine-member Stera Mahkama (Supreme Court), with justices appointed for 10-year terms by the president with approval of the Wolesi Jirga. A system of High Courts, Appeals Courts and a separate Afghan Independent Human Rights Commission was also established.

The supreme court, once established, attempted to act as a bastion of Afghan conservatism. But the appointment of an effective attorney general and several new supreme court justices by 2007 limited this political impact. Other courts were, by and large, either not established or were so corrupt that they have had a negative impact. The insurgents and narcotics traffickers targeted those elements of the judicial system that were effective. Alim Hanif, the chief judge of the Central Narcotics Tribunal, was assassinated in September 2008, among others. Law and order suffered as a result; there was no way to try suspects once they were arrested. Many have simply been detained indefinitely in overcrowded prisons, such as Kabul's Pul-e-Charki, site of many executions by the Afghan Communists and the Soviets in 1978–92. In June 2008, a National Justice Program to address these problems was approved by the Afghan government, but implementation has fallen short due to lack of resources or, in the opinion of many Afghans, because change would disrupt profitable corruption.

The failure of the Afghan judicial system has been a blessing to local strongmen and warlords. These non-judicial leadership figures, sometimes holding government positions, have access to patronage networks and armed force to back up decisions and have filled the vacuum in many areas. They often resolve disputes to their own enrichment. This was particularly the case in the south post-2001, where those nominally pro-Kabul Pushtuns that replaced Taliban authority often used this opportunity to impoverish tribal rivals. This is greatly resented by many Afghans who have instead looked to traditional institutions of tribal and local justice such as local shuras. One of the appeals of the post-2001 resurgent Taliban is that they claim to offer Afghans a route to traditional Afghan dispute resolution, rather than relying on a largely non-functional state system or rapacious strongmen and warlords.

State Power

The institutions of power—whether at the state, subnational, tribal, or local level—in Afghanistan are the playing pieces in the game of state power in Afghanistan. The nature of state power in Afghanistan has changed over the years. Who controls the state remains the focus of many of Afghanistan's conflicts, with each group wanting participants in the political process. Yet the concepts and requirements of state power in Afghanistan are, like much else, unique.

In the Golden Age, the generation before 1973, Afghanistan's national government was limited in its reach and impact and worked with local elites, limiting their power (provincial governors were appointed by Kabul and were usually from outside the province) while offering access to resources and prestige to ensure their cooperation. While the Afghan state was centralized, authority in rural Afghanistan was decentralized. Tribe and qawm were more important in adjudicating disputes than the provincial or district governor or the police, there to protect the government rather than the people. The local Afghans were primarily responsible for their own governance and were only involved with Kabul's authority when things went out of control. There were no state-supported ulema to displace the local mullah from his mosque. Conscription for the army was not enforced among the tribes of Paktia and Paktika, and the burden of taxation fell more lightly on Pushtuns, who tended to resent it more. The varied and heterogeneous people of Afghanistan precluded any unitary solution.

Occupying Afghanistan by force had hitherto been impossible. Since the Golden Age was ended by former prime minister Prince Mohammed Daoud's bloodless coup in 1973 that deposed the former king, seizing state power in Afghanistan has proven to be all too feasible. This seizure may be exerted by putsch, war, or internal penetration.

A military putsch following decades of internal penetration was how the Communist Khalqi military officers seized power in April 1978, killing Daoud and many thousands of Afghanistan's secular and religious elites. In December 1979, the Soviet invasion took over state power which was placed in the hands of Soviet clients from Afghanistan's Parcham Communist Party, rivals of the Khalqis. The Pakistan-supported Taliban occupied southern and eastern Afghanistan in 1994–96; in 1996, they were militarily able to oust the Islamic State of Afghanistan government from Kabul. While the Taliban occupied most of Afghanistan, they were never able to militarily prevail in the civil war. Al Qaeda effectively took control of the Taliban through internal penetration—exerting power inside Afghanistan through them—in the years preceding 2001.

The most recent seizure of state power in Afghanistan was with US and coalition support after 9/11 made it possible for the Northern Alliance (based on the Islamic State of Afghanistan that the Taliban had ousted from Kabul in 1996) to defeat the Taliban in 2001. The power of US intervention—made earnest by coalition airpower and the presence of a few hundred special operations troops and intelligence operatives on the ground—was more than sufficient to transform the Northern Alliance into a force capable of offensive action, just as the previous foreign interventions had allowed other Afghan clients to seize power (or, in the case of Al Qaeda, quietly take control of it from them).

Afghanistan's history of the importance foreign money—and how foreign support can seize state power—suggests a fundamental limitation of

Kabul governments dating back to the nineteenth century.[24] Formed as a buffer state rather than to be economically viable, Kabul and its adversaries in the form of the pre-1978 Communists and Islamists, 1978–92 resistance, 1994–2001 Taliban, and 2001 Northern Alliance have normally been dependent on foreign aid. Such aid is not always effective. Pakistan and supporters in Saudi Arabia and the Gulf provided the Taliban with extensive aid in its 1994–2001 civil war, but were unable to achieve battlefield victory or consolidate political success among Afghanistan's non-Pushtuns. In those years, the Northern Alliance received a much smaller amount of aid from donors such as Iran and India, but was able to hang on militarily, even if its political development remained weak. It was only when the US intervened in Afghanistan in 2001 that the Northern Alliance had access to the resources and patronage that enabled a rapid defeat of the Taliban and its Al Qaeda allies. Afghanistan is a country where patron-client relationships are key to power. Ironically, this applies to Afghanistan itself in the international field.

This fundamental limitation of Afghan state power—the reliance on foreign aid and the difficulty of collecting revenues—has applied to the post-2001 Kabul government. Al Qaeda demonstrated in 1996–2001 that in an extremely poor country, those having access to suitcases full of cash have a great deal of power. This power is magnified when there appear to be no other sources for income.

It would have been difficult in the best of conditions to re-assert state power over the Afghan grassroots post-2001. Nothing but grief had come from Kabul since 1978 or—in the case of groups such as the Hazaras—forever. Eshan Zia, Minister of Rural Rehabilitation and Development, saw the problems Afghanistan faced in 2009 as reflecting "top-down governance, the absence of a social contract, the gap between the government and people and an absence of civil society. Good development depends on good governance. Development and governance are two sides of the same coin. The challenge is how to connect the people with the government."[25]

Nowhere in Afghanistan was there a passive population waiting for the imposition of top-down governance. Rather, the decades of conflict had led to a divided—largely but not exclusively on ethnolinguistic lines—

radicalized and mobilized population, with both secular and religious non-governmental leaders seeking to thrive or at least survive in the post-Taliban Afghanistan. But the failure to reassert authority, when coupled by moves to de-legitimize the local strongmen and warlords who did have this authority, created a vacuum in Afghanistan that was filled (in parts of Pushtun areas in the east and especially the south), on the ground, by the insurgents; in the rural economic sectors, by narcotics cultivation and trafficking; and in Afghan culture, by the idea that the foreign presence is anti-Islamic and putting the future of Afghanistan at risk.

Patron-Client Relations

No single concept is more important to Afghanistan's internal conflicts than that of patron-client relationships and the patronage networks that these create. Afghanistan's conflicts are often those of competing patronage-client networks. Foreigners often fail to understand this, and their inability to use patronage relationships leads them to stress centralized organizations on their own models (whether Soviets post-1979 or the US and its partners post-2001). These outside powers tended to neither understand nor trust the patronage model. The Soviets found that it was unlikely to put and maintain committed pro-Moscow Communists in power. The US and international organizations found that those best able to use patronage often had attitudes, human rights records, or governing practices that were seen as unacceptable and undercutting the goal of creating an effective centralized government. By doing so, both the Soviets and the US found their ability to use Afghan policy tools limited. Afghanistan is a country of strong patronage networks and weak or incapable governmental institutions. Neither the heritage of the small but respected government that the Afghans created during the Golden Age nor the Soviet and US and international organizations' commitment to a centralized state had effectively altered this by 2008–10.

Patronage has been a traditional organizing principle of life and governance in Afghanistan and Pakistan. The patron-client relationship is not open to everyone. The relationship needs to be legitimate in Islamic and Afghan terms to work (which is why the Soviets proved poor patrons).

Membership in patronage networks is often hereditary and usually patrilineal.[26] Patronage is a way to link with others consistent with Afghanistan's patrilineal, collective, yet hierarchical society. Patronage provides security, jobs, and welfare. In the absence of government acting at the grass-roots level or in the rural communities where most Afghans live, patronage remains important. Leadership figures function as a patron, dispensing jobs and favors on the basis of relationships and political loyalty to create and maintain patronage networks rather than hiring on the basis of competence, ethnic balance, or other considerations.

After 1973, Kabul regimes were unable to effectively use the patronage networks in ways to support and extend the power of the state, as the former king had done. All of the actions the former king had taken to extend Kabul's control and capability did not last. In 1978–92, the Soviets and their Kabul-based clients were unable to make patronage work in most of Afghanistan. The Communists ended up creating their own patronage networks in Kabul and other parts of Afghanistan they controlled. The Pakistan-backed Afghan resistance parties' internal dynamics also reflected patronage. Pakistan-controlled creation of alternative patronage networks (based in Pakistan and dependent on resources provided by Pakistan) empowered those Afghans acceptable to Pakistan and helped marginalize others. These wartime patronage networks tended to focus on elite rather than mass followers. It was commonplace to see resistance political leaders as well as major resistance field commanders living well while their followers inside Afghanistan, fighting the war, often had nothing; this was consistent with obligations inherent in the patron-client relationship.

Afghan patronage networks are resilient. In some cases, multiple patronage networks can pull in reinforcing or competing ways. A provincial or district governor can be a fearless anti-drug campaigner while benefiting from narcotics traffic elsewhere in Afghanistan. Loyal Afghan police or soldiers can also supply ammunition to the insurgents.[27] Patronage networks hedged their bets throughout 1978–2001, often having members on both sides of each conflict just as resilient Afghans, elites and grassroots alike, that have not gone into exile have adapted to each change in government, wearing Western suits in the Golden Age, growing beards under the Taliban, working hard post-2001 but keeping in touch with the insurgents. In the eyes of many Afghans, this is less a contradiction than a survival strategy.

But not all patronage networks have remained effective over time. The Taliban effectively used patronage networks in their 1992–96 rise to power. Such networks proved more effective than the nominal institutions and links of state power that were in the hands of the Islamic republic of Afghanistan in Kabul. Yet the Taliban leadership's legitimacy was undercut when Mullah Omar stopped holding darbars and they effectively limited Afghans' former direct access for petitions and dispute settlement that they had practiced before their 1996 move to Kabul.

Since 2001, the traditional Afghan approach to patronage has often not worked. What has emerged to replace it in many areas—ministries in Kabul or provinces in the countryside—is a toxic adaptation rife with corruption. Alternative patronage networks are offered by Afghan insurgents, who, in return for loyalty, offer to kill today's extractive policeman. In response, foreigners push for institutions that, like their own, would not depend on patronage but would be built on Western models.

The clients' power lies in the fact that allegiance, like identity, is seldom fixed. A patron who is oppressive or ineffective will lose clients. This provides a check on top-down oppression, but also means that it is difficult for a patron to get clients to perform required dangerous or unpleasant activities (like cracking down on opium or giving up power). This dynamic only works where clients have the option to transfer allegiance away from a patron, as was the case in much of Afghanistan in 1978–92, when there were normally multiple local or regional leaders, each with their own patron in the form of a foreign-supported political party, competing for clients. There has been no such competition in much of Afghanistan since 2001. In many areas, the central government is ineffective compared to the foreign presence (in the form of military forces or aid donors). The only source of Afghan power has often been local or regional patrons, including warlords. As a result, there is less check on oppressive behavior, and violence and oppression spreads. In southern Afghanistan post-2001, such actions have created fertile ground for the emerging insurgency, which became an alternative source of patronage in much of that area.

The importance of patronage relations extends to the battle of ideas in Afghanistan. Afghans are exposed to many different and often competing sources of news, but there is a tendency to follow the views of the provider of patronage or other Afghans that they desire to emulate. This contributes to the prevalence and strength of conspiracy theories and rumors. The power and the speed with which rumors can spread even among a population of sophisticated and experienced consumers of international broadcasts is often astounding to foreigners.

In practice, in Afghanistan, even among the educated and elites, perceived truth is defined as what a dispenser of patronage or a person of high status believes. Even sophisticated Afghans tend to believe whatever their patron or others they admire and emulate believes, however objectively wrong or incredible it may be. Similarly, self-perceptions of victimization or persecution are often not supported by objective evidence, but are no less strong for that. Most of Afghanistan's major groups, regardless of how defined, consider themselves persecuted.

This leads to a vulnerability to the improved propaganda generated by Al Qaeda and spread by other aligned organizations.[28] It also contributes to the speed and power of "bazaar rumors" in Afghanistan, which could generate mobs in minutes even before there were over 6 million cell phones. Those Afghans perceived as losers—whose future patronage is unlikely to be good—are the usual targets of such rumors while winners—from whom future patronage is expected—become beneficiaries. This contributes to the speed with which setbacks in Afghanistan can become disasters and underlines the connection between legitimacy and patronage. Those unable to provide or sustain patronage have their ability to achieve legitimacy limited.

Qawms

Afghan society is the "human terrain" over which the conflicts defining Afghanistan are being fought. The qawm (affinity group) is the building-block of that human terrain. In Afghanistan, the qawm has traditionally been and remains strong; the state has, correspondingly, traditionally been and remains limited. The qawm remains the basic unit of community and subnational Afghan identity based on kinship, residence, and sometimes occupation.[29] Qawms can be family, clan, or tribal groups, but the term also applies to Afghans who lack a tribal identity. The qawm's local, more traditional, focus is as a solidarity group reflecting (or modeled on) kinship ties. The qawm, not the state, remains the basic unit of community and, outside of the family, the most important focus of individual loyalty.

Afghan social cohesiveness encompasses tribal clans, ethnic subgroups, religious sects, locality-based groups, and groups united by interests. All of these are reflected in the makeup of the qawms. Because qawms do not have to be homogenous in ethnolinguistic terms, though they often are, their importance prevents these divisions from being the primary key to Afghanistan's conflicts.

During the 1978–92 war against the Soviets, local resistance commanders usually initially represented and led individual qawms. During that war, the (externally imposed) political party structure (from Peshawar) or pro-Soviet groups organized and paid for from Kabul both had limited impacts (and that through patron-client relations) on clusters of qawm units with common identities.

During the course of this war, many qawms had new leaders (pushed forward by the war), access to foreign aid, new patrons (in the form of the resistance political parties and Pakistan), and a sense of larger community coming from the participation in jihad that was also a war of national liberation. Listening to foreign radio broadcasts such as the Voice of America, BBC, and Deutsche Welt also changed the focus of many Afghans away from the purely local. Larger ethnic, regional, and linguistic identities were encouraged by the qawms' patrons, either Peshawar-based mujahideen or Kabul-based pro-Soviets. Outside resources such as US aid to the mujahideen or Moscow's aid to Kabul were alike used to build new patronage networks to make possible this change.

Qawms were mobilized—normally through patronage—and politicized by all sides, generally along ethnic or regional lines. In some areas—with the notable exception of much of Pushtun Afghanistan divided by tribe—disparate qawms were unified through the emergence of regional leaders and shared patronage networks. This was seen especially in Dari-speaking Afghanistan. Ahmad Shah Massoud moved from the commander of the anti-Soviet resistance in the Panjshir Valley to the foremost regional resistance commander in northern Afghanistan in this way.

The transition of many of Afghanistan's qawms from the politically mobilized and often militarized elements of 1978–2001 has, since then, been challenging. The political, economic, development, and religious actions to re-integrate them into a peaceful Afghanistan did not affect much of rural Afghanistan where the grassroots lived. Pushtun qawms have given their loyalty to the insurgents in many districts.

Parties and Warlords

Afghanistan is today defined by conflict, and these conflicts are about power. Those that would use power must use it in the context of Afghan institutions and concepts—including patronage—in a way that is perceived as legitimate. Because use of power by the state is often weak or ineffective, parties and warlords play an important role in decisions and actions, either legal or illegal, that affect the entire population. Neither parties not warlords were part of traditional Afghanistan. But they shaped it in the years of conflict in 1978–2001. Their strengths and their limitations have the potential to further affect Afghanistan's current conflicts.

Party organizations were not permitted under Afghanistan's Golden Age experiments with parliamentary democracy. Those that emerged were, by definition, part of the two (then-illegal) oppositions, Islamist and Communist.

In 1978–2001, the party in Afghanistan was a social as well as a political institution. In Afghanistan, the political mobilization and polarization that accompanied the conflicts of 1978–2001 created another level of identity: that of the political party. The party was the institution used to carry out mobilization through militarization, and it facilitated awareness of inter-ethnic differences and intra-ethnic commonalities. In this period, the party became an alternative source of patron-client relations. This largely reinforced and hardened pre-existing patronage networks, and in some instances it replaced them.

In 1978–92, Pushtuns dominated one of Afghanistan's two

Communist parties and six of the seven Peshawar-based Sunni resistance parties (with the others dominated by Dari-speakers but including substantial Pushtun membership), creating organizations in Afghanistan that cut across tribal lines. The Hezb-e-Islami (HiH) of Gulbuddin Hekmatyar (a detribalized Pushtun from Kunduz) became the most powerful of the six Peshawar-based Pushtun parties in 1978–92. It had the highest priority for Pakistani aid and a strong top-down organization. HiH was able to overcome many of the divisions inherent in tribal and religious networks in the other parties. Hekmatyar himself perceived the party as adapting the tactics of a Leninist "vanguard part" to Islamism.

In 1978–92, Pakistan backed only a single Sunni predominantly Dari-speaking major resistance party among the "Peshawar Seven," Jamiat-e-Islami Afghanistan (JIA). This brought together the disparate Tajik geographical groups—Panjsheris, Heratis, Badakshis, and others. JIA's Islamist ideology had to extend to both traditional and revolutionary politics and religious orientation among Dari-speakers because there were no separate parties for them, unlike the Pushtuns.[30] Ahmad Shah Massoud, who started as the charismatic leader of anti-Soviet resistance in his native Panjshir Valley in 1978 (he had previously led a Pakistani-funded revolt there against Kabul in 1975), was in later years able to use the JIA to help build what became the Northern Alliance.[31]

The Taliban of 1994–2001 lacked an effective party organization but continued the party-originated move toward militarization as they attempted to politicize and, more lastingly, ethnically unify Pushtun Afghanistan and lead it in civil war against their opponents.

Post-2001 Afghan political parties were largely identified with the ethnolinguistic and ideological polarization associated with the decades of conflict. This contributed to the 2004 decision by Hamid Karzai—over international objections—to employ an electoral system intended to marginalize political parties in parliamentary elections. However, once the parliament was operating, parties proliferated; by 2008, there were 104 registered. But none has emerged as a viable, strong force, whether independently or as part of a recognizable coalition. "Afghanistan politics are very personalized; institution building has been taken hostage by personalities," in the words of Ambassador Mahmoud Saikal.[32]

In 2008–10, there were political parties on both sides of Afghanistan's conflicts. The post-2001 Taliban has moved away from the party model of organization. HiH remains a part of the insurgent coalition, although Hekmatyar's model has reportedly shifted to that of the Lebanese Hezbollah, embracing armed struggle while not ruling out political participation.

In the absence of effective state authority in much of Afghanistan, "warlords," who combined both local authority and armed force without the check of being part of a legitimate state structure and had emerged from the 1978–2001 conflicts, were important post-2001. Warlords are not a traditional Afghan institution. There is no agreement as to who are warlords. Ahmad Shah Massoud, the defense minister and de facto military leader of the Islamic State of Afghanistan, the mujahideen-based regime that tried to rule from Kabul in 1992–96 and was assassinated by Al Qaeda immediately before the 9/11 attack in 2001, was characterized as a warlord by many (especially Pushtuns), but in death he has become the national hero of post-2001 Afghanistan.

The absence of effective governance at the grassroots level post-2001 has ensured that warlords remain a part of Afghanistan's institutions. In much of Afghanistan, leadership figures from the 1978–2001 conflicts remain in de facto power, with or without the color of state authority. They frequently practice non-inclusive and extractive politics that are resented by their involuntary network of clients; other clients see them as the only viable alternative to what they perceive as a non-responsive over-centralized state that has little effectiveness outside of Kabul.

A Different Country

Influencing all of the conflicts that define Afghanistan is the fact that it is fair to conclude that Afghan society is overall inherently collectivist and Islamic, religious in its orientation and deeply conservative. Afghan cultural conservatism is at heart a survival strategy. Its effectiveness is demonstrated by the fact that many of Mountstuart Elphinstone's 1815 observations are valid today. It is based on the assumption that, at the end of the day, outsiders—Soviet, British, Arabs, American—will go home or vanish to smoke and the Afghans will be left with what they have always had: their land, their faith, and each other.

Foreigners who are trying to push change on polite but resistant Afghans may find cabinet ministers with doctorates from Western universities and village elders untroubled by literacy alike in their ability to deflect unwanted change while assuring the outsiders of their gratitude for wishing the best for Afghanistan. Neither ministries in Kabul nor shuras in remote villages are configured for bold and decisive change. Both are conservative institutions, aiming first to preserve the interests of stakeholders (which usually center on patron-client relations).

For Afghan government institutions and ministries, change is often resisted, a task made easier by a system that often combines the least responsive elements of traditional Afghan ways and Soviet-imposed central planning. Afghan government ministries tend to be profoundly conservative institutions. Not only do they defend their bureaucratic turf, as government institutions do worldwide, but they perceive a vital interest in blocking any change that they cannot control or that threatens the networks—especially the patron-client relations—which is how such organizations tend to operate in an Afghan context. "Lots of Kabul ministries mean nothing to people in the sticks. Further out [of Kabul] not much governance is going on," in the words of one UN official.[33]

Reconciling change with Afghanistan's conservative culture has been problematic. Rural Afghans are suspicious of change. Change has usually brought them nothing but grief and distanced them from the true path of Islam and an honorable life. But even conservative rural Afghans will support change if they are shown that it is consistent with their beliefs and goals and that it is effective. Only then will they take ownership and, most reluctantly, take responsibility for change. At the national level, the Afghans have taken ownership of the constitution and the parliament. They have generally accepted that female members of parliament and provincial councils are a good and useful thing, like female doctors. The grassroots may take pride and ownership over Afghanistan's Constitution, the Loya Jirgas and 2004 and 2005 elections, have been appreciative of schools, healthcare, and their cell phones (over 6.5 million in service by the end of 2008); but many, not limited to the uneducated rural majorities of all ethnolinguistic groups, were horrified at television showing Bollywood movies or Afghan women singing. Terrorists and insurgents have been quick to exploit this as examples of the infidel invader's aim of subverting Islam.

Elites have all too often seen change as a source of personal enrichment to provide security against the day when the outsiders go home and they may have to go back into exile. Yet many individuals—including President Karzai—still appear to be foreign creations. Traditionally, those pushing the hardest for change were urbanized educated middle class and elite Afghans, but this group was largely destroyed, marginalized, or driven into exile in 1978–2001 and has not managed to reconstitute itself as a viable Afghan political force (in terms of patronage and ability to get things done) since then. Despite the return of a number of exiles with access to foreign support, including those at the highest levels of government, they are still a much less powerful force than they were prior to 1978; they rely on their patrons, the international community and the aid donors, for their positions and what internal influence they possess.

Conversely, rural Pushtuns often appear to be most conservative element of Afghan society, though this differs greatly from place to place and tribe to tribe. Yet detribalized Pushtuns—often without the intermediating effect of tribal leadership and extensive kinship-based patronage networks—have in the past backed radical or extremist leaders, Communist and Islamist alike. Those Afghan ethnolinguistic groups without tribal divides tend to be more open to change, but even these are deeply conservative. Rural Badakshis are closer to rural Pushtuns in their worldview than they are to educated urban Kabulis, even though they share the Dari language and lack the Pushtuns' tribe and clan organization. Ties of family and kinship provide legitimacy. Afghans disparage another Afghan by saying "Who was his father?" (Part of President Karzai's strength is that his father, a chief of the Popalzai tribe of Durrani Pushtuns and a large landowner in Kandahar province, was widely known.) This attitude permeates Afghan life and politics, and leads to a deeply conservative cast to a society that tends to be shared even by those—such as Communists or Islamists—otherwise devoted to radical change.

When top-down change seems to threaten Afghan culture or the Afghan or Pushtun way ("Afghaniyat" or Pushtunwali), it has historically been resisted. King Amanullah in the late 1920s implemented change without securing support from elites. The result was years of bloody civil war. The Khalqi government in 1978–79 set about remaking Afghanistan using the bloodiest methods of their Soviet patrons' history. They had no need to legitimate themselves or rally Afghan support: the tide of history (and Moscow) was with them. The result was the largest national rising of the twentieth century, with Moscow feeling compelled to intervene militarily. The challenge facing those working to implement change in Afghanistan post-2001 is how to ensure that their efforts are not seen as following these unacceptable models. It is hard to get Afghans to take ownership, harder still to get them to take responsibility (reflecting the society's collectivist and qawm-based roots).

Since 2001, the Afghan insurgents have sought to portray themselves as defenders of culture as well as religion and nationality. Even more disconcerting for the conservative connection of Afghan culture to legitimacy has been the post-2001 non-Muslim foreign presence, with military convoys running farm carts off roads, the presence of unveiled women, and drinking. The negative cultural impact of the foreign presence in the eyes of many Afghans—even if they accept the security rationale for its presence—has made the association of President Karzai and the current Kabul government with the West a political liability. Cultural resentment of much of the negatively perceived impact foreign presence is, like Afghanistan's conservatism itself, shared by its ethnolinguistic groups, even those who originally welcomed the foreign presence and still see it as preventing a return to a disastrous civil war.

Cultural conservatism has presented the insurgents with a powerful weapon in the battle of ideas. They present Karzai as a current "Shah Shuja" (the nineteenth century ruler installed by the British before the First Anglo-Afghan War who was overthrown by a Pushtun revolt). Karzai is presented as being as much of a foreign tool and no more of a Pushtun than was Najibullah, the hated former secret policeman installed by the Soviets who was able to use Moscow's gold to govern from 1986 to 1992. Karzai's reacting to foreign pressure has also undercut his links to cultural legitimacy. When an Afghan accused of apostasy was allowed to leave the country under foreign pressure rather than be tried for what is a crime under Sharia law, it appeared to the conservative grassroots that Karzai represented the foreigners' belief systems, not their own, even if they were in favor of Afghanistan abiding by international agreements on human rights.

To the extent that the struggle inside Afghanistan is seen in terms of cultural values instead of reconstruction, it has undercut progress. This conservatism has led Afghans to reject—often violently—social change imposed top-down without securing support from a broad base of institutions, groups, and individuals and showing deference, respect, and support of Afghan sources of legitimacy and values. Conservatism has led some in Afghan society—especially rural Pushtuns—to reject the changes in governance and life to emerge since the fall of the Taliban in 2001 and oppose the foreign presence.

Yet the Western dichotomy of conservative and radical change is difficult to apply to Afghanistan. The original Taliban of 1992–96 succeeded for many reasons, including the fact that they could legitimate themselves to Afghanistan's Pushtuns in pre-existing social terms, a basically conservative action. The original Taliban was able to use the links of existing networks and patronage, especially that of the Pushtun clergy and tribal leaders, to legitimate themselves while at the same time creating radical change, especially in Kabul, Herat, and elsewhere outside their heartland. Yet the Taliban imposed radical change in religious practice, including their insistence on men growing beards, and gender relations, including their insistence on prescribing a dress code enforced by extrajudicial violence, banning women from the public sphere in general and in working outside the home in particular. The only previous Kabul regime in Afghanistan's history that had attempted that degree of radical change, using the force of state power to determine how each Afghan must treat the women in his family, was the polarizing Khalqis of 1978–79, who had Afghans of all ethnolinguistic groups in arms against them within months. The Taliban were able to use a combination of armed force as well as money and connections supplied by Al Qaeda and other outside allies to enforce this radical change. But even the Taliban's fighting men were outraged at the sight of Afghan women being beaten for transgressing the dress code, one reason why few were willing to fight for them once it became apparent that the US had intervened against them in 2001.

The collectivist orientation of traditional Afghan society has led to suspicion of the free market economy that has emerged since 2001. Since then, the appearance of goods (unaffordable to most Afghans) from the world market and the large houses built in Kabul or in the Panjshir valley have given Afghans much scope to exercise the propensity for envy that Mountstuart Elphinstone first noted back in 1815. Similarly, resentment of the West, coupled with envy of its material gains, dates back to the nineteenth century but required satellite television and DVDs in every village in Afghanistan to become a powerful force cultural force post-2001.

The post-2001 media revolution in Afghanistan resulted in a flood of new newspapers and television and radio stations. DVDs have arrived in even the poorest villages, giving people the ability to compare their quality of life to that of the outside world. The political implications of this media flood are enormous. If, prior to 2001, the average Afghan was content to interact with a distant world through shortwave radio broadcasts, they have since then had to contend with a much greater engagement with an outside culture that does not reflect Afghan culture and does not appear to value it, reflected in the appearance of satellite television and bootleg Bollywood movies that both fascinate and, often, repel the rural and uneducated majority. Afghanistan's insurgents have been able, in some areas, to transform this cultural unease into active or passive support for their cause. The first time the Afghan parliament overrode a presidential veto, in September 2008, it was to sustain a law restricting media rights, vindicating the cultural concerns of the grassroots while, conveniently, limiting press scrutiny of elite activities.

This deep conservatism is by no means an across-the-board rejection of change or nostalgia for the Taliban.[34] Most Afghans, including the most religiously conservative, point with pride to the constitution, the elections, the Loya Jirgas, and the parliament. Repeated polls show that Afghans of all classes support education and want their children—including the girls—to go to school.[35] The Hazaras—the poorest large ethnic group in Afghanistan—have since 2001 been in the forefront of pushing for girls' education and enabling women's involvement in the political process. The media revolution, following decades of exposure to international radio news and the widespread experience of being a refugee or working abroad, has brought the outside world to rural Afghanistan.

The future of Afghanistan will be determined by the implementation—not the formulation—of policies between summer 2011 (when the US will start to draw down its troop numbers) and 2014 (when the ANSF is scheduled to take over security). NATO and the US have pledged at Lisbon in 2010 to keep combat troops deployed until 2014. The May 2010 Karzai state visit to Washington and the January 2011 visit to Kabul of Vice President Biden led to reiterated promises of continued US commitment. Yet the commitment needed by Afghanistan may be undercut by the lack of strategic patience, domestic political support and willingness to provide resources in the US and the West. In 2010, terrorists and insurgents alike demonstrated that they remained adaptive, resilient and committed to achieving their policy aims, which are not limited to Afghanistan. In 2014, the end of the Karzai presidency is potentially treacherous, with an attempt to prolong his rule or designate an unpopular successor having the potential for a crisis.

CHAPTER TWO

DWELLERS IN THE VORTEX

"Rule the Punjabi, intimidate the Sindhi, buy the Pathan, and honor the Baluch."

—British colonial-era aphorism
attributed to Sir Robert Sandeman, c.1890

Geographically, the heart of the Vortex corresponds to the Pushtun world. This has meant that the shift from the Frontier to Vortex has had a tremendous—in some ways devastating—impact on life and culture in both Afghanistan and Pakistan. Because of the centrality of ethnic Pushtuns to the post-2001 conflicts, the politics and culture of the Pushtuns in Afghanistan and Pakistan have risen to a level of importance that is not shared and is often resented by the other ethnic groups in these countries. In 2008–10, those carrying out insurrections and supporting terrorists—as were those suffering from them in both Afghanistan and Pakistan—were largely Pushtuns, although both insurgencies were reinforced by substantial number of volunteers from Pakistan, especially Punjabis, and from would-be jihadis with worldwide roots.

In neither Afghanistan nor Pakistan was there large-scale violence between ethnic groups through armed organizations, the type of fighting that marked the conflict in Iraq at its height, though anti-Shia violence in

Pakistan has dramatically increased since a campaign was opened against the Touray Pushtuns near Parachinar in November 2007. If, in either country, the insurgency became widespread among other ethnic groups, such as Punjabis in Pakistan or Tajiks in Afghanistan, then it would transform the nature of the conflicts emerging from the Vortex. The conflicts waged by Pushtuns have an intrinsic ethnolinguistic firebreak. If it leaps over these firebreaks, then it will greatly enlarge the Vortex's heart of darkness and potentially engulf both countries, with global ramifications.

Other dwellers on the Pakistan side of the Vortex include Pakistan's security and intelligence services, especially the military's Inter Services Intelligence (ISI) but also the civilian Pakistan Intelligence Bureau (PIB), the Federal Investigation Agency, and provincial police Special Branch organizations. Pakistan's radical Islamic parties and their associated organizations also have a strong presence there. A third category of the dwellers in the Vortex (discussed in subsequent chapters) are those defined by their activities, including terrorism, insurgency (and crime), and narcotics cultivation and trafficking.[36]

The Durand Line

Sir Mortimer Durand actually knew what he was doing in 1893. The Durand Line, when it was the Frontier, was the limit of colonialism and of the post-Westphalia rational, ordered world of states, rulers and ruled, a seam between different civilizations and worldviews, the wild and the sown. In other ways, it is more comparable to the missing lines between countries in the Arabian Peninsula, put aside as too hard for mapmakers, independent sovereigns, or colonial administrators to draw. There are 350 known unofficial crossing places to the current Afghanistan-Pakistan border, many more in practice.

Much as Afghans will claim that the line is an arbitrary one imposed on Afghanistan to deprive them of control over the Pakistan heartland of what became Pakistan by the British Indian government at its Victorian zenith, there is actually a clear firebreak between the tribes that lived on each side, with a few exceptions primarily among traders (such as the Afridi, "lords of the Khyber") and truly transborder tribes (such as the

Mohmands and Wazirs, both of whom took up arms to oppose the line without the help of their neighbors). The line reflects a meaningful seam in the human geography of the Pushtun world, and the impact of over a century of separate history has increased pre-existing differences between the Pushtuns on both sides. The Pushtun world was so diverse that it required the policies of multiple Pakistani governments and the impacts of Afghanistan's 1978–2001 wars to change it from a Frontier to a line dividing an insurgency into two halves, helping the Pushtun insurgents on each side, enabling their own cross-border activities while preventing those of their opponents.[37]

The Durand Line was transformed by the migration of Afghan Pushtuns, over four million refugees who fled into Pakistan in 1978–92. The vast majority of the Afghan refugee camps were in Pakistan's Pushtun areas in the FATA and Baluchistan and North West Frontier Provinces. Pakistan supported the Durand Line as an international border, but its policy of aiming to control the Afghans through the Peshawar-based resistance parties and Pakistani institutions in the camps and elsewhere meant that they ended up encouraging resistance from Pushtun Afghans who did not accept the Durand Line and whose daily actions ran across it.

Resistance from Pushtuns—widespread in both Afghanistan and Pakistan—to the Durand Line ranges from traditional pre-1978 understandings intended to enable the movement of Pushtun Kuchi nomads to the widespread view of Pushtuns that the line should not to apply to them (though they do not see that other groups should be able to do the same). To the Government of Pakistan (and most of the international community), the Durand Line is a recognized international border. No Afghan government, even the pre-2001 Taliban that greatly depended on Pakistan for assistance in Afghanistan's civil war, has felt itself able to say the same, giving up its claim to the Pushtun borderlands. Younis Khalis, the Afghan 1978–92 resistance party leader, spoke for many Pushtun nationalists when he described the Durand Line as "written on water" a generation before Pakistani Pushtun insurgent leader Behtullah Mehsud said "there are no borders in Islam," universalizing its illegitimacy to all lines on maps that divide the umma and, implicitly, the governments that keep them divided.

The Pushtun World

The Pushtuns[38] share the basics of their culture: language, tribe, clan, collective tribal leadership, the idea of a shared patrilineal descent, and the importance of Pushtunwali (the code of the Pushtun). But there are vast differences between Pushtuns. Not all Pushtuns are part of a tribal structure. Many—especially those that have settled throughout Pakistan and those living in northern Afghanistan, where they were moved as a result of Kabul policies dating back to the nineteenth century—have become effectively detribalized. Detribalized Pushtuns in Pakistan or as far away as the UK, without the moderating effects of a tribal leadership, are frequently targeted for recruitment by terrorist or extremist organizations, according to Western anti-terrorism experts. In more peaceful times, Pushtun culture was a glorious mosaic of tribes and individuals.[39] By 2008–10, the insurgencies being waged by Pushtuns in both Afghanistan and Pakistan—despite the fact that most of their victims were other Pushtuns—were of global concern.

While predominantly Sunni and adhering to the Hanafi school of Islamic law, the Pushtuns' traditional practice of Islam, while intense, was heavily Sufic-oriented and reflected local or tribe-specific practices. Shia Pushtun tribes traditionally lived alongside Sunni neighbors; their shared Pushtun links outweighing the religious tension. In Pushtun culture, politics and identity are strongly linked. Traditionally, Pushtun tribes were governed by Pushtunwali as they understood it. The themes in Pushtunwali were melded with Sharia and were interpreted locally in a tribal context. While often at variance with Sharia law, the tenets of Pushtunwali are diverse but powerful. They include nanawatai (hospitality), badal (revenge), nang (honor), izzat (respect), and namus (women's honor). Traditional Pushtun culture reflects an overriding concern with honor, respect, and lineage, all in an Islamic context. Pushtunwali means men must defend their women to maintain not only their honor, but that of their family and lineage. For example, this makes searches of Afghan dwellings, especially by male foreigners, more than an inconvenience, a grave insult not only to the men involved, but to the core values of their society. Badal—revenge—is the only appropriate result. To the follower of Pushtunwali, honor is a powerful force. A world without honor would be a world unfit for anyone, especially Pushtuns, to live in.

In Afghanistan, Pushtun leadership has been primarily local and tribal/collective. Traditionally, in Pakistan and, to an extent, in Afghanistan, tribes were less interested in the national power than in gaining an advantage against other, competing groups, usually other Pushtuns. There has been a tendency for any ethnic Pushtun official with access to power to reflect patronage ties and support first his own village or clan.

In 2009, only some ten percent of respondents in a national poll cited Pushtun ethnicity as their primary identifier, ahead of Afghan nationality.[40] The educated Pushtun Kabuli or exile is more likely to see Pushtuns as a whole; his cousin who has never been a day away from his village is likely to define himself through his tribe, clan, or sub-clan. Urban elites may care about the competition between, for example, Ghilzay and Durrani Pushtuns or Pushtuns and Tajiks in general; but at the grassroots level, competition tends to be between a group and its neighbors in a perceived zero-sum competition for governmental support, irrigated land, or other benefits of patronage.

Pushtuns and State Power in Afghanistan

Power—especially state power—in Kabul has traditionally been held by Pushtuns. Mountstuart Elphinstone, the first Englishman to report from the then "Kingdom of Caubul" (though he never made it to the capital itself), was first among the many that equated Afghan with Pushtun. To him, this kingdom—not yet a country—was a Pushtun one. Those brief intervals when Afghanistan was not ruled by a Pushtun—the brief rule of Habibullah, an ethnic Tajik (known by his Pushtun enemies as Bacha-i-Saqao, "son of the water carrier") in 1930 and the Northern Alliance-dominated ISA of 1992–96—have been associated with governments with limited legitimacy and capability. Both were, not coincidentally, greatly resented by many Pushtuns (although both retained significant Pushtun allies). The legitimacy of these governments was limited in Pushtun areas, requiring them to try to impose authority through local officials that were independent operators owing largely nominal allegiance to Kabul.

No other Afghan ethnolinguistic group has comparable nationalist claims on the nature of Afghanistan. Others are merely "minorities" that are literally marginalized in the views of many Afghan Pushtuns. To Pushtun nationalists in Afghanistan, Persian-speakers were "junior partners" except if they were Shia Muslims, when they were not partners at all. The Turkic-speakers were conquered subjects. This view has remained strong among Pushtuns despite the challenge posed to Pushtun nationalism by Afghan nationalism. To other Afghans, this claim of Pushtun nationalist primacy is a direct threat. They have not fought since 1978 to return to living under Pushtun dominance.

The Pushtun nationalist vision of Afghanistan as the land of the Pushtuns (with other groups as minorities in a subordinate role) was never explicitly accepted even in the pre-1973 Golden Age (however much it was implemented in practice).

The 1978–92 war against the Soviets de-legitimated rule from Kabul and put weapons in the hands of Afghanistan's non-Pushtuns, who discovered that they could lead themselves while the Pushtuns were divided by tribe and subject to Pakistani influence. This reflected the divisions of the Pushtuns: tribal structure, religious differences, followers of particular Sufic leaders. Pakistan's forming six competing Peshawar-based parties with primarily Pushtun membership contributed to these divisions.

Non-Pushtuns created political and military organizations and institutions of their own which proved, on the whole, to be more effective than those formed by Pushtuns. It also reflected the more limited Pakistani control of non-Pushtuns and the emergence of men such as Tajiks Ahmad Shah Massoud from the Panjshir and Ismail Khan from Herat as strong leaders in the anti-Soviet resistance (Dostum, the ethnic Uzbek leader, was a Soviet collaborator until 1992).[41]

Despite this, in 1978–2001, Pushtun nationalism thrived in the exile communities, especially those from urban elites who maintained an emotional link with their tribal connection and a sense of entitlement to power. Without having the bitter but instructive experience of having to deal with other Afghans in the realities of fighting a war rather than the hothouse atmosphere of exile politics, they did not see that the "minorities" were politically mobilized, armed, radicalized, and unwilling to revert to a marginalized role or as subordinate to Pushtun power.

The pre-2001 Taliban, in practice, embraced the Pushtun nationalist worldview despite their extensive rhetoric about a universal Islamic umma. The pre-2001 Taliban made a point of recruiting a few members of non-Pushtun groups (usually Sunni religious figures) that were given posts of high visibility and no authority.[42]

The Pushtun nationalist vision has been rejected by the post-2001 Afghan political process aimed at creating a multiethnic democracy. It is also reflected in the Afghan refusal to consider formal divisions of administrative power or responsibility along ethnolinguistic, religious, or other divisions. Nor have the post-2001 Afghans redrawn provincial boundaries around ethnic lines.

This post-2001 change, however, while accepted by many ethnic Pushtuns—such as President Karzai—was ignored by some returning Afghan Pushtun exiles and Pakistani elites of all ethnicities, Punjabi as well as Pushtun. To them, Afghanistan is still land of the Pushtuns, and any arrangement of state power that does not reflect that is illegitimate. This has posed a challenge to establishing the legitimacy of the post-2001 Kabul government in the Pushtun heartland, a situation made worse by Kabul (and its supporters) failing to deliver effective governance and by the ability of insurgents to undercut arrangements. Others argue that Pushtun nationalism is reconcilable with a democratic, Islamic Afghanistan. According to Massoud Kharokhail, a Kabul-based scholar of Pushtun culture and politics: "Some countries have a core ethnic group, like the Punjabis in Pakistan. In Afghanistan, if you look at Kabul, post-2001, the president is Pushtun and most ministers are Pushtun." A veteran journalist in Kabul observed "Pushtuns are still convinced of their entitlement to state power and the status of other groups as minorities."

The US and other international organizations, in supporting moving more Pushtuns into the cabinet, did not solve the problems of reconciling power and ethnicity in Afghanistan. Post-2001, the presidency of an ethnic Pushtun (albeit a committed nationalist), Hamid Karzai, and the increasing number of Pushtuns (often replacing non-Pushtuns associated with the Northern Alliance that defeated the Taliban in 2001) holding cabinet positions, has led to a continued identification, among non-Pushtuns, of Afghanistan's state power with Pushtuns and resultant dissatisfaction at this shift of power.

By 2008–10, among non-Pushtuns, the heavily centralized power held in Kabul was widely perceived as Pushtun power. President Karzai and a large number of cabinet members, were Pushtuns. Post-2001, the goal of empowering Kabul was widely seen as being a way to empower Pushtuns at the expense of other groups. That it was backed by the US (especially identified in Afghan eyes with Ambassador Dr. Zalmay Khailzad, himself an ethnic Pushtun) increased the suspicion of non-Pushtuns. Those insisting on the primacy of central government power in Afghanistan are often seen as using it as a tool to ensure the primacy of ethnic Pushtun power. By 2008–10, there was increasing support among non-Pushtuns to amend Afghanistan's constitution to make power less centralized.

This perception that the Pushtun ethnicity of those in positions of power and authority consistent with their (estimated) demographic proportion was sufficient to prevent "Pushtun alienation" was not accepted by many Afghan and Pakistani Pushtuns. These have attacked the Pushtuns holding leadership positions in post-2001 Afghanistan as "false Pushtuns," as many saw Karzai himself. Massoud Kharokhail sees extensive alienation from Kabul among many Pushtuns who are not rallying to the insurgents. "Pushtuns do not feel represented by the government."[43]

Pushtuns and Their Neighbors

Centuries of encounters between Pushtuns and their neighbors built the foundation for the Pushtun self-image: spiritual, utopian, literally on the cutting edge of Islam and a threat to any, Muslim or otherwise, that falls short of their own ideas of social justice. It was a strategy of cultural resistance and self-preservation in the face of state power that collided with traditional Pushtun society. Indirect control—with money, opportunities for state service, and advancement for relatives—was widely practiced by governments on both sides of the Durand Line. It led to the malik system in Pakistan, in which the Pushtun leadership figures who interacted, with the government, through its political agents, with the government were eventually seen more as state representatives than as members of the tribe, increasingly de-legitimating them in recent years. "Being Pushtun does not mean you represent Pushtuns. Links to the tribal system are very important. There are no links with grassroots for Pushtun elites, unlike [the Afghan Taliban's leader since 1992] Mullah Omar," said Massoud Kharokhail.

Pushtun nationalism evolved in its present form not through the narratives of the tribes and lineages, but largely through barriers to participation in the politics of Afghanistan and Pakistan. When ethnic Pushtuns have voted in open elections in either country, they have not elected standard-bearers for nationalism but rather fellow Pushtuns committed to working with other ethnic groups at the national level. Yet despite this, by 2008–10, substantial minorities of Pushtuns in both Afghanistan and Pakistan were participating in or, more often, passively supporting insurgencies that had an explicit aim of ending the multiethnic democracies in both countries and replacing them with an ill-defined Islamic regime that would, in practice, incorporate or enforce Pushtun rule.

In pre-1973 Afghanistan, although state power was in the hands of Pushtuns, in practice, rule in Afghanistan's Pushtun areas was indirect, through tribal leaders. Provincial governors were brought in from other areas or were often urbanized Kabulis who did not have access to the local tribal system (which assured their loyalty to Kabul). Tribes that cooperated with Kabul received development, irrigation projects, roads, schools, and scholarships for the children of leadership figures (all largely paid for with foreign aid). Those tribes that refused to cooperate received none of these benefits.

The pro-Soviet Afghan governments of 1978–92 had no desire to follow this model. The Khalqi governments of 1978–79 targeted many Pushtun tribal leaders for death as "feudal remnants." The 1986–92 regime of Najibullah, the Soviet-appointed ethnic Pushtun former secret police chief, tried to revive this approach, but by then Kabul had little legitimacy or capability. Najibullah himself, in his efforts to maintain power, increasingly turned to Pushtun nationalist approaches.

The Pakistan governments of 1978–92 used as their instruments of power not the Afghan Pushtun tribes but six of the seven Peshawar-based resistance parties that were predominantly Pushtun. The outside supporters of the Afghan resistance—especially the US—found that the Pakistani military was unwilling to share control of the resistance parties' politics. Rather than use traditional Afghan institutions (such as tribes), Pakistan used the distribution of aid to "buy" control. When Pakistan's "chosen instrument" among these parties, HiH, failed to gain state power in 1992–94, the Taliban emerged as their replacement, a status it still, in some ways, retains as part of the insurgency fighting inside Afghanistan.

The actions of outsiders, whether in Kabul, Moscow, or Islamabad, set back for a generation the emergence of independent, non-dependent Pushtun political leaders. Outside patrons gave their Pushtun clients the resources to choke out alternatives, either by killing them, driving them into exile, or politically marginalizing them. Such leaders have every interest in preventing elections, for in both Afghanistan and Pakistan Pushtuns have elected moderate leaders. Those seeking to influence Pushtuns rely on bribery, so it is not surprising that the most effective Pushtun political leaders to emerge since 1978 have generally been political fanatics with outside support who have been the most ruthless toward Pushtun competitors: Najibullah, Gulbuddin Hekmatyar, Mullah Omar, Behtullah Mehsud, Siraj Haqqani.

Pushtuns have been both instigators and victims of the post-2001 insurgencies in Afghanistan and Pakistan. Pushtun nationalism has been a powerful force in motivating and mobilizing insurgent support from the population, building on resentment and the widely shared feeling that state power in Afghanistan must be equivalent to Pushtun power and that, in both countries, the insurgents are fighting an unjust, corrupt government supported by anti-Islamic foreigners. To some, Pushtunwali is under attack. The theme that the conflicts in Afghanistan and Pakistan are part of a global attack on Islam by the US has struck a responsive chord among many Pushtuns. In retrospect, the attack on Pushtunwali—the code of the Pushtuns, the champions of Islam—is seen as having gone on for decades, marked by the rise of the cash economy in the Pushtun world, when men came to care more about money than honor and when tribal chiefs cared more about attaining comfortable exiles than helping their suffering kinsmen.

Pakistan in the Vortex

The Frontier did not become the Vortex overnight, nor in the short time between Al Qaeda and the Afghan Taliban arriving from Afghanistan in 2001 and the Pakistani Army's disastrous South Waziristan campaign of 2005.[44] In fact, by 2008, the Pakistani military had lost more soldiers fighting the insurgency in Pakistan than the US and NATO had lost fighting the insurgency in Afghanistan. It took decades of decisions and policy implementation from multiple parties and players to create a disaster this large. The policies of Pakistan, especially its security services, including the military's Inter Services Intelligence (ISI) directorate, however, were instrumental in creating it. While these policies have changed as the insurgencies emerging from the Vortex threatened both Afghanistan's and Pakistan's continued existence by 2008–10, their impact continues to affect all the conflicts in both Afghanistan and Pakistan.

The British stressed divide-and-rule along tribal lines. Institutions or individuals—secular or religious—that had the potential to have a cross-tribal appeal and could provide a matrix for Pushtun integration therefore had to be countered and kept under strict control. This approach was different from the practice in Afghanistan. Governments in Kabul since King Abdur Rahman were also historically practitioners of divide-and-rule tactics, tribally based throughout the Pushtun areas, but there was never the need to place a firewall between the tribes and Pushtun-controlled state power in Afghanistan like the British did.[45]

When the British Empire left, there was less need for a firewall between the tribes and the government of Pakistan. The Pakistan military withdrew frontier garrisons that the British (like their Mughal and Sikh predecessors) had maintained; shared Islamic identity rather than armed force would support state power in the borderlands. Instead of being seen as a threat to the new state, cross-border Pushtun loyalties were seen as a strength, and Pakistan relied on traditional lashkars raised on both sides of the Durand Line as their main fighting force in the 1948 Kashmir conflict with India.

For their firewall, Pakistan decided to create the FATA. The tribal agencies that make up the FATA, under Pakistan as they had been under the British, is a place where, off the main roads and aside from narcotics, the laws of Pakistan do not run. The firewall included the political status of the FATA; its institutions, especially those of the political agents and maliks, the Frontier Corps, the banning of political parties in the FATA, and the enforcement of the British-drafted Frontier Crimes Regulations (FCR) with its emphasis on collective responsibility and punishment rather than the laws of Pakistan, all remained. While Prime Minister Yousaf Reza Gilani called for abolition of the FCR and extension of the laws of Pakistan to the FATA in his 2008 inaugural address, it remained in place.

The population of the FATA is uncertain. It is estimated at about four million, about two percent of the population of Pakistan. In the 1980s it also contained two to three million Afghan refugees in a small (the size of Massachusetts) resource-constrained area. An estimated 88 percent of the land is unused, with three percent irrigated, eight percent under crops, and one percent under the remaining forests. The lack of development affects the people as well as the land. Overall literacy is estimated at 17 percent, compared to a national average of 42 percent. Female literacy in the FATA is about three percent, while there are over 8,000 people per doctor there as opposed to about 1,500 in the rest of Pakistan. This degree of underdevelopment was not the result of insurgency or Islamic radicalization, but of decades of Pakistan's governance.

The FATA did not even have voting privileges until 1996. Political parties remain banned. The widespread dissatisfaction with the banning of political parties and activities in the FATA means that in recent decades it has been the mosque that shapes political action under the cloak of religious activity. By doing this, the Pakistani government policy effectively provided years of monopoly to the religious organizations in the FATA without the competition from other political parties that they face for Pushtun votes in the NWFP, Karachi, or elsewhere in Pakistan.

Pakistan started in the 1970s to line up support behind the groups that were the ISI's chosen instruments for controlling events in Afghanistan.[46] Linked to this was the policy of multiple Pakistani governments to make the nature of the government in Kabul the focus of Pakistan's Pushtun politics (rather than contesting for power within Pakistan). Former US ambassador to Afghanistan James Dobbins described this policy by Islamabad as the "aspirations of Pakistan's Pushtuns are to be projected onto Afghanistan by the Government of Pakistan rather than being focused on Pakistan."[47] An extremist Muslim infrastructure appeared along the Afghan-Pakistani frontier: religious seminaries (madrassa), numerous training camps and staging areas for international Islamist action as a tool of Pakistani statecraft. To the ISI, building this religiously based infrastructure and its networks that ran throughout Pakistan and, eventually, globally, was consistent with then-president Zia ul Haq's embrace of Pakistan's religious parties. He believed that the Islamic dimension was one way Pakistan could counter India's superior battlefield strength. Zia was suspicious of Afghan secular nationalism, blaming it for Pushtunistan crises of previous decades and offering India, in return for a trivial amount of aid, a chance to encircle Pakistan through cooperation with Kabul. At the same time, Zia distrusted Pakistan's secular Pushtun organizations, such as the Awami National Party, seeing them as potentially secessionists and having a heritage of links with New Delhi. Pakistan believed that religious-based insurgent groups were, in the end, something that it could control and could make a powerful counterbalance to Pakistan's national security dilemmas, both in terms of the competition with India and combating the Soviet "southern thrust." Pakistani government policies including supporting the "Afghan Arabs" (Muslim foreigners who volunteered to take part in the jihad against the Soviets). Networks established in the 1980s for bringing in funding for Deobandi and (neo-) Wahabi-based Islam were the forerunners to what Al Qaeda would use to create a worldwide terrorist threat. In the words of Pakistani Ambassador Husain Haqqani, "This political commitment to an ideological [Pakistani] state gradually evolved into a strategic commitment to jihadi ideology."[48]

How this commitment played out was most clearly seen in Peshawar, the headquarters of the seven Pakistan-supported Afghan Sunni resistance parties, and the refugee camps in the 1978–92 anti-Soviet conflict. Islamic radicalization became the guiding ideology. Pakistan aimed at empowering those Afghan Pushtuns that espoused this radicalism, most notably Gulbuddin Hekmatyar and his Hezb-e-Islami Hekmatyar (HiH) party.

Afghanistan's Shias were also losers in Pakistan's policies in 1978–92. Pakistan largely refused to recognize any Shia Afghan resistance parties (leaving the field open for Iran to pull together its eight-party alliance of Shia parties) or, until 1987, take actions that would pull together the bitterly divided Shia Afghans. President Zia was afraid that this would lead to integration of Afghan Shia groups with Pakistan's restive Shia population, with the result being subject to Iranian influence. When Afghanistan's Shia groups did come together in the late 1980s, it was largely in spite of rather than because of Pakistan and reflected Iranian efforts.

In the 1970s and 80s, the secular military ISI ended up creating infrastructure and networks that included mainly religious institutions and organizations. Former Afghan military officers were marginalized in the Pakistan-based leadership of the war against the Soviets. Secular Afghan elites, especially leadership figures, were driven into exile from Pakistan by the repressive atmosphere attending the creation of what became the Taliban culture. In Pakistan during the 1970s and 80s, the emergence of the Taliban culture also reflected both the systematic weakness in civil society and the marginalization of the FATA in terms of political participation and economic development. The failure of the state school system in Pakistan was a powerful impetus to the rise of the madrassa network that provided the groundwork for the Taliban culture.[49]

At the same time, the existing tools of Pakistani control over the Frontier were allowed to atrophy, replaced by direct influence by the ISI and other security services or indirect control through the actions of favored groups, either Pakistani or Afghan.[50] The malik system among the Pushtun tribes fell into disrepute. The positions of political agent in each of the seven FATA agencies, considered by their predecessors to be the most challenging posts in all of British India, were now given to junior civil servants.

The ISI created a network of camps and support systems on both sides of the Durand Line. The ISI, starting in the 1980s, brought in groups waging a cross-border insurgency in Kashmir, plus allies whose focus was on Pakistan's domestic policies. Thousands of radical Arabs and other foreign extremists were processed through this infrastructure en route to jihad against the Soviets in the 1980s and against Afghan Muslims opposing the Taliban in the 1990s, although, increasingly in the late 1980s, Kashmir became the main focus until the Kargil crisis of 1999 led Pakistan to change its policies away from a support for transborder insurgency there. In the 1990s, the network spread into Afghanistan, making use of the Pakistan-supported Taliban's control of areas along the Pakistan border. This gave Pakistan even more deniability. By the late 1990s, the Taliban, Al Qaeda, and Pakistani intelligence cooperated with groups supporting the insurgency in Kashmir like the Harakat-ul-Mudjahedin (formerly Harakat ul-Ansar), Lashkar-e-Taiba (Tayyaba), Jaish-e-Mohammed, Al-Badr Mudjahedin, and the Hizb-ul-Mudjahedin, which was the Kashmiri militant wing of Pakistan's largest Islamic radical political party, the Jamaat-i-Islami. They used training camps and other facilities in Afghanistan, especially in Paktia and Nangarhar provinces, that were also used to support the increasing Pakistani involvement of these groups in Afghanistan's 1992–2001 civil war. On the Pakistani side, there were networks for logistics, communications, transportation, safe houses, and a population expected to be supportive and ask no questions.[51] One veteran Afghan political observer, whose work with Pakistani intelligence dates back to the 1970s, described this network as "the privatization of terror."

While the creation of this infrastructure was paralleled by the rise of Islamic inroads into the Pakistan military, its creators were by no means all or even primarily Islamists. They were primarily uniformed but also civilians and Pakistani nationalists first and foremost. Since the decision in 1948 to counter the Indians in Kashmir with Pushtun tribal lashkars (armed groups) recruited from both Afghanistan Pakistan, secular nationalists counted on cross-border Islamic and tribal-based links as a way to redress the balance of power with India and saw this as a way for Pakistan to confront threats on its borders without the threat of a conventional conflict that it would likely lose. Building on a strength Pakistan has, namely its connections with transnational Islam, which its opponents could not match, and trying to use them to achieve its policy aims against the Indian and (pre-1989) Soviet threats, helped create the Vortex.

This network survives today and runs inside Afghanistan, providing support for the insurgents.[52] However, the degree of control in ISI hands is uncertain. The ISI claims to be unable to turn the network off. Post-2001, Pakistan was unwilling to close it down. In 2008–10, the insurgency was so powerful inside Pakistan that it was unable to do so.

Creating the Vortex: The Crisis of Pushtun Authority

Traditional sub-national Pushtun governance in both Pakistan and Afghanistan was primarily tribal and secular. This does not undercut the important of religious leaders in Pushtun society and culture. In the past, in what became Pakistan, when frontier tribes did unite, it was usually under a charismatic religious figure that could cross tribal lines and bring together tribally divided rivals under an Islamic cause. This was seen in the 1830–31 Barevli jihad against the Sikh kingdom, the 1897 frontier rising, and the 1930s revolts led by the Fakir of Ipi.[53] But in Afghanistan, secular leaders were the primary leaders of political actions that cut across tribal lines, not religious figures.

The existence of the Frontier shaped how Pushtuns were governed. Pushtun politics worked as long as they took place in two parallel contained systems at the edge of civilization. Competing forces could be kept in balance: between national and subnational loyalties, between tribal and religious leaders, between Pushtowali and Sharia, between different Islamic practices. Each victory for one competitor would bring a reaction, often financed by external patrons, which would restore equilibrium.

During the 1970s—the decade when the Frontier started to become the Vortex in earnest[54]—challenges to the system of secular Pushtun leadership arose from the increasing opportunities to make money for Pushtuns in Karachi and the Gulf. This meant that there were numbers of Pushtuns with money but shut out of power. In 1970s-80s Pakistan, the absence of electoral politics in the FATA meant that tribal politics were the only avenue open to these Pushtuns unless they wished to remain elsewhere in the country. The nature of the government-maintained malik system effectively choked off political participation in the

FATA. In Afghanistan as well as Pakistan, such Pushtuns became "tribal entrepreneurs," with power and authority but often operating outside the traditional collective decision-making of the tribe.

As more Pakistani Pushtuns moved to Karachi and other cities in Pakistan, they participated in electoral politics and lived under Pakistani law. At home in the FATA, they had no vote until the 1990s and no party politics even after that. The FATA remains governed by the colonial-era Frontier Crimes Regulations (FCR) with its emphasis on collective responsibility and collective punishments rather than the same law as the rest of Pakistan. The Pushtun diaspora, in Pakistan, the Gulf, and the UK, has grown throughout this period of instability and has been estimated at up to six million. They provided money and access to outside resources that allowed "tribal entrepreneurs" to challenge a system of power and control that, in Pakistan, increasingly no longer seemed legitimate.

However, under Pakistani president Zia al Haq, the separateness of the FATA was affirmed. His predecessor, Zulfiqar Ali Bhutto, had looked to assimilate it into Pakistan. Zia stressed the importance of Pushtun religious leadership rather than the power of the maliks and the government political agents in the FATA. This policy direction was applied to Afghanistan during the 1978–1992 conflict, when ISI's policies enabled the rise of mullahs as Pushtun resistance leaders and the emergence of the Pakistan-established Afghan Sunni Peshawar-based political parties as alternative patronage networks, Pakistan-funded using international aid. In Pushto-speaking Afghanistan, the emergence of religious leaders—with the resources directed to them by the seven Peshawar parties, six of which were themselves headed by religious figures—to lead the qawms of Afghanistan into their transition to guerrilla organizations to fight the Soviets was in line with Pakistani strategy. Religious leaders were thought likely to be committed to a conflict even where there was no easy path to victory.

In Afghanistan, the assault on Pushtun leadership carried out by the Communists soon after they seized power was bloody and had a lasting impact. Non-Communist sources of authority in Pushtun Afghanistan—tribal leaders and major Sufic religious authority figures among them—were in many cases killed or arrested as feudal remnants by the Afghan Khalqi regime in 1978–79. Those tribal leaders who avoided murder by the Khalqis were forced into exile in Pakistan, along with their tribes. There, they found a Pakistani official policy of marginalizing them, ensuring that authority would be with either the Pakistani government or Afghan religious figures. Many Afghan Pushtun tribal leaders were threatened with violence. As a result, they tended to leave Pakistan for the West—often using their superior connections and access—and were in many cases the spearhead of the worldwide Afghan diaspora. Their connections with grassroots Afghans, either fighting the war at home or in the refugee camps, suffered as a result, as did the perceptions of the legitimacy of those who had gone into exile returning to claim positions of authority.

In part because alternative leadership figures were killed or forced into exile, in much of Pushtun-speaking Afghanistan in 1978–92, the ulema of Pushtun Afghanistan, especially local mullahs, became the primary decision-makers. Seven political parties were operating in refugee camps inside Pakistan. These parties were subject to Peshawar law and Pakistani authority, yet they are operating as part of a shura of Muslim clergy, even though many members of these parties only nominally abided by sharia law and their view of Islam is closer to Pushtun folk traditions and Deobandi-influenced madrassas, customs that are common in the FATA region, where many of these men studied prior to the fall of the Taliban in 2001. In the Afghan refugee camps in Pakistan, the refugee Afghan clergy had access to religious patronage networks—often funded by foreign money—that allowed them—not the nominal tribal leaders— to benefit their own clients among their tribe or group. Many of the surviving Afghan Pushtun leaders, while their nominal clients were in the field waging jihad or in the refugee camps, did not share this experience with them, but went instead into exile in Peshawar or to the west, taking advantage of their superior contacts with high-level patrons. Those secular leaders—whether tribal chiefs or army officers—who went to Pakistan ended up largely peripheral to both the direction of the conduct of the war in Afghanistan and to humanitarian efforts, both cross-border and in Pakistan. During the war against the Soviets, Pakistan's government and international aid organizations made decisions of resource allocations on behalf of the predominantly Pushtun Afghans in Pakistan rather than the Afghans making their own decisions.

The Pakistanis were able to do this because Sunni Afghan political leadership was largely controlled by the seven Peshawar-based parties, all dependent on Pakistan. The great fear in Pakistan during the war against the Soviets was that the Afghans, fighting men and refugees, would remain if the Soviets managed to consolidate their rule in Afghanistan and that they could link up with discontented elements of Pakistan's Pushtuns to mount an armed challenge to Pakistan's political authority on the model of "Black September" in Amman in 1970 (when Zia was Pakistan's military attaché to Jordan). Part of his lesson was that, having seen secular Palestinian organizations try to overthrow the secular Jordanian monarchy, religious links need to be stressed if Muslims were not to kill each other but unite against a common enemy, which to Zia was the threat created by the Soviet thrust into Afghanistan and the continuing security competition with India.

Inside Afghanistan, during the 1978–92 conflict, tribal shuras in the border provinces of Paktia, Paktika, and Kunar found themselves unable to defend their home territory against extractive activity, especially clear-cutting of trees, by cross-border entrepreneurs linked to the transport and timber mafias in Pakistan. These often made alliances with local Pushtun "tribal entrepreneurs" that did not represent a majority leadership view but were important figures because of their access to money. Such figures became more important on the Pakistani side post-2001 as the traditional leadership came under attack.

Tribal entrepreneurs with a limited claim to tribal primacy but with important outside contacts that allowed access to networks extending outside the Pushtun borderlands (or even worldwide) have emerged to become major insurgent leaders, such as Jaluladin Haqqani in the 1980s and Behtullah Mehsud post-2001. These leaders received financial support from the Pushtun diaspora, anxious for change in their homeland.

These events brought crime into the Pushtun world, where it remains important to the present. Most of this is connected with narcotics traffic, but it has its roots in the "timber mafia" and the "transport mafia" in Pakistan, dominated by ethnic Pushtuns, who have become important players since enriching themselves as a result of Afghanistan's 1978–92 war against the Soviets. By 2008–10, crime and insurgency had become increasingly integrated across the Afghanistan-Pakistan border.

The rise of the Taliban culture and especially the insurgency in Pakistan has seen a redoubled assault on secular and tribal Pushtun leadership. The widespread killing of maliks and tribal elders (khans) by transnational terrorists, especially Al Qaeda and the IMU, in cooperation with the Pakistani Taliban started soon after 2001. South Waziristan saw an especially bloody campaign of murder and intimidation. This contributed to the rise of what would become the Pakistani Taliban. The victims were replaced as decision-makers by shuras of nominal ulema that were the backbone of what would become the Pakistani Taliban, much as their Afghan counterparts had been during the rise of the Afghan Taliban in the 1990s.

The mullahs that emerged as leadership figures among Pakistan's Pushtuns are not all ignorant venom-spewing preachers. Many are well educated and have access to a range of governmental and non-governmental support networks. The Pakistani Pushtun mullahs that have emerged as the leadership figures in the FATA and, subsequently, the NWFP have to compete with the entrepreneurial tribal jihadi leaders, most notably Behtullah Mehsud, who targeted and killed Wazir tribal elders who would not go along with being superseded.

After 2005, in many areas of the FATA, alternative malik systems emerged. These new maliks remained the tribe's interface with the government of Pakistan but were selected by a tribal shura, rather than by the government. The government of Pakistan, in 2008–10, remained committed to trying to use the old system of political agents and maliks in a FATA now marked by an intense insurgency and with many areas controlled by the insurgents and off-limits to the government. This approach has had success in some areas. In mid-2009 the Wazir tribe in Waziristan was rallied by pro-government maliks to oppose the rival Mehsud tribe that was linked to the Pakistani Taliban through their then-leader Behtullah Mehsud.

These changes in Pakistan's Pushtun leadership reflected a decades-long process that has, in the Vortex, created a leadership vacuum. This vacuum has, since the 1970s, been filled by other than traditional secular Pushtun leaders. By 2008–10, it was increasingly being filled by two competing new Pushtun leaderships. One is the secular and religious leaders, radicalized by the Taliban culture but not limited to the Pakistani Taliban. The other is the secular leadership represented by the democratically elected Pushtuns who sit in Pakistan's parliament or the parliament of Pakistan's NWFP. The previous source of secular Pushtun leadership in the form of tribal chiefs and the malik system has effectively been sidelined in much of the FATA—although in some tribes, such as the Wazirs, increased government support had revitalized them by mid-2009. By 2008–10, the conflict between these two groups of Pakistan's Pushtun leaders and their competing vision of the future for Pakistan's Pushtuns had assumed great importance for both Pakistan and Afghanistan.

Born in the Vortex: The Rise of the Afghan Taliban

The original Afghan Taliban was much more than a Pakistan-supported Pushtun movement to seize state power in Afghanistan or a fundamentalist Sunni religious movement that sought to transform political Islam, although it was both of those things. In part, the original Afghan Taliban represented the nexus of the bazaar, madrassa, and mosque of southern Afghanistan, cut out of the context and put down in the harsh terrain and refugee camps of the FATA, Baluchistan, and the NWFP.

During the war against the Soviets in the 1980s, the Afghan Taliban was a strong element in the local indigenous resistance to the Soviet invasion, especially in Helmand and eastern Kandahar provinces. However, they declined later in the war as the resistance became more dependent on external support from Pakistan and direction by Peshawar-based parties. The Taliban was transformed in 1994 as a fundamentalist reaction to the failure of the post-Soviet mujahideen government to bring either social justice or order. In 1992–94, support from Pakistan to revive an alterative to the situation in southern Afghanistan where trucks were being stopped and detained—or at least forced to pay bribes—at multiple checkpoints led to the revival of the Taliban. They also represented a response to what was seen as a lack of social justice in southern Afghanistan, with Pushtuns, under the nominal authority of the post-Soviet Islamic State of Afghanistan, extracting resources from local inhabitants. Tribal feuds and disputes were waged with no recourse to effective outside authority. But it was not until 1996 that the Taliban was able to fully displace the

Hezb-e-Islami of Gulbuddin Hekmatyar (HiH) as Pakistan's chosen instrument of policy in Afghanistan.

The original pre-2001 Afghan Taliban emerged not from old Afghanistan or from traditional Pushtun culture, although it drew elements from both; rather, its roots were in the refugee camps along the Pakistani border in the 1980s. The Taliban culture grew in the 1980s with the marginalization of much of traditional Afghan Islam in the refugee camps in Pakistan. These were dominated by the "rupee mullahs," who used rupees—foreign funding—to buy sound-amplification systems to literally drown out those with otherwise greater religious authority. To this was added, in the 1980s, a mixture of Pushtun tribal conservatism, poorly understood Deobandi reformism from the subcontinent, and Wahabi fanaticism associated with support from Arabia and the Gulf. The Taliban's gender policies reflected the realities of the camps, a totally cash-based economy. Traditional subsistence agriculture and herding, which depended on women, was limited or impossible. Male heads of families signed the roll for rations. The economy was unlike that of rural Afghanistan, where female labor was valued because it was necessary. The depopulation of much of rural Pushtun-speaking Afghanistan by the Soviets, along with accelerating the pre-1978 trend of a shift away from an economy based on subsistence agriculture to one based on cash transactions and top-down distribution reflecting the impacts of patronage networks, paved the way for the rise of the Taliban culture.

Apologists for the Taliban—in both their Afghan and Pakistani forms—claim that "the Taliban culture is simply Pushtun culture." But the Taliban differed significantly from traditional Pushtun life in key issues such as religious practice, with the Taliban stressing Wahabi-influenced Deobandi-origin practices against the Sufic-influenced traditional Pushtun practices. The Taliban stressed the power of the mullahs rather than the Pushtun balance of tribal, secular, and religious authority. In what became their most controversial policies, both in Afghanistan and internationally, the Taliban made female absence from the public sphere a religious obligation, while Pushtun traditional society realizes that without women's work in a society dependent on subsistence farming and herding, everyone starves. In the final analysis, Pushtuns value independence and the Taliban proved willing to be used by outsiders such as the ISI or Al Qaeda to achieve their goals.

The original Afghan Taliban differed from the 1978–92 Afghan resistance that fought against the Soviets, even though all of the present Taliban leaders are former mujahideen. They were able to use the networks created by the ISI, international Islamic NGOs (whose numbers and significance greatly increased over the course of the anti-Soviet jihad in Afghanistan), Pakistani religious parties, the "Afghan Arabs," and the Pushtun diaspora. The most important were the networks of Pushtun religious figures, educated at the same Deobandi-inspired madrassas in the FATA.

The origins of the madrassa network in the FATA go back to the early years of the twentieth century and were seen by many Deobandi clerics as a way of creating a generation of ulema out of reach of British law or "modernizing" elements of Islam from the subcontinent. The growth of the madrassa network—also reflecting the failure of Pakistan to put in place an effective state school system in the FATA—was accompanied by a rise of Deobandi-influenced mullahs. Their practices started to displace the Sufic-influenced Islam traditional among the FATA's Pushtuns even before the 1978–2001 conflicts. This was made possible by funding from elsewhere in Pakistan, Saudi Arabia, and the Gulf. This also led to increasing tension with the FATA's minority population of Shia Pushtuns in the 1980s, forcing them to seek support from Iran in response.

It is often stated that the Taliban were welcomed by the population of Pushtun Afghanistan in 1994–96, who saw them as deliverers from local tyrants and criminals and absent rule from a Kabul government of limited capability and legitimacy, dominated by Panjsheris whose control of state power was seen as a departure from Afghan ways. As with much that is "common knowledge" about Afghanistan, this sentiment is not true.[55] It is an accurate description of some parts of Kandahar province, where the crime situation was compounded by the tribal dynamics, the presence of potentially valuable prey (the truck traffic from Pakistan), and the unwillingness of the then-ISA government in Kabul to upset the dysfunctional local situation because it needed the support of those in charge. Even had the ISA wished to remove the local leadership from power in 1992, they lacked an effective way to execute their will.

In much of Pushtun Afghanistan, however, the Taliban had to use armed force or, more often, a mixture of force and persuasion to gain power. This is why it was only in 1996 that they were able to seize the momentum that took them from Logar (where they absorbed most of HiH's forces that had been waging the civil war, including those that had intensively rocketed Kabul) to Jalalabad to Kabul, despite having seized Kandahar two years before. The key change between 1994 and 1996 was that Pakistan's ISI had made the decision to drop HiH as their chosen instrument of Afghanistan policy and replaced them with the Taliban.

The pre-2001 Afghan Taliban essentially offered a competing system that connected elements of the Pushtun Sunni religious leadership with shared links to Deobandi-based madrassas in Pakistan. These networks linked primarily the non-Sayid ulema from southern Afghanistan that had studied there, Durranis and Ghilzays alike, with former students (talibs) from these madrassas. These networks competed with the longer-established traditional religious authority of Sufic brotherhoods. These had been especially important in southern Afghanistan but, like all traditional Afghanistan institutions, had been weakened by the impacts of the war and exile in Pakistan.

The 1990s Afghan Taliban was the ulema, especially non-sayid, of Pushtun Afghanistan in arms, often able to use mullah-to-mullah ties that could cross ethnolinguistic barriers. The original Taliban's supporting networks also included tribal leaders (reached through kinship ties), bazaar merchants, hundi/hawala bankers, weapons dealers, land speculators, and small industrialists. Access to Pakistani government support helped it access more powerful interconnected interests—the transport mafia, oil smugglers, timber mafia, the increasingly-important narcotics mafias (linked through Pakistan to international markets), and their own networks of dependent growers (increasingly important under Taliban rule), and smugglers of consumer goods (the bara bazaar network in Pakistan).

This cemented the link between the nominally "law and order" Taliban and criminals. While the Taliban came to power in southern Afghanistan in 1994 with their reputation burnished by clearing away checkpoints on highways and suppressing extraction from local inhabitants, their links to the different mafias operating cross border-trade soon spread to narcotics cultivation and other criminal activity. As a result, the Taliban seemingly attracted every fugitive from the Islamic world in 1994–2001, aware that no extradition warrants were being served. This trend accelerated after 2001. By 2008–10 the activities of criminal groups, especially banditry and kidnapping, in southern and eastern Afghanistan were indistinguishable from the Taliban insurgency. Indeed, much of the criminal activity has been by individuals and groups that claim to also be Taliban.

The Afghan Taliban believe that the government in Kabul rightfully belongs to Pushtuns and the Durand Line is no barrier to those who need to retrieve this prize, kept from them by non-Pushtuns, infidel foreigners, and takfir Afghans. The Taliban offered a return to the Pushtun nationalist vision of "Afghanistan as the lands of the Pushtun." While the 1994–2001 Taliban welcomed non-Pushtun Sunnis and appointed some to positions of titular (but not significant) authority, their insistence upon submission to their own authority effectively ensured that, in practice, non-Pushtun Afghans had no greater rights in Afghanistan—and in practice much less—than those associated with any other Muslim.

The Afghan Taliban have had an international dimension since their inception. Mullah Omar assumed the title of *Amir al Mumineen* in 1994, a title requiring obeisance by all Muslims, across frontiers. Though starting as a Pushtun movement, there was never a sense that their message was limited to that group. The shift from the more traditional Pushtun internal worldview to one that increasingly saw themselves as part of a global struggle for Islam initially reflected the camps' location in Pakistan, support networks running to them from throughout the Islamic world (which, in the 1980s, saw a growth of non-government organizations), and the ISI's desire to carry the war to then-Soviet central Asia, which they saw as vulnerable to Islamic resistance. With guerillas and aid crossing the Durand Line daily to fight the Soviets, the Afghan Pushtun view that it was not a border that was legitimate to them or should restrict their movements became widespread. "The Taliban were raised in the refugee camps in Pakistan and, rather than a sense of Afghan nationhood, were indoctrinated in an Islam without borders," said a veteran Afghan political observer.

The pre-2001 Afghan Taliban's Islamic universalist and cross-border ideology, which was often difficult to reconcile with its more parochial Pushtun roots, was not brought in bin Laden's luggage, but was there from the roots of the movement in Pakistan in the 1970s and 80s. The Taliban's ideology easily evolved, from the belief that the Durand Line should not be a barrier to the Pushtuns it divided, to a belief that "there are no borders in Islam." Mullah Omar and the Taliban leadership's attraction to the goal of a restored Sunni Khalifait in which they would play a major role predated Al Qaeda's transnational appeal.

All these factors made the original Afghan Taliban a formidable force. They were able to achieve a degree of legitimacy with Pushtun Afghanistan that HiH, their predecessor and rival, was unable to achieve despite having the full backing of Pakistan and a more sophisticated party organization. In the final analysis, HiH's explicit Islamist ideology—looking to Islam as a modernizing force that will transcend the backwardness of tribal, divided, underdeveloped Afghanistan—was less attractive to the conservative Afghan Pushtuns than the Taliban's implicit fundamentalist ideology, looking back to an Islamic past of piety which, if as imaginary as Pushtun tribal lineages, was no less powerful for that fact.

Shaping the Vortex: The Post-2001 Afghan Insurgents

The post-2001 Afghan Taliban, revived in Pakistan, has since been re-exported—by cross-border insurgency and propaganda—into southern and eastern Afghanistan. What has emerged in the Vortex is different from the pre-2001 Taliban in Afghanistan. The pre-2001 Taliban had lost legitimacy, and this was further undercut by the scope of their military defeat.

Driven into sanctuaries in Pakistan following their defeat in Afghanistan in 2001, the remaining Afghan Taliban were largely cut off from their bases of support back home. With little interest shown by the winners, Afghan and foreign, in cutting them in on the post-conflict settlement, they had no choice except to transform.

The beaten Afghan Taliban of 2001 became part of an insurgent coalition that by 2008–10 threatened the future of both Afghanistan and Pakistan. They rebuilt where the "Taliban culture" was strong and state institutions weak in both countries. Motivation was provided by Al Qaeda-developed propaganda and the alienation of many Pushtun leaders. The failure of post-2001 Kabul and its foreign supporters to use effective patronage, strengthen the institutions that meant something to Afghanistan's rural Pushtuns, create effective and legitimate governance, and provide meaningful conflict resolution, when combined with the aggressive Taliban culture, meant that the insurgent threat has gained strong inroads where its predecessors were defeated a decade before.

The Afghan Taliban and their insurgent allies that have emerged from the Vortex are not the same pre-2001 organizations.[56] In 2002–06, the Afghan Taliban in Pakistan accelerated their cross-fertilization from other organizations that had marked the later years of their rule in Kabul. This included participation in the rise of the Pakistani Taliban. The government of Pakistan refused to move against the Afghan Taliban in their sanctuaries in Pakistan.

In Pakistan, Afghan insurgent groups have access to networks running outside the FATA, and money from Karachi, Lahore, and elsewhere made involvement in Pakistani internal politics even more important. In 2001, the Taliban had found few willing to fight to the death for them except some foreigners. By 2008–10, there was no shortage of insurgent fighters: Afghans, Pakistanis, and a new generation of foreigners. Despite the increased internationalization of the conflict, the leaderships of all major Afghan insurgent groups are Pushtuns. Those Afghans fighting in the insurgency were, in 2008–10, mainly Pushtuns. The current Afghan insurgents have, like the 1994–96 Afghan Taliban, been able to present themselves internally as the banner carriers of Pushtun nationalism and the restorers of Pushtun power in Kabul while holding fast to a transnational ideology of Sunni Islamic radicalism.

The post-2001 Afghan insurgent groups rely on the networks used by its pre-2001 Taliban predecessor and also share them with Al Qaeda and other threats, terrorist and insurgent alike. Post-2001, the Afghan Taliban and other insurgent groups have managed to come out from under Osama bin Laden's effective control. The post-2001 Taliban has become the leading Afghan insurgent group, dominating but not controlling a diverse insurgent coalition, but has retained its links with Al Qaeda. But while Al Qaeda focused on its global mission, the post-2001 Afghan Taliban instead aims at seizing state power in Afghanistan as part of an insurgent coalition that includes, among other groups, its pre-2001 rival HiH.[57]

It remains, however, that the insurgents, including the post-2001 Afghan Taliban, have not been able to claim the allegiance of all the ulema that had given at least passive support to its predecessor. Many of those with links to Kabul and those that still retained ties to the Sufic orders have not supported the insurgents, although signs that the Taliban have been increasingly penetrating brotherhoods in southern Afghanistan in 2008–10 have been disconcerting.[58] Other pro-government mullahs continue to resist the insurgents.[59]

Before 2001, many of the cultural restrictions that made the Taliban a brutal occupying force in Kabul or the Hazara Jat were applied more leniently—or at least more haphazardly—in the Taliban heartland of southern Afghanistan. The current Afghan insurgency combines some of this approach. In many areas, the insurgents make use of outreach to local inhabitants where possible. But more brutal and direct methods associated with the cross-border insurgency are also widespread. The Afghan insurgency is a mix of Afghan Taliban Pushtun origins and a potential Islamic Khmer Rouge. Xenophobia has been exalted, reflecting the need to de-legitimate the foreign presence that supports Kabul and reflecting the Al Qaeda-provided narrative that Afghanistan is one front in a global struggle against Crusaders and Zionists. It builds on a shared sense of deep humiliations to Muslims worldwide.

The worst crimes of the pre-2001 Afghan Taliban and their allies— the massacres in the Hazara Jat and Mazar-e-Sharif, the despoliation of the Shomali Plain, the repressive rule in Kabul and other cities—are likely to be the standing operating procedures of their successors. In south Afghanistan by 2008–10, the murder of pro-government religious figures and aid workers, and the massacre of civilian Afghans, have been widespread. Perhaps most telling, the intimidation of rural Afghan Pushtun leadership figures has forced many to flee to Kandahar, Kabul, or Dubai. Many of these were the bedrock of local support for the pre-2001 Afghan Taliban. The Afghan insurgent coalition is a different type of force.

CHAPTER THREE

PAKISTAN IN THE VORTEX

"The most dangerous geography on earth."
—Ambassador Richard Burt, 28 February 2008

I t is questionable whether there can be any lasting improvement in the security of Afghanistan, and with it the lives of Afghans, without addressing the conditions and policies in Pakistan that turned the Frontier into the Vortex. Many countries, organizations, and individuals created the Vortex. But the government of Pakistan, through overt action and enabling or not countering the actions of others, began the creation on its own territory, with the intention of affecting Afghanistan. But, from the start, Pakistan has been reaping the unintended consequences of these actions.

"Pakistan does not want to own Afghanistan, just run it, like the [pre-1919] Brits" is the view of one veteran journalist. In 2008–10, for Pakistan's military and elites, the goal of their Afghanistan policy is the creation of what eluded them in the past: a Pakistan-friendly, Pushtun-dominated (often styled "moderate Taliban") government in Kabul. They believe that the US and the coalition are preventing the achievement of this goal, even though it is also in their interest. By 2008–10, the US had become wildly unpopular in Pakistan, both among elites and in mass sentiment. The US is seen as waging a war on Islam both in Afghanistan and through their links with India and Israel. US policies are seen as being aimed at destabilizing or dismembering Pakistan to weaken or eliminate a nuclear-armed Muslim state.

Many Pakistanis see US policies since 2001 as having led to the emergence of the radicalized Taliban movements that by 2008–10 threatened both Afghanistan and Pakistan. They still believe that, in the end, the US and the coalition forces will disengage from Afghanistan and that their Afghan allies and the current Kabul government will flee into exile at that point. The non-Pushtun Afghans—perceived as a minority—will deal with Pakistan's enemies and rivals—India, Iran, and Russia among them—to try and hang on to power, setting the stage for a potential resumption of the Afghan civil war that the US could have avoided by supporting Pakistan's goals.

The continued cross-border nature of the terrorism, insurgency, and narcotics traffic make Pakistani policy decisions vital to the future of Afghanistan. The future of Afghanistan is more dependent on what happens in Pakistan than any other country (including the US and its coalition partners). It is questionable whether there can be any lasting victory over terrorism, insurgency, and narcotics in Afghanistan and with it improvement in the lives of Afghans without solving the long-running crisis of governance problems in Pakistan.

There remain significant differences between the conflict in Pakistan and the one in Afghanistan. No one wants to secede from Afghanistan, while the greatest threat to Pakistan is that their insurgency may cause the country to come apart at its ethnolinguistic seams. The insurgency in Pakistan—emerging from the Vortex but not limited to it—was widely recognized by 2008–10 to have become a threat to its future.

Creating the Vortex: The Roots of Pakistani Policy in Afghanistan

Pakistan's involvement in Afghanistan has been more extensive than any other regional power and has played a direct role in events back to the 1970s. Pakistan's involvement in Afghanistan is inherent in the contradictions of Pakistan's political and cultural identity; it is not just the conflation of issues and actors. It dates back to when Pakistan recruited

Pushtun tribal lashkars (armies) from both Pakistan and Afghanistan to fight the Indians in Kashmir in 1948. Pakistan later withdrew the regular military from its garrisons in the FATA; it would embrace the Pushtuns and their ethos—while denying them the vote and access to Pakistani justice, and underdeveloping their heartland in the FATA—and not be an occupying power like the British.

Pakistan's long-standing perceptions of national security have led to a necessity to shape the political situation in Afghanistan. This has led to participation as a frontline state in the conflicts in Afghanistan. Pakistani strategy in Afghanistan reflects what can be seen as a succession of two geostrategic thrusts.[60] The first (from the 1950s until 1989) was southward by the Soviets. The Soviets threatened Pakistan through their actions in Afghanistan: first, widespread aid, trade, and internal penetration; and, in 1979–89, through invasion and a major military commitment. The Soviet relationship with India in these years further increased Pakistan's fears that the Soviet goal was to surround and destroy Pakistan and achieve access to the "warm waters" of the Indian Ocean. This provoked a Pakistani northward thrust. Pakistan saw Soviet and Indian support for this Afghan policy as being much more important than the minimal amount of cross-border violence that resulted from Kabul's Pushtunistan claims. Indian influence in Kabul encouraged Afghanistan to create and use the Pushtunistan issue as a lever to dismember Pakistan. Even though Afghanistan did not militarily cooperate with India in any of its conflicts with Pakistan, the Pushtunistan issue contributed to the lasting concern Pakistan has about threats that may emerge from Afghanistan.

Pakistan's northward thrust became a political and military search for the elusive "strategic depth," otherwise denied it by geography, that put most of Pakistan within easy striking range of India. This strategy was always viewed through the prism of its security competition with then-Soviet ally India on one hand and domestic (especially dealing with military and ethnic Pushtun access to power) politics on the other.

The northward thrust was viewed as a counter to the two threats that Pakistan's military thought could destroy the country. These were outside attack by India (aided by the Soviet Union), or outside-aided internal strife that would pull Pakistan apart. Because of India's links with both the government in Kabul and Pakistan's own Pushtun population—both dating to before partition in 1947—the strategy had both an internal and external dimension.

The northward thrust began in the 1970s, after Pakistan's defeat by India in the 1971 war and the secession of East Pakistan to become the independent state of Bangladesh. In 1971, the Pakistani military perception was that their outside supporters—the US, China, and Saudi Arabia—could not prevent India pulling off a piece of Pakistan or aiding movements aiming to secede from Pakistan. In their mind, at the end of the day, Pakistan could not count on outsiders. Therefore, Pakistan needed to build a strategy on national and especially religious bonds that would prove solid under pressure.

To counter previous decades of Soviet and Indian involvement in Afghanistan, Pakistan's involvement also started with internal penetration. Pakistan armed and trained anti-Kabul Afghan Islamist insurgents (including both Gulbuddin Hekmatyar and Ahmad Shah Massoud). These were launched in an abortive uprising against the Afghan government, the 1975 Panjshir revolt. Pakistan policy evolved to providing support for the Afghan war of national liberation after the 1978 Communist putsch seized power in Kabul.

Pakistan's military and especially the Inter Services Intelligence (ISI) directorate has remained the main internal generator and implementer of Pakistan's Afghanistan policies. The ISI is both a military intelligence agency and the military's "directed telescope" inside Pakistan. This military control of Afghanistan policy generation was not total and complete but was often to the exclusion of the Pakistani foreign ministry and other civilian governmental organizations (including, for example, the political agents in the FATA). While different Pakistani governments—military and civilian—have tried to involve other organizations, the military has remained the prime determinants of Pakistan's Afghanistan policies.

Since the Panjshir revolt, the Pakistani military's main agents of change in Afghanistan have been Afghan guerrillas, who are motivated by Pushtun ethnicity and Islamist or fundamentalist ideology. Pakistan has enabled—either by direct support or an indirect hands-off

approach—these guerrillas to fight against other Afghans and their foreign supporters (the Soviets in 1979–89, the US and ISAF more recently)
opposing Pakistan's policies.

The 1979–89 Soviet invasion of Afghanistan transformed Pakistan's
northward thrust into part of overall Cold War strategy. In those years,
Pakistan was a frontline state and its actions received support from the
US, China, Saudi Arabia, and others. The Pakistan-based Afghan resistance received extensive aid from the US, China, Saudi Arabia, the UK,
France, and many other donors. Pakistan insisted on retaining control
of both their own strategic vision and their relations with the Afghans
waging the war and sheltering in their territory.

The Afghan guerrillas of 1979–92 had the benefit of a seemingly
open sanctuary in Pakistan that was, in the end, always denied by the
government in Islamabad and a massive aid flow. The Afghan resistance
managed to prevent Soviet political consolidation in Afghanistan until
Moscow's war effort was swept away by the final unsolvable crisis within
the Soviet state. While Pakistan, unlike the Soviets, put much smaller
numbers of military men—hundreds rather than some 150,000—into
Afghanistan in 1979–89, their presence was much better thought out,
their actions shrewder, and their impact more long-lasting.

By 1987–89, the Soviet Union was coming to an end and their southward push was failing. Instead of aiming to counter the southward thrust,
Pakistan now believed that its strategic interests required that state power
in post-Soviet Afghanistan be held by Pushtuns, that a government in
Kabul be "friendly" to Pakistan and Islamic in character, and that Indian
involvement in Afghanistan be marginalized. Pakistan added to the
strategic requirements motivating the northward thrust, re-opening central Asia after over a century under Russian rule. To the other strategic
requirements were added that Pakistan now must have unfettered access
to central Asia for trade and energy pipelines, with Karachi as the main
port on the Indian Ocean for the landlocked nations that were formed
from former Soviet territory in central Asia.

The Soviet defeat in Afghanistan reopened the Kashmir issue, as
India's superpower ally was now in retreat. The ISI planned to achieve
victory in Kashmir much as they had perceived that it was already being

achieved in Afghanistan, through the use of Pakistan-hosted guerilla groups in a cross-border insurgency. The revival of conflict in Kashmir and the tensions with India that resulted lasted through the Kargil conflict of 1999 and beyond. A cross-border insurgency directed at India would require strategic depth, a source of manpower, and a deniable support infrastructure. Pakistan looked to post-Soviet Afghanistan to provide all three.

In 1992, as the Soviet-installed government in Kabul collapsed, Pakistan backed a force led by HiH, supported by a strong force of foreign volunteers from the Islamic world, the "Afghan Arabs," to seize Kabul and establish a government that would meet Pakistan's strategic requirements: pro-Pakistan, anti-India, ethnically Pushtun and Islamic in nature. However, HiH was preempted by the Northern Alliance forces, led by Ahmad Shah Massoud that, in a bloody battle, held Kabul and made possible the creation of the Islamic State of Afghanistan (ISA), drawn from the Pakistan-based anti-Soviet resistance leadership, in Kabul. To Pakistan, the power of the Northern Alliance—led by Massoud and made up of guerillas from Tadji, Uzbek, and Hazara coalitions—made the ISA government unacceptable. They therefore decided to back HiH in proxy war against the ISA in Afghanistan. This started with rocket attacks on Kabul in August 1992.

Pakistan backed HiH through much of Afghanistan's civil war, transferring its support to the Taliban starting in 1994 and culminating just before the Taliban took Kabul from the ISA in 1996. But, following this success, Pakistan saw its influence with its Afghan Taliban clients challenged by the arrival of Osama bin Laden in 1996 and the rise of Al Qaeda in Afghanistan; by the late 1990s, Pakistan was interested in creating a "moderate Taliban" leadership to replace what they saw as increasingly non-responsive Taliban regime (president Karzai's father was murdered, presumably by Al Qaeda or the Taliban, following an approach for participation in this stillborn group).

With its political control eroded, Pakistan increased its commitment to the proxy war being waged against the predominantly non-Pushtun Northern Alliance forces, whose (limited) support from India, Iran, and Russia Pakistan perceived as a challenge to its national strategy. Pakistan and Al Qaeda alike backed the Afghan Taliban for what they hoped would be the final military defeat of the Northern Alliance. In 2001, the 9/11 Al Qaeda terrorist attacks brought about US and coalition intervention. The military situation changed rapidly. The Taliban collapsed. Al Qaeda fled. The end of the Pakistan military commitment in Afghanistan came when Pakistan had to ask US permission to airlift trapped ISI officers from northern Afghanistan, alongside the Taliban and Al Qaeda.[61]

Post-2001: The Vortex and Pakistani Policy

In 2001, Pakistani President General Pervez Musharraf's military government had supported and enabled the US-led coalition in their intervention in Afghanistan. To Musharraf, this US intervention was seen as inevitable after the 9/11 attacks and he hoped that Pakistan's support for the US would lead to more security aid for Pakistan in the short term and a renewed relationship with the US—previously soured by Pakistan's acquisition of nuclear weapons—in the longer term. To many in Pakistan—including much of the military and civilian nationalist elites—this spelled disaster. With the arrival of the Al Qaeda (and its foreign allies) and Taliban in the FATA, NWFP, and Baluchistan after their retreat from Afghanistan in 2001–02, the war literally came home to Pakistan.

A similar "blowback" also happened following the Musharraf government's ending of Pakistan's transborder guerrilla operations in Kashmir in 2003–04. The infrastructure, systems, and networks created to support these two failed proxy wars stayed and grew even stronger.

After 2001, Pakistani policy was based on cooperation with the US (at least against "foreign" Al Qaeda) and providing continued support for the Bush administration Global War on Terrorism. The government of Pakistan did not take the opportunity to disrupt the Afghan political process—which excluded Pakistan's Afghan clients—that started at Bonn in 2001. Pakistan did not interfere in Afghanistan's politics throughout the Bonn process, including the Emergency Loya Jirga and the Constitutional Loya Jirga leading to the new constitution and the 2004 presidential and 2005 parliamentary elections. This Pakistani restraint, following Pakistan's 2001 response to the US requirement for access to Afghanistan and its support for American military operations there, earned President

Musharraf the gratitude and support of President Bush. Musharraf's rhetoric, his talking of starting long-needed reforms to revitalize Pakistan's civil society and capability for governance, was well received in the West. But the results proved limited: US support for the Musharraf regime focused on capturing a limited number of high-ranking foreign Al Qaeda leaders.

Nevertheless, Pakistan's long-standing strategy of the northward thrust did not go away. The Pakistan military became the strategic opponents of the US at the same time as they were cooperating in the US Global War on Terror and counting on US arms aid to redress the balance of forces with India. Post-2001, Afghanistan replaced Kashmir as the main focus of Pakistan's security competition with India. Pakistan's military saw the improvement in the US relationship with India, which had begun earlier in the 1990s, as a threat; Afghanistan could be the site of future US-Indian cooperation. The Pakistan military looked with concern at improved US-India and Israel-India relations. The US war in Iraq was seen by many Pakistanis as a reaction to Muslims having weapons of mass destruction, raising concerns among Pakistan's government and elites—not just the military—that Pakistan, as the only openly nuclear Muslim state, would be the next target. US actions are seen by elites and grassroots alike as being part of a concerted effort to destabilize Pakistan.

Post-2001, Pakistan's Afghanistan policy was seen by the Pakistani military leadership—as well as many civilian leaders throughout Pakistan's political spectrum—not as part of a Global War on Terror. While Pakistan was willing to cooperate against Al Qaeda, it did not perceive the Afghan insurgents operating from its territory and their allies among their own Pushtun population as an imminent national security threat.

Post-2001 Pakistan—not just the ISI—saw no threat from the exiled Afghan Taliban and other Afghan and Pakistani radical groups. Rather, Pakistan saw its Afghanistan policy primarily as part of their competition with India and secondarily an extension of domestic policies and politics, especially regarding Islam in government and the ethnic Pushtun population's access to state power in Pakistan. Pakistan would cooperate against Al Qaeda and other foreign (non-Afghanistan or non-Pushtun) terrorists. The Pakistan military was willing to act against terrorism aimed at

Pakistan outside the borderlands or at the US and UK because it saw this as a threat to themselves and their outside patrons. This met the primary US Global War on Terror goal and also pleased China and Saudi Arabia, Pakistan's other key foreign supporters, who feared indigenous terrorists in Al Qaeda's camp.

The trust gap between the US and Pakistan widened starting after 2001.[62] Pakistan was alarmed at developments in Afghanistan. Even while Musharraf was seen as an ally of the Bush administration's Global War on Terrorism, Pakistan's military leadership was pre-occupied with walking a tightrope between meeting the demands of the US-led coalition and rebuilding its Afghan policy on the same lines (operating through proxy forces) that had failed in 2001. Pakistan saw the US as undercutting its national security interests by blocking its need for a Pakistan-friendly government in Kabul. It saw the initial post-2001 cabinet positions held by members of the Northern Alliance being easily bought or manipulated by Iran or India. It also saw a government not dominated by Pushtuns as unacceptable. Karzai, educated in India, was expelled from Pakistan when an ISA diplomat in the 1990s. He has few friends and admirers in Islamabad, fewer still in Rawalpindi (where the military and intelligence headquarters are). Pakistan has never seen Karzai as Afghanistan's proper leader.

In actuality, the post-2001 Musharraf policy was largely aimed at maintaining Pakistan's capabilities for implementing its pre-2001 policies—including the proxy war in Afghanistan—while waiting out the US and coalition military departure from the region. While Pakistan's cooperation against Al Qaeda was genuine, if limited, Musharraf's rhetoric proved hollow. Pakistan aimed to maintain ISI leverage over the Afghan Taliban and other radical Afghan and Pakistani factions now rebuilding in the Vortex, which they believed they could control and provided Pakistan with a vital national security capability. Pakistan's post-2001 policy first became evident when Pakistan limited its military efforts to round up Al Qaeda and Taliban fugitives coming over the border after Operation Anaconda, the Battle of Tora Bora in 2002. The preoccupation of the Pakistani military with its long-standing Indian opponents after the 13 December 2001 terrorist attack on the Indian parliament raised tensions and meant that there were few resources on the ground on the Pakistani side of the Durand Line. Pakistan's cooperation against "foreign" Al Qaeda terrorism continued. The Musharraf government proudly pointed to its anti-terrorist cooperation with the West, most notably in the trans-Atlantic airliners conspiracy that was revealed in 2006. More senior Al Qaeda personnel have been caught in Pakistan than any other country, reflecting the continued presence of their leadership as well as Pakistan's cooperation with the US and UK.

Continued ISI coordination with Pakistani religious parties and its Afghan clients made the infrastructure, systems, and networks along the Afghan-Pakistani frontier that had existed since the 1970s available for future use inside Afghanistan following 2001. The ability of the post-2001 terrorist and insurgent networks to make use of this infrastructure is apparent by the fact that all Al Qaeda members with ISI links that have been captured in Pakistan have been found in safe houses connected with Sunni Kashmir groups. These same training camps established for the Afghan resistance in the 1980s in Mahsehra, Miranshah, Shamshutta, and elsewhere were supporting insurgents post-2001.[63]

To the Pakistan military, the US 2005 decision to turn the security of southern Afghanistan over to NATO was seen in Pakistan as leading to imminent US disengagement, leaving a vacuum in Afghanistan that, if Pakistan did not fill, its rivals—India, Iran—certainly would. The US seemed to be on track to disengage from Afghanistan, first because of Iraq and then because of a lack of political will to sustain a commitment.

By 2006, the sanctuary that Afghan insurgents were receiving became a major issue in US-Pakistan relations. Individuals within the Pakistan government, especially under Musharraf, were obviously strong supporters of the Afghan insurgents, including passing intelligence.[64] The open work of the Quetta shura, the Afghan Taliban's ruling body, and other insurgent command organizations, the flow of logistics support and casualty evacuation, and the well-known location of training camps all suggest more than simple complicity.[65]

Only one senior Al Qaeda figure was caught in Pakistan in the 2005–08 period. Overall arrests of Al Qaeda went down in that period. Yet Musharraf still received the support of the US government that was to endure even when it appeared that his government's legitimacy was rapidly waning in 2007–08. The 2008 worldwide economic downturn hit Pakistan early and hard, adding desperation to their strategic worldview. The "fatal problem was too much faith in Musharraf," according to US terrorism expert Bruce Hoffman.[66]

In 2007–08, the always complex and troubled Afghanistan-Pakistan relationship reached a nadir. The attempted assassination of Afghan President Hamid Karzai was publicly blamed on Pakistan-based terrorists. Afghan frustration at Pakistan's claims to be an innocent victim of insurgency, while at the same time harboring and supporting those fighting in Afghanistan, rose. Press reports of ISI involvement in terrorist actions in Afghanistan, such as the bombing on the Indian embassy and funding Taliban insurgents, increased the tension. In 2009 polling, some 91 percent of Afghans had an unfavorable view of Pakistan and 86 percent had a negative view of Pakistan's role in Afghanistan.[67] By 2008, the end of the Musharraf government and an improved military relationship between Afghanistan, Pakistan, and the US, including the establishment of the first of a series of tripartite intelligence fusion centers near the border at the Khyber Pass, improved Pakistan-Afghanistan relations.

The 2008 elections in Pakistan started to turn around the relationship. There has been considerable improvement since 2008 when, in the words of Mohamed Mahmud Stanekzai, former Afghan minister of communications, "Afghanistan and Pakistan, with elected governments, could start efforts to negotiate from both sides."[68] In 2008, MG Mark Milley, deputy commander at Regional Command East, saw an improvement in cross-border coordination from previous years: "I talk to the Pakistanis almost every day. We are linked in at all levels. We coordinate operations with the Pakistani military."[69] A series of Pakistan-Afghanistan peace jirgas have been organized; these have demonstrated cooperation but lack the participation of a number of important players, both within each country and from the region as a whole. Canada has taken a hands-on role in the Dubai process for government-to-government Afghanistan-Pakistan contacts on cross-border issues and security.[70] But suspicions remain. The Tripartite Commission, set up in August 2008, is supposed to alternate meetings between Pakistan and Afghanistan but has been slow to get under way. Joint operations between Pakistan and ANA or coalition forces are still not taking place, although there is a greater degree of coordination, such as reporting troop movements in the border area to avoid inadvertent firefights.

The US campaign of using armed UAVs against Al Qaeda, Afghan, and Pakistani insurgent leaders on Pakistani territory has proven effective. But killing a number of leaders, while potentially valuable, has never in the past proven decisive in defeating a large-scale insurgency. These attacks are unlikely to improve the perceived legitimacy of the government of Pakistan. Neither the US nor the government of Pakistan has sought to explain the UAV attacks or justify them in terms of Pakistan's security. Dr. David Kilcullen, an Australian expert on counter-insurgency warfare, said of the UAV campaign in 2009: "We need to call off the drone attacks . . . the drone attacks are highly unpopular. They are deeply aggravating to the population. And they've given rise to a feeling of anger that coalesces the population around the extremists and leads to spikes of extremism. The current path we are on is leading us to loss of Pakistani government control over its own population."[71]

However, this negative impact would be much greater if there were additional on-the-ground incursions into Pakistan by US or Afghan forces. The outcry over such a perceived incursion in 2008 showed that for all the costs of the UAV campaign, it is apparently effective and it limits the direct liability of both the US and Pakistan.

Attempts to target bin Laden himself have been ongoing—without success—since 2001. It is accepted as fact throughout Afghanistan and Pakistan that this is evidence that the US is not really interested in him as a target but actually is using him as a rationale either for the continued war against Islam, for those that are anti-US, or for geopolitical reasons for supporters of the US.

The Vortex and Pakistani Strategy

Pakistan's national security strategy remains the province of the military. Despite the 2008 election and the return to democratic rule, the Pakistani military still remains in control of security policies, including that dealing with Afghanistan. Pakistan still insists on the marginalization of other regional players in Afghanistan and the exclusion of India; a government in Kabul must be friendly to Pakistan to avoid encirclement from India. Pushtun-dominated government in Kabul also remains a major policy goal, driven by internal Pakistani politics. However, the goal of access to central Asia appears to have fallen by the wayside. The concept of "strategic depth" that motivated much of the original thinking behind the northward thrust has become less important in terms of a security competition in which the India-Pakistan nuclear balance plays a major part. The international presence in Afghanistan and the multiethnic democratic elected government in Kabul continue to be largely seen alike by ISI as at best passing phases or, at worst, part of the attempted encirclement of a nuclear Pakistan.

Pakistan's governmental and non-governmental elites, much as they may resent the military, are more likely to align with and trust them than the highly polarized, distrusted, and frequently corrupt elected officials. In the view of the ISI, the security threat to Pakistan has greatly increased since 2001, but it was only in 2009 that they began to see the insurgency as part of this. In the words one of former Pakistani officer, "Show where the threats to Pakistan have gone away and only then can our Afghanistan policy go away." To this, a veteran Afghan political observer replied "that is because Pakistan's Afghanistan policy has actually created many of the threats that they face, including the insurgency and out-of-control Islamic radical groups."

In 2008–10, Pakistan's military's role in governing at home was undercut by the unpopularity of the later years of the Musharraf regime, although the lack of capability demonstrated by the elected government shows signs of reversing this trend. Yet the military still sees itself as the custodian of Pakistani nationalism and statehood. This has made the events of the Musharraf years, including the decision to enable the US-led intervention in Afghanistan in 2001 and the decision to halt the cross-border insurgency into Kashmir in 2003–04, hard for them to embrace. Both have largely been seen as examples of where Pakistan has given in to external pressure and received only a diminished national security posture in return. The military, even if it is reluctant to return to running the country, is fighting hard to retain its political and economic power and it has no interest in change that would undercut this. There-fore, they cling to the Indian threat and their hold in Afghanistan much tighter.

There has been a basic overall consistency in implementing Pakistan's Afghanistan policies. Both military and civilian governments in Pakistan, at the end of the day, have relied on the ISI. While the degree and extent of ISI operations in support of Afghan insurgents remains uncertain, it is not a "rogue" operation or a "state within a state," two clichés frequently encountered in Western reporting. The ISI had operational freedom and independence to implement policies within broad guidance, but it remains under military control. The Pakistani military remains united and disci-plined, if largely ineffective against terrorism and insurgency on its home territory. While the Pakistan military is hardly monolithic—reflecting service, personal, and political divisions—it is not factionalized.[72]

The ISI will not act against the interest of Pakistan's military. The ISI is many things, but it remains basically a professional military organiza-tion. It is not a tool of radical Islam, though it has certainly cooperated with it and used it to advance its own policies at times. Even today, despite the changes in Pakistan and its army that have taken place since the 1970s, the ISI's operational capability lies with its field-grade officers, and these remained largely secular nationalists. The ISI has also, since the 1980s, been subjected to greater interest by outside governments and intelligence agencies than any other institution of the Pakistani govern-ment, other than perhaps the nuclear program. The ISI includes relatively few supporters of bin Laden, nor even of Mullah Omar; its secular mili-tary leadership is highly nationalistic, but this has not prevented them from supporting groups defined by a radical Islam to the point where they threatened the existence of Pakistan. But the ISI does resent what it sees as a history of US intrusions on Pakistani sovereignty ranging from conditionality on aid to the armed Predator UAV attacks on targets in Pakistan from bases also in Pakistan. It is not only extremists in Pakistan who fear that improved US security relations with India (and Israel) may eventually lead to confrontation with a nuclear-armed Pakistan. All of these factors influence the ISI's development and implementation of Pakistan's Afghan policy.

Yet the paradox of this support and the 2008–10 insurgent threat to Pakistan remain. In the words of former US Ambassador James Dobbins, "Pakistani intelligence provides clandestine support [for the Talibans], despite their attacks in Pakistan and killing Pakistani soldiers."[73] US Secretary of Defense Robert Gates said of Pakistani intelligence involvement with the insurgents: "Look, they're maintaining contact with these groups, in my view as a strategic hedge. . . . They are not sure who's going to win in Afghanistan. They're not sure what's going to happen along that border area. So, to a certain extent, they play both sides."[74]

Pakistani military and security services, spearheaded by but not limited to ISI, extending covert support to Afghanistan's insurgents is likely to become an increasingly explosive issue as US and coalition casualties mount. While acknowledging that some of the ISI-created support networks still work in the insurgents' favor, COL Patrick McNiece, USA, deputy director of intelligence for ISAF in 2008, saw "no high level government support," although he acknowledged that there were reports to the contrary: "There are piles of intelligence on ISI guys meeting, doing training, but any outsider in the FATA is called ISI."[75] He saw as more substantial the lack of action against Afghan insurgent leadership. "If Pakistan is really serious, they could roll them up rather than cherry pick to appease the west. They are more serious in Bajaur [where there is the anti-Pakistan insurgency]."

Pakistan's political choice in 2010 was not to use military force against the North Waziristan sanctuaries of insurgents fighting in both Afghanistan and Pakistan. Operations in South Waziristan, while disrupting and displacing insurgents, did not lead to lasting gains. Despite the deployment of over 130,000 troops to the western borders in March 2010, there has been little military progress in 2010. This led to an increase in US UAV attacks in the FATA starting in September 2010. The danger of decreased governmental legitimacy and increased radicalization can be seen in the reaction to the assassination of Salman Taseen, PPP governor of the Punjab, on 4 January 2011 and the continued hostility to US policies by elites and mass sentiment alike.

PART TWO

THREATS FROM THE VORTEX

CHAPTER FOUR

TRANSNATIONAL TERRORISM

"I am the spirit that always negates and rightly so, because everything that
comes to be is worthy of its own destruction."
—Mephistopheles, in Goethe's *Faust*

A l Qaeda and its associated transnational terrorist organizations, such as the Islamic Movement of Uzbekistan, defeated
in Afghanistan in 2001, reestablished themselves in the Vortex.
There, despite years of efforts by Pakistan to target Al Qaeda's leadership, this organization and its allies have been able to use the pre-existing
Taliban culture and the infrastructure developed by ISI and others over
previous decades to enable insurgent operations in Afghanistan and
Kashmir for their own purposes. Al Qaeda has been able to put in place
new leaders to replace those it has lost, train new recruits, establish a
headquarters, and reinforce its transnational networks of support. These
networks now run from the Vortex to "franchised" groups that carry on
the Al Qaeda name and run a campaign of terror in turbulent regions
worldwide. Groups such as the Pakistani Lashkar-e-Taiba, originally
formed to take part in Pakistan's cross-border support of the insurgency
in Kashmir, have carried out their own terrorist attacks, such as that in
Mumbai in 2009. Al Qaeda is now a decentralized parallel movement in

several countries, while rooted in the Vortex, a networked group, taking direct action when required but also willing to work indirectly or through local "franchises."

Networked Transnational Terrorism

In the wake of Al Qaeda's retreat from Afghanistan in 2001–02, senior US officials though it was defeated. But Al Qaeda quickly found what amounted to a sanctuary in parts of the FATA, places where individuals cannot be traced, policemen cannot operate, and even avenging armies march slowly and with great difficulty. It took advantage of Pushtowali to claim protection and invoke loyalty from some Pushtuns. Al Qaeda's access to resources from Arabia and the Gulf gave their personnel additional opportunities to arrange local marriages that further cemented their ties to the region and their hosts.

Al Qaeda has evolved over the years and has become politically more sophisticated, at least in its rhetoric and in its participation in the battle of ideas. Al Qaeda has replenished its decimated leadership cadres. It has often replaced lost Arabs with more-competent Pakistanis with local ties and cachet, although bin Laden himself remains apparently at the heart of an impenetrable Arab inner circle.

Successes—publicized and otherwise—by the US, UK, and their international partners have effectively destroyed the pre-2001 leadership of Al Qaeda. Since 2001, it had lost three-quarters of its leadership and over 4,000 personnel worldwide. While Osama bin Laden remained the focus of Western efforts to disrupt the leadership, Pakistanis took over a larger role in the leadership, displacing Arabs and Egyptians. Yet despite many successes against Al Qaeda, the US Government National Intelligence Estimate (NIE) of July 2007 suggested that Al Qaeda was still creating more terrorists than are being taken out of action by US efforts.[76]

Al Qaeda has deepened its connections with and support for the wide variety of militants mounting insurgencies in both Afghanistan and Pakistan. Al Qaeda relies on multiple networks to link their leadership in Pakistan with the operational cells, the recruiters, the ideologues and information warriors and those providing logistical and financial support across the world. It has trained and planned for operations worldwide while enabling regional terrorism. It has become a multi-regional group, not just revolving around a single headquarters in Pakistan, and has embraced franchises of local groups where it does not aim to have its own presence.[77] For example, the formation of Al Qaeda in the Maghreb—a local franchise group—was created to attack targets in Algeria and penetrate France via the Algerian community. Because of this Algerian connection, Al Qaeda operatives now have French passports, even French names, and thus operate with greater ease in Al Qaeda's "distant" targets, namely America ("the head of the snake") and Western Europe.

Before 2001, the Taliban's war and Al Qaeda's war in Afghanistan were the same war. Since then, they have become separate but overlapping ones. Today, Al Qaeda, the post-2001 Afghan Taliban, its insurgent and criminal allies, and the Pakistani insurgents all remain loosely allied and co-located in the Vortex, sharing the same networks and support systems, even though their broader policies, paths, and other global alliances have diverged. Al Qaeda is continuing to wage transnational jihad from the Vortex, aimed at distant targets including the US and UK as well as the Islamic world as a whole. Al Qaeda will fight alongside the Afghan and Pakistani Talibans as well as other insurgent groups. They remain united by their opposition to the US, the non-Muslim foreign presence in Afghanistan, and their desire to overthrow the governments of Afghanistan and Pakistan, as well as a shared Islamic radical ideology.

Al Qaeda is part of the transnational terrorist threat to the US, the UK, and the West, as well as taking part in terrorism and insurgency in Afghanistan and Pakistan. Al Qaeda has been unable to recreate an attack on the US comparable with those of 11 September 2001. Whether it has the ability to do so remains uncertain.[78] Al Qaeda's desire to acquire weapons of mass destruction apparently also remains strong.[79] The 2009 terrorist attacks in Mumbai show that the Al Qaeda approach to terrorism, with spectacular multiple attacks targeting soft targets, has been adopted by other terrorist groups. Mumbai also served warning that future Al Qaeda-style attacks may be mounted by other groups, sharing Al Qaeda's goals if not operational planning and with better access to the target or more effective resources. "Al Qaeda has suffered serious setbacks, but it remains a determined, adaptive enemy, unlike any our nation has ever faced," said former Director of Central Intelligence Michael Hayden.[80]

The new transnational terrorist model adopted by Al Qaeda included multiple types of relationships, ranging from direct top-down control of high-value operations to franchising the Al Qaeda name to allied groups or sharing a support infrastructure and goals. Since 2001, Al Qaeda has outsourced much of its targeted violence in Afghanistan and Pakistan to groups that had their origins in the conflict in Kashmir and so had access to the support networks put together by the Pakistani security services, and has thus been more effective than if Al Qaeda had tried to carry out these actions directly. Al Qaeda has also put an increased emphasis on producing propaganda.

It was in Taliban-controlled Afghanistan that Al Qaeda first demonstrated the benefits of working at the center of an enabling network, leaving other groups responsible for the kinetic activities. During the 2000 Air India Flight 814 hijacking incident in Kandahar, Al Qaeda let Kashmiri groups and the Afghan Taliban take the blame and receive worldwide attention, while maintaining a low profile, despite apparently having planned the hijacking.[81] Similarly, Kashmiri groups' willingness to use direct terrorist action to try to move India and Pakistan toward confrontation and radicalize Indian Muslims was seen in the 2002 attack on the Indian parliament and the 2008 attack in Mumbai. While there was no direct link to Al Qaeda in either one, both furthered Al Qaeda objectives. It remains uncertain whether either attack could have taken place without Al Qaeda support.

Since 2001, Al Qaeda has also demonstrated its ability to cooperate with dissimilar groups (e.g., "secular" Palestinian groups). Al Qaeda has been able to use its franchises and networked connections to indirectly link up with groups that lack its commitment to violence but excel in building networks worldwide and running clandestine organizations, such as Hezb-ut-Tahrir, which operates covertly with its leadership believed to be on the West Bank. Such extremist groups, while not sharing a commitment to terrorism, are often well organized and offer a capability that can be used by other, more violent, groups. Even though these groups themselves have not relinquished their opposition to terror, their pre-existing organizations worldwide are targets for internal penetration by Al Qaeda.

Al Qaeda's War of Ideas

The networked Al Qaeda that has emerged since it was forced to retreat from Afghanistan in 2001 has, while retaining its predecessor's commitment to violence, embraced many of the tactics of emerging high-technology social movements: the Internet, cell phones, DVDs, and direct access to the global media. In 2007, Al Sahaab, Al Qaeda's media outlet, had an audio or video release every three days to "outside" media, primarily in Pakistan and Afghan, and its efforts have greatly increased in both quantity and quality since then.[82] Al Qaeda's skills at propaganda and psychological operations have become a powerful asset. Even if they have not repeated the bloodshed of 9/11, they have managed to do much damage in less kinetic ways, often through Afghan insurgents.

Al Qaeda's propaganda and information operations capability has evolved to be far more robust than its pre-2001 predecessor. From havens in the Vortex, Al Qaeda can draw adherents from across the globe, without respect for borders and simultaneously attacking the state system that imposes them. Al Qaeda aims to influence Muslim societies by a combination of violent terror and effective propaganda, going over the heads of governments to target the youth of the Islamic world, many facing nonresponsive governments and weak social structures, and exploit the challenges of a demographic bulge and lack of economic and political opportunity facing entire generations.

The Islamic world as a whole—perhaps to a greater extent than just Afghanistan—faces an overwhelming crisis of purpose, memory, and knowledge involving everything about the way they live and think. Al Qaeda aims to seize the high ground and provide an answer to this crisis, one that will set those who hear it against the "Zionist-Crusader" enemy and make their own governments, if not the enemy, irrelevant. This propaganda is not limited to Afghanistan and the Pakistan border but has had an impact throughout the Islamic world. It offers the listener a coherent worldview that makes sense of a world that seems hostile, if not completely insane, while at the same time validating and valuing their own self-image. It answers the great question "If we—our religion and/or our culture—are so great, why are we so screwed up?" It's not their fault, Al Qaeda says. It is externally imposed evil-doers—Zionist-Crusaders, takfir governments—that make your life hard, stupid, and pointless, while you deserve both social justice and material comfort. And we, Al Qaeda, can give you this. This narrative is not just aimed at the people of Afghanistan, where conspiracy theories and bizarre rumors can be easily accepted, but at Muslims worldwide who Al Qaeda has targeted as their potential supporters and sympathetic media that repeat the narrative.

In 2008—10, the Al Qaeda versions of events—including, for example, the brutal murder of a foreign aid worker in Kabul claimed by the Afghan Taliban in October 2008—were picked up and used by the global English-language media while the Afghan government and the international coalition forces, despite their large expenditures of spokesmen and psychological operations, took several news cycles before they had their version before the world media. The view that could have been put before the people of Afghanistan, that this murder has violated their obligation to hospitality and has shamed them by killing a young woman who came a long way to help injured Afghans, never appeared. The divided "information warriors" of the Afghan government, independent news media, US, and ISAF, each conscious of its own turf and subject to external constraints and multiple layers of bureaucracy, conceded this particular battle of ideas to Al Qaeda. That terrorists and insurgents kill both Muslims and those foreigners that have come to help them must be brought before the people of Afghanistan and Pakistan.

Narratives are important in the Vortex. The tribal lineages of the Pushtuns are narratives. The Northern Alliance's pride in withstanding first the Soviets and then the Taliban is a narrative, one that cannot be matched by returning exiles or those that fought with the Soviets, and hence it has been used to legitimate the claims of their leadership of access to power. Narratives transmit Pushtowali and Afghaniyat, rather than an explicit code. In creating the narrative that inks many of its efforts aimed at Afghanistan in its war of ideas, Al Qaeda has sought to portray the current conflict in Afghanistan in terms of Izzat (honor).[83]

Al Qaeda has used its narrative of an assault on the Islamic world to justify insurgency in Afghanistan.[84] Al Qaeda created and gave to the post-2001 Afghan Taliban the narrative "Islam is under attack" as well as using it themselves. Al Qaeda was able to claim their own powerful narrative—that of resilience after defeat and of the US thwarted—that has become all the more compelling as memories of 11 September 2001 faded and the costs of wars in Afghanistan, Iraq, Lebanon, and Gaza increased. These are sophisticated psychological and information operations that produce effective propaganda and make conditions in both Afghanistan and Pakistan more difficult and dangerous.

During the war against the Soviets and even during Afghanistan's internal conflicts of 1992–2001, Afghans generally did not see themselves as part of a larger struggle affecting the entire Islamic world. That many now do is in part because of the access to multiple media sources, but it is also the result of Al Qaeda's strength in the battle of ideas, which has enabled it to define conflicts in Afghanistan in ways that make them harder to resolve, as well as the failure of post-2001 Kabul and its foreign supporters to effectively respond. More so than their pre-2001 predecessors, the Afghan Taliban and other insurgents are increasingly willing to link their struggle to an international resistance to what they portray as US-Zionist invasion and oppression. Afghans were in the past less concerned about Israeli-Palestinian issues than their own crises. In place of this worldview, Al Qaeda has offered to what proved to be receptive audiences the theme that "non-Muslims are invading the Muslim world" and that the natural leaders of resistance are the Afghans, who have never been conquered by an outside invader, be they British or Soviet. Al Qaeda has helped add Americans to that list. They have helped define the US and coalition presence as occupiers rather than guests in the eyes of many Afghans. Even among Afghans that have never heeded Al Qaeda, the years of friction inherent in a foreign military presence, of nationalist sensibilities offended, road accidents with convoys, collateral damage incidents, house searches, raids, and detention, have caused more of them to oppose a continued foreign presence.

Al Qaeda-inspired themes have been powerful in Afghanistan and Pakistan for many reasons, but none has been more important than the Western presence in Afghanistan. Resentment of this presence has been successfully tied to Islam as well as nationalism, mobilizing many of Afghanistan's Pushtuns against a government that can be presented as a client of a Zionist-Crusader war on Islam as well as corrupt and failing to deliver social justice.

The Vortex also fits with Al Qaeda's internal narrative and its self-image. Al Qaeda's leaders see themselves as *firkan* (knights) that go forth from a stronghold to do great things autonomously.[85] This fits too with the traditional Pushtun view of the Frontier—especially on the Pakistani side—as a place from which raiders, representing an exemplary and exceptional Islam, strike against targets in the plains, whether governed by infidels or takfir Muslims.

Shia Muslims are, like the Zionist-Crusaders and the takfir Muslim leaders that accommodate them, a target of Al Qaeda's narrative. Anti-Shia ideology contributed to the Pakistan Taliban attacking the Shia Touray Pushtuns starting in November 2007 and has inspired an increasing level of anti-Shia violence in Pakistan by 2008–10.

Transnational Terror from the Vortex

The transnational terrorist threats emerging from the Vortex include: those aimed at Afghanistan, those aimed at Pakistan (and India), and that targeted at the primary enemy: the US, UK, and the West. The global mission is more important to Al Qaeda than the war in Afghanistan they use to justify their narrative of Islam under attack. The main task of Al Qaeda in Pakistan is to prepare for new attacks on the primary enemy. According to Bruce Riedel, a US counter-terrorism expert and retired CIA officer, "Al Qaeda is recruiting and training individuals with Western European passports in their camps in Pakistan. There's only one reason they're doing that. They don't need guys with British and French passports to attack the Marriott Hotel in Islamabad."[86] If the conflict in Afghanistan and Pakistan appears remote in the West, their connection to Al Qaeda and its allies literally has their name on it; they are targeting the West and, just as Al Qaeda started this campaign years before the Western interventions in Iraq and Afghanistan, even a future withdrawal would be unlikely to bring it to a halt.

Even when Al Qaeda dominated Taliban-ruled Afghanistan in the years before 2001, terrorism did not spread across its borders isotropically. Rather, the Afghanistan-based Al Qaeda's Declaration of War on America issued in 2000 promised war not in Afghanistan but against the West. Al Qaeda's choice and their timing has reflected their focus on the "primary enemy" in America and Europe, such as the 2004 Madrid bombing attacks, immediately before the Spanish election. Awareness of the importance of timing was also seen in the October 2000 terrorist attack on the destroyer USS *Cole* in Aden harbor, at a time when its proximity to the US presidential election made retaliation appear unlikely. Bin Laden's appearance on television on 29 October 2004, immediately before the US presidential election, was thought to be intended to remind the US electorate of the Al Qaeda threat. When Al Qaeda acts, it reflects its nature as a transnational threat.

Al Qaeda has been able to use its relationship with Pakistani-based groups to implement its strategy of striking at the "primary enemy" worldwide, even though these groups had previously limited their operations to striking at targets in the region. Pakistani journalist Ahmad Rashid said "These people are militants who have been fighting in Kashmir, who have been fighting in other places and who are linked to Al Qaeda and are providing assistance to Pakistani groups worldwide. We saw, for example, the London [transport] bombing in July [2005]. They were clearly linked back to some of these Pakistani militant groups, who in turn were linked back to al Qaeda."[87]

The Vortex's connection to transnational Islamic terrorism in the Anglo-American world has been revealed by attacks, arrests, and prosecutions. The support infrastructure in the Vortex, accessed by insurgents and terrorists alike, is attached to a network powered by a metaphorical "main circuit cable" that runs the Atlantic, from the US to the UK to Karachi all the way to the FATA, the origins of much of that metropolis's population, and from there runs to Afghanistan.[88] Significantly, Pakistani groups such as Jaish-e-Mohammed, TTP, and Lashkar-e-Taiba have moved beyond their focus on India and Kashmir to participate in global terrorism. This has enabled them to use this same support infrastructure to present a terrorist threat to the US and UK, building on Al Qaeda's model.[89]

Al Qaeda has been able to work with other transnational jihadist organizations, through shared networks, to tap into the "culturally uprooted" among Europe's Muslim population. Al Qaeda has uniquely positioned itself to feed and then take advantage of the social and psychological factors that are driving its members or those sympathetic to terrorist organizations' goal even if not their methods. Most of the people that it has attracted to Al Qaeda or linked groups are not driven by poverty (except vicarious poverty) or by a longing for reform in their home country. Rather, many are motivated to exact retribution for real or imagined transgressions by the West against Islam.[90] Al Qaeda has demonstrated an ability to appeal to individuals who, although neither poor nor uneducated, feel lost or have a deep-seated desire to empower themselves and serve a higher purpose. Those who feel themselves to be second-class citizens with no future even if they are nominally in the middle class, and those experiencing cultural victimization and political pointlessness, are particular targets for Al Qaeda or similar groups (especially those Pakistan-based groups that had their origins in the Kashmir insurgency, such as Lashkar-e-Taiba).[91] Marginalized individuals, such as those in prison or converts that need to prove their sincerity as Muslims, are often among those recruited. In Europe, successful professionals have gone on to become suicide bombers. Terrorism is nothing if not empowering.

The links between the UK and terrorist organizations operating in the Vortex are strong. The UK security services are aware of attempts by subversive and terrorist organizations to infiltrate and radicalize British Muslims dating back to the 1980s.[92] In 2004, the Home Office estimated that Al Qaeda and aligned terrorist groups had some 10–15,000 supporters in the UK.[93] It was estimated that some 3–4,000 British Muslims, most of Pakistani background, had been trained in camps, most in Afghanistan or Pakistan.[94] A smaller number were trained in Yemen or elsewhere. Some subsequently left the UK, including those who joined insurgents in Iraq or Afghanistan. Few have been sanctioned, and most remain living in the UK.

While the number of active terrorist cells in the UK's Muslim population is small, Al Qaeda and associated organizations provide these terrorists, as they do with the Taliban in Afghanistan, specific direction for high value operations as well as sharing planning and tactics, techniques, and procedures (TTPs). The 7 July 2005 terrorist bombings of London were carried out by native-born British terrorists, using the tactics of simultaneous attacks on soft targets and the use of powerful peroxide-based liquid explosives that originated with Al Qaeda.

Starting in 2005–06, Pakistan-based Al Qaeda exerted greater hands-on direction of their networked supporters in the UK and Europe than in those Islamic countries where there was a "franchise" Al Qaeda presence. British intelligence sources have changed their characterization of the UK-Pakistani threat from a mere characterization to the assertion that the "command and control is provided by Al Qaeda in Pakistan." Dame Eliza Manningham-Butler, then director general of MI5, said in a public speech in November 2006 that Al Qaeda's command and control was still linked to "numerous plots to kill people and to damage our economy. . . . What do I mean by numerous? Five? Ten? No, nearer 30 that we currently know of. These plots often have links back to Al Qaeda in Pakistan and through these links Al Qaeda gives guidance and training to its largely British foot soldiers here on an extensive and growing scale."

The "foot soldiers" she referred to are largely provided by radicalized individuals of the estimated 800,000 Pakistanis in the UK. In contrast to the relatively large number of supporters or even those that have undergone training, Western anti-terrorism experts estimate that there are hundreds of supporters with an active commitment to terrorism, certainly a much smaller commitment to political violence than was seen in home-grown movements such as those in Northern Ireland in recent decades. The UK's Pakistani community has a greater degree of societal integration with the UK as a whole than most of the Muslim communities on the continent and has the ability to travel on a British passport for attacks on the US. There are an estimated 400,000 trips between Pakistan and the UK a year, many of them lasting several months, beyond the capabilities of any monitoring system to keep track. Only a small percentage of this community needs to embrace terrorism to create a formidable terrorist threat.

The Transatlantic airline terrorist plot, whose members were arrested in the UK in August 2006 following a joint Anglo-American investigation with Pakistani cooperation, demonstrated the importance of Vortex-based Al Qaeda in directing the UK-based terrorist threats through directives and resources that moved down the main circuit cable from the FATA. The targeting of no less than 10 airliners—to be destroyed simultaneously, cutting the main transatlantic air links between the US and UK—was consistent with the Al Qaeda focus. The tactics also had the Al Qaeda mark. They apparently already had 20 volunteer suicide bombers trained. Some had already made their martyrdom videos.

The 2006 airline plot was significant in that it was not being carried out by a haphazard collection of individuals but rather represented a cohesive action by teams of self-radicalized terrorists, directed by Al Qaeda in Pakistan as part of a multi-year, well-planned, and nearly well-executed process. It marked a break of post-2002 Al Qaeda action in striking soft targets, instead hitting a hard target set, civil aviation, and using advanced-technology liquid explosives. This was not the degraded Al Qaeda's first apparent attacks post-2001, hitting soft targets such as synagogues in Tunisia and weddings in Amman. Rather, it appeared to aim at nothing less than provoking a US-UK military response against Al Qaeda's base in the FATA that would, ideally for them, have the impact of splintering the Pakistani state and putting them in the position of helping their Pakistani allies put together the pieces.

The failure of the airliner plot did not end the threat from the Vortex but was merely an indication of the new direction Al Qaeda had taken and an additional indicator of the importance of this region in world affairs. The 2007 plot for attacks in Copenhagen was reported to have been organized from Pakistan.[95] In Germany, the 2007 plot for an attack on Ramstein Air Base also had links back to Pakistan.[96] In Belgium, suspects arrested in 2008, thought to be planning a suicide attack, included members trained in Afghanistan.[97] Senior western European government officials have identified Pakistan-based terror as the biggest single threat to western Europe, eclipsing that originating with alienated indigenous communities.

The threat of indigenous radicalization with links to Al Qaeda has now spread to the US, even though, by 2010, relatively few US citizens or permanent residents had been established to have trained with Al Qaeda and then returned to the US.[98] In the eight years after 9/11, 693 terror suspects, a third of them citizens, were prosecuted in the US, a third of them for terrorism.[99] The US, with its diverse population with worldwide links, is said to have connections with terrorist networks in 60 countries. Al Qaeda has been targeting recruits in the US.[100] While the death of the first US-recruited suicide bomber (in Somalia in 2009) and other homegrown US terrorist threats had no immediately apparent Al Qaeda links, the impact of the 9/11 attacks and the subsequent prosecution of what were seen as home-grown "sleeper cells" has led to concern that such potential terrorists may be able to follow Al Qaeda's example or even, through personal contacts, draw on Al Qaeda-related expertise.

The Terrorist Threat to Afghanistan

Al Qaeda has retained its vanguard nature and is still trying to achieve leadership through conflict in the Islamic world. Afghanistan is but one front in Al Qaeda's global offensive, with its most important role being seen as helping to rally Muslims against the "Zionist-Crusader" invasion. The director of the US Defense Intelligence Agency, LTG Michael D. Maples, said, in 2006, "Al Qaeda will remain engaged in Afghanistan for ideological and operational reasons."[101] In 2008, Al Qaeda was estimated to have 150–500 cadre and fighters in the Pakistani borderlands plus operational control over one to two thousand central Asians.[102]

While numerically small and not a major combatant force in the insurgency in Afghanistan, Al Qaeda is important in providing outside ideas, concepts, and personnel, according to COL Patrick McNiece, ISAF deputy director of intelligence in 2008.[103] He qualified it in this way: "Afghans are proud enough that they will not be led by Al Qaeda, but they will take money, ideas and, for many, TTPs [tactics, techniques, and procedures]." "Al Qaeda is very involved in training and facilitating the arrival of foreigners," including the teenage madrassa students from Pakistan and elsewhere that make up many of the suicide bombers.[104]

Afghanistan itself is not a hotbed of terrorists, nor do Afghans have a history of participation in terrorism. No Afghans participated in the

11 September 2001 attacks or other high-profile attacks in the West. The long and bitter Afghan jihad against the Soviets in 1978–92 did not include a campaign against Soviet or third-country targets outside of the region. Indeed, it was marked by an almost complete absence of such activities. Afghanistan's history of physical and intellectual remoteness from the ideas running through the Islamic world included resistance to multinational terrorism. When Afghans showed up carrying weapons outside their country in the 1990s, as in Bosnia or Chechnya, they were largely low-level former mujahideen in search of money and status (many married local wives) unavailable to them at home. Just as availability of employment and education did not prevent middle-class young men from the Arab world and Europe's Islamic communities from being involved in terrorist action in the West, the lack of these same opportunities, conversely, did not lead to Afghans becoming terrorists.

No single country has been as affected by Al Qaeda and transnational Islamic terrorism as Afghanistan. Al Qaeda made pre-2001 Afghanistan the headquarters of its campaign to establish a global Khalifait. It operated in close alliance with, and ended up controlling, the Taliban—which, while they shared Al Qaeda's worldview, was primarily concerned with waging Afghanistan's bloody civil war and bringing Afghan society and life into line with its fundamentalist view of Islamic practice. Al Qaeda and its allied Pakistani terrorist groups such as the Sipah-e-Sahaba added additional horrors to that of Afghan's 1992–2001 civil war, massacring Shia Afghans in Mazar-e-Sharif and devastating the Hazara Jat and the Shomali Plain. Pre-2001, Kabul under the Taliban had attracted not only Al Qaeda but also other terrorist groups and a large number of Muslim common criminals. Lashkar-e -Taiba operated in Afghanistan in 2010.

The impact of transnational terrorism in Afghanistan was seen when two Al Qaeda assassins killed Ahmad Shah Massoud on 9 September 2001. The Al Qaeda plan brought in two killers from Europe. It took over a year of Al Qaeda's meticulous planning to get them in striking range of Massoud. It appears to have been the work of the same Al Qaeda planners that made possible the suicide bombing of the USS *Cole*. Even after 11 September 2001, Al Qaeda's history of violence in Afghanistan, both providing fighting men in the civil war and carrying out atrocities, means that it has still killed many more Afghans than Westerners.

While Al Qaeda is apparently not looking to recreate the effective control of a state it enjoyed in pre-2001 Afghanistan, they make effective use of the new sanctuary that has emerged in Pakistan's borderlands. Since 2001, Al Qaeda has apparently learned that it is counterproductive to take over states or build mass movements. They now focus on escalating, extremely violent terrorist attacks. Al Qaeda will also act to take advantage of vacuums created by an absence of state power, especially in Pakistan.[105]

In 2008–09, Al Qaeda's military commander for Afghanistan was an Egyptian, Mustafa Abu al Yazid (known as Shaikh Said), who was reported killed by the Pakistani military in 2008 but was apparently still operating in 2009.[106] He is thought to be part of the core of Al Qaeda's Pakistan-based leadership, along with Osama bin Laden, Ayman Al-Zawahiri, and Abu Yahya al-Libi. His statements have pointed to the number of non-Afghans fighting inside Afghanistan (for which Al Qaeda is claiming responsibility) as well as terrorist attacks in India as a reflection of the fact that they are winning the conflict. By 2008–10, the improving security situation in Iraq and the increasing hostility toward foreign fighters meant that many would-be jihadis instead made their way to Pakistan to fight in Afghanistan. Veterans of Al Qaeda in Iraq were providing training to Afghan and Pakistani insurgents as well these incoming foreigners.

Terrorism in Afghanistan since 2001 has reflected the actions of Al Qaeda and its transnational allies as well as the Afghan Taliban and its insurgent allies. The rapid increase in these attacks from 491 in 2005 to 1127 in 2007 was an indication of the start of the deterioration of the security situation that had reached crisis proportions in 2008–10.[107] In 2008, there were widespread Western press reports, citing intelligence sources, that the Pakistani ISI had had a direct role in several of that year's terrorist actions in Afghanistan. These included the bombing of the Indian embassy in Kabul and attacks aimed at Karzai or leadership figures, most notably the 2008 Karzai assassination attempt and the 2007 Baghlan suicide bombing. Such attacks have also targeted Kabul-based Afghans and foreigners, as seen by the 2007 Hotel Serena attack, the

2008 Ministry of Culture and Information attack, and the 2009 suicide attack on the Ministry of Justice.

To Al Qaeda, suicide bombing is not just effective terrorist tactics against an infidel that lacks resolve; it is a key part of their ideology and appeal to those it recruits.[108] While the Taliban was already aware of suicide bombing techniques through their links to the Tamil guerrillas in Sri Lanka, it was Al Qaeda that introduced suicide bomb attacks to Afghanistan, starting with the assassination of Ahmad Shah Massoud on 9 September 2001 by attackers who Al Qaeda had recruited in Europe. By 2003, suicide bombers had emerged as part of the Afghan insurgency. But it was only after Al Qaeda's recruiting and training foreign suicide bombers started to have an impact in 2005–06 that the numbers of attacks increased.[109] More recently, the suicide bombers have been reportedly predominantly from Afghanistan and Pakistan. Former interior minister Mohammed Hanif Atmar said "Central Asians are used as expendable assets by terrorists. Uighurs have not been seen in Afghanistan as yet, though we do have reports they are harbored across the border. Al Qaeda has run out of assets."[110]

But the suicide bomber remains an alien concept to the region, which is why the Taliban in both Pakistan and Afghanistan have put an emphasis on murdering religious and leadership figures that criticize suicide bombers.[111] Mass-casualty attacks, suicide or otherwise, against soft targets, leaving lots of bodies, Muslim or otherwise, have generally not been the terrorist tactics of choice in post-2001 Afghanistan. In Afghanistan, the terrorists have been more selective, primarily sending suicide bombers against targets where there is a generalized antipathy, even if not outright hostility, among the Afghan population. But the amount of collateral damage remains high. Large numbers of Afghan civilians have been killed in such attacks, including a group of schoolchildren killed by the 2007 Baghlan attack.

In addition to the terrorist threat coming across the border from Pakistan, terrorism is certainly one of the Afghan insurgency's most important tactics. Most modern insurgencies have made use of terrorism as a tactic in the theater of operations or in the enemy homeland. But they have generally maintained a unity of command, effort, and objective. It is uncertain how much that is the case in Afghanistan. An example of a politically active leader who participates in both the terrorist conflict and the insurgency is Sirajjuddin Haqqani, who has links to both Al Qaeda and the Taliban but is a member of neither and has been linked to the Serena Hotel attack in Kabul in 2007. To Atmar, "Terror attacks represent weakness, not strength. . . . No one with a political objective would be so careless about the population. The fact that they do not care about their image shows their hopelessness. They can still threaten life but have no capability to derail processes or challenge the government."

The Obama administration's March 2009 Afghanistan-Pakistan strategy identified its core objective to be: "The strategy starts with a clear, concise, attainable goal: disrupt, dismantle, and defeat al Qaeda and its safe havens."[112] US involvement in Afghanistan has been driven by the counter-terrorist focus before it was involved in the conflicts threatening the future of that country and Pakistan. But defeating Al Qaeda will mean more than killing or capturing bin Laden and the elusive high-level leadership: it will be creating a situation where whatever comes after them will not find even better conditions for transnational terrorism than bin Laden did when he returned to Afghanistan in 1996.

Terrorism is not a threat that, even if individuals are taken out or plots are thwarted, can be totally defeated. It can be marginalized, weakened, or contained.[113] Negotiations with those carrying out terrorism (as opposed to insurgency) are unlikely. Al Qaeda is not interested in returning to Kabul or functioning as governors in rural Afghanistan. They are more interested in showing Afghanistan as one of many fronts in the invasion of the Islamic world by the enemy. Restoring peace, a functioning civil society, and a private sector economy in Afghanistan would not even be guarantees against terrorism. The ability of numerically small terrorist organizations to pose a threat even to highly developed nations with proficient intelligence and security services is a warning not just to Afghanistan, but to all nations. They are reminders that it is not just or even primarily the poor and oppressed who have made terrorist campaigns long and costly.

Removing Western forces from Afghanistan or even the whole of the Islamic world would not remove the oxygen from the terrorist threat to "The Primary Enemy." Al Qaeda's mission is not about removing troops anyway. It is about changing the Islamic world to conform to their ideology. The appearance of foreign troops in the Islamic world is just an example of how degraded current regimes are, that they require armed infidels to protect them from the devout. The groundwork for Al Qaeda's terrorist offensive grew in the 1990s when there was minimal Western involvement in Afghanistan and the Arab-Israeli peace process was progressing. Even then, Al Qaeda had no qualms about targeting the Strasbourg Cathedral Christmas Market in an abortive plot in 2000 or destroying Indonesian churches in the Christmas Eve 2000 bombings.

Nor will development in Afghanistan or Pakistan by itself provide an effective counter to future terrorism. A peaceful and affluent democracy with well-developed governmental and social welfare institutions is certainly no barrier against terrorism, as the history of a previous generation of European terrorist organizations demonstrates.

The terrorist war against Afghanistan is not likely to succeed. Nor is it intended to. Al Qaeda leaders such as bin Laden's lieutenant Ayman al-Zawahiri have explicitly condemned negotiations, which is how insurgencies tend to end, along with any acceptance of partial or temporary solutions en route to ultimate success.[114] Al Qaeda's specialty is destruction. The extremist essence of Al Qaeda makes it hard for them to work with anyone, including the Afghan insurgents who, in 2008–10, constituted the major threat to Afghanistan.

The Terrorist Threat to Pakistan

Pakistan is no stranger to terrorism. In the 1980s, the Soviets and their Kabul regime allies waged a bloody campaign of state-supported terrorism in Pakistan. Since 2005, however, the terrorist threat emerging from the Vortex now has the potential to affect Pakistan far from terrorists' remote sanctuaries. Pakistani terrorist groups see the creation of a fundamentalist government in Pakistan as their foremost priority. In her last interview with a Western journalist, days before her assassination by Pakistani terrorists, Benazir Bhutto, who certainly had no interest in minimizing the threat these terrorist groups posed to her country to Western audiences, said "I now think Al Qaeda can be marching on Islamabad in two to four years."[115]

Al Qaeda's impact on Pakistan has grown considerably since 2001, the same time as Musharraf first raised expectations for the revitalization of civil society. Al Qaeda has participated in the terrorist networks that have targeted Pakistan's secular institutions and leadership figures. Musharraf was the target of up to nine assassination attempts, not all by Al Qaeda. Al Qaeda has attacked Western-related and international targets in Pakistan, such as hotels and the Danish embassy in 2008.

Terrorist victims in Pakistan include those supposedly protected by the security services, such as Benazir Bhutto in 2008 and the Sri Lanka cricket team in 2009. Terrorist organizations may have penetrated the Pakistani security apparatus and are able to act with inside information or the support of the organizations. The only Pakistani arrested in Pakistan in connection with the 2006 plot on transatlantic airliners escaped from ISI custody.[116] Attacks in 2007 inside Sargodha Air Base and the ISI compound in Rawalpindi Cantonment raised fears of inside cooperation with terrorists. Benazir Bhutto was convinced the Pakistani security services were involved in the plots against her, as they had refused to allow her to bring in expatriate bodyguards.[117] Three thousand and twenty-one Pakistanis were killed by terrorists in 2009.

Terrorist attacks in Pakistan have increased in intensity and in number since 2007. In 2009, there were 87 recorded suicide attacks in Pakistan, in comparison to 45 reported attacks in all of 2007. Suicide attacks with heavy casualties occurred in Islamabad, Rawalpindi, and Lahore. By 2009, the number of terrorist attacks had quadrupled over two years.[118] The Pakistani Army had, post-2001, believed it would not be a terrorist target because of its willingness to deal with both Afghanistan and Pakistani insurgent groups and because those terrorist figures turned over to the US were limited to "foreigners." Despite this, the military has found itself increasingly to be the target of terrorism, starting in 2007, when there were 36 attacks on the Pakistani Army, two on the ISI, and one on the Army's elite Special Service Group (SSG).

Terrorism in Pakistan inevitably has a nuclear dimension, as it faces the most intense terrorist threat of any nuclear-armed country. The potential penetration of Pakistani security services by the terrorists and their insurgent allies has raised concerns worldwide. Al Qaeda still wants weapons of mass destruction, which fits with its overall strategic goal.[119] Pakistan may appear to Al Qaeda as the most viable source to obtain them.

The Future of Al Qaeda

Al Qaeda apparently continues to believe that it needs to prepare for ever-larger terrorist attacks, especially against the US and other Western enemies, to maintain their image as the one force striking back at those they claim are waging a global war against Islam. Al Qaeda has never aimed at being a mass organization, but its record of attacks and assassinations shows that it has a powerful capability to prevent a stable government from taking hold in Afghanistan or Pakistan. Al Qaeda are not builders but inspirers and, above all else, destroyers, which meshes with their continued commitment to the acquisition and use of WMD and their focus on Pakistan as a likely potential source.

It is likely that the next, predictable, Al Qaeda-driven crisis will occur when a large-scale terrorist attack in the US or Western Europe is traced to Pakistan. Kinetic options against Al Qaeda in Pakistan must walk a fine line, and by 2009 the US UAV campaign had apparently been effective. The question remains whether it has been worth the cost to the legitimacy of the government of Pakistan.

Despite its extensive adaptation and pervasiveness, the revived Pakistan-based Al Qaeda has real limitations as a terrorist organization. Al Qaeda's commitment to Salafist practices, its brutality and love for public executions and its impatience with local political and social realities have undercut its ability to create a viable alternative to current governing arrangements, whether in the FATA's South Waziristan or Iraq's Anbar province, regardless of the ability to interact in different ways created by its networked organization within the Vortex. Al Qaeda's disdain for negotiations and political settlements, although this historically has been the way outsiders come to power, and their willingness to kill Muslim civilians and condemn other Muslims as takfir, are, taken together, likely to be increasingly divisive. For all its attempt to portray a rhetoric of "third-worldism," diversity is not something Al Qaeda tolerates well.

Another detriment is that Al Qaeda lacks a positive vision.[120] In the end, Al Qaeda seeks not to build a better world, but to destroy and clear away all that has grown up since the rise of Islam. What shall emerge after, in their view, is a Wahabi-inspired Khalifait (something that has never existed) in which there shall be no place for infidels, Shias, or takfir Muslims. Al Qaeda provides no social services. Its guiding idea of restoring the Khalifait has little direct appeal to most Muslims. It is unable to provide the patronage that is vital to power relations in Afghanistan and Pakistan. It has a limited ability to tie itself to nationalism while retaining a commitment to an Islam without borders, as Pushtun insurgents have done in Afghanistan and Pakistan. Its single-minded fanaticism toward acquiring WMD and using them to create mass casualties has not proven a recruiting tool except against those select few that feel aggrieved at a highly personal level toward the US and the West. Al Qaeda has done little toward achieving the social justice that is the appeal of Sharia law for many people.

These characteristics have led to widespread Muslim opposition to Al Qaeda, most notably embodied by the fatwa issued against terrorism by the Darool-Uloom Deoband, associated with the root school of the Deobandi-influenced madrassas that were the roots of the Afghan Taliban leadership.[121] The Iranians have offered the Hezbollah model as a competing vision to the world's Islamic revolutionaries, Shia and Sunni alike. Since 2001, Al Qaeda has seen its efforts fail to have their desired impact despite terrorist campaigns in Iraq, Saudi Arabia, and Southeast Asia. In addition, these campaigns led to grassroots counterreactions in Jordan, Saudi Arabia, and Iraq. In Afghanistan, Al Qaeda's actions and attitudes were widely resented and helped undercut the legitimacy of the Taliban regime pre-2001. While there is not yet a groundswell of anti-terrorist sentiment in Afghanistan and Pakistan, this history suggests that it may happen there as well.[122] Even under repressive regimes, where the local population gets to hear the blasts and see the bodies, they have turned against the terrorists, demonstrated by a failure to win mass support to the terrorists' cause. Pakistani radical Islamic parties, with their links to terrorism and their disinterest in secular patronage, remained marginal politically. For example, in Pakistan in 2009, popular opinion turned violently against the insurgents in Swat when video of them enjoying the beating of a young woman was widely broadcast on Pakistan television. In the words of US analyst Audrey Kurth Cronin, "A backlash among Muslims against terrorism is well under way."[123]

It has been argued that Al Qaeda has a self-generated internal tendency toward marginalization and implosion that the US and its coalition partners have largely disdained to exploit, both in terms of the conflict in Afghanistan and worldwide.[124] The insistence by both Al Qaeda and insurgent groups in Afghanistan and Pakistan that democracy is an infidel concept that can have no place in an Islamic regime shows little evidence of being widely accepted; internal corruption instead appears to threaten democracy to a much greater extent than radical ideology. Instead, despite deep societal conservatism and commitment to Islam, there is sympathy for democracy, empowerment, and change, for a better future that is not on offer from terrorists and insurgents.

The bad news is still that Al Qaeda has the potential to clear the way for future groups that may not share their self-inflicted wounds. Al Qaeda has pioneered effective tactics, techniques, and procedures for the use of the Internet, computers, and global communications.[125] It has already demonstrated its ability to contribute to the actions of radical Islamic terrorists worldwide as well as Afghan and Pakistani insurgents. While India had once claimed that all of the terrorist threat it faced was cross-border, it has not repeated these claims in recent years, a recognition that Islamic radicalism has metastasized and is now internal.[126] Bangladesh now has the potential to be a second front for terrorism. It has a diaspora community in the UK now larger than that of Pakistanis. So far, despite a long-standing relation with Bangladesh terrorists, Al Qaeda has not penetrated that country's corresponding UK community in the way it has made inroads with Britain's Pakistanis, who have proven critical in expanding their presence and capability in Europe.

Future terrorist groups may seek to build not only on Al Qaeda but also on the networks and organizations associated with transnational Islamic groups that are explicitly peaceful, such as Hezb-ut-Tahrir and Tablighi Jamaat, which bring together large numbers, mobilize them, and create trusted links between them. As advocates for a Sunni Khalifait operating in a world of nation-states, Hezb-ut-Tahrir normally operates in a clandestine cell-like organization even in the UK. Al Qaeda's limitations have not reduced the risk that, even if these organizations remain peaceful, they can be penetrated and used by terrorist organizations. Their members could be recruited or their clandestine organizations used to support terrorist activities, even if they may not share the terrorists' commitment to violence. Both the numbers of individuals and the extensive networks involved with such organizations suggest that these could be powerful tools. They, along with the diaspora communities, represent prime targets for penetration and influence by a powerful and skillful terrorist threat. Such groups may also come to share the "leaderless" approach of Al Qaeda, in which the network executes the specifics of broad policies that are publicly announced by leaders who focus more on inspiration than coordination. Pulling the different elements together, there is a real possibility that what emerges from the Vortex, regardless of whether it keeps or discards the Al Qaeda "brand," may be much more dangerous than the current threat. A potential new group, regardless of name, would have an ability to serve as a focus for grievances about governments, European or third world; globalization; cultural decay; social change; and much else, effectively embracing terrorism as a tool to counter the trends in the postmodern world that have disconcerted or marginalized so many.

In 2010, terrorist groups including both Al Qaeda (in Kunar and Nuristan) and Lashkar-e-Taiba (in eight provinces) put an increasing number of cells into Afghanistan. Transnational terrorism remains cheap. LeT's annual budget is an estimated $5.25 million. Funding from donations and charities in Saudi Arabia and the Gulf is unabated. Al Qaeda's rhetoric equating the distant and primary enemies and groups such as LeT and TTP (the May 2010 attempted bombing in New York) becoming threats on a global basis, it remains that these terrorists have been prevented from inflicting casualties in the US and the West for some years. Whether this can be continued in a world reflecting the changes in Afghanistan likely post–2014 is one of the questions inevitably confronting policy makers.

CHAPTER FIVE

AFGHAN INSURGENTS

"For you will be delivered to life in a world where, at the worst, no horror is now incredible, no folly unthinkable, no adventure inconceivable."
— Rudyard Kipling, Rhodes Dinner, Oxford, June 1924

Throughout Afghanistan, in the immediate aftermath of the 2001 defeat of the Afghan Taliban and their Al Qaeda patrons, anyone suggesting that by 2008–10 these organizations would be waging a cross-border insurgency that would threaten the future of both the country and the regions it borders would have been ignored as a crank. Yet that is precisely what occurred. The Afghan insurgents amount to a "coalition of the unwilling" that were either opposed to, or not included in, the post-2001 political process in Afghanistan, joined by those who had originally welcomed the defeat of the Taliban and Al Qaeda but have since been motivated to take up arms alongside their successors.

The insurgency is not a national Afghan movement, unlike that which emerged victorious from the 1978–92 conflict. While their motivations are diverse, the insurgents collectively amount to a xenophobic, anti-secular, anti-Western ethnolinguistically Pushtun opposition. They do not require, nor receive, broad-based support inside Afghanistan as a whole. But by 2008–10 they had managed to achieve such support in a large number of the districts of the five southern provinces where the heaviest fighting is concentrated plus other districts throughout the east and north of Afghanistan, some close to Kabul in Wardak, Logar, and Nangarhar provinces. The insurgency is limited geographically. Where there are few ethnic Pushtuns, there is a limited insurgent presence.

The majority of Afghans are probably not Pushtuns and, despite widespread frustration and disappointment at the ruined hopes of a better life that were so widespread in 2001, not intrinsically xenophobic or anti-Western. The Afghan insurgents have been able to tap into widespread support from government and government-tolerated sources in Pakistan, the Taliban culture in both Pushtun Afghanistan and Pakistan, and a semi-clandestine network of supporters that exists throughout Pushtu-speaking Afghanistan and Pakistan. While the Taliban Culture has drawn strength from Pushtun roots, its followers are not all Pushtuns. It is less about Pushtun nationalism than it is about Deobandi-influenced Sunni Islamic fundamentalism.

The Afghan Taliban and their insurgent allies that have emerged from the Vortex are not the same pre-2001 organizations.[127] In 2002–06, the Afghan Taliban in Pakistan accelerated their cross-fertilization from other organizations that had marked the later years of their rule in Kabul. This included participation in the rise of the Pakistani Taliban. In Pakistan, Afghan insurgent groups have access to networks running outside the FATA and money from Karachi, Lahore, and elsewhere made involvement in Pakistani internal politics even more important.

In 2001, the Taliban had found few willing to fight to the death for them except some foreigners. By 2008–10, there was no shortage of insurgent fighters: Afghans, Pakistanis, and a new generation of foreigners. Those Afghans fighting in the insurgency were, in 2008–10, mainly Pushtuns. The current Afghan insurgents have, like the 1994–96 Afghan Taliban, been able to present themselves internally as the banner carriers of Pushtun nationalism and the restorers of Pushtun power in Kabul while holding fast to a transnational ideology of Sunni Islamic radicalism. Post-2001, the Afghan Taliban and other insurgent groups have managed to come out from under Osama bin Laden's effective control. The post-2001 Taliban has become the leading Afghan insurgent group, dominating but not controlling a diverse insurgent coalition, but has retained its links with Al Qaeda. But while Al Qaeda focuses on its global mission, the post-2001 Afghan Taliban instead aims at seizing state power in Afghanistan as part of an insurgent coalition that includes, among other groups, its pre-2001 rival HiH.[128]

Before 2001, many of the cultural restrictions that made the Taliban a brutal occupying force in Kabul or the Hazara Jat were applied more leniently—or at least more haphazardly—in the Taliban heartland of southern Afghanistan. The current Afghan insurgency combines some of this approach. In many predominantly Pushtun areas, the insurgents make use of outreach to local inhabitants. But more brutal and direct methods are also widespread. The Afghan insurgency is a mix of Afghan Taliban Pushtun origins and a potential Islamic Khmer Rouge. Xenophobia has been exalted, reflecting the need to de-legitimate the foreign presence that supports Kabul and reflecting the Al Qaeda-provided narrative that Afghanistan is one front in a global struggle against Crusaders and Zionists. It builds on a shared sense of deep humiliations to Muslims worldwide.

The worst crimes of the pre-2001 Afghan Taliban and their allies—the massacres in the Hazara Jat and Mazar-e-Sharif, the despoliation of the Shomali Plain, the repressive rule in Kabul and other cities—are likely to be the standing operating procedures of their successors. In south Afghanistan by 2008–10, the murder of pro-government religious figures and aid workers and the massacre of civilian Afghans have been widespread. Perhaps most telling, the intimidation of rural Afghan Pushtun leadership figures has forced many to flee to Kandahar, Kabul, or Dubai. Many of these were the bedrock of local support for the pre-2001 Afghan Taliban. The Afghan insurgent coalition is a different type of force.

Despite, and in some ways because of, the unprecedented coalition military effort in Afghanistan post-2001 (with 49 countries contributing in 2010) and a number of major battlefield successes, the Afghan insurgency has continued to gather strength. Insurgent and terrorist attacks rose from a maximum of 400 per month in 2005 to 1,000 per month in 2007. By 2008, attacks in the provinces around Kabul, increased crime, and attacks inside the city led to the US decision to commit an additional 17,000 personnel in early 2009. Following a strategic review by the incoming Obama administration in Washington, the senior US and NATO leadership in Afghanistan completed their own reassessment that showed a need for further coalition assets and an expansion of the Afghan National Security Forces (ANSF) to eventually take over the burden of the conflict. Despite battlefield success in 2010, this will need to be implemented before things can get better.

Insurgents in Afghanistan

"The insurgents share the same short term goals, to get rid of the foreigners and get rid of the governors. They have no common vision of the future but work together well and their differences have not been sufficient to drive a wedge between them," in the words of COL Patrick McNiece, USA, ISAF deputy director of intelligence in 2008.[129] The Afghan Taliban is the largest single member of a diverse coalition fighting inside Afghanistan. The Afghan Taliban continues to demonstrate an ability to unite Pushtuns in both Afghanistan and Pakistan, cutting across tribal and local loyalty, a reason why the Pakistani security services have used them as a tool of national strategy in Afghanistan in the past. The Afghan Taliban may have had had their origins in Pakistan's goal, dating back to the 1970s, to use Afghanistan for "strategic depth"; post-2001 it turned out that it was Pakistan that was providing the Taliban and their allies with their own "strategic depth."

Part of what GEN David Petraeus called the "syndicate of extremists that are the problem in Regional Command—East"[130], other insurgent groups include the Hezb-e-Islami (HiH) of Gulbuddin Hekmatyar, who was no longer involved in the day-to-day command of operations by 2009. Another affiliated insurgent group is led by Jaluladin Haqqani, a 1978–92 field commander with strong "Afghan Arab" ties, in who was in failing health or possibly deceased by 2009 and his son Sirajjuddin Haqqani. There are also Wahabi groups including Arabs, Pakistanis, and Afghans operating mainly in Kunar and Nuristan. A large number of basically criminal groups and narcotics traffickers claim nominal allegiance to the insurgency.

Except for some of these latter—crime knows no ethnicity—the members of insurgent groups appear to mainly consist of Afghan Pushtuns and Pakistani Pushtuns fighting together, reflecting the insurgents' ideology that the border dividing them is illegitimate. All these groups also have some (under 10 percent) foreigners, mainly non-Pushtuns from Pakistan but also Arabs and even Muslim volunteers from the UK and Europe. Pakistani insurgent groups fighting in Afghanistan such as the Tehreek-e-Nafaz-e-Shariat-e-Mohammadi (TNSM, Movement for the Enforcement of Islamic Law), Jaish-e-Mohammed (Arm of Mohammed), and the Pakistani Taliban umbrella group, Tehrik-e-Taliban Pakistan (TTP, Students' Movement of Pakistan), are also fighting in Afghanistan.

Afghan and Pakistani insurgents fighting in Afghan, as well as those fighting in Pakistan, have been able to draw personnel, funding and support from Deobandi-influenced Islamic radical groups in Pakistan which have overlapping memberships, such as Jamiat-ul-Ulema-e-Islam (JUI, Union of the Clergy of Islam), Jaish-e-Mohammed, and Lashkar-e-Taiba (Army of the Righteous). These groups have shown an ability to change identity and focus, able to adopt new names or present themselves in Pakistan as a charitable group. The Pakistani Jamiat-e-Islami (JI, Union of Islam), which has exclusive membership, has been an exception; it has long-standing links with the Afghan HiH and its members have tended to support that group. The large numbers of non-Pushtun Pakistanis that have fought in Afghanistan since the 1990s were in large part recruited through these Pakistani Islamic radical groups.

These Pakistani groups and individuals have been important for the insurgency in Afghanistan as well as that in Pakistan. Even after Pakistan ended its support for cross-border insurgency in Kashmir, links with exiled Kashmiri militants in the FATA and Baluchistan continued to be fostered by Afghan insurgents. Such Pakistani groups and their members were already mobilized and radicalized, in many cases, and easily transitioned to other Afghan and Pakistani insurgent organizations. Even the Pushtun nationalist Afghan insurgents, bitterly fighting their own non-Pushtun countrymen, welcomed non-Pushtun Pakistani volunteers as honored guests. For example, many of the original Pakistani Taliban in the FATA's Bajaur agency were JUI members from areas outside the

FATA, who only took up the Taliban name to gain Pushtun recruits after the initial insurgent successes in South Waziristan. JI members played a major role as auxiliaries to the ISI in Pakistan's brutal counter-insurgency campaign in what was East Pakistan in 1971.

In practice, all these Afghan and Pakistani insurgent groups have some links, ranging from close integration to limited cooperation, with Al Qaeda and other transnational terrorist groups. This has included sharing technology and tactics, even among groups where there is not an ideological link, and has allowed blowback from Iraq and lessons from other insurgencies to affect Afghanistan and Pakistan. This has ranged from more lethal improvised explosive devices (IEDs) and roadside bombs to adapting effective political and propaganda themes.[131] Afghanistan and Pakistani insurgent groups have been widely reported to share access to logistics, infrastructures, and networks running throughout Pakistan and to the sources of support outside the country. They included the networks between Al Qaeda and other transnational terrorist organizations; what remains of the support networks created by the Pakistani security services to support guerrillas in Afghanistan and Kashmir and sympathetic movements and political parties at home; networks of patrons and clients enabled by resources provided from outsider supporters; and networks of religious leaders, linked by roots in the same madrassas. ADM Eric Olson, former combatant commander of US Special Operations Command (SOCOM), has said the Afghan insurgency is "about genealogy and theology more than ideology."[132]

Yet, despite shared access to these networks, it appears that what coordination exists between the different coalition members, much as in the 1978–92 war, is through local coordination between field commanders backed up by a top-down resource allocation process imposed by outside aid donors. Yet at the operational level, the different insurgent groups have demonstrated an ability to pull together coalitions for major operations. For example, the force that attacked and defeated a US-ANA outpost in the Pech valley of Kunar province in July 2008 was estimated to be over 200 strong and included large numbers of Pakistani insurgents as well as Afghan Taliban. An even larger force overran a US–ANA outpost outside Komdesh in Nuristan in October 2009.

This does not all work smoothly; Mullah Omar has supposedly been in conflict with Behtullah Mehsud, head of TTP until his death in an UAV attack in August 2009, over the latter's strong links to Al Qaeda. Another source of the conflict was that Behtullah Mehsud was threatening the same Pakistani military that was providing Mullah Omar and the Quetta shura effective sanctuary in Baluchistan.

The insurgency in Afghanistan brings together groups that would often just as readily fight each other, even to a greater extent than the fractious Afghan resistance of 1978–92. Some of these conflicts have been long-running and violent. In Kunar and Nuristan, HiH and Wahabi-funded groups have been rivals since the 1980s. Many of the foreign insurgent fighters in Afghanistan, Pakistani well as Arab, are ignorant of local ways and often disdainful of the Afghans. This often leads to resentment and violence. Indeed, in much of Pushtun Afghanistan, the mosaic of tribal and sub-tribal divisions means that Pushtuns from another (or rival) tribe can encounter as much xenophobia as the Punjabis or Arabs that often make themselves hated by the local inhabitants. They can be considered foreigners as much as Europeans, despite the ties of shared Islam. Often, tensions over religious practice lead to divisions or violence.

The Afghan Taliban

There is no central Afghan insurgent command nor a central source of money or logistics, although the different groups may share and overlap. Mullah Omar remains the titular head of the Afghan Taliban, as he has been since at least 1994, but his power and authority have changed. He no longer provides the direct charismatic leadership and dispute resolution that he did during the Taliban's rise to power in the 1990s.

In 2008–10, the inner Quetta shura was reportedly able to make strategic decisions and allocate resources to implement them; the spread of the Afghan insurgency among Pushtuns in northern Afghanistan and to target troops from Germany, Italy, and Spain to encourage their withdrawal was reported to have been the results of such high-level action by the Quetta shura.[133] The Quetta shura has also, when practical, issued precise operations orders and conducted structured "lessons learned" processes, including a formal campaign review at the end of each year, at the end of which Mullah Omar announces guidance and intent for the coming year.[134]

The involvement of the Quetta shura in decision-making increased in 2008–10, apparently reflecting the heavy losses of mid-level commanders, especially in southern Afghanistan, in 2005–07, especially when the Taliban tried to hold their ground against coalition forces. "The high-level guys' command and control is from Quetta by cell phone; mid-level guys do not like being led in this way. It takes higher level guys to do coordination," said COL McNiece.[135]

The Afghan Taliban of 2008–10 is part of a loose coalition where their pre-2001 predecessor was a failed attempt at a unitary organization. This makes it hard to negotiate a settlement with an organization largely created to wage insurgency on autopilot. In many cases, the insurgent groups may share the same name without being part of a unitary organization. The Taliban has followed Al Qaeda's franchise approach, allowing their name to be used by associated groups. The multiple groups that made up the Pakistani Taliban have never been under the operational control of Mullah Omar. The groups had called themselves "Taliban" for years before 13 of them eventually joined together in December 2007 to become the Pakistani Taliban umbrella group, Tehrik-e-Taliban Pakistan (TTP, Students' Movement of Pakistan). Other groups, including those involved in criminal activity, appear to have adopted the name without permission. All of this is evidence that the Taliban remains a powerful "brand name" that apparently has an appeal not limited to Afghanistan and the Pakistani borderlands. The suicide bombings in central Asia in summer 2009 suggest one direction where the Taliban may spread instability through example even if it is not an explicit policy. The IJU and IMU have both modeled themselves closely on the Taliban, even though most of their recent support has been from Al Qaeda.

There are no explicit factions. All of the Afghan Taliban owes at least nominal allegiance to Mullah Omar and the Quetta shura. The Afghan Taliban's Quetta shura has functioned largely openly since 2001; and this appears to be their major decision-making body. Pakistan claimed to have shut it down in mid-2008, forcing its dispersal to smaller villages in Baluchistan, but there is no evidence that this is the case. However, the Quetta shura reportedly was by 2008–10 meeting in different locations, including Karachi.[136] Along with Mullah Omar, participants are thought to include Mullah Birader Akhund (captured and released by Pakistan in 2010), his lieutenant and first deputy. The shura has about 18 members.

Maulavi Abdul Latif Mansur, pre-2001 Minister of Agriculture, is the head of the Quetta shura's political committee. Abdul Qabir, the former head of the political committee, is the Afghan Taliban's military commander for eastern Afghanistan since 2007.[137] He was reportedly captured by Pakistani security forces in 2005 but has apparently returned to action.[138] Mullah Abdul Jalil, foreign minister pre-2001, is thought to be an advisor to Mullah Omar and possibly the Quetta shura's shadow Minister of the Interior. Mullah Agha Jan Mu'tasim, finance minister pre-2001, has been reported to be the former head of the Quetta shura's finance committee and the former or current head of the political committee. Abdul Zakir and Akhtar Mansur were announced as deputies in 2010.

These men have been Mullah Omar's comrades in arms since the 1980s. They mainly have their roots in Ghilzay tribes in Durrani-dominated (Birader is Durrani) provinces in the south. They tend to tolerate of necessity but distrust Sufic-influenced religious practices as non-Islamic and tribal loyalties as divisive and instead embrace a fundamentalist Islam without borders. They went to the same Deobandi-influenced madrassas in the FATA and fought together against the Soviets, owing at least nominal allegiance to the "Peshawar seven" parties, first to the Harakat-e-Inqilab-e-Islami of Mohammed Nabi Mohammedi and, as that declined, to the Hezb-e-Islami of Younis Khalis. Only Zakir is younger.

Other Afghan Taliban shuras in Pakistan operated by 2008–10. Regional commanders work with regional shuras. There is also a Rahbari (leadership) shura, a subset of the Quetta shura chaired by Mullah Birader. This organization reportedly handles coordination between the Quetta shura and senior field commanders, who are also members. There is reportedly a Peshawar shura that, despite its name, is based in South Waziristan and a Miran Shah shura that are both reportedly concerned with military operations while the Karachi shura handles logistics and the all-important outside funding.[139] US MG Mark Milley described the Afghan Taliban as having "no unitary actor, no charismatic leader, a diffuse organization with similar—but not the same—structures."[140]

The Afghan Taliban has appointed shadow provincial and district governors for Afghanistan.[141] Originally, many of these Taliban-appointed governors remained in Pakistan, but by 2008–10 a number have moved inside Afghanistan.[142] Several of these Taliban governors have been targeted and killed or captured, including those for Kandahar and Helmand provinces. In 2008–10, the Afghan Taliban claimed they were operating governing shuras in several southern provinces.[143] They have installed Sharia courts, enforced taxation, and conscripted Afghans for fighting and labor. They have also publicized that there exist mechanisms for complaints against Taliban officials inside Afghanistan to be received. Ashraf Ghani, the former Afghan minister of finance, said, in 2009, "The Taliban has appointed governors, but these do not function in providing services to the populace on the model of the Chinese Communist or Malayan insurgents. They do have an ombudsman against their own officials, because the number of those that present themselves as Taliban and perpetrate terrible crimes has increased."[144]

Taliban leaders at the lower level tend to be young, many too young to have fought in the anti-Soviet jihad. Few held power under the pre-2001 Taliban regime (and so did not share their loss of legitimacy). While Mullah Omar's inner circle is still drawn largely from the Ghilzay tribes that provided most of the pre-2001 Afghan Taliban's leadership, most of the other leaders have Durrani backgrounds.[145]

One of the most significant Taliban leaders who was not a comrade of Mullah Omar in the 1980s is the commander of the Tora Bora Front, Anwar-ul-Haq Mujahid, who is reportedly the current military commander for Nangarhar province. He is the son of the late Younis Khalis, head of the Hezb-e-Islami (Khalis) (HiK) party, an Islamist party that was one of the "Peshawar Seven" Sunni Afghan resistance parties supported by Pakistan in 1978–92. Mullah Omar and his inner circle were reportedly nominal HiK members in the late 1980s. Mujahid remains the nominal head of HiK. He has extensive Khogiani Pushtun tribal links in Nangarhar.

Hekmatyar and Haqqanis

The Afghan insurgency has attracted few Afghan elites, secular or religious. The senior Afghan Taliban, some Pakistan-based Taliban, Hekmatyar, and Jaluladin Haqqani are veterans of the 1978–92 war against the Soviets and the 1992–2001 civil war. But many of the insurgent leadership come from the new generation, Pushtuns who spent 1978–92 growing up poor in a refugee camp or village in the FATA and attending the local madrassas.

The Afghan insurgents are strongest in areas where their leaders are already established. For example, Gulbuddin Hekmatyar remains popular among Pushtuns in his home town of Kunduz, even though he himself lacks a strong tribal identity and, as an Islamist and a modernizer, is ideologically opposed to the tribal system, though the Pushtun ethnicity of his supporters means he has had to pay lip service to it in the past. His group is most significant in Kunduz and elsewhere in the north. They are important in Kunar and Nuristan where they can muster a significant number of fighting men. They have also launched suicide attacks in Kabul and other cities. Hekmatyar remains popular among some Afghan Pushtuns. If he chose to run for parliament in Kunduz, he would probably win in a fair election.

Hekmatyar has been a major figure in Afghanistan's politics since 1975, when he was one of the leaders of the Pakistan-backed abortive Islamist revolt against the Afghan government of President Prince Mohammed Daoud. Starting in 1978, he led the most radical Islamist of the seven Peshawar-based Sunni resistance parties, his personal faction of Hezb-e-Islami (HiH). This had the highest priority in receiving outside aid through much of the war against the Soviets. Hekmatyar's group saw much fighting in Afghanistan, but he positioned himself to ultimately seize power in Kabul. This included carrying out an assassination campaign against pro-Western Afghan elites living in Pakistan and fighting against other resistance groups inside Afghanistan, especially those associated with Ahmad Shah Massoud.

HiH was Pakistan's chosen policy instrument in Afghanistan from the 1980s to 1996, but his radical politics and lack of a tribal base made him unable to rally Afghan's Pushtuns and he was displaced from favor with Pakistan by the Taliban. Since then, Hekmatyar has been in exile in Pakistan and Iran. After 2001, Hekmatyar made up with the Taliban, despite their ideological gap. Hekmatyar's origins were as an Islamist, looking to religion to modernize a backwards Afghanistan, while the Taliban's ideology is largely fundamentalist. They may use cell phones and laptops but have no use for modernization except to better promulgate Islam. Yet their reconciliation has been to their mutual advantage. Hekmatyar's years of exile in Iran has given him links to the leadership, especially of the Revolutionary Guards, the bitterly anti-Shia Mullah Omar and the Afghan Taliban lack. Hekmatyar also has long-standing links to Al Qaeda; the "Afghan Arabs" fought on his behalf in 1992, trucked to Kabul by the ISI to try and displace Ahmad Shah Massoud's Northern Alliance forces.

By 2008–10, Hekmatyar was said by several Afghan political figures to desire a settlement that would allow HiH to function in Afghanistan much as Hezbollah does in Lebanon, participating in parliament but retaining an armed militia, criminal-economic networks, and strong links with foreign patrons.[146] If this is true, it would distinguish his own group from the Afghan Taliban's insistence on the primacy of an armed struggle to ultimate victory. HiH is likely to demand top-down negotiations to achieve this goal.

Yet there has been little evidence of Hekmatyar being open to negotiations, despite reports of talks being held with representatives of the Karzai government in Saudi Arabia. Only a few lower-level HiH figures, mainly from Nangarhar, have joined with Kabul. Other former HiH leaders have joined with Wahabi-backed groups in the Kunar valley in a competition dating back to the 1980s. Hekmatyar and his inner circle of "hard men," despite many rumors to the contrary, remain aloof and intact.

Jaluladin and Sirajjuddin Haqqani can claim a block of support from their Jadrani Pushtun tribe. They also controlled, in 2008–10, a sizable area of Pakistan's North Waziristan. They also have access to funding from Saudi Arabia and the Gulf and strong links to both Pakistani radical parties and Al Qaeda, as Osama bin Laden himself fought alongside the older Haqqani against the Soviets. Siraj also has close ties to Pakistan's ISI.[147] David Rohde, a *New York Times* reporter held prisoner in the FATA in 2009, has written: "My suspicions about the relationship between the Haqqanis and the Pakistani military proved to be true. Some American officials told my colleagues at *The Times* that Pakistan's military intelligence agency, the Directorate for Inter-Services Intelligence, or ISI, turns a blind eye to the Haqqanis' activities. Others went further and said the ISI provided money, supplies and strategic planning to the Haqqanis and other Taliban groups."[148]

"Siraj is part of a younger, more aggressive generation of Taliban senior leadership that is pushing aside the formerly respected elders," said Army LTC Dave Anders, former director of operations for Combined Joint Task Force-82 in 2007. "Now, the Haqqani network is clearly in the hands of Siraj, and the face of it is evolving, becoming more violent and self serving." MAJ Chris Belcher, then spokesman for CJTF-82, added that Sirajjudin's links have increased his capabilities and Sirajjudin's "extended reach brings foreign fighters from places like Pakistan, Uzbekistan, Chechnya, Turkey and Middle Eastern countries into Afghanistan."[149]

The Haqqanis gained prominence in January-February 2002 as they were able to organize, secure, and feed many of the Al Qaeda and Taliban "bitter enders" that retreated into the FATA from Tora Bora in Afghanistan following Operation Anaconda, the ultimately unsuccessful US military operation to cut them off. In 2008–10 he has been involved with organizing attacks against Kabul itself. "Most suicide bombs here [Kabul] are Haqqani. Haqqani is most responsible for suicide bombings. He is the closest to Al Qaeda of any insurgent [leader]," according to COL Patrick McNiece, ISAF deputy director of intelligence in 2008.[150] In 2010, Pakistan tried to mediate talks between Siraj and Kabul.

A Diverse Insurgency

The insurgency is limited on an ethnic (almost purely Pushtun or foreign) basis. While most terrorist/insurgent action has cross-border roots, from Pakistan, internal insurgency has been increasing, especially in five key southern and eastern provinces. The insurgency is heavily cross-border. In 2008, the amount of cross-border activity increased 28 percent, and previous years had seen increases of ten to twenty percent.[151] In 2008 "72 percent of the incidents happened in ten percent of the territory and [directly] involved six percent of the population," according to BG Richard Blanchette, Canadian Armed Forces, the ISAF spokesman.[152] Polling shows that the impact of the insurgency on Afghans is also concentrated; in 2009, while only 14 and 23 percent of Afghans in war-torn Helmand and Kandahar provinces respectively have a positive view of local security, 75 percent of those in Kunduz (which has some ongoing insurgent activity) and 76 percent of those in secure Balkh province did.[153] The insurgency has been growing. GEN David Petraeus said: "2009 showed a sixty percent increase in security incidents above 2008, which in turn was an increase over 2007. . . . The total spiked at 900 in July 2009. In 2009 Badghis and Kunduz provinces [in the north] included a district in red [indicating 51–100 security incidents] which were not there before."[154] 2010 saw a spreading insurgency.

Mainly Pushtuns are fighting and some Uzbek and Nuristani with the exception of a relatively few individuals groups. The Afghan insurgents are unwilling to accept a major Western presence in Afghanistan. They include Pakistani radicals, many of them focusing on Afghanistan rather than Pakistan. Former pre-2001 Afghan Taliban members are one of the largest insurgent groups along with former Khalqis (who largely found their Pushtun ethnicity and anti-urban mindset suited them to cooperation with the Taliban) and those linked to them by religious practice.

In 2008–10, the insurgency had evolved into several different areas, each with different insurgent (and counter-insurgent) groups. The south is the heart of the insurgency, in Kandahar, Helmand, Uruzgan, and Zabul provinces, corresponding to the coalition Regional Command South (RC-S).[155] It extends also up the main road to the west, to Herat and in pockets beyond, almost to Turkmenistan. This insurgency is rooted in the infrastructure and networks created in Pakistan's Baluchistan. The insurgents are primarily those identified as Afghan Taliban, but with many foreigners based in Pakistan. The number of foreign fighters has increased in 2008–10, reflecting the heavy losses to local Taliban in 2005–07. Supposedly, the Afghan Taliban's Quetta shura and Mullah Omar have the closest links and most direction over this area. It is also the area where the Pushtun tribal system is still the strongest. But all politics is local, and in these provinces, local politics are Pushtun tribal politics. These provinces are also the heart of Afghanistan's poppy production, and this is the area where the insurgency is closely linked to it. Over 80 percent of insurgents fight near their homes.

The east is where the insurgency has been less successful but the proximity of Pakistan has ensured that this remains an area of bitter fighting, although in 2007–08 only one of the top five provinces for insurgency action—Paktika—was in the east. The areas in the east suffered some of the most intense devastation and depopulation during the war against the Soviets. Tribal structures differ between the provinces, with Khost having the most intact and functional tribal system. The east corresponds largely to part of the coalition Regional Command–East (RC-E), but effectively is divided into divergent southeast and northeast insurgencies.

The southeast insurgency focuses on Paktia, Paktika, and Khost provinces. The insurgency there is rooted in Pakistan's FATA. The insurgents are primarily but not exclusively Afghan Taliban (which still includes increasing numbers of foreigners and especially Pakistanis in their ranks). Pakistan's TTP operates across the border there. This is the area where the Haqqani network is strongest, drawing on its pre-2001 base among Afghanistan's Jadrani Pushtuns and its external links to the "Afghan Arabs" with a logistics base in Parachinar. While the tribal authority remains significant here, the traditional leadership structures were damaged by the 1978–92 war which included widespread depopulation and devastation of this area by the Soviets. Opium cultivation has been greatly reduced in this area, but drug laboratories and trafficking routes are in this area. Much cross-border trade is in the hands of Taliban-aligned "mafias," which have links to Pakistan's security services dating back to the 1980s.

The northeast insurgency is most active in Nangarhar, Kunar, Kapitsa, and Nuristan provinces, using bases in the FATA (especially the Bajaur Agency), NWFP, and other areas as far north as Chitral. This is the area where, in addition to the Afghan Taliban, HiH, TNSM, and, in the Kunar, Wahabi groups are strongest. The tribal system is important, but less cohesive than that farther south. The Afridis and Shinwaris are made up of independent khels, committed to cross-border trade. The Mohmands retain a strong cross-border structure. The Kunar's tribal structure has been fractured ever since the former king cleansed the valley of its Safi Pushtun inhabitants in 1944, replacing them with loyalists from elsewhere in Afghanistan. The Nuristanis are divided by clan, tribe, and dialect. This remote province, poor and undeveloped even by Afghan standards, has seen much violence. This area, especially Nangarhar, was previously the site of intensive opium cultivation, but by 2008–09 this had been greatly reduced. In 2010, Nangarhar had been poppy-free for three consecutive years, a remarkable achievement in a province where, after 2001, poppy fields were visible from the main highway to Kabul. This achievement reflects not only the actions of Afghan and coalition Counter Narcotics programs but also that Nangarhar has greater access to development, markets, labor (in Kabul or Pakistan), and other sources of incomes than the insurgency-plagued provinces in the south where poppy cultivation has been concentrated. It also reflects the commitment to narcotics eradication of the Nangarhar provincial governor, Gul Agha Sherzai. Even his critics concede his effectiveness, although they argue his motivation was increasing the market share of his own investments in Kandahar-grown opium. Kunar and Laghman provinces also saw poppy cultivation drop to insignificant levels by 2008.[156] The northeast area has seen company-size coalition operations defeated either in forward operating bases or in the field and forced to withdraw, such as the US in the Pech Valley of Kunar and the French at Sarobi Gorge in 2008 or the joint US-ANA outpost overrun at Komdesh in Nuristan in October 2009.

In 2008–10, a central front in the insurgency emerged near Kabul, including Wardak, Logar, and Laghman provinces, some within an hour's drive of the city. HiH groups have returned to areas where they were strong in 1992–96. Some of the strongest groups, especially in Wardak, were pre-2001 Afghan Taliban returned from exile in Pakistan to reawaken old alliances with local and tribal leaders. Cross-border Pakistani groups have also been operating in this area, as have a large number of criminal groups using insurgent cover.

In 2009–10, the north, relatively quiet in previous years, emerged as a front in the insurgency.[157] Provinces such as Kunduz and Badghis have sizable ethnic Pushtun populations dating back to the nineteenth century, when King Abdur Rahman resettled them there. These populations were reduced in size during the 1978–2001 conflicts, many fleeing to exile in Pakistan or southern Afghanistan. Tensions with their Dari or Turkic-speaking neighbors have been high. The northern insurgency has diverse roots, with many of those near Kunduz receiving support from HiH groups in the east and those in Badghis receiving support from the Taliban in Helmand (where many local internal refugees fled). Operating in the north also allows insurgents to help secure some of the narcotics trafficking routes running through the former Soviet Union.

The insurgency is not a mass movement of the people of Afghanistan or the Pushtun world. It is not popular with grassroots Afghan opinion, unlike the 1978–92 mujahideen. Multiple polls taken with a range of methodologies in Afghanistan suggest that support for the insurgents does not exceed 10–18 percent nationally; consistent with the type of support a fringe party would receive even in a developed country. GEN McChrystal's report in August 2009 was basically accurate when he said "popular enthusiasm for them appears limited."[158]

Even in the Pushtun heartland of the south, there were originally few areas where a majority supported the insurgents. These increased by 2008–10, with many of the districts in Kandahar, Helmand, Uruzgan, and other provinces being someplace where no one is likely to ask polling questions and where intimidation and kinship and local loyalties can compensate for limitations in support for the insurgent cause. Among the Pushtuns of eastern and central Afghanistan there is generally less support for the insurgents than in the south. 2009 polling suggests that nationwide support for the Taliban is only seven percent, with 25 percent in the Pushtun southeast and 17 percent in central Afghanistan; only eight percent nationwide believe the insurgents are likely to win the conflict.[159] "Insurgents need 30 percent to sustain a political program or seize power" is the view of MG Mark Milley.[160] He added: "The insurgents are popular with ten percent of the people; in no country have they taken power with that."[161] Even if these figures are optimistic and the polling methodologies limited, it shows that by 2008–10 the insurgents did not have the active support of anything approaching a majority of Afghanistan's Pushtuns.

The widely differing attitudes identified by polling in early 2009 about the insurgents in Wardak and Laghman provinces reflects that in the former they are perceived as follow-ons to the guerrillas of 1978–92 and the Taliban of 1996–2001, while in the later they are seen as alien invaders.[162] When asked whether the insurgents had become more moderate in 2009, 58 percent of the Afghans in Wardak agreed, but only 14 percent of those in Laghman.[163] This may reflect the Taliban's massacre of a bus full of Afghans from Laghman in October 2008. This was followed by three to four days of province-wide protests. In the words of Massoud Farivar, Afghan journalist, "Laghman is a conservative province. It has lots of Taliban sympathizers. But the people rose up and said that was savagery."[164]

In 2008–10, a majority (albeit diminishing) of Afghans supported the foreign military presence, as an ABC news poll showed. Afghans remain painfully aware that, in the absence of the foreign presence, polarized Afghan factions and, most importantly, their cross-border supporters would plunge the country back into civil war.[165]

With the continued lack of a functioning civil economy in much of Afghanistan, especially with the 2008 rise in energy and fuel costs, this has created many desperate people in Afghanistan. Such people have a willingness to accept desperate solutions despite limitations as long as they can cross the threshold of legitimacy in Islamic and national terms. When ethnicity is added to the mix, as in the Pushtun areas, it has contributed to the strength of the insurgency. Outside pressures such as effective Al Qaeda-inspired propaganda, US and coalition policy failures, Pakistan policy, and foreign money would have been hard-pressed to fuel an insurgency in Afghanistan post-2001 without it having a degree of legitimacy—even if not support—in Pushtun Afghanistan. Much of this was provided by Al Qaeda, injecting the widespread perception that the Muslims have been subject to repeated invasion by non-Muslims, and repeated by the media in both Pakistan and Afghanistan until it is widely believed even among the majorities in both countries that do not support insurgents or radicalization.

"Yet it is a force that can regenerate itself, yet not so deeply rooted" even in the demographic of southern Afghanistan where "there are two million people, 45 percent under 15, and some 490,000 potential fighters, yet the total [insurgent force] is 5–10,000," according to BG Marquis Hainse, CF, who commanded Canadian troops in Regional Command-South in Kandahar in 2007–08.[166] MG Mark Milley estimated the insurgent force in October 2008 as 15–20,000.[167] Former interior minister Mohammed Hanif Atmar spoke of some 10–15,000 insurgents in 2009.[168] Later in 2009, US estimates of the number of full-time insurgents had increased to 25,000, an increase of 25 percent since 2008.[169] The 2008–09 bottom line is that some 80–85 percent of the Afghan population are not pro-insurgency. Even Afghanistan's most nationalistic Pushtuns are pragmatic and tired of conflict. "More people are pro-government than we think, though they may not be so overtly. 80 percent of the people in the south say that they believe in government institutions. This shows that if we do this right, we can have success. It is important that we capitalize on success. Tactical and operational success do not translate to strategic success," said BG Hainse.[170]

Crime is part of the insurgency, with many criminal combatants using the insurgents' rhetoric, and so difficult to distinguish from it. The inability of the Afghan government to counter criminal activity has hurt Kabul's legitimacy in provinces that have seen few insurgents. Crime affects many Afghans. Atmar, reviewing the 2008 crime statistics, said: "Organized crime is increasing. Daily there are over 50 incidents, a sixty percent increase over 2007."[171] 2009 polling showed that 17 percent of Afghans had been victims of crime or violence; of these only 9 percent reported the insurgents as the cause, compared to nine percent for foreign forces and 7 percent for Afghan National Security Forces.[172] Crime and insurgency have become increasingly interrelated throughout Afghanistan, but especially in the center, where the country's most functional local economy, that of Kabul, provides enough money to make crime pay. Kabuli criminals target Afghan elites, often kidnapping them or their children for ransom. There is widespread frustration with the government and their foreign supporters for not providing security.[173] By 2008–10, widespread crime in Kabul had done more than the insurgency in the south and east to lead to capital flight and discourage investment in Afghanistan.[174] This further encourages the culture of corruption, as other Afghans see this and look to extract resources to enable their own escape.

The appeal of the insurgents inside Afghanistan is not that they are the Taliban or their allies, but that they are Pushtuns (unlike a multiethnic Kabul government), not the government (with its lack of capability, corruption, and failure to met high grassroots expectations) or (infidel) foreign troops (with their intrusive searches and collateral damage). They can also make promises—and sometimes deliver them—of better security. "Crime, narcotics, and endemic corruption create a population susceptible to facile solutions, even from sources like the Taliban," in the words of US terrorism expert Bruce Hoffman.[175]

Insurgent Strategy

What has made the insurgency an existential threat to Afghanistan is not so much the weakness of the Afghan state, the internal conflicts of Afghanistan, or the failures of US and coalition policy, but rather the fundamental trans-border nature and its ability to find receptive supporters in some parts of Pushtun Afghanistan, especially in the south. Insurgencies with sanctuaries support and funds from across the border tend to win or, failing that, are able to negotiate themselves a favorable settlement. In recent decades, they have tended to be successful, even against effective practitioners of counter-insurgency warfare. The cross-border nature of the insurgency is complicated by the parallel internal conflicts on each side; neither the transnational terrorists nor the narcotics traffickers want to see the insurgency end, as it would undercut their own position. Rather, both thrived when the Afghan Taliban held power in Kabul pre-2001.

Insurgencies are normally ended by cutting some of the insurgents and their supporters in on the deal of running the country. This is limited in this case because the Taliban culture pushes towards a maximalist Islamist solution that would have to include the reduction of foreign influence in Afghanistan, reopening it to Pakistani control and, in effect, restarting the civil wars of 1992–2001. Settlements—either top-down, negotiated with the leadership; or bottom-up, negotiated with one insurgent sub-group or subordinate leader at a time—set the terms for insurgent participation in the post-conflict political process.

Splitting off a "moderate Taliban" has proven even more elusive since Pakistan first proposed it as a policy in the late 1990s and Musharraf reiterated it in 2007.[176] Those cited as actual or potential members of such a group, suitable parties for negotiation, usually include marginal figures without real authority.

A senior Pakistani official was quoted as saying in 2009: "We've already been talking to the Taliban. If the US helps the process, some arrangements can be worked out for political arrangements."[177] This is essentially the failed 1990s Pakistani policy returning. Pakistan has urged the US and Afghans to negotiate with the Afghan insurgents, with the goal being creation of a government in Kabul that would meet Pakistan's perceived security needs (to the detriment of Afghanistan, especially its non-Pushtuns). But the Afghan Taliban, as the major insurgent group, shows little interest in negotiations. In 2008–10, Afghan Taliban leaders appeared assured that time was on their side. They had no interest in any future that did not include the withdrawal of the foreign support for Kabul and did not embrace their views on Islamic practice. In 2008–10, while the Afghan Taliban were willing to reassure regional powers that they posed no threat to them, they offered few indications of any lessening of their pre-2001 enmity toward Afghan's non-Pushtuns.[178] Mullah Omar has even been willing to reassure the West that he would not be under the control of Al Qaeda.[179] But there has been little reassurance offered to Afghanistan's non-Pushtuns. In Kabul, there was concern among non-Pushtuns that negotiations with the insurgents may be used to increase Pushtun power and exclude non-Pushtuns. In October 2009, one (ethnic Pushtun) former cabinet minister justified negotiations with the Taliban: "All of the warlords are criminals; some of the Taliban are criminals."

In 2008–10 there were a number of parallel negotiation attempts with Afghanistan's insurgents. The US was supporting efforts to identify those insurgents—within the Taliban or in different groups—that could be brought into the government through a settlement. There were separate negotiations running with Kabul, either directly or through an interme-diary, including Saudi Arabia. These were not with local leaders but the Taliban's leadership and Gulbuddin Hekmatyar. In 2008–10, both of these felt they held the upper hand and were reluctant to deal.

The Afghan insurgents' current commitment to a fundamentalist Islamic vision and the insistence on the illegitimacy of the infidel for-eign presence—which ensures Pakistan, which has officially denied any presence or role in the conflicts, would control Afghanistan—and their association with the control of state power by ethnic Pushtuns gives little apparent room to compromise. Ideas that a "moderate Taliban" might be created and would be suitable subjects for negotiations if, at the end, they had the prospect of being brought into power—a policy Pakistan has held out since the late 1990s—is less likely because those willing to talk are not those able to have authority over the fighting men or the flow of resources. Even if local deals were made with insurgent commanders, they would become a magnet for assassination attempts and suicide bombers, as former Afghan Taliban local leader turned district governor Mullah Salam has been in 2008–10 in Musa Qala in Helmand province.

The most useful approach is likely to be bottom-up, paying off local Afghan Taliban leaders to come over or at least halt offensive operations until reforms in security and governance allow Kabul to be more effec-tive; a strategy for the long term. This has been the objective of the PTS (Program Takhim-e-Sohl, strengthening peace), although the number and importance of the insurgents this has brought in has been limited. The local level is largely where the negotiations were focused in late 2008, largely on the pattern of the Anbar awakening in Iraq and many local negotiations in Afghanistan's 1978–2001 conflicts. Recent surveys show 71 percent of Afghans supporting reconciliation efforts with "anti-government elements."[180] As Central Command combatant commander GEN David Petraeus said: "reconciliation of 'reconcilables' has been identified as a priority. We need to establish who they are, identify them, separate them from the irreconcilables and make reconciliation."[181]

The Afghans are not intrinsically warlike. That the Afghans are sick of war and want peace was used by the Taliban in 1994–96 to expand their control of Pushtun Afghanistan. People wanted peace so much, they would accept rule by a group that otherwise would not have been able to legitimate their rule even among their own ethnolinguistic group. By 2001, the Afghans' desire for peace meant that few Afghan Pushtuns were willing to fight to the end for the Taliban; many joined forces with the Northern Alliance to displace them. By 2008–10 the insurgents were counting on this to help increase their control of Pushtun Afghanistan, that even a bad peace may seem preferable to an unending insurgency. Yet current insurgents (unlike Pakistan) have no interest in offering Afghanistan's non-Pushtuns a peace that would not see them marginalized. In practice, the insurgents offer the potential for peace to Afghanistan's Pushtuns and the certainty of civil war or worse (especially in the case of Shias) to non-Pushtuns unless they submit.

In 2008–10, Afghan insurgents looked to increase the at-home impact against Afghans, US, and coalition forces alike. Anti-election efforts aimed at the 2009 Afghan presidential election began with the start of the voter registration campaign in 2008, with the Taliban threatening to behead Afghans caught with a voter registration card. However, as Election Day came closer, the Taliban limited this campaign. The pre-election surge of US and coalition forces was intended to drive insurgents into Pakistan and prevent them from interfering with the vote. When the presidential election was finally held in September 2009, the insurgents launched over 400 attacks as Afghans went to vote, following months of an overall "spike" in violence. The overall turnout for the election, at 38 percent, was just over half that of 2004. But the damage done to governmental legitimacy internally and internationally by Afghans trying to rig the election was far more widespread than that inflicted by the insurgents.

The insurgents are also capable of undertaking offensive action targeted at different coalition national contingents at times meaningful for their own political calendars. The insurgents are capable of identifying and targeting the seams in the coalition and the differences in perceived levels of will and the national caveats that indicate a limited liability commitment of many coalition partners. This has become "fuel for insurgents to break up the alliance," in the words of BG Marquis Hainse.[182]

The insurgents are aware that every tactical action can have strategic implications. "Most opposition groups learn that they can impact foreign capitals. Do something in Ghazni, it has impact in Warsaw," LTC Chris Cavoli, who commanded an infantry battalion of the US Army's 10th Mountain Division in northeast Afghanistan in 2007, said.[183] "They focus on weakening the will of the international community," agrees Rahim Wardak, Afghanistan's defense minister.[184] This was seen as contributing to the spread of insurgent operations into northern Afghanistan by autumn 2009. These apparently had a goal of inflicting German casualties—along with a threat of Al Qaeda attacks directly against targets in Germany—to influence that country's September 2009 election and inflicting Italian casualties to force that country to withdraw.[185] This is a change from the pre-2001 Taliban, with minimal understanding of the outside world, and reflects the Al Qaeda influence on the insurgents and their continued cooperation with transnational terrorists.

Another change from pre-2001 Afghanistan is the intense coverage of its conflicts by the international news media. BG Marquis Hainse said that when he was commanding Canadian and coalition forces in Regional Command South in 2007–08: "We hear about each NATO soldier that dies."[186] The degree of political judgment and operational timing that led to the 2004 Madrid railroad station bombing has come to Afghanistan.[187] The Internet and the rise of the 24-hour news cycle have become great levelers, enabling a few clever insurgents with laptops to successfully fight against the infinitely better-resourced coalition and Kabul (with the benefit of large numbers of foreign experts and consultants).

Insurgency Against Legitimacy

The insurgents seek to justify their warfare against Kabul and its foreign allies primarily in Islamic terms, secondarily in ethnolinguistic terms (as the avengers of Pushtun rights), and to a lesser extent as the authentic voice of Afghan nationalism and as the expression of a wide range of grievances ranging from the highly local (absence of jobs) to the global (the perceived US-directed war against Islam). Their great strength, however, is not their policies but their persistence. When Afghan or coalition troops leave an area, the insurgents—especially the Taliban—move in, exact retribution, destroy the benefits of contact with the outside, and stay. They cannot build or create, but it takes only limited numbers and resources to be spoilers in a region where there is little enough of anything to spoil.

At the same time, the insurgents seek to prevent the Kabul government (and this, in light of the limited capability building post-2001, means its foreign supporters) from taking acts that would legitimate itself (especially in Pushtun areas) by providing reconstruction and security, making possible economic activity other than narcotics cultivation and trading, and by not having to rely on non-Muslim foreign troops. Where there is no functional economy, the insurgents can buy all the fighting men they need cheaply in the absence of alternative employment. Where there is no security or development, the insurgents can profit from the activities that can flourish, especially narcotics and the extractive activities of the mafias. To do this, the insurgents have—so far successfully—waged a battle of ideas to legitimate their own actions in Islamic, Afghan, and Pushtun terms that has gone largely uncontested by Kabul and their coalition supporters, who have watched as the reservoir of goodwill and support that they enjoyed post-2001 among the majority of Afghans of all ethnolinguistic groups has eroded away. By 2008–10, many of the rural Pushtuns of southern Afghanistan have become more Talibanized than democratized.

"The Taliban needs an absence of governance to succeed," in the words of LTC Cavoli.[188] Such an absence of (non-corrupt) governance is one thing that has marked much of southern Afghanistan since 2001. Where it has been present, the building of roads, schools, and mosques has been outweighed by the years of extractive action by local officials or warlords—claiming their share under color of Kabul authority—and corrupt police. Some have seen the roots of insurgency in the south in extractive practices under the color of Kabul's authority that were widespread in 2001–05. These were almost all done by Pushtuns against other Pushtuns (with the targets for extraction often reflecting long-standing tribal divisions and rivalries). That they were less endurable than elsewhere in Afghanistan reflects the fractured nature of Pushtun politics, especially in the south (an earlier version of the same intra-Pushtun politics had led Pakistan to support the Taliban to take control there in 1994). More cohesive local politics in the east, in provinces such as Nangarhar, Paktia,

Paktika, and Khost means that while these are not peaceful, the impact of the insurgency was less there in 2008–10. The Helmand province intelligence (NSD) chief, Dad Mohammed Khan, was considered particularly extractive, but also happened to be good at his job; when he was finally fired in 2006, the insurgents gained more ground in the province.[189] That the officials carrying out these unpopular actions have almost all been, in the south, ethnic Pushtuns brought Kabul no benefit. "The people who are pro-Kabul created the situation in Kandahar, Helmand and Uruzgan, not the Taliban, [it was] the wrong policies post-2001," in the words of Massoud Kharokhail of the Kabul-based Tribal Liaison Office, a non-governmental development organization.[190]

It was not simply a matter of extractive or rapacious ANP or other government officials. A series of governors and other Kabul appointments diminished the perceived legitimacy of the government in Kabul in the south and—by their concentration on corruption rather than governance—undercut the ability of the government to deal with the initial stages of the insurgency.[191] Other Pushtun leaders led Afghan Military Force (AMF) units post-2001 in the south and east. These often sought to operate as independently as possible from the Defense Ministry in Kabul (then under Panjsheri control). Power and land grabs, backed up by armed force, became commonplace. Where such leaders were from rival or outside tribes, they were in many cases resented more intensely than would any non-Pushtun.

The insurgents have pushed Afghans to embrace xenophobia. They have succeeded to an extent, radicalizing their own ranks and imbuing a hostility to outsiders that was alien even to the pre-2001 Afghan Taliban. The Afghan insurgents have to show that a continued foreign presence in Afghanistan remains illegitimate and a threat to Islam and Afghan nationalism. They have done this, in part, by successfully embracing the theme that they are fighting a global war on Islam that has targeted Afghanistan and that Afghans need to be concerned about the oppression of Palestinians, Kashmiris, Bosnians and others by non-Muslims. Most important is resentment toward what is seen (however unrealistically) as an infidel-controlled non-Pushtun government in Kabul and its actions that threaten Afghanistan's culture: perceived failure to be responsive to local concerns and unwillingness to engage with grassroots Pushtuns. The issue was often seen as whether their family, clan, or tribe had been treated justly. The cumulative impact—of extractive officials and police, a government and coalition that cannot keep them safe or seems to favor local rivals, of collateral damage and lack of economic opportunity—is too often negative. In the words of GEN McChrystal in 2009, "We run the risk of strategic defeat by pursuing tactical wins that cause civilian casualties or unnecessary collateral damage."[192]

In parts of Pushto-speaking Afghanistan, the insurgents had local leaders to direct those with grievances in their direction, where Kabul did not have a counterpart capability. On the insurgent side, many of the lower-level leadership that emerged under the Afghan Taliban, especially in Kandahar and the south, were not de-legitimated along with the national leadership and so it was not widely accepted when they were cut out of power post-2001. The new would-be leaders that Kabul put in place in the south post-2001, despite being largely ethnic Pushtuns, did not enjoy a presumption of legitimacy from the local population that had shared the hardships and risks they had fled in 1994–2001. In a number of cases, inter-Pushtun rivalries made these leaders more hated than any non-Pushtun. It was easier for many to find the insurgents more legitimate than Kabul, Karzai's government, and foreigners.

The Afghan insurgents have acted to try and discredit the strategy of trying to increase legitimacy through provision of developmental aid: "the road is for infidels to drive on." The perception that the international community is doing nothing to benefit the average Afghan, as a result, has remained strong in much of Afghanistan. US ambassador to Kabul LTG (rtd) Karl Eikenberry's statement that "The Taliban begin where the road ends" sums up the link between lack of reconstruction and development in Afghanistan and the areas where the insurgency has been successful. Yet development itself does not cause insurgency to fade or create security.

Nor has action by the government or parliament aimed to preempt the social policies that the Taliban had used to legitimate their rule proven successful. Urban Pushtun elites had come to dominate Kabul politics. Non-Pushtuns pointed at Karzai's desire to win the allegiance of Pushtuns. Many non-Pushtuns resented the centralizing influence on the process of US ambassador Dr. Zalmay Khailzad, himself an ethnic Pushtun. The insurgency in Afghanistan has grown rather than declined in scope since 2004 as Northern Alliance-connected figures (including all Panjsheris) have left the cabinet and key provincial governorships. In 2008–09 none of the power ministries were in Panjsheris' hands. Another Northern Alliance regional leader, Ismail Khan, was the minister of energy, kept away from his former home base of Herat. Cabinet reshuffles to achieve ethnic balance alienated many non-Pushtuns, failed to attract Pushtuns to support Kabul, and helped retard the initial steps toward creating a functioning Afghan government.

Appointments within each ministry (as well as at the provincial and subnational level) also became problematic as the patrimonial model of Afghan politics reasserted itself. Many cabinet ministers or provincial and district governors treated their responsibilities as personal fiefdoms and filled positions with those to whom they were tied by blood (tribe in Pushtun areas) and patronage. The familiar Afghan pattern is where a member of one group gets control of patronage and surrounds himself with those who have such ties to the exclusion of everyone else, regardless of issues such as competence or representation, leading to resentment. Some of the Afghans who received their positions due to kinship ties proved surprisingly effective, reflecting their access to patronage networks and a desire not to let family members in power down.

While the insurgents do not provide a positive vision of the future for grassroots Afghanistan, they can provide some elements of the social justice Afghans demand: suppressing bandits and adjudicating disputes. While there have been a state legal system and codified laws since the nineteenth century, in pre-1978 Afghanistan, dispute resolution was not purely or even primarily a governmental function. Religious leaders, especially *sayids*, were used as arbitrators in the land and water disputes that mean so much in rural Afghan life. The pre-2001 Afghanistan Taliban's willingness to settle land and water disputes was seen as important to restore peace to rural Afghanistan.

There appears to be a concerted policy by the Afghan insurgents to infiltrate governmental and non-governmental organizations, especially the security forces and police. The Afghan Taliban also creates shadow provincial and district leaders. These apparently are located mainly in Pakistan, but they reportedly will receive petitions and listen to and resolve disputes, especially about land and water rights. Tribal or other local groups that have been radicalized or need a counterweight to rivals have looked to insurgent support. The Afghan Taliban were able to use long-standing tribal feuds to their advantage when Kabul appointed officials or provided aid to one group, alienating the other, as with Barakzai and Noorzai Pushtuns in Kandahar province. A perceived Kabul bias in favor of the Popalzai, Karzai's tribe, has led some of their rivals to side with the insurgents. Those Afghan leaders with links with Kabul tend to use these to benefit their own kinship or affinity group almost exclusively, largely because these are the only people they believe they can trust.

The losers in this process are natural recruits to the insurgency. The insurgents have demonstrated an ability to focus on the voids in Afghan society and move to take advantage of kinship, tribal, or patronage ties. These are based, in large part, on tribal loyalties and links between Pushto-speaking clergy. The Afghan Taliban (as with their Pakistani Taliban counterparts in the FATA) has made a practice of reflecting tribal representation in their appointments. For example, in 2006–09 the coalition found parts of Kandahar Province's Maiwand District "bandit country" because the population, largely resettled there pre-1978 to occupy irrigated lands from other parts of southern Afghanistan, had turned to the Taliban for support against their neighbors, envious and eager to dispossess them.[193] In 2008–10, in Logar and Wardak, the insurgents built on local ties, tribal loyalties, old HiH links (strong in Logar pre-1996), and leadership personnel dating back to the war against Soviets. In the Kunar, the insurgents have made common cause with timber mafias marginalized by Kabul's actions. In Kunduz, insurgents rallied Pushtuns feeling threatened by more numerous Tajik neighbors. These insurgent tactics have not always been successful. The situation in Wardak was reportedly helped by co-opting many insurgents into local police forces in 2008.[194]

Insurgency and Development

The Soviets threw a great deal of money and effort at aid programs, especially in Kabul, but it did not buy legitimacy or security for them or their Afghan clients and thus was largely ineffective. In non-Pushtun Afghanistan, there is increasingly widespread resentment that post-2001 development spending has been perceived as concentrated in the Pushtun areas, while everyone else's problems are ignored.

But the insurgency is not motivated primarily by the lack of development and reconstruction, as clearly the insurgents have brought none of these things and are still finding support. Throughout post-2001 Afghanistan, it has become evident that it is simplistic to equate the provision of the benefits accorded by development—schools, clinics, wells, and roads—with security.

By 2008–10, in much of Afghanistan, perceptions of aid were that it does not prevent, but rather contributes to, instability, with insurgents being paid protection money by donor-funded contractors. "Building something" without insisting on local approval and participation—often frustrating because the Afghans will insist that their own patronage networks benefit—undercuts the local leaders who have been bypassed. Aid that bypasses local or traditional authority damages their perceived legitimacy and weakening them for challenges by competitors, such as insurgents or warlords. The competition for aid resources has been used by insurgents to recruit resentful losers to their side. The availability of aid resources has fueled the culture of corruption. Those benefiting have used their resources and power for resource extraction rather than enabling a better life of Afghans. Grassroots Afghans, especially in Pushtun areas, will not take ownership and—hard to achieve in a kinship or tribal-based collectivist society—take responsibility for it. But aid projects built without this degree of local involvement have gone undefended and the insurgents then destroy it easily. In Pushtun areas, outside aid that does not receive community support creates more for the Afghan insurgents to burn. In the areas of Afghanistan where there is the most need for development, notably in the provinces in the south where the insurgency is most intense, there is also the least capability and motivation for development to occur. There cannot be development without security, yet there is still progress despite the continuing security setbacks. "Even in the south there is more construction than we think, especially where we have seen communities stand up to the Taliban," according to BG Marquis Hainse, CF.

That said, development by itself cannot avail in Afghanistan without legitimacy; and legitimacy, in the eyes of Afghans, requires security from outside attack, which the government in Kabul is not doing, especially in much of the south and east. This was the thinking behind the Pakistani-inspired tactic of rocket attacks on Kabul in both the 1980s and 1992–96, which was intended to demonstrate to Kabulis that the government could not defend them. It also suggests the importance of the lack of a functioning national civil sector economy that will provide a degree of unity to Afghanistan and repair the damage caused by decades of fighting, corruption, and instability. It also points out the importance of the lack of alternative employment for young men, making them easy targets for insurgent recruiters or further susceptible to criminal temptations.

But the Afghan insurgents have an interest in development or making life better for Afghans only as far as it advances their goal of attaining power and answering the one existential question: how best to live in conformity with their vision of a Deobandi-influenced Sunni Islam. In some areas in 2008–10 the Taliban made local deals to permit schools, even for girls, to operate and basic health services to be provided (both under strict supervision). Largely, the Afghan insurgency has aimed to prevent meaningful development. The Taliban burned down 1,089 schools in Afghanistan in 2005–07 alone.[195] In the same period, over 40 health workers were killed or kidnapped while delivering services; and at least 36 health facilities were shut down in the east and south due to insecurity.[196] Some 5,000 schools have closed in Pushtun areas.[197] As a result of conservatism and the insurgency being concentrated in the south and east, only 44 percent of Pushtuns have access to girls' schools while the figures for other groups are over 70 percent.[198]

As the insurgents in Afghanistan destroy clinics and state schools, they largely do not replace them with their own clinics or maktabs (Mosque schools), though there have been some examples of this being done in Kandahar, Helmand, and other southern provinces in 2008–10.

The Taliban has also provided protection to narcotics traffickers where they have funded clinics. The Afghan Taliban has made a major effort of discouraging positive work and prefers disorder and chaos, aiming to present the rigor of their rule as the only viable alternative. In the south and other areas where there are many foreign fighters among the insurgents, most humanitarian work is seen as being in league with Kabul and the Western infidels. One of their initial successes of the insurgency was in forcing the withdrawal of NGOs and most reconstruction and development programs from most of southern and eastern Afghanistan. Burning clinics and schools and the killing of "spies" and collaborators are the message the insurgents wish to send to their potential supporters.

This is a major difference between the pre-2001 Taliban and the current insurgents. The pre-2001 Taliban wanted Western aid and were willing to compromise to some extent to get it as long as their overarching ideology was maintained, at least until the US cruise missile attacks of 1998 and the increasing influence of Al Qaeda cut off the potential for accessing those resources. The insurgents object more to the source of aid—a Western involvement they see as illegitimate—than the concept of aid. In a number of places in Taliban-controlled Afghanistan, where institutions like schools have been adopted and embraced by the local community and do not have the fingerprints of outsiders on them, only these have been allowed to remain. Schools, mosques, and the like, built by the West, become targets of destruction. Aid is accepted only in some parts of Afghanistan by the current insurgency. In Wardak and Logar provinces in 2008, for example, insurgents made deals with NGOs to allow projects such as basic health services to be implemented by Afghan staff.

The diverse insurgent factions, with their shared links to the Al Qaeda-inspired battle of ideas, have been flexible enough, however, to be able to shift the focus in their war on legitimacy from structures and military operations to politics. These same groups all decided not to engage in widespread offensive actions, and did not attempt to block voters from registering for the 2009 election. They had also previously refrained in the 2004 presidential and 2005 parliamentary elections, reflecting an unwillingness to openly disenfranchise those they were looking to for at least passive support. By 2007, they were even promulgating a "Taliban constitution" for Afghanistan. It was uncertain how much of this document represented a formal commitment by insurgent leadership (and, if so, what process had led to its adoption), or whether it was an instrument of psychological warfare.

Horror and Hearts and Minds

The Afghan insurgents' influence and inroads are not without significant flaws. "The Taliban inability to modulate the use of violence has led to overreach," in the words of LTC Cavoli.[199] As conflicts in Afghanistan are essentially about legitimacy, unrestricted implementation undercuts claims to legitimate Afghan or Islamic authority. In 2009, the Taliban leadership issued a code of conduct to its members. But the overall message has been a powerful one: that the foreigners and the ANA will eventually leave, but the insurgents will stay and take retribution. Over 70 percent of Afghan civilian casualties in 2010 were Taliban-inflicted.

The insurgents' maximalist view of warfare and religious practice alike has made it hard for them to achieve control of the true center of gravity in any insurgency: the Afghan population. "[The insurgents] use extremist measures even at the risk of losing connection with the population," said BG Marquis Hainse, CF.[200] Yet their worldview takes them easily into moving the battlefield into other areas that may prove more decisive, such as culture, economics, and family life, in a way that their opponents have found difficult. Before 2001, the Taliban made their point by hanging bandits and exploiters. In Musa Qala in 2006, when they reentered the town after the British left, they hanged a 16-year-old that had participated in a government work-for-food program.[201] Refugees from areas where the insurgents have seized control and have fled to Kabul or Kandahar city tell of schools being closed, clinics shut down (the sick were instead offered raw opium or folk medicine), and retribution exacted on local villagers. In southern Afghanistan in 2008–10, Pushtuns that had lived in their home districts under the pre-2001 Taliban were increasingly fleeting their current counterparts for the greater security of Kabul or Kandahar city.[202]

The insurgents have demonstrated an ability to moderate some policies. The Afghan Taliban groups have not reintroduced all of their pre-2001 social repression: destruction of tape players, beard inspections, mandatory haircuts. In 2008–10, Mullah Omar had urged moderation, ombudsmen have been appointed and the "taliban constitution" publicized, yet the use of intimidation and terror remains their prime persuasive approaches to the Afghan population. "In Taliban expansion areas, they rely on intimidation rather than a positive agenda. . . . Don't underestimate intimidation," in the words of LTC Cavoli.[203] Zoran Milovic, a public opinion researcher who has worked in southern Afghanistan, said in 2009: "You're not going to criticize the Taliban in the south once you see what happened to the mullahs who did that."[204]

Recruiting Insurgents

Despite heavy casualties since 2005, the different Afghan insurgent groups are unlikely to run out of recruits any time soon, as the Taliban culture is likely to provide them with all the Kalashnikov-carriers they will ever need. The current Afghan insurgents reflect the demographic realities of the borderlands: large numbers of young men with limited education and career and family prospects. Despite the large numbers of recruits from Pakistan and elsewhere now taking part in the Afghan insurgency, the vast majority of the insurgent fighting men are Afghans.

Warfare has become commercial in Afghanistan, a way for extended families to support themselves and achieve access to patronage, a trend that emerged during the anti-Soviet war and has continued since then. The large generation of young men far exceeds the numbers of jobs available to them. Cut off from the old ways of traditional Afghanistan or the Pakistani borderlands, the shift to a cash-based economy and the failure to develop attractive alternative livelihood has meant that the traditional agriculture of rural Afghanistan holds little appeal for them. The lower-level Taliban members are largely drawn from the unemployed and underemployed. This trend continued through 2008–10. A 2009 US government estimate was that 90 percent of the insurgents were local, often recruited by money or kinship, ethnic, and patronage links, while some 10 percent were ideologically committed.[205] The Canadian military reported that the vast majority of the prisoners captured in 2007 gave as their reason for fighting with the Afghan Taliban simply that they would pay them and no one else would.[206] Despite this, in 2008–10, many insurgents in the south fought without receiving a regular salary. A significant minority of the Afghan Taliban were pushed to join the insurgency by collateral damage by allied airpower, heavy-handed house searches, or extortionate Afghan policemen. One-third of a group of 42 Afghan Taliban prisoners taken by Canadians in 2006 had lost relatives to collateral damage.[207] These incidents build on each other to create an atmosphere favorable to the insurgents. Insurgent IED attacks, in some areas, are blamed on Kabul or the coalition forces; every villager who goes to look for work in Pakistan or the Gulf is said to be in a secret USA prison at Bagram Air Base. But non-presence is certainly not an effective option. "The insurgents will control the population where the ANA is not protecting them," in the words of COL McNiece, and then all inroads, strategic, cultural, and social, would be lost.[208]

Insurgent Tactics, Techniques, and Procedures (TTPs)

As mentioned before, the insurgents have demonstrated a capability to evolve. "The Taliban does not fight very well" was LTC Cavoli's judgment based on his 2007 tour of duty.[209] However, since then, they and the other insurgent groups have visibly improved both their actions on the battlefield and, more significantly, their ability to use a range of asymmetric tactics that give them capabilities off the battlefield. By the end of 2008, overall insurgent attacks had increased over 40 percent from the previous year.

The Afghan insurgents, including but not limited to the Taliban, have increasingly turned to asymmetric tactics over the course of the insurgency, rather than relying on any single tactical approach including standing and fighting as they did against Operation Medusa in Panjwai district in Kandahar province in 2006 or indirect fires and the use of mines and improvised explosive devices (IEDs). The number of IED and roadside bomb incidents increased from 307 in 2004 to 4,000+ in 2009.[210] The trend continued. There were 217 IED incidents in Afghanistan in August 2007, 386 in August 2008, and 969 in August 2009.[211] IEDs caused 69 percent of ISAF casualties in 2008, increasing to 77 percent in the first six months of 2009.[212] This shift to asymmetric tactics was reportedly after action reviews that led to orders issued from Pakistan by Mullah Omar, the Afghan Taliban leader.[213] This shift to asymmetrical tactics was seen between 2007 and 2008, when insurgent offensive actions decreased from a 50 to a 40 percent ratio of direct fire. The use of IEDs and mines increased from 20 to 30 percent. Indirect fire attacks remained at 30 percent. The number of attacks did increase overall, however, in part as a reflection of additional coalition and Afghan troops operating in contested areas.[214] By 2008–10, more sophisticated ambushes, widespread suicide bombings (frequently integrated with other attacks), mine warfare, urban terrorism, and widespread targeted assassinations had all increased.

Coordinated suicide attacks, often in urban areas, have been one type of asymmetric tactics where the insurgents have demonstrated increasing sophistication, capability, and boldness. Such suicide attack tactics were not seen in Afghanistan in the anti-Soviet conflict of 1978–92 or the 1992–2001 civil wars. "The suicide bomber is not there in Afghan culture," BG Richard Blanchette, Canadian Forces, ISAF spokesman, said in 2008.[215] Suicide bombers are frequently seen as being adapted from foreign groups, especially Al Qaeda and their allies among Pakistan-based groups; the attack on the Indian parliament in December 2001 is often cited as a model.[216] In Afghanistan, suicide attacks as such started later, in May 2003, but increased steadily until the number of volunteers, especially foreigners, picked up to disturbing levels in 2005. By 2006, suicide attacks in Afghanistan reached an average of ten per month.[217] Suicide attacks since then have increased in sophistication and damage. The coordination of attackers—both vehicle-borne and on-foot, with explosives and with rifles and grenades—and the targeting of high-value targets with political impact has been a feature of many Afghan insurgent suicide attacks. Dates with political impact have been selected for these attacks. A series of high-profile suicide attacks have had an impact on Afghan political legitimacy, showing the government's inability to provide security. These have included the November 2007 attack in Baghlan province, the January 2008 attack on the Serena Hotel, the April 2008 national day attack, the July 2008 Indian embassy attack in Kabul, attacks on the Ministry of Information in October 2008, three sites in Kabul including the Ministry of Justice in February 2009, and a police head-quarters in Kandahar in March 2009.

The evolution of suicide attacks since they were introduced to Afghan-istan has led to increased sophistication, featuring, instead of individual suicide bombers, multiple coordinated attacks, building penetration, taking of hostages and execution of prisoners (especially government employees).[218] Embedding the actions of suicide attackers in a larger operation also helps ensure that the attackers retain direction and that they will not have to carry out their missions in isolation. There was con-siderable Afghan resistance to adopting suicide tactics in the initial years of the insurgency. The Taliban assassinated ulema that spoke against suicide attacks.[219] Even in 2008, Maulavi Abd-al-Hadi "Pash Wa'l" bin-abd-al-Hakim, identified as Taliban military commander in Laghman province, was defensive about these tactics, indicating that they are still of questionable legitimacy. "We carry out martyrdom-seeking operations when needed. This happens when we cannot use other military tactics, therefore, we have used the tactics of martyrdom-seeking operations against the Crusading forces only once."[220]

The move by different Afghan insurgent groups away from direct opposition to coalition and Afghan forces applies to other tactics, not just the recent spectacular suicide attacks. "Last year [2007], we had 50 guys attack a FOB [Forward Operating Base], now 10 men each [objec-tive], a shift to more asymmetry, more events per insurgent, less loss per event," COL McNiece said in 2008.[221] He also saw it as part of a more sophisticated insurgency, better able to apply appropriate tactics and that "someone, somewhere is learning to combine IEDs, direct [attack] and indirect [fires]." "Smaller, decentralized, and more asymmetrical warfare" was how BG Blanchette described the insurgent trends of the past year in 2008. Yet this trend did not mean the insurgents had given up a capa-bility to mass forces when required. Groups of several hundred insurgents have made attacks, including the one that overran a joint US and Afghan National Army outpost at Komdesh in Nuristan in 2009.

On the battlefield, despite the insurgents' access to clandestine arms markets and funding streams, as of 2008–10 neither their weaponry nor their battlefield skills match those of the anti-Soviet Afghan resistance of the late 1980s. Yet the insurgents have demonstrated a number of considerable strengths. They have an ability to use effective cell and small unit organizations that have contributed to their resilience and ability to quickly reorganize after setbacks. They have effectively used surprise and deception in their attacks. The spread of IEDs and other guerrilla techniques suggests that the current insurgents can draw TTPs and equipment from diverse sources, such as the Chechens and Tamils.[222] Many of the Afghan guerrillas today have high-quality equipment, often bought on the international market. Other equipment appears to have been bought from the Afghan security forces.[223] The availability of funding and access to world weapons markets makes the absence of certain types of weapons among the insurgent forces significant. The insurgents have used no anti-tank guided missiles (ATGMs) and few surface-to-air missiles (SAMs), even though these weapons were both used in the later stages of the 1978–92 conflict. This suggests that there has been a decision by someone to limit insurgent access to these weapons. It is unlikely that shortages of funding, training, and logistics facilities or availability of these weapons on the world market were keeping these weapons out of the hands of the Afghan insurgents in 2008–10.

Other sources of supplies to the insurgents have also been limited. Iran has limited its supplies to a few Explosive Formed Projectile (EFP) warheads for use in roadside IEDs and Chinese-made man-portable HN-5 SAMs. GEN Petraeus in 2009 described Iran's "malign activity" as including, "to a limited degree, arming the Taliban in western Afghanistan as well."[224]

Funding Insurgency

Former finance minister Ashraf Ghani has described the Afghanistan insurgency in 2009. "One of the best financed insurgencies, more diverse and consolidated. They can buy a lot in a cash economy."[225] To compound an already-complex threat, the Afghan insurgency is cheap to run and has no shortage of funding.[226] Like the transnational terrorism with which it shares its support network, the Afghan insurgency has access to multiple, redundant sources of funding, and narcotics cultivation and trafficking is often reported to be one of the most significant. "Powerful

economic forces not run by fanatics living in caves bankroll these movements," in the words of former AP Pakistan correspondent Gretchen
Peters.[227] Richard Barrett estimated that 20–30 percent of the total insurgent funding, some 60–70 million dollars, came from narcotics, with the
bulk of the remainder coming from Saudi Arabia and the Gulf.[228] GEN
Petraeus put the percentage of insurgent funding from narcotics at about
a third, with the remainder coming from donations, remittances, and
criminal activity.[229]

The insurgents' non-narcotics funding coming in from sources in
Saudi Arabia, the Gulf, and other Islamic countries is hard to estimate
but is clearly extensive, as indicated by the level at which Afghan insurgents are able to operate. The relatively few names of Saudi and Gulf state
nationals on the UN sanctions lists for such activities suggests more how
little is known rather than the lack of support coming from there. The
Afghan insurgents' infrastructure of financial support includes not only
the *hundi/hawala* money transfer system that has attracted much interest
since 9/11, but also networks of legitimate financial institutions, couriers,
facilitators, and sources of funding that are shared by transnational terrorists, Afghan and Pakistani insurgents, and narcotics traffickers alike.
In 2009, the US government estimated the Afghan insurgents' donation
income in the past 12 months at about 106 million dollars, compared to
70–400 million dollars from narcotics in differing estimates.[230]

In areas such as Pakistan's FATA and Afghanistan's Kumar valley
and Nuristan, Afghan and Pakistani insurgents alike have continued the
practice of making extractive use of natural resources, especially clear-
cutting forests, to feed the timber mafia in Pakistan. Some of the Afghan
timber-cutting groups have been recruited, mainly by HiH, to join the
insurgents when Afghan government action ended their lumber trade in
the Kunar valley and Nuristan by 2008, with the unemployed Afghans
and Pakistanis alike being paid to fight US forces. The cross-border
ethnic Pushtun transport mafia that controls much of Pakistan's long-
distance trucking was also a long-standing ally of the pre-2001 Taliban
and had links with the ISI and other Pakistani security services. While
gem mining and trafficking is a relatively small percentage of the overall
income, it has been carried out since the 1980s. It has now spread to

Pakistan from Afghanistan as a source of insurgent funding. The TNSM took over gem mines in Swat in 2009.

Insurgents also seek to extract money from all other aspects of daily life in Afghanistan. Cell phone companies have had their towers and facilities threatened by insurgents who demand they pay protection money. The Afghan insurgents have embraced kidnapping as a major part of their tactics of intimidation. Criminal gangs have been known to "sell" wealthy or well-connected Afghan kidnap victims up the chain to insurgent or terrorist groups to whom they may be of value as a hostage, contributing to the increased crime that undercut Afghan security in 2008–10.[231]

"Greed and grievance" is a powerful force for instability in Afghanistan.[232] Experiences with other insurgencies have shown that the most enduring insurgent groups are those that have access to an independent source of contraband funding.[233] This also leads to conflicts over the source of such unaccountable resources.[234] Narcotics cultivation and trafficking is the most significant such resource in Afghanistan.

In 2010, the Pakistani military was urging Afghan insurgents towards negotiations, through them, with Kabul. They want the US to help put in place a "moderate" successor government in Kabul, delivering the non-Pushtuns to prevent a renewed Afghan civil war that would undercut Pakistan's goals of excluding Indian, Iranian and Russian influence. Pakistan may be more aware they cannot control Afghan insurgents, but they are still using them in a proxy war.

CHAPTER SIX

AFGHAN NARCOTICS

"If we do not eliminate drugs, drugs will eliminate us."
—Hamid Karzai, President of Afghanistan, 2006

The global implications of narcotics cultivation are enormous. The country produced over 92 percent of the world's opium in 2008–09. Narcotics trafficking is the Vortex's third facet of international conflict, one that may indeed have the largest global reach.

Narcotics cultivation has greatly increased in Afghanistan since 2001.[235] It has been intense in key provinces in the south. The area north of the Hindu Kush has been relatively quiet. There have been reductions in what, in the 1980s and 90s, were areas of opium cultivation, such as the plains north of Mazar-e-Sharif and Badakhshan. The UN estimated that the 2008–09 growing season produced some 6,900 tons of raw opium. Poppy cultivation in 2007–08 increased in overall yield even while the area cultivated declined 19 percent. In 2009, opium prices reached a ten-year low and more was being seized; poppy cultivation dropped by 22 percent and opium production by ten percent.[236] Faced with falling world prices, in 2009 it was estimated that the Afghan insurgents have a stockpile of some 10,000 tons of raw opium that they are holding to manipulate market prices.[237] Prices per kilogram of opium declined by up to a third from 2008 to 2009 but then rebounded ($29 to $77 per pound) in 2009–10. Yet 14 provinces in Afghanistan have no eradication program at all. In 2008, with the target goal of eradicating 50,000 hectares of land from poppy production, only 5,480 hectares were eradicated and in the southern province of Helmand, where the area used for poppy cultivation has tripled since 2006.[238] Opium and refined narcotics from Afghanistan are distributed throughout diverse regional markets in Afghanistan, the former Soviet Union, and to Iran and Pakistan and throughout the end-markets in Europe, America, and Asia. Heroin from South Asia has taken up an increasing share of the market in North America.[239]

Years of Afghanistan's foreign supporters enabling the Kabul government's efforts increased the number of drug-free provinces in Afghanistan from six in 2006 to 18 in 2008. Yet there is still have a long way to go when it comes to dealing with narcotics. In 2008–09 close to 98 percent of the remaining cultivation had been concentrated in seven provinces where the insurgency is strong: Helmand, Kandahar, Uruzgan, Daikundi, Zabul, Farah, and Nimruz.[240] In 2010, this led to a rise in opium prices.

Opium requires instability and lawlessness for its cultivation as much as it needs labor to tend it and minimal levels of fertility and rainfall. Without these conditions, neither growers nor traffickers will make investments in both cultivation and infrastructure that assume they will make money before any outside force will take action to close them down.

Many of the tactics aimed to defeat narcotics have the potential to help spread the insurgency. By effectively chasing opium production into those provinces where the insurgency is strong, the insurgents secured a powerful revenue stream to support their operations. But outside these provinces, narcotics are still trafficked; this has powered the culture of corruption throughout Afghanistan, including the opium-free provinces. Even "opium-free" provinces play a role in Afghanistan's narcotics.[241] Cannabis and hashish cultivation goes on in these provinces, replacing opium in many cases; in some opium-free northern provinces, the cannabis crop is reportedly yielding a higher cash return per hectare under cultivation than did opium a few years ago.[242]

The Origins of the Threat

The initial rise of opium cultivation in Afghanistan followed a US-urged campaign of suppression in Pakistan in the late 1980s. Much of the cultivation was chased over the border into Afghanistan. There was already some opium cultivation in Afghanistan, but it was largely low-intensity and small in scale. During the anti-Soviet conflict, Helmand province was one of the first areas where pro-Soviet Afghan Communists and Islamic resistance leaders, both committed to ideologies that were anti-narcotics, alike realized that the income from poppy cultivation could be vital in buying local loyalties. As so often occurred in subsequent years, ideological concerns yielded to the need for income. In the 1980s, Ismailis in Badakhshan were cultivating narcotics and, unlike other Afghans, actually using some themselves. While narcotics use among Afghans was initially rare, it expanded during the decades of war until it reached a crisis level in 2008–10, spreading to the ANSF.

In the late 1980s, new varieties of opium poppy and fertilizers were introduced to Afghanistan by following trans-border trading "mafias," mainly ethnic Pushtuns with ties throughout Pakistan, especially in the FATA and Karachi, who were making inroads across the border in Afghanistan. Once the number of Afghans with opium-growing skills reached "critical mass," cultivation spread.

The rise of the Taliban followed the initial rise of narcotics cultivation in Afghanistan in the early 1990s. Dissatisfaction with the increase in narcotics cultivation that had taken place in southern Afghanistan in 1992–94 helped fuel the Taliban's initial success in that area. The Afghan Taliban was originally opposed to narcotics cultivation. Their initial anti-opium positions reflected the widespread grassroots Afghan suspicion of opium as potentially falling under the Koran's prohibition of intoxicants like alcohol.

Yet soon after they had consolidated their hold on southern Afghanistan, the Taliban embraced opium cultivation for its financial and political benefits. Narcotics growers and traffickers who largely share the Taliban's Pushtun ethnicity joined "mafias" as part of a pro-Taliban coalition, sharing money and credit.[243] In the heyday of Taliban support for opium, it became the cash crop of choice in many areas. Even non-farmers would cultivate it for the chance of a quick profit, and in 1996–2000 the Taliban grew and exported 15 kilotons of opium.

The July 2000 Taliban prohibition called for a stop to opium cultivation, but not export, and was widely thought to be a move to increase market prices by creating artificial scarcity. Yet its primary effect was to deepen the debt by farmers to opium traffickers who had paid them in advance for their crops and so to further the trafficker's hold on the local population in the areas of most intense cultivation. Because of this prohibition, the price of raw opium rose some one thousand percent. Exports from existing stockpiles continued, gaining additional income for the traffickers but not for the local cultivators. Mullah Omar personally rescinded the ban after 9/11 in an attempt to rally wavering grassroots Afghan support, but his regime's attempt to manipulate prices proved to be one of the many actions that undercut its support even among its supporters.

The post-2001 Afghanistan government in Kabul, however, has not wavered from its commitment to make narcotics cultivation and trafficking illegal. Not only Afghan law but traditional justice systems do not accept the claims by cultivators and traffickers that either poverty or the desire to extract revenge on the infidel occupiers justify cultivation of a substance considered prohibited by international standards and the Koran alike. Yet the fact remains that one of the most important reasons for the rise of narcotics cultivation in many areas of Afghanistan after 2001 was the lack of alternatives, which Kabul and its foreign supporters have found providing problematic. According to the UN Office on Drugs and Crime (UNODC), some 98 percent of Afghanistan's poppy cultivators would be willing to turn to another crop if it provided as much as half as much as they earned from their current crop.[244] The reason why opium cultivation has become concentrated in seven southern provinces with a strong insurgent presence is that this makes presenting alternatives impossible, and so the cultivation continues.

The Nature of the Threat

As with most activities in Afghanistan, it is difficult to generalize about narcotics cultivation and trafficking, which has historically varied greatly between and even within provinces.[245] In parts of Afghanistan, even the good guys grow poppy. In places such as Kandahar and Helmand provinces, the cultivation is so widespread and ingrained in the local economy that no major landowner or local official can avoid dealing with cultivation. If there was no cultivation, there would be few viable alternative sources for income or services in much of those war-torn areas. The strength of the insurgency in those areas means that Kabul and its supporters are in no position to offer an alternative to the crop that provides insurgents with much financial support.

"The Taliban and other groups are not running the drug trade but work in service of it," in the words of Gretchen Peters.[246] All of the terrorist and insurgent groups operating in Afghanistan are involved to a greater or lesser extent in narcotics. The Afghan Taliban is the largest single Afghan group involved in narcotics, but Haqqani and HiH are also known to be involved. In some areas, insurgents are participants in the narcotics-based violence. Elsewhere, traffickers have their own armed men. In 2005–06, HiH was widely believed to have murdered crop substitution aid workers in Helmand.[247] Other groups involved are basically criminals that have adopted Islamic names and alliances as a matter of convenience. As with everything else in Afghanistan, there is no central command and there is extensive, often violent, competition between groups, with many Afghans trying to call in Afghan security forces or coalition airstrikes on rivals to give them a greater market share. Many insurgent commanders that have been killed or captured were targeted in this way, indicating the tensions between different insurgent groups and terrorists and insurgents and the traffickers.

Afghan groups appear to have control over the opium traffic within the borders of Afghanistan. Afghan insurgents offer protection for growers and opposition to counter-narcotics efforts in exchange for funding. They seek to use the traditional Afghan approach to patronage relations to create a culture of dependency. Since 2005–06 more and more laboratories and refineries dedicated to opium have moved in to take advantage of the insurgency. After the 2007 increase in the crop, large-scale stockpiling of opium by traffickers appears to be taking place, to prevent flooding the market and as insurance against the time when Afghanistan may not be able to produce, if the counter-narcotics efforts can be extended throughout the country.[248] By 2008–10, the insurgency was taking a more hands-on role in this process, as the Afghan Taliban and other insurgent groups are now being reported as running their own laboratories and providing protection and transportation for those laboratories run by outside traffickers, who pay for this service.[249] Since cultivation of the poppies from which opium is extracted attracts less money than those actions higher up the value-added chain such as refining or sales, the traffickers set the farmgate price so that they usually pay the Afghan farmers only a little more than they would get with a legal crop, usually wheat. This means that if a farmer or laborer can earn four dollars a day or more from a legal crop, the appeal of opium will be undercut.[250] Yet there is in many areas none of the infrastructure necessary for legal commodities to succeed in the global market the way Afghanistan's poppies have done.

The opium traffickers have, in many cases, created the only thing resembling a social support network in much of southern Afghanistan. Narcotics traffickers also provide other vital services for their farmer clients, including providing credit. Others provide capital equipment or maintain services, including health clinics in some areas. Since the economy of rural Afghanistan has traditionally run on credit and, with the population largely too high in debt by 2001 to borrow further, this has been an area where crop substitution programs were often not adequate, giving narcotics traffickers an additional hold over the cultivators. After years of drought, warfare, and the impact of the Taliban, rural Afghanistan faced a total lack of new credit. There was no one willing or able to extend credit. Traditional sources of credit—kinship and patronage—were almost at maximum capacity, leaving many Afghan farmers desperate.

While lending money at interest is impermissible under Sharia (or legal codes based on it), a buyer, including a narcotics trafficker, may pay a farmer in advance for crops through a Salam contract. These contracts were written so that the farmer could never actually pay off the debt, so that each year he would become more heavily indebted. Because the debts are usually denominated in kilos of opium (especially in provinces such as Kandahar and Helmand), price rises increase each farmer's debt. This created a cycle that, once the farmers were in debt, they could not get out of and to even stay even required delivering increasing amounts of opium, further binding them to the narcotics cultivators.

Because debts may remain even if the cultivation of opium is halted, suppression of opium (and removal of the source of credit) has often led to other social ills, such as debt bondage and child labor, which increased notably in Nangarhar in 2007–08 as opium cultivation was reduced. Elsewhere, especially in Kandahar and Helmand provinces, opium traffickers have guarded their investments by forcing the cultivator to bear the risks of falling prices. The drop in opium prices in 2008–09, as with earlier price reductions, led to widespread hardship, including families without possessions having to turn over children to creditors.[251]

Relapses in areas that had halted growing opium for a few years have proved common, both after the Taliban's 2001 prohibition and in the case of several provinces that the UN declared opium-free in 2005–07.[252] Other opium-free provinces, especially Nangarhar, have the potential to relapse if the security situation deteriorates. Security and viable alternative livelihoods are conditions that must precede any effective eradication of Afghanistan's narcotics. In 2007–10, where security has been present, the cultivation of narcotics has been reduced, even in provinces threatened by insurgents such as Nangarhar, although the possibility of a relapse if market prices shift remains a threat. To combat this, the UK's Department for International Development (DfID) was, in 2009, aiming to implement a new agricultural program to prevent poppy-free provinces from relapsing.[253] It will be years before it can be implemented and its effectiveness assessed. Narcotics traffic goes through many such poppy-free provinces, but the corruption that keeps this trade flowing has given local leaders, including warlords, a degree of independence from Kabul's authority, allowing them to conduct business as usual. By 2005, a senior US Drug Enforcement Administration (DEA) official in Kabul estimated that 90 percent of the police chiefs in Afghanistan were involved in corruption through narcotics.[254] This is not a comforting statistic for a country trying to establish rule of law. Narcotics money has rendered much of the culture of corruption financially self-sustaining, even in areas where no poppy is currently being grown. There are multiple levels of Afghans, ranging from the ANP to local patrons and members of parliament, to be paid off. "Corrupt state actors move more than insurgents" is the view of Gretchen Peters, former AP correspondent in Pakistan.[255]

The Impact of the Threat

The economic impact of narcotics is perhaps the most powerful one, more so than its role in financially aiding the Afghan Taliban and other insurgent groups. In 2007–08, narcotics cultivation and trafficking was estimated to be about half the size of Afghanistan's legal gross domestic product (GDP).[256] The UNODC reports: "Opium permeates much of the rural economy, with critical links to employment generation, access to land and credit. Opium markets, prices and traders populate the Afghan landscape and provide important signals for economic actors. Drug money is a very important, often dominant ingredient in the informal financial transfer system (hawala), which is also the main vehicle in Afghanistan for payments and transfers of funds, including remittances and much aid. Through protection payments and connections the drug industry has major linkages with the local administration as well as high levels of national government."[257] The concentration of opium cultivation in southern provinces has made it increasingly intertwined with the insurgency.

While terrorist and insurgent propaganda seeks to justify opium cultivation and traffic as striking a blow against the infidels, in reality it is Muslims that have suffered. Since 2001, addiction rates have soared in Afghanistan, Pakistan, Iran, and central Asia (Kazakhstan reportedly has over two million addicts), not Europe or America. "Over one million Afghans are now using. The park near the cinema [in central Kabul] is full of needles. 2009 will show increasing addiction," according to one UNAMA official.[258] By 2008 Afghanistan had established 17 health facilities for treating addicts.[259] Iran, after waging a large-scale "war on drugs" since the 1980s which included large-scale clashes between paramilitary forces and well-armed traffickers, has now evolved its own "culture of corruption" which is being used by Afghanistan's terrorists and insurgents.[260] The Iranian government remains opposed to Afghanistan-based narcotics trafficking, which they see as supporting the insurgency. Iran estimates 2,500 tons of opium entered the country from Afghanistan in

2008, 700 tons of which are used in Iran and over 500 tons of which were seized (some of this later being resold).[261]

In previous years, corruption fed narcotics cultivation, especially in the years following the fall of the Taliban in 2001 when police checkpoints and extractive officials made legal crops in much of southern Afghanistan noncompetitive with those from northern Afghanistan, let alone imported from Pakistan. Today, narcotics cultivation both causes corruption and is caused by it.

The real money is made by the refiners and traders, providing value-addition along the chain of trafficking that stretches from Afghanistan to addicts in London and New York. Some of the money is evident in the large houses of politically connected Afghans in Kabul and Dubai. Most of it never comes to the everyday Afghan in any form; even those involved in cultivation usually sink further into debt. What does come to Afghanistan goes to the insurgents. The insurgents tax the opium trade for support—most readily apparent in a ten percent tax (*ushr*) usually paid in kind at the farm gate—and receive money paid for protection by traffickers of opium fields, laboratories, and trafficking. Drug laboratories and refineries inside Afghanistan and Pakistan are both usually taxed by local insurgents. In March 2009, GEN Bantz Craddock, USA, then-Supreme Allied Commander in Europe (SACEUR), told the Senate Armed Services Committee in Washington that of the 60 billion dollars created by the narcotics trade in Afghanistan, some 4 billion remained in Afghanistan, but this went largely to the insurgents. Zalmay Afzali, spokesman to the Ministry of Counter Narcotics in Kabul in 2008, estimated the total Afghan opium income at five billion dollars, of which just a third of one percent (0.3 percent) went to the farmers.[262] "The real drug traffickers are not in Afghanistan," he said. In 2007, the United Nations Office on Drugs and Crime estimated that the insurgents, major traffickers in their own right, earned 156 million dollars in ushr, 133 million dollars in taxes on refineries, over 250 million in protection fees, and tens of millions in benefits to the insurgents through access to equipment and support services funded by the traffickers and also used by them.[263] In 2009, estimates on the Afghan Taliban's income from narcotics ranged from 70 to 400 million dollars.[264]

There have been many instances where shared economic interests in opium have brought the insurgents and the rural population together.[265] Ali Shah Mazlumyar, a tribal elder from Marja District of Helmand province, said: "The [poppy eradication] campaign destroyed lands belonging to pro-government farmers. . . . Then the Taliban showed those farmers that they could protect them. So even the pro-government farmers took up arms and stood with the Taliban when the interior ministry came."[266] Zalmay Afzali said that Afghans "have to face eradication at several levels. Resistance comes not from the farmer, but from the terrorists. Seventy seven policemen were killed doing eradication in the most recent [2008] growing season, many by landmines and suicide bombs, things that farmers do not do."[267] There is a considerable contingent that does not want Afghan narcotics cultivation to cease even if the proverbial magic wand could replace opium with an alternative crop that yields as much and employs as many people per hectare. This sentiment means that creating viable agricultural alternatives is likely to require more than mere crop substitution.

In Search of a Viable Counter-Narcotics Approach

The failures of the US and its coalition partners to address narcotics cultivation and trafficking after the fall of the Taliban contributed greatly to the reemergence of terrorism and insurgency in the Vortex. The UK was initially responsible for counter-narcotics after the fall of the Taliban, under the US-developed system of sectorial "lead countries." However, in addition to inadequate resources, this approach took the narcotics problem out of its larger social and economic contexts, which any potential solutions must also address. Being seen by coalition members and Afghans alike as a British responsibility essentially ensured that the problem would get out of hand. In reality, it is impossible to treat narcotics as a problem independent from the creation of governance and a viable economy in rural Afghanistan. The British were not the "lead country," nor were they given the proper resources to deal with the broader social and economic context of restoring a legal economy to rural Afghanistan, nor were they prepared to address the demobilization of Afghan fighting men, both former Taliban and their opponents. Yet all these factors proved to be critical in the reemergence of narcotics.

As a result of the limitations of this initial effort, the US took a larger role in counter-narcotics, allocating some 1.468 billion dollars in 2005–08 compared to 1.545 billion dollars by the UK; yet the US effort was described by Ambassador Richard Holbrooke as "the most wasteful and ineffective program I have seen in 40 years in and out of government."[268] About half of the US effort was devoted to eradication efforts. Because the US emerged as the largest donor, eradication efforts came to dominate the efforts by Afghans and foreign supporters alike. Most of the US eradication efforts focused on the poppy fields, rather than potential targets higher up the value-added chain.

The successor to these initial policy limitations emerged with the June 2007 Rome Conference on the Rule of Law in Afghanistan that resulted in aid pledges for 360 million dollars from a wide range of donor countries and international organizations and in a timetable for establishing a National Justice Program being set. The UN Security Council passed Resolution 1817 in June 2008 to curb narcotics exports and the flow of precursor chemicals. The NATO decision at its 2008 Budapest conference to become more involved in counter-narcotics operations made it possible for ISAF forces to target transport, chemicals, and laboratories, as well as high-value individuals (including chemists, mainly from Pakistan and Iran, who have been recruited). "We need more involvement of international forces," said Zalmay Afzali, Ministry of Counter Narcotics spokesman, in 2008.[269]

But implementation of effective counter-narcotics operations did not follow the decision at Budapest. Many coalition members are limited by their own national law or policy from using military forces in Counter Narcotics missions, regardless of NATO policy. Many Europeans are still not convinced of the urgency of the problem, despite the fact that their countries are the end-destinations of much of this Afghan opium; they are reluctant to let their troops be used even against laboratories and convoys, let alone growers.[270] And so many countries participating in the coalition retain their national caveats preventing their forces from acting against narcotics in Afghanistan; others have to refer back to their home parliaments where political realities are unlikely to permit action. The potential cost in operations funds and casualties of operating against narcotics has deterred many coalition members. In Afghanistan, the rumors circulating among the population cited this as further evidence that the US and the West were not really interested in making things better in Afghanistan.

The ability to reduce the number of provinces engaged in narcotics cultivation has reflected an increase in Afghan law enforcement presence and the availability of internationally supported programs providing alternative livelihoods, especially for farmers who are making use of crop substitution. As of 2008–10, there have been some moves against major Afghan figures ("kingpins") in narcotics trafficking by the Kabul government, with 1,700 corruption cases opened as of October 2008. Yet on the whole, neither Kabul nor its foreign allies have been willing to target mid- and high-level Afghan officials or others close to them for involvement in narcotics. The political cost of such action is seen as being too high by many Afghans.

Money from narcotics is so pervasive in Afghanistan that anyone operating there cannot avoid it, and many Afghan leaders are thus involved to a degree. Removing all officials from the Afghan government who have benefited from narcotics, while appealing, is as impractical as closing down all the farms that grow it. However, ending narcotics-based political corruption will reduce not only the incentive to participate in cultivation and trafficking in the end but also the willingness to tolerate it. Ending the ease with which narcotics money enters the system through political and social corruption would yield more immediate results versus closing down all cultivation and trafficking through eradication and force, which would also have the added negative effect of alienating many Afghans even more.

The Options

A country such as Afghanistan simply cannot afford to destroy half of its rural GDP[271] in the middle of an existential conflict, even if it is opium-based. But the Afghanistan Compact committed Kabul to "a sustained and significant reaction in the production and trafficking of narcotics with a view to complete elimination." Thus Afghanistan and the coalition find themselves at an ideological and practical impasse.

Narcotics cultivation is not politically popular among Afghans. Anyone who has talked with Afghans—including those with no political affiliation or geopolitical understanding—can attest to how much they want Afghanistan to be a country like any other. They are willing to embrace international standards, including a willingness to counter narcotics cultivation and trafficking rather than proclaim Afghan exceptionalism to international norms. Even when foreigners suggest that the Afghans should not be made to pay for the vices of wealthy foreigners, and that narcotics prohibition has probably done more harm than good in the developed world, it is ultimately the questionable status of narcotics under Sharia that renders Afghans unwilling to defend it. Afghans are not willing to challenge the world for a crop of doubtful Islamic legitimacy. Polling in 2009 showed that only twelve percent of Afghans polled in opium-dependent Helmand province and three percent nationwide believe opium cultivation is justified.[272]

Eradication targeted on poppy crops in the field has been the most controversial of the drug-war tactics. It has been used effectively by Afghan law enforcement, backed up by coalition non-military specialists. The US Drug Enforcement Agency (DEA) identified the poppy-free status of Balkh province, achieved in 2006, as a success for eradication.[273] The provincial governor, Ustad Mohammed Atta, a veteran anti-Taliban commander and a former warlord, disagreed with this characterization. He claimed that the lack of overall economic development has undercut the positive effects of eradication and that the end of opium cultivation has actually led to a decline in income for many people in that province.[274]

While eradication had been previously advocated by the US as an effective tactic, in June 2009 it was announced that interdicting narcotics supplies and cultivating alternative crops would be stressed instead.[275] US policy shifted to end eradication because, unless it is linked to an effective rural reconstruction program, it had the potential to create additional recruits for the insurgents. The US had considered cultivation eradication as just one element of an integrated counter-narcotics strategy, as has been set out in Afghanistan's current National Drug Control Strategy (NDCS). The change reflected an emerging consensus that the impact of eradication efforts was felt by farmers and rural laborers rather than those further up the value-added chain. GEN Petraeus said "We are reducing eradication, which often gets the little guy, while increasing the pressure against the big guys."[276] Ambassador Richard Holbrooke added that he believed eradication "did not reduce the amount of money the Taliban got by one dollar."

However, US-funded eradication in Afghanistan is still carried out by the Afghan government. In 2010, this spread to poppy-growing districts in Helmand. Eradication efforts have been a vehicle for corruption (which is one of the reasons the US had pushed for aerial spraying). Reports of the poppy fields of poor farmers being burned out while their better-connected neighbors' fields down the road remained intact have been commonplace.[277] Widespread corruption weakened the credibility of enforcement efforts.[278]

Winning the Conflict

Stable, non-corrupt governance in rural Afghanistan appears to be the most effective counter to narcotics. However, it remains out of reach in much of the country. This is just one facet of the solution. Effective counter-narcotic policy needs to provide a substitute for practically everything the traffickers provide and their clients currently need. This includes marketing infrastructure, credit against future crops, and help with growing crops.[279] Simple crop substitution by donating seed and fertilizer is not sufficient.

Alternative livelihoods, if security, infrastructure, and markets permit their implementation, can effectively replace opium cultivation in a number of areas. This is because the narcotics buyers set the amount paid artificially low, so that the Afghan farmer receives just enough to ensure that he receives more cash and is able to employ more people (allowing him to establish patronage) than he would with any other crop, thus providing a marginal incentive but not so large that these farmers are wedded to poppy-farming into perpetuity; the traffickers rely on the cycle of debt created by credit payments for future crops to have that effect. The fact that the rising food prices of 2008 encouraged some Afghan farmers to replace poppies with wheat shows that crop replacement can be done.

However, transitioning from a poppy-based economy in those parts of rural Afghanistan where it has dominated agriculture is likely to take longer than a few years and will require institutions and infrastructure that are currently lacking outside of those provided by the traffickers. As of 2008, the Afghan Ministry of Counter Narcotics was working with the Ministries of Agriculture and Rural Rehabilitation on microfinance schemes that could be applied in opium-producing provinces and could start the first step of replacing the traffickers' use of credit to control the local economy. Kabul and its coalition supporters should use existing institutions such as the *hawala* system to provide alternatives to narcotics financing, help jumpstart social and economic development at the grassroots level and would give those who run the system a legal stake in success in Afghanistan, making them less vulnerable to the temptations of drug money and cooperation with terrorists and insurgents.

Subsidizing legal crops, if done through a mechanism where there is some assurance that the farmer will be able to earn a decent living and that the funding will not vanish through corruption, has some potential to reduce the appeal of opium. "If commodity prices stay up for wheat, it can replace poppy," said GEN David Petraeus in 2009.[280] But by 2008–10, the corruption of the Afghan government made approaches such as agricultural price supports for legitimate farmers almost impossible to implement.

Large-scale conversion of Afghanistan's opium crop to licit uses has been suggested.[281] This course of action has been opposed by other countries such as Turkey and India that are currently involved in licit opium for morphine production. Poppy has potential use as a biofuel. Licensing opium production, if serious legal, political, economic, efficiency, security, and religious obstacles could be overcome, has the potential to weaken the threat posed by the current illicit traffic and possibly alleviate the pressure to find another replacement crop.[282]

Zalmay Afzali said in 2008 of Counter Narcotics policy, "You cannot do this by force. The Afghan farmer listens. You tell him it [narcotics] brings a chaotic situation to his family. Force is not the answer."[283] Targeting the Afghan farmer as the most vulnerable part of a value-added chain that runs from there to the addicts of Europe and America runs the risk of benefiting the insurgents. Military action against laboratories and refineries or even the suppliers of precursor chemicals and the transporters of narcotics themselves all represent options far more likely to yield better results than crop eradication that targets the poppy fields. Degrading the ability to pay and transfer money would also be a powerful blow to the traffickers. It is also less likely to drive the local Afghans into the arms of the insurgents, especially if there is an ability to re-insert Afghan governance into former opium-dependent areas. Whatever tactics are employed, they are likely to prove ineffective unless accompanied by a parallel move to address Afghanistan's overarching culture of corruption, especially in Kabul, targeting and removing officials that are heavily involved in narcotics trafficking. This corruption is widely believed to reach all the way up to the highest level officials in Kabul, including the Ministries of Interior and Counter Narcotics, as well as in provincial and district governments and in the security forces.[284] Corruption spreads by enabling Afghanistan's narcotics networks to be effectively supported by the state at all levels across the country. Wealthy (and politically connected) Afghans and outsiders with links to narcotics are not targeted, but should be. An extradition treaty with the US remains a moot issue with the Afghan parliament, as many of its members would be reluctant to see such people dragged off to the US in handcuffs, even if extradition would be a powerful weapon against narcotics traffickers, known terrorists, and others who are involved in this widespread ring of crime and corruption.

Rural Afghanistan requires an effective narrative showing that cultivation is *not* reconcilable with Islam nor with the Afghan tradition of self-definition based on the weighty pillars of the concepts of honor and respect. This narrative must also be backed up by demonstrating that they will not suffer, either at the hands of the insurgents or from lack of income or credit, if they turn away from opium, and then the coalition and Kabul must be prepared to protect them from those two things; otherwise the betrayal that these people will feel will be very real and unforgivable. In the longer term, prediction of success in the conflict against narcotics can best be indicated not by a decrease in the acreage under poppies, for that can change with the next growing season, but with achieving security and economic viability in rural Afghanistan.[285]

The problem with creating poppy-free provinces is the same problem facing the creation of insurgent-free areas. It can be done, but the real challenge is keeping it that way—just as, in the past, coalition ground forces have managed to force Afghan insurgents from an area, only to find that there is no capability to backfill this new power vacuum with effective government and security forces. When the coalition ground forces are needed elsewhere, the insurgents just move back in. When a province or district is said to be poppy-free, it needs to fill this vacuum with an economically viable alternative, not just crops but credit, markets, and infrastructure. Otherwise, like the insurgents, the poppies will find their way back in and—more dangerous still—they may be welcomed anew by the local Afghans as having provided something that the government and the foreigners did not. Narcotics pose their own unique challenges, but they do still feed into the insurgency, and both can be countered by the eventual creation of a secure, legitimate uncorrupt government and a viable economy. Just as the insurgency is fed by narcotics-generated funds, narcotics require the insurgency to continue to prevent Counter Narcotics efforts being effective. Eliminate one and you are halfway to eliminating the other. Fail at one, and the impact is twofold.

In narcotics, as is the case elsewhere, in Afghanistan the root issue tends to be about the concept of legitimacy. To defeat narcotics requires that opium cultivation, trafficking, and the corruption it entails be de-legitimatized in both Afghan and Islamic terms. To remove the conditions that have allowed the concentration of opium cultivation in the south requires an increased military presence that will have to be followed up by effective governance, including a demonstrated ability to provide alternative livelihoods and protect those that take these up from further violence or retribution from traffickers and their insurgent allies. In parts of southern Afghanistan, the insurgents manage to provide the local inhabitants with what most Afghans want and the Kabul government and its foreign allies cannot assure: a chance to work their fields and make a living in peace. They would rather the crop not be opium, but when there is no alternative that provides this security, many see it as a necessity. There needs to be a concrete strategy and policy in place that offers incentives for cooperation and penalties for resistance; only in this way can there be hope of effectively curtailing both problems.

CHAPTER SEVEN

AFGHANISTAN'S INTERNAL CONFLICTS

"It is not enough to do one's best. What is required is that one does what is necessary for success."

—Winston Churchill

"The general character and situation of a people must determine what sort of government is fit for them."

—Edmund Burke

S hattered states have taken decades to recover and reestablish themselves after less punishing histories. When the Taliban fell in 2001, Afghanistan was suffering from damage—physical, societal, economic—caused by the conflicts of 1978–2001. Since then, recovery has been slow and uneven. The effect of the gains made in the generations before 1978 have faded. Internal strife, reflecting both long-standing ethnolinguistic and cultural divisions and the pervasiveness of corruption, combined with poor government and limited economic development, now threaten the future of Afghanistan that was wrested from the Taliban and Al Qaeda in 2001.

A Land Defined by Conflicts

Afghanistan has seen impressive achievements in the years since the fall of the Taliban. The majority of Afghans remain proud of their achievement in creating the new constitution and the instruments of government and civil society, but this pride alone is not sufficient to secure an Afghan future. Other sources of national pride, however small, are seized upon by Afghans of all groups, such as the first-ever winning of an Afghan Olympic medal by Ruhollah Nikpai, who won the bronze in men's taekwondo in 2008. An ethnic Hazara, he was cheered by Afghans from all groups.

The most obvious of Afghanistan's divisions are ethnolinguistic. Outside observers have a tendency to focus on them, but there is a mosaic of conflicts, with origins that reach through politics, tribes (especially within the tribally divided Pushtuns and, to a lesser extent, Uzbeks), attitudes toward modernization, religious issues (between different Sunni practices and Sunni-Shia), leadership (who exactly rules in Kabul, in terms of individuals, ethnicity, and Islam), corruption (extractive processes by state and substate authorities), center-periphery (Kabul, regional, and local authority all seeking power and security), economic (no working national economy), land and water rights, patronage, gender (what are the appropriate cultural and socio-political roles for women, and who exactly gets to determine them), and relations with foreigners, Muslim or otherwise. There are also the new conflicts that arose out of the divisions of Afghan society during the conflicts of 1978–2001. Former mujahideen, returning exiles, technocrats, former Taliban, former Communists—each with their foreign supporters and different ethnolinguistic and political links—still view each other warily and so far have had difficulty in pulling together for the greater good and unity of the Afghanistan that they all love and wish to preserve (there are no secessionists here). The result has allowed narrow self-interest and corruption to run rampant and enabled the insurgents to present themselves as an alternative.

Afghanistan is not a land of centuries-old ethnic rivalries that doom it to internal conflict, but rather continues to suffer from the results of ethnolinguistic polarization and mobilization during the conflicts in 1978–2001. Afghanistan's history is marked much more by cooperation across and between groups rather than conflict. Intragroup conflict has been more common than conflicts between groups. Yet the rise of corruption and dependency inside Afghanistan has undercut the ability of Afghans to resolve conflicts by their own means. The ability of the US, coalition partners, and international organizations alike to manage conflict in Afghanistan has decreased with the deteriorating security situation. There has been a failure to fund a shared "golden tomorrow" that should reward cooperation. Aid has instead created alternative patron-client networks between foreign donors and Afghan recipients, often pushing Afghan government institutions to the side. Other moves, such as cabinet reshuffles, often reflecting US or other foreign donor dissatisfaction with the incumbents and the wish to see Afghans they believe are competent and who they feel comfortable working with, have succeeded in putting a few highly competent individuals into positions of authority, but they have too often proved limited in their ability to improve Afghanistan because this myriad of underlying issues makes significant progress toward stability or economic and social development problematic. Government institutions are often less effective than patron-client relationships in getting things done. In many areas, power brokers and warlords who have access to force and patron-client relationships remain more important than the government.

Ethnolinguistic Conflict

"The main argument has become an ethnic issue and this is a dangerous thing," Saleh Registani declared in 2008. As a member of parliament for Panjshir province, he has a view of the overarching dynamic of Afghanistan's politics.[286] Ashraf Ghani, former minister of finance and presidential candidate, said: "Ethnicity is problematic. It is not toxic yet. Ethnicity can become toxic from elite competition and mobilization."[287] The ethnolinguistic dimension of conflict reflects the increasing binary division of Pushtun vs. non-Pushtun that has resulted from the exclusively Pushtun insurgency threatening Afghanistan (as discussed in chapter 2).

Afghanistan is still determining the post-2001 rules of ethnolinguistic power. Many foreigners perceive this as requiring, for example, that the elected president in practice be an ethnic Pushtun and the two vice presidents be non-Pushtuns, views not shared by many non-Pushtuns who see it as keeping them from access to centralized power. The current Afghanistan constitution avoids requiring explicit ethnic shares for government positions. In both the 2004 and 2009 presidential elections, Hamid Karzai was supported by a considerable percentage of non-Pushtuns, reflecting his support by foreign donors (especially in 2004) or leaders of some non-Pushtun groups, including those he ran with as vice presidents, in 2009. In Afghanistan, the effects of ethnolinguistic divisions are not set in stone.

In Afghanistan, enmities between ethnolinguistic groups have tended to be localized rather than nationwide divisions. Tensions between neighboring groups often reflect issues such as differing economic spheres, such as the competition between urban Pushtuns and rural Tajiks in Kunduz. Competing agricultural practices include conflicts between Pushtun herders and Hazara and Uzbek farmers, long-standing in places such as Bamiyan and Jowzjan provinces. Conflicts between loyalties to competing warlords became widespread after the 2001 defeat of the Taliban. Most were between Pushtuns, but some, such as that in 2002–04 between Mohammed Atta's largely Tajik and Dostum's largely Uzbek supporters near Mazar-e-Sharif that led up to corps-size clashes including artillery and armor, brought different groups into conflict. The ever-present land and water disputes also frequently bring groups into conflict.

However, the longest-lasting and most severe division is that between Hazaras and Pushtuns. This reflects the generations of identification of state power with Pushtun ethnicity and Hazara resentment at having gotten little from Kabul since being brought under its rule by force of arms in the late nineteenth century. Multiple factors—race, religion, language, land use, water rights, social status—have lined up to increase tensions between Pushtuns and Hazaras, exacerbated most recently by the brutal pre-2001 occupation of the Hazara Jat by the Taliban and its foreign allies. The Shia, Mongol-descended Dari-speaking Hazaras, were historically at the bottom of Afghan society. Mobilized and organized as a result of their participation in the 1978–2001 conflicts, the Hazaras have little desire to return to a subordinate status. The current insurgency is seen by Hazaras as the latest Pushtun campaign to bring them under their domination.

In Afghanistan since 2001, terrorism, insurgency, and narcotics cultivation alike have been largely carried out by Pushtuns. Most of the post-2001 violence in Afghanistan has been within the same ethno-linguistic group, mainly Pushtun insurgents killing Pushtuns living in Afghanistan. Infighting has prevailed within clans and families. Cousins are often competitors for a kinship group or clan's resources, leadership, or access to patronage (a dynamic termed tarborwali in Pushto). This reflects the impact of decades of conflict on the social structure. In many Pushtun tribes, especially in the south, there is no agreement as to who the leadership figures are or should be, resulting in competing or authority-less chiefs or shuras. The acephalous nature of Pushtun society means that each male is a potential leader. As a result, after decades of conflict, there is often no clarity or agreement about where authority or leadership, tribal or otherwise, lies.

However, there is still significant tension between the largely non-Pushtun regions in the north, central, and western parts of Afghanistan and the Pushtun regions in the east and south, where the insurgency and narcotics cultivation are concentrated. In areas where Pushtun and non-Pushtun groups are mixed, there is local tension and competition. The non-Pushtuns of Afghanistan resent the large share of state power in Pushtun hands, the Pushtun role in terrorism, insurgency, and narcotics, and the allocation of a large share of development and other state resources to the site of the insurgency in Pushtun Afghanistan. "We should take up arms against Kabul and we would receive more aid" is a frequently heard remark from dissatisfied non-Pushtuns in Afghanistan. Non-Pushtuns see Kabul and foreign donors effectively rewarding the Pushtuns through concentrating aid in their areas. To those allocating aid, using it to counter the insurgency is an obvious priority. This is an area where Mountstuart Elphinstone's identification of envy as among the Afghan's most intense (and enjoyable) vices has remained valid. As Afghanistan became more dependent on outside aid for development and coalition forces for security, every Afghan became convinced that his or her group was being cut out.

Within Pushtun areas, the rivalry is especially severe between tribes and clans. The insurgents often capitalize on resentments that the coalition or Kabul may have created. Every time one tribe benefits from Kabul's actions, its rivals, aggrieved, often turn to the insurgents. This has been matched by Pushtun resentment of non-Pushtun claims to a share of power commensurate with their numbers (which Pushtuns answer with probably inaccurate, but nonetheless passionately believed, claims to be an absolute majority). The failure of the national leadership to interact with the Pushtun grassroots in a way consistent with Afghan expectations of legitimate authority, governmental or otherwise (including holding darbars, receiving petitions, and resolving disputes), has contributed to the Pushtun alienation from the Afghan government that has been motivated by the rise of the Taliban Culture and radicalization. In any context, alienation can easily morph into extremism, with the Pushtun insurgents offering an alternative. The emerging Afghanistan media may offer a potential alternative way to interact with the grassroots, but this has yet to be demonstrated or effectively used.

Ethnolinguistic conflict is complex due to the fluid multiple nature of Afghan identity. The Taliban's 1994–2001 demands that a unitary Sunni Islamic religious identity trump all others (in theory) were never widely accepted in practice even by their supporters and were hard to reconcile with the overlapping, competing, and often fluid representations of Pushtun identity. In addition to Islam, links to the nation as well as family, clan, and tribe remain important to the Pushtuns of Afghanistan.

By 2008–10, relations between ethnolinguistic groups were deteriorating, reflecting the insurgency and the continued political polarization in Afghan politics. President Karzai, whatever his failings, was a sincere, if romantic, Afghan nationalist at his core. This image has been undercut, especially among non-Pushtuns, by the perceptions of increasing reliance on Pushtun power to rule during his first term, culminating in the extensive corruption reported in the 2009 elections. Karzai's willingness to personally declare allegiance to Massoud in his conflict with the Taliban and Al Qaeda in 2000 and his original lack of interest in advancing a Pushtun ethnic or especially tribal agenda, or in taking up the trappings of a khan that belonged to him after the Taliban's assassination of his father, has reduced his support among many Pushtuns, who initially saw this nationalist approach as an ethnic betrayal. To the Pakistani military, Karzai's pre-2001 allegiance to the Northern Alliance, his lack of links to Pakistan, and his education in India makes him a likely tool of Pakistan's enemies.

These nationalist origins were part of the hope for a better future that Afghans of all ethnic groups embraced after the fall of the Taliban. Karzai was put forward by his foreign supporters but had broad-based Afghan support, reflected in the 2004 presidential election. Since then, this support has eroded. Non-Pushtuns see Karzai as an instrument of Pushtun power, while many Pushtuns have turned against him for failing to adequately represent their interests. The result has been the tainted 2009 election, ethnic polarization, and an unpopular presidency: 2009 polling showed that Karzai's support in his native Kandahar province has dropped to 16 percent from 90 percent in 2004.[288] Additionally, Karzai is blamed for Kabul's failure to provide security and economic opportunity. He is derided by Afghan Pushtun nationalists as a "fake Pushtun" set in place by the foreigners to serve at the behest of minorities and prevent genuine Pushtun power in Kabul.[289] In response, Karzai has appeared as a spokesman for Pushtun concerns, denouncing collateral damage by coalition airpower and raids by special operations forces. The appearance of presidential incompetence and ineffectiveness and the power of Karzai's family despite widespread beliefs of their links to narcotics and political patronage have tended to dominate other perceptions and undercut the trappings of legitimacy in the eyes of both Pushtuns and non-Pushtuns. By 2009, polling showed that all Afghans, not just Pushtuns, holding a favorable view of Karzai had declined to 52 percent—still enough to win the election—from 83 percent in 2004.[290] The impact of the 2009 election diminished it further. His popularity among Pushtuns, despite widespread disappointment, is still significantly higher than that nationwide.

What has killed more Afghans than violence between ethnolinguistic groups in post-2001 Afghanistan has been conflict within groups. Tribes, localities, and kinship groups all compete for patronage, access to irrigated land, and trade, as well as to exercise long-standing resentments. In Afghanistan's Pushtun areas, tribal dynamics dictate why some areas tend to be more cohesive supporters of Kabul and the foreign presence while others send men across the borders to join the insurgents. Such divisions are not limited to Afghanistan's Pushtuns—they also have led to conflict among Afghanistan's Nuristanis and other groups—but among no others are they as severe nor have they led to as much conflict.

Religion

Religious alliances have been used to cross ethnolinguistic boundaries in Afghanistan's conflicts but have not been determinative. The Sunni Islamist Ahmad Shah Massoud opposed the Sunni HiH and was able to make alliances with the Shia Hazara Hezb-e-Wahdat party and with Dostum's Uzbek Junbish party, whose roots were as a pro-Soviet militia. When the Afghan Taliban invaded the Hazara Jat in the 1990s, their Pushtun mullahs were able to make common cause with Tajik mullahs to persuade Sunni Afghans of different ethnicities to wage a campaign of destruction against the Shia Hazaras. The post-2001 Taliban have attempted to reach out to non-Pushtun Sunni mullahs (Shias being beyond the pale) as common defenders of Afghan Islamic culture against the foreign infidel presence.[291]

While the original Taliban regime saw its legitimacy erode prior to its rapid collapse in 2001, it still retained at least the nominal allegiance of the informal patronage-based networks of mullahs and other religious figures that cut across Pushtun Afghanistan and into Pakistan's borderlands of the FATA, Baluchistan, and North West Frontier Province. When the Taliban were defeated, the majority of these religious figures did not flee into Pakistan. They remained where they were, central pillars (in the absence of effective secular authority) of Afghan society. Neither Kabul nor their foreign supporters came after them to remove them.

The Afghan ulema have better internal links and an ability to mobilize Afghans, through the mosques, than does Kabul. The inability to win over much of the Afghan ulema to the government and their continued opposition to the foreign presence (largely from its cultural impacts) raises a cloud over the legitimacy of the government. The trends are not running in favor of the religious practices of old Afghanistan: "Older alims retire, the new ones are graduates of Pakistani madrassas," said Haroun Mir, an Afghan political observer.[292] Another pro-Western Afghan scholar said in 2008: "In my mosque in Kabul, every Friday the sermon is about the evils of the foreign presence and the need to banish them. Goodness knows what they preach down south. In Egypt, where they have state-controlled ulema, they would end up in jail or at least lose their financial support from the government for such preaching. In

Kabul, it is simply accepted." The Afghan government and its foreign supporters are losing—or, frequently, not even participating in—one of the most important parts of the battle of ideas, that taking place in the mosques throughout Sunni Afghanistan.

One of the most capable networks in Pushtun-speaking Afghanistan, ulema linked by their madrassa educations or Deobandi-influenced teachings in Pakistan, is effectively controlled by the insurgents. Despite this, it is likely that in 2008–10 only a minority of the Pushtun ulema supported the insurgency.[293] Many have strong links to Kabul or anti-insurgent sources of patronage. Others, with ties to the Sufic brotherhoods, oppose the insurgents. As the Taliban increasingly overcame or penetrated the Sufic brotherhoods that were part of traditional religious practice in southern Afghanistan in 2008–10, this has reduced their capability to organize resistance to them.[294] Mullahs continue to resist the insurgents for many reasons.[295] But all of these alike have increasingly been targeted for assassination (three a week average in 2010).[296]

The days when power of the village mullah or a madrassa's maulavi was limited to the moral, not the political, realm are unlikely to return to Pushtu-speaking Afghanistan, especially in the light of the continued weakness of secular and tribal leadership in many areas and Kabul's inability to assert effective secular governance or provide any sort of service at the grassroots level.[297] The local mullahs in Pushtun Afghanistan, because this group provided much of the resistance leadership in the war against the Soviets as well as grassroots leadership under the Taliban, have not reverted to being the subject of jokes as they were in the Golden Age. The Pushtun ulema of rural Afghanistan remained in their villages after the Taliban leadership fled to Pakistan in 2001–02. These mullahs were marginalized and became bitter and resentful. They did not see themselves as benefiting from the new political order the Bonn process put in place. Kabul had little interest in or capability for outreach. The US seemed intent on sending as many Afghans as possible to Guantanamo. In many cases, it was the mullahs' contacts and networks—which they maintained when their previous allies the Taliban leadership ran across the border—that turned what started as a cross-border insurgency in 2003–04 into one which by 2008–10 had a grip on districts throughout Pushtun Afghanistan.

Today, traditional Afghan religious practices demonstrate only a limited ability to reassert themselves, especially in Pushtun Afghanistan, where the past three decades of violence have caused great disruption and social damage. Moreover, the intervening decades have seen the rise of Islamist demands for the enforcement of the Sharia (Islamic law) in Afghanistan as well as throughout the Muslim world. The Sunni response to the Shia Iranian Revolution as well as the rise of militant religious power in Afghanistan over the years has also hurt traditional Afghan Islam's ability to re-assert itself. Perhaps more significantly, there has been limited aid or governmental assistance reaching traditional Afghan Islam. Deobandi and Wahabi influences that had been strong among Afghans in the refugee camps in Pakistan starting 30 years ago have not faded in Pushtun Afghanistan despite the defeat of the Taliban in 2001. Mullahs that are followers continue to receive outside funding. The Deobandi funding comes from religious parties in Pakistan, many with links to the ISI. Wahabi funding comes largely from Saudi Arabia and the Gulf states, either directly or through NGOs. In many cases, covertly pro-insurgent Afghan ulema (not all Pushtuns) have been able to make common cause with conservative Afghan or Islamist religious leaders, including those in Kabul that are supporters of the government or members of parliament. They have been able to use shared concern over Afghan culture being threatened by exposure to foreign influence and a realization that an effective secular government would undercut their power.

Whoever "wins" the conflict over Afghanistan's religion will determine what form of Islamic practice will help shape Afghan government and society. Political Islam is far from a dynamic and revolutionary force: rather, it currently serves as a conservative force, motivating parliamentary and judiciary opposition to the Karzai government, filling a vacuum that existed in the absence of a tradition of parliamentary loyal opposition and waving the nationalist flag to oppose foreign-backed social changes. What has given the issue of the direction of Afghan religion additional importance is the religious basis, through Sharia law, of the secular legal system of Afghanistan. Chief Justice Faisal Ahmad Shinwari (who held that post in 2001–06) and his allies aimed to make the judiciary a bastion of religious conservatism against socio-political change. This changed with the appointment of Karzai allies to judicial positions.

Religion also has a direct impact on how dispute resolution reaches the Afghan grassroots. In much of rural Afghanistan, dispute resolution falls not to the largely distrusted or nonexistent state-run judicial process; rather, the local population administers traditional justice themselves, through the hoqooq (a specialist land-and-water-rights body), jirga, shura, or other local organizations. While the centralization of power in Kabul and its state institutions under the constitutions had led to these subnational institutions being undervalued and unsupported after the fall of the Taliban, they were by 2008–10 receiving more support from aid donors. In some areas, especially in the omnipresent land and water disputes, the mediative role of *sayids* (descendants of the Prophet Mohammed) continues as it has for centuries. In other areas, the insurgents have offered their own rough justice—with a veneer of Sharia law for acceptability included—administered by local insurgent shuras or, more often, individual mullahs—seldom with the qualifications to be a *qazi* (Islamic jurist)—or insurgent commanders, often from outside the local area.[298] The insurgents have targeted *jirgas, shuras*, mediation, and other local approaches to dispute resolution as unIslamic, as such traditional justice undercuts their claim to totalitarian authority.

There is no Afghan tradition of state-supported ulema. The size of the Afghan ulema, an estimated quarter million, would make such state support unfeasible. Kabul has tried to instill loyalty by forming ulema councils at a national and provincial level. The National Ulema-e-Shura (NUS) (Council of Clerics), a group of 100 religious leaders from around the country, headed by Shinwari, meets monthly in Kabul and provides Karzai with a stamp of approval. Three thousand mullahs receive a monthly NUS stipend. The clerics are financed directly from Mr. Karzai's office, according to the secretary of the council, Fazel Ahmad Manawi (a Karzai ally, former deputy chief justice, and a member of the 2009 Independent Election Commission).[299] Each province is supposed to have a comparable organization, although not all are apparently active. These efforts have not been effective, with some exceptions such as the Kandahar council which includes religious leadership figures related to

Karzai and senior ulema respected by all sides in the conflict. Kandahar's and Nangarhar's Ulema-e-Shura have been active, issuing *fatwas* against the insurgents and especially suicide bombing. In return, their members have been targeted for assassination, deterring ulema in areas within the reach of the insurgency from cooperating with the government or from preaching anti-insurgent messages. Ulema seen as having links to Kabul have been targeted, and many have been murdered by insurgents.[300] In some areas, such as Uruzgan province, the security situation is too dangerous for the council to operate. Elsewhere, such as Paktika province, the council was formed by local ulema who complained they received no support (or help with security) from Kabul.

The Afghan government has also used ministries to create positions for ulema on the government payroll to ensure loyalty. Starting in 2007, the Ministry of Border and Tribal Affairs in Kabul has in effect put more "conservative" mullahs from some Pushtun tribes on the government payroll. But this has been seen more as a concession to appease conservatives than an attempt to affect what is preached in the mosques on Fridays.

The Karzai government has tried to get its message across through the mosques, for example by sending a message on International Women's Day to be preached; however, as the imams tend to add their own interpretation at the end, the results may not be as Kabul intended. Many Afghans see the government's interaction with religion as inept and ineffective. Three thousand mosques received government funding in 2010.

The religious dimension of Afghanistan's conflicts is too important to be conceded to the enemy. Much of the post-2001 outside aid to Afghanistan had failed to make life better for the average Afghan in that it had tended to avoid agriculture and religion, the two areas of life that Afghans depend on for material and spiritual well-being. The purely secular approaches that the West is most comfortable with do not connect with this world where religion is central to life and society and is at the heart of the challenge posed by terrorists, insurgents, and narcotics traffickers alike. Religion (like agricultural development) was too often ignored by aid donors post-2001 despite their shared importance to the daily lives of Afghans at grassroots level. In practice, this has meant that in much of Pushtun-speaking Afghanistan, what is preached in the mosque reflects outside influence and hostility to Kabul's non-Muslim foreign supporters. The Sufic brotherhoods and their networks received some outside support but have been unable to demonstrate strength comparable to the Deobandi-influenced networks that have allowed the insurgents to mobilize ulema throughout Afghanistan. In the words of US political philosopher Michael Novak, "Mere secular force will not do when the fundamental battle is spiritual."[301]

Corruption

Afghanistan has never been free of corruption.[302] Yet it was much less prevalent in the generation preceding the 1978 Communist takeover. And despite the inflow of aid rubles and dollars in the Cold War years, Afghanistan's relative isolation from the international economy and the relatively small number of educated Afghans involved in this process kept overall corruption in check. Because this relatively small group of people had to work together over the course of their lifetimes, reputation was all-important, making officials less likely to be tempted by bribes or building personal patronage at the expense of governance. "When I was a junior officer in the Royal Afghan Army, stationed at Kargha, someone lost one submachine gun; they turned the place upside down looking for it and its loss ended peoples' careers," nostalgically recalled Afghan Defense Minister Rahim Wardak in 2008.[303]

"Corruption of leaders (entirely unacceptable), administrative corruption, road tolls and illegality, and connection with narcotics"[304] was overwhelming Afghanistan in 2008–10, according to former Interior minister Mohammed Hanif Atmar, who lost his position in large part because of his personal reputation for rectitude. The threat to Afghanistan from corruption is different from anything that was seen in the past. President Karzai has been forthright in recognizing the problem corruption causes for Afghanistan's future and has spoken strongly against it.[305] Yet Karzai himself is frequently identified as contributing to corruption, benefiting from fraudulent 2009 election results and tolerating the unchecked activities of his family and clients in Kandahar and adjacent provinces that have reportedly involved them in land, narcotics, and other questionable dealing. In 2010, polling showed that 85 percent of Afghans considered corruption a problem, already up from 72 percent in 2007.[306] Yet, in another poll, more than half the population said they had no personal experience of corruption.[307] The recent rise in corruption challenges the very legitimacy of Afghan governmental institutions, threatening the country's future. It has undercut the ability of Afghans and foreign supporters alike to create effective Afghan political and societal institutions. This widespread corruption creates a destructive game of beggar-my-neighbor through shady resource allocation, with different groups and localities competing against each other. This widespread corruption has also hurt economic growth and development, diverting resources away from where they are needed. "The difference is between *baksheesh* [traditional gift-giving and wheel-greasing] and high level corruption. Provincial and police chiefs are deeply on the take," according to US Ambassador Richard Holbrooke in 2008.[308]

Traditionally, inter-Afghan relations had been based on patronage, compromise, and deal-making. It was, after all, a nation of carpet merchants and horse traders. What is often seen by outsiders as corruption can co-opt groups and give them a stake in avoiding further conflict. It can buy off opponents and rivals, putting together operational coalitions where state institutions are weak. But the tradition of "give a little, get a little" has been hard to adapt to today's reality when benefits come not from exchanges among equals, but from top-down donors. Then, corruption's awesome powers to destabilize and destroy a society have been demonstrated. Outsiders have often not realized how their well-intentioned actions have helped create corruption. Many Afghan elites have felt entitled to take their share.

Because benefiting the life of Afghans at the grassroots level was not a priority of pre-2001 Afghanistan governments, winning over elite loyalties and servicing patronage networks were the traditional goals. When, post-2001, outside resources in terms of aid or foreign support were available, the inclination was to divert them to these objectives. While Afghan elites and grassroots alike may have embraced the hope created in 2001, the weakness of government institutions and the fragmenting and damage to society limited their ability to realize this hope in terms of concrete change.

Starting with putting together the coalition of Afghans that ousted the Taliban in 2001–02, especially ethnic Pushtuns, there has been a perceived need for outside donors to secure support inside Afghanistan by providing access to resources. As a result, every time an Afghan leader or ministry in Kabul—or, less often, a qawm, village, tribe, or district—benefits from outside aid, it creates envy and resentment among those who did not receive anything. These people then devote themselves to preventing further progress until they or their group benefit, which obviously may never happen. Every such unshared benefit is seen as a result of corruption. Former finance minister Ashraf Ghani said in 2007: "Corruption has become a major problem in Afghanistan. It is a cancer that has eaten through. No high-ranking official of the government has been prosecuted for corruption and sentenced and unless that happens, there will be disgust."[309] By 2008–10, the disgust was widespread.

Since that statement, there have been increased efforts to prosecute officials involved in narcotics trafficking—a powerful contributor to the culture of corruption—and others have been quietly moved out of power. Yet despite these efforts, trans-border narcotics-trafficking leaders such as Haji Juma Khan[310]—arrested in October 2008 and in custody in the US—and Haji Bashir Noorzai (also prosecuted in the US and sentenced to life in prison in 2008)[311] have left still-viable networks and enduring and virulent rings of corruption behind them. President Karzai's brother Ahmad Walid Karzai has been identified as having been able to benefit from the disruption in narcotics-trafficking networks caused by these arrests.[312] Afghan security forces, especially the Afghan National Police (ANP), often behind in their pay, proved bribable in many areas and would often do the bidding of whoever paid them the most money, closing down rival operations and confiscating their opium to assure their patrons a higher market share. Embassies, Afghan civilians, Afghan law enforcement, international organizations, and NGOs alike all had their own lists of those in Kabul and provincial capitals they considered corrupt. But even the worst offenders remained in power, thanks to protection from family clout or other influential patronage relationships, as long as they could effectively use patronage networks. Many of those on these lists claim they have been put there because they put Afghanistan's (or their clients') interests above those of the foreigners or the Afghans compiling the lists. There remains a risk that, if these men are targeted for prosecution, they will either make common cause with the insurgents or narcotics traffickers to save themselves and their position or, if they are removed, there will be no one able to replace them. This new power vacuum could then be filled by insurgents, criminals, or warlords, a likely possibility considering the difficulty of recruiting and keeping competent and clean Afghans into government, with many less frustrating and high-paid alternatives in the private sector, working for NGOs or foreign countries open to them.

The culture of corruption than afflicts Afghanistan has its roots in the culture of dependency that was created in Afghanistan during the 1978–92 jihad years and contributed to the political failures of the 1990s. Afghan groups emerging in Pakistan from the jihad, like those created inside Afghanistan to support the Soviet presence, failed to achieve independent Afghan political legitimacy. They were then used by the outside powers that funded them, starting a cycle of dependency on outsiders rather than cooperation with other Afghans. In Peshawar and Kabul alike, Afghans were dependent on their foreign patrons rather than building effective coalitions with other Afghans to achieve their goals. Traditional Afghan patterns of patrimonial authority appeared in a new context. The constraints previously imposed by Afghan society, notably the importance of reputation for dealing with other Afghans, were removed. Many of the old elites were forced into exile. The potential for abuse was increased by the availability of new outside sources of resources; the line between "clean" outside aid money and "dirty" self-enrichment was never distinct. In Pakistan, the Afghan population spent, in many cases, a decade or more in refugee camps, drawing rations rather than earning a living. To survive required corruption, bribing officials to get on camp rosters or be put on a list for medical care. Western aid donors cared more about how much they spent than how effectively this money was helping Afghans. As a result, the money flowed disproportionately to a corrupt few, not to those actually fighting inside Afghanistan who had no access to the outsiders' resources. In Peshawar, international aid flowed freely in the late 1980s, and it was commonplace to see resistance political leaders and field commanders (mainly ethnic Pushtuns) living in expensive rented houses and driving new four-wheel-drive vehicles while their followers in the refugee camps and in Afghanistan had nothing but the clothes they stood up in. The Afghan people saw this firsthand, and it only reinforced the notion that this kind of money was the only way to get by. More recently, the culture of corruption has been assimilated by many as being consistent with traditional Afghan patronage. In the words of a Western reporter covering the fraud in the September 2009 presidential election, "As the men relaxed and smilingly described the election day, it became clear that what would constitute large-scale fraud in western context meant little more to them than the usual haggling over chicken or vegetables in a market."[313]

Corruption has become, in effect, a domestic issue on its own terms as well as a factor contributing to terrorism, insurgency, and narcotics. It has done more damage to post-2001 Afghanistan than much of the violence. The spread of corruption in Afghanistan has been in large part facilitated and encouraged by an international aid system that siphons off aid to donor-country administrators, consultants, and a pyramid of contractors and sub-contractors until only a fraction of every dollar pledged at international donor conferences actually reaches Afghans. This has led to a nationwide crisis that has undercut both the capability and legitimacy of current Afghan government to implement any effective policy as well as the well-meaning actions of foreign supporters, including the US and UN.

Conflicts in Afghanistan are about legitimacy. Legitimacy comes from providing or enabling fair dispute resolution, from providing security and enabling the population to be able to earn a living from lawful occupations or trade (not opium). Corruption undercuts Kabul's claim to be the legitimate government of Afghanistan, weakening the already tenuous hold they had on state power and control. Although the pre-2001 Afghan Taliban proved corrupt in practice when they came to power in Kabul— Al Qaeda bought and paid for them—the current insurgents have been able to reclaim some of the sheen of Islamic rectitude that the Taliban used to enable their 1994–96 rise to national power.

If it is law that builds the land, Afghanistan remains broken. This state of lawlessness and non-functional state institutions has led to increased corruption at all levels of society that poses a threat not just to the current government: it poses an existential challenge to its future as a nation. This growing corruption has made narcotics cultivation and trafficking easy and profitable, which has helped make the overall population, especially among Pushtuns, receptive to the insurgents that enable this livelihood. If this downward spiral is not stopped, it will create a situation where a future setback—however limited it may appear at first—can snowball and lead to collapse. Corrupt governments are not resilient governments. A battlefield setback, a natural disaster, or the withdrawal of foreign patrons can bring down the whole house of cards.

Immediately after the fall of the Taliban in 2001, the interim Afghan leadership at the national and subnational (province and district) levels secured access to the initial flow of foreign aid and started to divert it to their own personal use, building their own patronage networks or enriching themselves. Some anti-Taliban leaders that had fought with the Afghans and their foreign supporters were able to use their place in post-war Afghanistan to establish extractive relationships, securing themselves land and income from Afghans who lacked their access to power or their ability to use armed force with impunity, reflecting, first, that they could, having no alternative sources of power or authority to oppose them and, second, a sense of entitlement. Many Northern Alliance veterans in the government, seeing that they were being cast aside by the increased number of Pushtuns brought into the government under Karzai, saw they had better take their "due" now. Others, rather than direct enrichment, made their goal the construction of improved patronage networks that would cement them in power, as Marshal Fahim aimed to do with the Afghan Military Forces while he was Minister of Defense. Many of the returning exiles had a similar short-term view. They were entitled to regain what was rightfully theirs and they were not going to make a long-term commitment to Kabul or to the social and economic future of the nation as a whole. This entwined sense of resentment and entitlement by Afghan elites helped accelerate Kabul's move toward a culture of corruption that has come to threaten the very legitimacy of the government. The large amounts of money injected into the economy by foreign aid, Kabul development, and, of course, narcotics meant that there were immediate rewards available to those taking part in this fluid corruption culture.

The second great boost to corruption came with the increasing perception in Afghanistan and Pakistan that the US and its allies were not going to be in the conflict for the long haul. Now was the time to start extracting money that could be used to buy a viable exile for them and their families in the near future. By 2008–10, the numbers of high officials with real estate or family outside Afghanistan had become a running joke. More seriously, it led to the unspoken but important separation between those Afghans with a way out and those with no alternative but to prevail in Afghanistan. This last may require adapting the traditional Afghan survival strategy of switching sides and joining forces with a winner, if they will have you.

Afghanistan's path in the Berlin-based Transparency International annual index of perceived corruption has been steadily downward.[314] By 2007, it had reached 172—just seven away from the title of world's most corrupt—and had beaten out all its neighbors except Uzbekistan. By 2008, Afghanistan was holding steady at 176 out of 180. Only Haiti, Iraq, Myanmar, and Somalia were rated lower. In 2009, Afghanistan was second from the bottom in Transparency International's "Corruption Perception Index."[315] While this measures perceptions, and Afghanistan's corruption has received a great deal of attention because of the interest of international donors and the presence of the world media in Kabul, it suggests that the trend lines in corruption, as with much else in Afghanistan, were running in the wrong direction.

By 2008–10, in much of Afghanistan, corruption undercut governance. In the judicial sector and in the police, constant demands for bribery have discredited these institutions. In Pushtun Afghanistan, the insurgents have been able to take advantage of this. In non-Pushtun Afghanistan, the problem of corruption is less intense but still has undercut Kabul's claim to legitimacy. This crisis has only shortened the horizons of those in authority, which in turn begets more self-interested yet ultimately destructive extraction. In the final analysis, corruption is more a symptom than a cause of Afghanistan's crisis of governance. In the words of Ashraf Ghani: "The Afghan political class has failed to offer a national vision to the people. They have pursued their personal interests at the expense of the national interest and corruption has resulted in disappointment."[316] More than prosecuting corrupt officials, dealing with the root cause requires changes to how Afghanistan is governed that will make it more effective and legitimate and will provide renewed hope to the Afghan people for a future with security, development, and stability, because, with anything else, many Afghan elites are going to enrich themselves when they can and switch sides when they must.

Afghan election corruption at the 2004 presidential level increased to that seen in the 2005 parliamentary elections, while the 2009 presidential election was seen as tainted as early as the registration process starting in 2008, so the widespread accusations of fraud on election day were no surprise. While the 2004–05 elections were conducted with joint UN-Afghan efforts, since then they have been conducted under the authority of the Afghan Independent Election Commission (IEC), which lacks international acceptance. The main vehicle of corruption has been bloc voting, in which a local leader is able to offer the votes of his real or fictitious followers, especially women, whose voter registration cards are not required to have a photograph. Registrars, for a share of the proceeds, have often been happy to issue voter registration cards for fictitious Afghans. In the 2005 election, this was most evident in places such as remote conservative Pushtun Paktika province, where more voters were registered than in densely populated Kabul, many of them women, though local attitudes limit the acceptability of the female franchise. By the spring of 2009, in provinces such as Nuristan and Panjshir, there were more registered voters than the estimated total populations. Allegations of voter fraud marred the 2009 campaign, with Ashraf Ghani, running for president, claiming the Karzai government "has already committed substantial fraud in voter registration," while former ambassador to the United States Sayid T. Jawad countered that "he has no interest in muddying the waters because he is ahead of everyone by substantial margins."[317] Corruption undercut the government's already weakened legitimacy by undermining one of the few areas—voting—where they has previously received general public acceptance and approval. Making the election particularly damaging was that support had split on ethnolinguistic lines. Pushtuns supported Karzai and considered his election legitimate. Non-Pushtuns opposed him and were outraged by the widespread fraud, especially in Kandahar and other Pushtun areas. This differed greatly from the 2004 election, when many non-Pushtuns supported Karzai because that was seen as what the US and the coalition wanted; by 2009 both Karzai and the US had less appeal. Ambassador Peter Galbraith, the deputy head of UNAMA who was fired over protesting that organization's acceptance of the election results, wrote that "The fraud has handed the Taliban its greatest victory in eight years of fighting the United States and its Afghan partners."[318] In the 2010 parliamentary elections, insecurity, more than corruption, reduced Pushtun representation.

The culture of corruption has enabled the (old) patronage system to influence and, in some places, control the (new) universal franchise. The importance of local leaders among a population that has been mobilized along ethnolinguistic, tribal, or local (rather than national) lines has helped make it possible for a particular patron to be paid for delivering the bloc votes of his clients. Much of the vote-buying is aimed at meeting the needs of the patronage system, especially in light of the particular ideological and political edge voting has acquired in recent years. Competing claims of family, clan, ethnicity, and politics divert the minimal flow of resources. The pre-1978 government had at least a competent and devoted civil service in both Kabul and provincial capitals. Some of these men and their successors have throughout the years, accommodating Communists, mujahideen and Taliban alike, tried to maintain order and at least a modicum of the rule of law. Neither Peshawar nor Kabul cared much about competence in 1978–92, but rather promoted those with proven political loyalty and familial or patronage ties. There were a considerable number of competent and loyal Afghans in both systems, but this was in spite of, rather than because of, the incentives. Only inside Afghanistan did the harsh Darwinism of waging an insurgency and the need to forge coalitions with other Afghans bring forth a generation of more effective leaders in those years, especially those, such as Ahmad Shah Massoud, who escaped control from Pakistan.

In 2008–10, efforts were started to combat official corruption inside Afghanistan.[319] The High Office of Oversight was established in June

2008. Each of Afghanistan's cabinet ministries is forming inspectors-general offices. Transparency was considered a condition for increased Afghan government involvement in receiving and spending aid funds. The US and other donors had deployed experienced personnel to train Afghans to combat corruption. In 2009, one of these estimated that it would take ten years of hard work for this to become effective.

But all corruption in Afghanistan is not equal. The West has also insisted that Afghans meet their standards, but have demonstrated little capability or investment in making better the lives of individual Afghans, undercutting their claim to be protecting them from corrupt officials and police or rapacious warlords. As a result, just about every Afghan leader who depends on homegrown support rather than outsiders for authority is considered corrupt by many foreigners. In reality, as with narcotics, targeting every Afghan who benefits from the activity, in the absence of an economically viable legal alternative, is not a viable option.

Corruption has become so pervasive that even a strenuous effort—let alone a few prosecutions to please the foreigners—will not suffice. Just as narcotics cannot be effectively addressed without dealing with the economic and social context of rural Afghanistan in which it exists, combating corruption requires a broad-spectrum approach. In the long term, only a reformed, decentralized government that will involve Afghans at the grassroots level as well as Kabul and a functioning national private-sector economy that allows Afghans to earn and retain wealth legally can displace corruption. Even so, corruption can mutate as fast as any virus and is prevalent in many developing countries much more stable and peaceful than Afghanistan. If corruption is to be held in check, the constraints of pre-1978 Afghanistan, of a concern for keeping face, family honor, and a reputation for fair dealing, needs to be encouraged, like much else, to reappear.

Modernization

In Afghanistan, political and social competition has often been between the different strains of urban, modernizing, and centralizing forces, both secular and religious, and how different vectors were diametrically opposed by other rural, religious, and traditional forces, aiming to secure the status quo or responding to change by a return to tradition. Foreign supporters have generally been proponents of modernization, and so aid money has financed many of the recent changes and development, as it has those attempted over the preceding century. But evidence, both recent and historical, suggests that for all the diverse peoples of Afghanistan, modernization proves problematic unless they were directly involved and invested in the process. Much of the actions of international involvement in Afghanistan has led to "top-down" or "trickle-down" modernization that ignores this lesson and, as of yet, has not involved or benefited the ordinary Afghan to an appropriate degree.

The failure of modernization that is imposed from the top down stems from its inability to have the Afghan grassroots in the process to both participate in and take responsibility for change and what it achieves (jobs, infrastructure, etc.). Top-down modernization has often been resisted, and even when its implementation by Kabul governments does not have disastrous results, it leads to unused schools, built by foreign aid, that are used as storehouses or, especially in the south and the east, burned by the Taliban.

Those seeking to change Afghanistan often rely on foreign patronage. King Abdur Rahman created Afghanistan as a state with British support in the late nineteenth century. King Zahir experimented with democracy in the Golden Age, paid for by both sides in the Cold War. The Khalqis attempted to remake the country in a neo-Stalinist model in 1978–79 with Soviet support. The Islamist HiH has relied on Pakistani support from the 1970s to the present. The rise of the fundamentalist Taliban— no modernizers but bent on radically changing Afghanistan—was only made possible by the Pakistani military, money from Saudi Arabia and the Gulf states, and eventually Al Qaeda support.

Afghans are deeply conservative by nature, especially the rural populations of all ethnicities. Under King Zahir, Afghanistan's modernization policy was supposed to support Kabul's domestic and foreign policies while social and economic modernization was more limited. The top-down approach of these policies failed to create a sizable grassroots constituency in support of modernity except in Kabul and other cities, as well as among modernized groups such as military officers. These groups and the urban elites also spawned the Communist (and Islamist) opposition that were, with foreign help, eventually to bring the slow-moving modernization process to a violent stop. On the other hand, the ulema and traditionally educated communities in rural areas, especially Pushtuns, grew more religious as a reaction to change—a trend that would accelerate throughout the 1978–2001 conflicts—and became hostile to urban elites, mostly linked to the Kabul government. In Pushtun areas, tribal leadership weakened, removing a buffer between modernization and the conservative grassroots.

The conflicts of 1978–2001 brought much destruction as well as modernization. Traditional society was undercut. New organizations such as political parties emerged. Afghans were politically mobilized, polarized, and radicalized. Grassroots Afghans listened to international radio news, becoming aware of the larger world. The original Afghan Taliban emerged from this upheaval as a fundamentalist force, looking backward to an idealized Islamic Afghanistan. The Taliban success in the 1990s was, in many ways, a victory against modernization.

Modernization will largely be identified with the foreign presence until its Afghanistan constituency is recreated. However, there remain core groups committed to modernization in Afghanistan. Even the grassroots, ambivalent about modernization, want the access to education and jobs it has the potential to provide. The new Afghanistan media, with its multiple outlets, has the potential to provide a platform for modernization.

Center–Periphery

The power struggle between the center and the periphery in Afghanistan was reignited in Kabul in 2001, in the wake of the defeat of the Taliban. The vision of a centralized state was, with foreign urging, supported by Afghans of all ethnic and political groups. At Bonn, there was no foreign support for the vision of a federal system in Afghanistan. There was concern that federalism would lead to state fragmentation and invite destructive foreign support for regional figures. A federal system or an investment in subnational power was also seen, by Kabulis or returning exiles, as potentially empowering rivals. During the Constitutional Loya

Jirga, at US urging, Afghanistan became a highly centralized state under a president with extensive powers. Many Afghans, especially non-Pushtuns, were concerned that, in the words of Dr. Abdullah, the former foreign minister and 2009 presidential candidate, "Reviving Abdur Rahman's entity using democratic tools can only discredit democracy."[320]

Provincial governors, never chief executives in Afghanistan, became second-level functionaries, subordinate to the Minister of Interior. They have no independent taxation or budgeting capability. Whatever they have financially is provided by Kabul. Proposals to have provincial governors elected, while popular among delegates to the Constitutional Loya Jirga (who saw themselves likely candidates) were put aside (with US support).[321] In today's centralized Afghanistan, not only has the Karzai administration moved governors around the country to prevent them from developing competing local power bases, but moving teachers between schools and police chiefs out of stations requires action by often non-responsive ministries in Kabul. Other factors contributed to turn the Afghan desire for a cohesive national vision instead into a highly centralized if largely incapable state after 2001. International organizations and aid donors alike concentrated on Kabul, both in terms of governance and economically, until 2008–10.

Since 2001, Kabul and the centralization of power in Afghanistan have been identified with current President Hamid Karzai. Karzai presided over the Bonn process in Kabul and was elected president by a considerable majority in a generally fair 2004 election. Karzai was elected, in large part, because Afghan voters thought that he was what the US wanted, and thus his election would be followed by increased aid and thus an improvement in the quality of life. The widespread accusations of fraud after Karzai's reelection in the 2009 elections diminished the stature of the process. Ashraf Ghani, who ran for president in 2009, said: "No one calls the election fair or legitimate."[322]

Karzai's administration, which had opened so hopefully, was now largely identified with the incapacity of the Afghan government and the rise in corruption, appearing to favor Pushtuns in practice, while repeating nationalist rhetoric to non-Pushtun audiences, on top of the lack of security, rule of law, and governance. Kabuli intellectuals complained that he was not among Afghanistan's "best and brightest" and therefore cannot claim to be a deep or original thinker.[323] Ashraf Ghani said in 2009: "I worked for Karzai in 2002–04. The only way to manage him [sic] is to give him options and timelines. . . . When he became the elected president, he would sit on decisions for two years. . . . Karzai focuses on tactics, not strategy, which is why he is so flexible. He is willing to engage with any party and any process."[324]

Karzai's reputation has been undercut by actions of his family members, including reports of involvement in narcotics—albeit, as largely absentee landowners in Kandahar province, where it is ingrained in the rural economy, there is not much they could do to prevent this. However, by 2008, "He cannot control his own family, so how can he control the country?" had become a catchphrase even among supporters in Kabul. The patrimonial aspects of Afghanistan governance made US and coalition support for the centralized Kabul government appear to be support for an increasingly unpopular Hamid Karzai. Dr. Najibullah Lafraie, who served in the post-1992 Afghan Foreign Ministry with Karzai, wrote: "I highly respect President Karzai and admire his integrity and patriotism. However, he has proved to be a very incompetent leader and administrator. He not only lacks a strategic vision but also the necessary decisiveness and he has been incapable of curbing factionalism within the cabinet he inherited from the Bonn conference as well as within the ones he has appointed himself."[325]

Prior to 2001, no central Afghan government ever did much to improve the lives of individual Afghans out in the provinces. The government allocated resources to different provinces to strengthen patronage ties or avoid elite challenges to Kabul's authority. This often became a source of resentment. The tax revenue from the prosperous north was perceived to be mostly spent in the southern Pushtun areas, which did not pay much tax as it was. While Afghanistan is today collecting relatively little internal revenue, the burden to collect at all has fallen heavily on non-Pushtun provinces, in large part because tax collectors would be a target for insurgents in many Pushtun areas. This of course has led to resentment in the non-Pushtun provinces. The lack of a conflict in their area has meant that resources from taxation and outside aid alike are directed elsewhere, largely to pacify Pushtun areas, in effect penalizing them for maintaining order and a civil society.

Kabul has a thriving civil-sector economy. Outside Kabul, the failure to redevelop a national economy in the wake of the Taliban still reverberates today, with the regional economies in effect continuing to function as low-cost supplements to the stronger economies of neighboring countries rather than making Afghanistan an economic entity. This—along with the continued tension with Pakistan—has helped limit provincial Afghanistan's integration with the regional and global economies.

The challenge facing Afghans and policy makers around the world today is making the government in Kabul relevant and capable of making material improvement to all Afghan groups. Kabul's legitimacy was not quickly bolstered and rebuilt after the fall of the Taliban, giving times for its cracks to deepen and resentments to fester. The non-Pushtun areas of the north, center, and west have evolved over the past thirty years and are now mobilized to voice discontent and demonstrate a renewed dissatisfaction with Kabul. Today, Kabul is, in many ways, back where King Zahir was at the start of his reign, almost seventy years ago.

Political Leadership

Afghans still believe in Afghanistan. 77 percent of Afghans told pollsters in 2010 that they saw themselves primarily as Afghans as opposed to only 23 percent that put an ethnic identify first. This suggests that the national vision remains strong at the grassroots level; there is a reason no one is talking about dividing up Afghanistan.[326] What is missing has been the inability of Afghan political elites or their foreign supporters to unite such diverse identities. The post-2001 Kabul government and its supporters have proven ineffective in exerting governance on much of rural Afghanistan. Because there are few Afghans willing and competent to backfill behind US or coalition forces when they are able to push insurgents out of an area, governance has been denied in much of Pushtun rural Afghanistan even by what remains an unpopular insurgency.

Because Afghan institutions are weak, personal leadership in Afghanistan is critical to any hope of success. While the failure of leadership has contributed to this crisis inside Afghanistan, there are, in actuality, too many leaders and too little authority available to create effective governance. Competition for power, legitimacy, and access to patrons and foreign supporters and donors has increased and has created a more divided and factionalized Afghan political system than even during the two-party Communism under the Soviets in Kabul or the seven parties in Peshawar in the 1980s. In 2008–09, different ministries in the Kabul government and different aid programs each had "their" particular foreign sponsors. Because most of the foreign money was given directly to the recipients rather than through the Kabul government, what little impetus there was to cooperate with other Afghans evaporated, encouraging them to build relations with foreign patrons.

For most outsiders, dealing with Afghans has only resulted in extreme frustration. Even the mighty and ruthless Soviets, who had power of life and death over their clients in Kabul for a decade, found themselves repeatedly defied and thwarted in the most frustrating ways. Part of this inherent resistance to outside direction stems from traditional Afghan independence of thinking and general bloody-mindedness. Rather than thinking of a bottom line or effective or enabling decisive decision-making, Afghans consider all their actions in terms of kinship, patronage networks, and the complex society of which they are a part, which includes their relationship with Islam. However, in today's Afghanistan, few decisions are purely in Afghan hands. Foreign interests—patrons, investors, donors, or soldiers—are currently an inextricable part of the equation.

Educated Afghanistan is a small place. Everyone thinks they know every other educated Afghan or at least someone else who knows them. In the Golden Age, this led to a low level of corruption; people had to maintain their reputations (and those of their kinship groups). Besides indicating how few educated Afghans there were and currently are, it poses another problem because there is a great deal of personal "who's-who" knowledge about other Afghans within this limited group, there is also a great deal of personal distrust and unwillingness to work toward a shared common good. In Afghanistan, the near-total brain drain that took place before 2001 has only been reversed to a limited extent. A sizable number of educated Afghans have proved willing to come back to Kabul, but finding educated Afghans that are willing to do difficult jobs out in rural Afghan, whether as government administrators or teachers or doing development, is limited. "The scarcity of educated Afghans is the key limit in all fields," said Eshan Zia, Minister of Rural Rehabilitation and Development.[327] This makes short-term solutions to many problems elusive. The same Afghan political conflicts can be seen in microcosm at the local level.

Warlords and Power Brokers

Combining access to governance and to non-state sanctioned armed forces, many Afghan warlords were originally local commanders whose leadership originated from resistance against the Afghan Communists and the Soviets. When a leader has been killed or becomes too old, his son, brother, or nephew usually succeeds him, in line with the Afghan reliance on kinship ties.

Afghan attitudes toward warlords are often ambivalent. When asked what was the biggest danger to Afghanistan, only 6 percent of Afghans in 2010 polling said local commanders (compared to 64 percent saying the Taliban, 14 percent drug traffickers, and 6 percent the US).[328] In 2009 polling, only 37 percent of Afghans said they had confidence in local militias—often associated with warlords—and 54 percent said they had no confidence.[329] The term "warlord" itself—*jang salaran* in Dari—is pejorative. Yet many Afghans see value in their own particular warlords, local leaders, and power brokers. Some warlords may be unpopular, but tend to deliver for their clients without imposing harsh extraction in return (but are still willing to use violence or repression to turn back challenges to their authority).[330] To many Afghans, the anti-Soviet war of 1978–92 was the greatest event of their lives and the leadership figures that had their roots in that conflict have a strength and presumption of legitimacy that the returning exiles, technocrats, and former Communists that many in the international community find more acceptable cannot match. Many warlords had experience in putting together coalitions or using patronage that other Afghans lack. With this wartime experience, many warlords have a degree of legitimacy independent of any positions they may hold under color of the Kabul government's authority. There is no tradition of warlords in Afghanistan. They resulted from the conflicts of 1978–2001.

For example, Pushtun warlords, in order to survive post-2001, had to show Kabul and the US forces that sufficient differences existed between themselves and the Taliban. It was individuals from this group that held power under Kabul's authority after 2001. Many were repressive and provided no economic development. The tribal dimension—favoring their own group to the exclusion of others—and issues of cross-border influence from Pakistan have made Pushtun warlords generally more divisive than their non-Pushtun counterparts. When, at the insistence of the US and the international community, these warlords were transferred to other positions or marginalized and removed from power, along with the militias and the patronage networks they controlled, it actually contributed to the rise of the insurgency, rather than subverting it by removing the source of local grievances as the US thought it would. They might have removed warlords contributing to the problems of Pushtun-speaking Afghanistan. With nothing to replace them with, removal actually made the situation worse. Replacing and bypassing warlords removed a layer of leadership that could have acted to mediate the demands of the population toward Kabul.[331]

Other warlords were part of the Northern Alliance that with coalition help defeated the Taliban in 2001. In the Hazara Jat, warlords and party organizations have been part of the local governance that has led to that area being the most peaceful in Afghanistan despite the devastation caused by the Taliban.

Among Afghanistan's Uzbeks, the figure of former Communist militia leader Abdul Rashid Dostum, who brought down the pro-Soviet Najibullah regime in 1992, continued to have a strong impact on politics in 2008–10, despite a year in exile in Turkey following accusations of extensive criminal activity. He is hated by many Pushtuns, especially in the south where he fought on behalf of the Soviets and is often accused of personal aggrandizement and violence toward rivals.[332] He has been accused of causing the deaths of large numbers of Taliban prisoners, mainly Pushtuns and Pakistanis, in 2001, by keeping them confined in airless shipping containers, revenge for their massacres in Mazar-e-Sharif years earlier. He returned to Afghanistan as a pro-Karzai figure during the 2009 election campaign and has continued to work with the government, much as this has enraged foreigners, most notably US Vice

President Joseph Biden and special representative Ambassador Richard Holbrooke, immune to the charisma that has served Dostum among his Uzbek supporters.[333] The welcome given Dostum in 2009 and Karzai's looking to him, rather than more traditional Uzbek leaders, to deliver the vote in the 2009 election showed his importance both to the national leadership and the grassroots.[334]

Another Northern Alliance figure was Ismail Khan, a Dari-speaking former army officer who was the leading resistance commander in his native Herat province in the anti-Soviet conflict. Captured by the Taliban in 1996, his Iranian allies bought him out of prison and enabled him to play a major role in driving the Taliban from Herat in 2001. Restored to the governorship of Herat in 2001–04, he had strong relations with Iran. He was removed from this position at US urging in 2004 and made minister of energy in Kabul. He retains considerable support in his home area of Herat, especially among Dari-speakers, and his governorship is often looked back on with nostalgia.[335] In many ways, security has been perceived as having deteriorated in Herat since his replacement. Some 98 percent of Afghans polled in Herat in 2009 identified corruption as a problem, the highest percentage in the entire country.[336]

"Disbanding Illegal Armed Groups" (DIAG) has been the focus of international accords, including the 2005 Afghanistan Compact. To many non-Pushtuns, especially leadership figures (warlords and more benign figures alike) in the Northern Alliance, programs to disarm the militia forces associated with warlords such as the UN-supported Disarmament Demobilization and Reintegration (DDR) were aimed directly at them. To Tajiks (especially Panjsheris), Hazaras, and Uzbeks, the strong emphasis on marginalizing warlords by the US and its allies, along with the creation of a centralized Afghan state, seemed intent on curtailing the power of the warlords. In the Hazara Jat, disarmament of Shia militias was met with increased distrust of Sunni authority in general. To all these peoples, the perception was that disarmament was not indeed to remove non-government armed organizations as much as it was rather to preclude future armed resistance in case a future Pakistan-backed Pushtun force should again try to control Afghanistan. Conversely, to Pushtuns it seemed that the DDR process ensured that the Panjsheris that provided much of the leadership of the Northern Alliances' forces reserved the best jobs (and, increasingly, opportunities for corruption) for themselves.[337]

The US and the coalition are frequently criticized for "not doing enough to get rid of the warlords"; yet in many areas, there was no alternative authority. Local notables or tribal leaders were dead or stripped of legitimate clout. The warlords provided the only functional patronage networks. There was no capability to provide an alterative to them that ensured acceptable governance.

The amount of power held by these warlords became an issue after the fall of the Taliban because they were receiving governmental positions and material and financial support from Kabul or directly from the US and did not have to secure their positions by keeping their patron-client relations among the local people intact. Post-2001, many warlords—especially Pushtuns—became increasingly extractive to the local Afghans, through forced land acquisitions, bribes, toll collections, forced marriages to secure relationships, and violence toward potential rivals. Kabul support negated their need to receive consent from the local population or even specific groups of people within their "constituency." Consent, usually as part of a patron-client relationship, had continued to play an important part in Afghan internal politics in most of the country even in the dark years of the 1980s and 1990s, and now it was rapidly deteriorating. Competition between regional leaders for the support of local qawm leadership figures had then often limited crime or harsh extractive policies by warlords or would-be warlords. In most cases, if such leaders proved too extractive or unable to provide benefits for clients, their clients and the local inhabitants would find someone else who could meet their needs, either from one of the other Peshawar parties as in 1978–92 or from the other side in the civil conflicts. Now there was no check or balance like this on warlord power, yet there are few viable replacements for them either, as there had been in the past. The ability for a qawm, village, or other group to switch allegiance from an oppressive leader became much more limited if not impossible, allowing such warlords to "rule" with impunity.

Kabul has aimed to reduce warlord power by limiting their support. By 2002–04, few warlords were getting direct money from Kabul or foreign supporters. Ashraf Ghani, as finance minister, had taken a strong stand against such payments as undercutting Afghan government capability or even sovereignty, although his opponents saw him as acting to reduce competition to centralized Pushtun-dominated power in Kabul. In some areas, warlords or their supporters engaged in opium cultivation or trafficking. Others used their fighting men to secure what remained of their status, especially in key areas that cannot be ignored such as a local bazaar, a district, or a valley, or other such strategic position, like a mountain pass. By 2008–10, with their income limited and lacking outside patrons, warlords had either transitioned to being allies of the Karzai government or were increasingly absent from national-level politics.

The return of the Northern Alliance's former military leader Marshal Mohammed Qassam Fahim—who, as defense minister in 2002–04, promoted himself to field marshal to command over 2,500 generals, aiming to secure his position with what seemed the largest and most costly patronage network in Afghanistan's history—as one of Karzai's vice-presidential candidates in the 2009 election was greeted with dismay by many foreigners. But the fact that he is not seen as overpowering other Afghan leaders by his access to his old patronage-based organization shows how much these have declined since the 2003–04 period, when Fahim was highly influential in Kabul.

Many, especially returning Pushtun exiles, Kabulis and technocrats, along with their foreign or Pakistani supporters, have been critical that stronger action has not been taken to exclude the warlords from Afghan politics and life. But even had Afghanistan not been threatened by terrorism, insurgency, and narcotics, it would have taken a generation for the warlords to be replaced by state institutions as they were rebuilt. Nor does it appear that there was or is strong support among non-Pushtun warlords' clients and their ethnolinguistic groups for excluding them. Where warlords have not acted to enrich themselves or oppress the locals, they have considerable opportunity to strengthen bonds, pass on information, perform charity and redistribution of resources, and even provide security. In short, carry out the duties expected of Afghan "patrons."

Returning Exiles

While many Western observers tend to equate exiles with moderates and the pre-1978 regimes in which they flourished, this is not necessarily the case. Because many exiles did not have the bitter but instructive experience of battlefield cooperation against the Soviets, they retain their pre-1978 expectations of power in Afghanistan untouched by intervening events. Because a higher percentage of Pushtun elites was in exile than non-Pushtun elites, these expectations often include an identification of Afghan state power with Pushtuns in a way that is not necessarily a viable option any longer.

To many exiles, the men who fought and resisted were often seen not as the heroes who had battled first the Soviets and then the Taliban, but as human-rights violators. They were held responsible for the civil war of 1992–2001 and its widespread devastation, especially in Kabul. Many returning exiles looked to the international community to put them on trial and remove them forever from Afghan politics. This motivated the Afghan parliament in 2007 to pass an amnesty law preventing the state from independently prosecuting Afghans for war crimes from past conflict, to the personal benefit of many members of parliament.[338] For some former Afghan fighting men, the insult "*sag shoy*" (dog washer), coined by a former HiH commander, summed up their visceral dislike of some of the returning exiles. One veteran Afghan political observer believed "The contribution of the resistance was totally ignored" by the new government in Kabul and their foreign supporters.

The exiles ended up using their superior relationship with the US and other international donors to come out on top. Some of the "dog washers" had been just that. Other, more senior returning exiles received jobs because they offered foreign donors and allies at least the appearance of greater competence and less corruption than did their counterparts in the (predominantly non-Pushtun) Northern Alliance. However, their success has been limited to Kabul or other areas where the foreign influence is determinative. In the countryside, their foreign ties held little sway. Compounding this division is the fact that once an Afghan leaves the country, it is hard for him to re-establish himself on the local scene. Afghan expectations of legitimacy largely include that of shared experience, especially those as traumatic and violent as the conflicts of 1978–2001. It was difficult for returning exiles to re-integrate themselves. In the words of one long-time Kabul-based observer of Afghanistan, reflecting the attitude of a large portion of the population, "Afghans like to follow a winner. Winners don't run away."

Yet in a country where warfare and violence have outweighed political discourse since 1978, the expectation that the returning exiles would function effectively when thrust into a heavily armed, radicalized and polarized political system was unrealistic. Some of their foreign supporters looked to ISAF to use their good, clean, European non-American force to sustain these returning Afghans. Some returning exiles, indeed, had resumes and backgrounds that would qualify them for cabinet-level positions in just about any country. Others had fought themselves as anti-Soviet guerrillas before going into exile. By 2007–09, the returning exiles had broadened their base by reaching out to former Communists, Kabulis, and technocrats. Widespread resentment against former Communists by the former mujahideen had kept them out of cabinet-level positions in previous years. Foreign supporters pressed Karzai to bring in former Communists who had proven capable and had reputations for rectitude to important positions, including that of Minister of the Interior and Minister of Counter Narcotics. Others now hold command positions in the ANA and ANP. Many of those brought in to the government in this way were Pushtuns, leading many non-Pushtuns to see this as a move by the Karzai government to strengthen its ethnolinguistic constituency.

Land and Water

Conflicts over land and water rights underlie a lot of Afghanistan's internal strife, including those relating to corruption and even terrorism. Arable land and water are both scarce in what is generally an infertile country, and this scarcity adds to their value as a source of income and status in an overwhelmingly agrarian society. This is perhaps the main area where the inability of the Kabul government to put an effective civil system in place has the most direct impact on rural Afghanistan and thus their hold on power throughout the provinces. In the absence of a state system to allocate water resources and adjudicate land titles, a mixture of traditional law and force has tended to resolve disputes, delegitimizing Kabul even further and giving insurgents and warlords a hold on power that they would not otherwise have.

Traditional law approaches tend to stress the use of *shuras* or *jirgas*. The *hoqooq*, a local traditional dispute-resolution body, made up of experts on land tenure and ownership, is still used in some districts. Mediation by *sayids* is also used. In some areas, the state judicial system has been able to supplant these traditional mechanisms. In insurgent-controlled areas, these have been replaced by rough justice under a veneer of Sharia law, and those who take in traditional dispute resolution are frequently murdered. Much of what is called warlord oppression is their ability to resolve disputes over water and property in favor of themselves or those close to them. Many of these conflicts turn violent, a fact often lost in the larger concern about the insurgency, narcotics, and crime. It is estimated that several hundred Afghans a year are killed in land and water–related disputes.[339] A non-corrupt local government or court system was absent in the sites of many of these disputes.

Allegiances and orientations are frequently determined, at a local level, by Kabul's willingness to favor one mode of agriculture over another. In the 1970s and 1980s, the conflict between Pushtu-speaking Kuchi nomadic herdsmen and Uzbek or Hazara sedentary pastoralists was based on competition between different agricultural practices; Pushtun-dominated governmental authority looked away as cattle were driven over standing crops. Dostum's original Uzbek militia, formed in the 1980s, was intended to halt this practice. In the 1980s, some of Soviet-occupied Kabul's strongest rural allies were not committed Communists but those who depended on the central government to allow them to hold on to irrigated land against the claims of their neighbors, especially in areas such as those around Khost and in Kandahar province's Maiwand district. It is not surprising that in 2001 the Taliban's strongest supporter in the south, Mullah Abdul Wahid in the Baghran district of Helmand province, was an "upstream" leader, who had been able to keep scarce water for local use due to his personal relations with the Taliban. Since then, he has skillfully kept on good relations with both Kabul and the insurgents, which has enabled him to remain politically important in Helmand through his ability to affect the water supply.[340]

Some of the water and land–use conflicts cross international and eth-nolinguistic borders. The years of drought pre-2001 led to the rise of opium cultivation, which requires little rainfall. For example, the Wazirs, with close links to Pakistan's transport mafia and timber mafia (both Pushtun-dominated), have been clear-cutting vast areas of Paktika and Paktia provinces since the mid-1980s. This has put them into direct con-flict with the local Kharoshti Pushtuns from different tribes. Elsewhere, like the Kunar valley, where the Kabul government's ban on timber exports had finally stuck by 2009, unemployed low-level timber mafia members found an alternative source of income as foot soldiers for HiH and proved formidable enemies to US Army units.[341]

Gender

The nature of Afghan culture puts great significance on gender relation-ships. Control of paternity is vital to a patrilineal, patrimonial society in which lineage and blood ties remain key determinants of political ori-entation and alliances. Marriage in Afghanistan tends to be arranged, a political and economic alliance between two lineages. The companionate marriages of the West are viewed with hostility by some Afghans across the political and social spectrums as an implicit threat to Afghan and Islamic ways. Reflecting the widespread use of Islamic and traditional Afghan themes to mobilize and radicalize Afghans in the conflicts of 1978–2001 and the pre-2001 Taliban regime's making the enforced absence of women from the public sphere a core value, control of female life in general and sexuality in particular is often emphasized to the point of obsession. A man who cannot control "his" women is often seen as not much of a man, or, worse still, a man without honor, as it is also a way of controlling his lineage and holding on to power, at least domesti-cally. Control is often seen as requiring withholding women from outside employment, education, or contact with non-family members.

Just as Afghanistan, though now defined by conflict, traditionally saw more cooperation than bloodshed, the worst elements of gender-related oppression also stem from the societal dislocation and polarization stemming from decades of warfare. The irony is that an insurgency that claims to be motivated by Islamic requirements to safeguard the honor of women (and the men that must protect them) from the threat inherent in an infidel foreign presence has helped create an Afghanistan where widows beg, farmers sell their daughters to opium traffickers to compensate for falling income, and forced marriage or rape is used to create power relationships for the benefit of warlords, terrorists, insurgents, and narcotics traffickers alike. None of this was part of the old Afghanistan. Such gender oppression is still limited in scope and application. But the results of this and other conflicts—the insurgency and those about religion and modernization—have the potential to make life much worse for the future of Afghan women. Conversely, the potential to make life better, though real, remains more limited and incremental.

In 2003, Afghanistan signed the Convention of the Elimination of All Forms of Discrimination Against Women without reservations, unlike most other countries that base their personal status laws on Sharia. Article 7 of the 2004 Afghan constitution specifically identified Afghanistan as being required to abide by the UN Charter and the Universal Declaration of Human Rights as well as treaties and conventions. Afghanistan has a Ministry of Women's Affairs (MoWA) and has ensured that governmental development plans, including the Afghan National Development Strategy (ANDS), have emphasized gender mainstreaming. What is significant is the disconnect between the policies implicit in these actions and the political realities of an Afghanistan defined by its conflicts.

To many Afghans, the need for the patriarchal head-of-family to keep control over his family's honor mandates a rigid separation of the private from the public. The position of women in Afghanistan life and society does not reflect any particular Afghan or Islamic pathology but is comparable to that of other poor and underdeveloped countries. Indeed, Afghanistan has traditionally proven resistant to some of the more severe gender-related practices that resulted in oppressive outcomes in the sub-continent or elsewhere in the Islamic world. Yet this area remains a source of conflict. Any action by outsiders that has the potential to affect, let alone benefit, Afghan women is transformed by rumors and the Taliban culture to be an assault on honor and an attempt to defeat Islam and the Afghan patrilineal society. Any veteran aid worker in Afghanistan or the refugee camps in Pakistan can tell of programs or activities intended to benefit Afghan women, even those teaching basic sanitation or handicrafts, that resulted in foreigners being accused of enabling immoral behavior and causing men to lose control of their family and lineage, shaming their kin.

Gender emerged as a source of tension in Afghanistan starting with the changes in the 1960s and 1970s. This included acid-throwing attacks against Afghan women in Kabul dressed in Western clothing. Its importance has been fueled by failed attempts first by the Communists and then Afghan Taliban to use state power to transform gender relationships in order to bring their own version of the future. This meant "liberation" from the norms of Afghan and Islamic culture for the Communists and a withdrawal from the public sphere for the Taliban. These were the only Afghan governments to attempt to dictate the terms of gender relationships within the family. The Communists (especially the Khalqis of 1978–79) and the Taliban, despite their ideological differences, were both totalitarians, demanding state involvement in personal life; both parties "told us how we must treat our women," in a common Afghan characterization. The Soviets tried to use the women of urban Afghanistan as a surrogate proletariat to strengthen their political consolidation in the 1980s, who would receive resources (jobs, money, access to education, cheap food) in return for political loyalty. This policy helped bring stability to urban centers, but could not turn around the widespread hatred of the Soviet presence. Most Kabul governments throughout history have treated the division between public and private as a firewall and do not aim to interfere with domestic life. Actions seen as interfering led to widespread resistance to Communist and Taliban rule.

The harshest of the pre-2001 Afghan Taliban's impacts on gender relationships were, in practice, reserved for areas they saw as a threat to their control, especially Kabul and the Hazara Jat. Educated Afghan women—indeed, most of the educated elites of any ethnicity—were effectively totally marginalized, losing jobs and being excluded from economic or social activity, helping the Taliban consolidate their hold. The Taliban was less repressive in their heartland of southern

Afghanistan. Some women in Kandahar kept their jobs. In rural Pushtun areas, women's labor, especially the drawing of water and the gathering of firewood, continued much as before without the all-enveloping burqa (the one-piece covering with a view slit) that was enforced on urban Afghan women. This was because the Taliban did not view them, or their kin, as a threat to their hegemony.

Similar contradictions were also apparent in the Taliban's harsh policies affecting male homosexuals (the Taliban apparently did not believe in female homosexuality). The Taliban made a point of nominally turning against the traditional Afghan attitudes of toleration and willful ignorance by imposing harsh, even fatal punishments on a few individuals who were known homosexuals. But, in reality, the Taliban widely used sexual degradation and relations with boys as a tool of establishing power. In Kabul, the Hazara Jat, and elsewhere, this included taking custody of boys from the local population and sexually abusing them. The use of boys, especially singers and dancers, as catamites by powerful men, *bacha bazi* (play by boys), was part of the Afghan traditions the Taliban rhetorically opposed. Throughout Afghanistan, girls were pressed into forced marriages, often as second or third wives, with Taliban supporters that would otherwise have not had the resources or status to marry. Where this and other examples of the pre-2001 Taliban's failure to achieve the rectitude they claimed became known, even to their supporters it was a powerful blow to their legitimacy. That the Taliban used sex as a tool of political power and degradation of opponents has led to non-Taliban and anti-Taliban Afghans adopting these tactics in retribution, and it remains widespread.[342]

It was apparent long before Dr. Freud ventured into political philosophy that frustrated manhood could find expression in political and social action, seldom for the better. Gender issues are used to rally the insurgency as shorthand for the insurgent's claim to defend Afghanistan's culture and religion from destruction by Western intervention. "Foreign influence makes our women immoral and destroys our honor" has been a widespread rallying cry, reinforced by such Western counter-insurgency tactics as house searches. Other Western imported practices are presented as being as much an attack on Afghan and Islamic ways as those brought by the Communists. This reflects the insurgents' maximalist approach to Islamist practice, especially toward those they believe are lax in their Islamic devotion. If Islam requires modest dress in women, then it is better still to prescribe an all-encompassing dress like the burqa and insist on women's exclusion from the public sphere, versus any other previously accepted social practice.

Since 2001, there has been much that seems to threaten Afghanistan's honor in the eyes of conservative Afghans, not just the insurgents. The "gender issue" is essentially the final straw, but still part of an amalgam of cultural conflicts. The arrival of television opened a new front in Afghanistan's cultural conflicts that is still ongoing, while the arrival of large numbers of foreigners in Kabul—imagined by many Afghans to be drinking and fornicating behind their compound walls—made their living apart from, and their often imperious and disrespectful attitude toward, Afghans they claimed to be helping even less tolerable. Many foreigners involved in Afghanistan perceived their mission in terms of moral uplift and insisted that Afghanistan have the benefits of advances in gender equality and suffrage that had only come about in their own countries in the past generation, and this after a century of male and female literacy and democratic institution-building. The Afghans often respond with a lack of comprehension, failing to see what they mean in terms of Afghan life or Islam. In some ways, it is like imposing post-modern views of women on the Europe of previous centuries, yet in other ways the Afghans have been receptive to these outside influences when presented to them as being congruent with their core values.

The Afghan and Pakistani insurgents share a devotion to maintaining and expanding gender-defined boundaries to relationship, power and behavior. These are believed, in most cases, to be ordained, inviolate, and compulsory upon all Muslims. As with much else in the Islamic practices embraced by the insurgents, these beliefs represent Pushtun folkways for which Islamic legitimacy is claimed and held. In 2008–10, insurgents in both Afghanistan and Pakistan were reported to be targeting clinics that provide contraceptives.[343] Imposing dress restrictions, separate education, and ultimately exclusion of women from the public sector is increasingly being seen as a goal of radical parties through Pakistan, including areas remote from the insurgency.[344] The more the West is seen as being the source of gender equality, the harder these groups will push for repression.

The fact that serious Islamic theologians around the world would not support these actions does not make the insurgents' approach to gender relationships any less powerful or compelling to their followers. Gender relations have been at the heart of the narrative Al Qaeda, the Taliban, and other insurgent groups produce in order to mobilize their followers and legitimize their actions against the West and elected governments in Muslim countries. The 1990s saw Western press reports of demands by ulema associated with the Taliban in Kabul that pop-culture figures like Michael Jackson and Kate Winslet be turned over to them for harsh punishment for crooning songs or appearing in films that extolled romantic love rather than arranged marriage. These were only precursors to the widespread theme of today that the infidel outside world is seeking to destroy Islam, starting with Afghanistan and the Pushtuns, by attacking their culture through an intrusive foreign presence that specifically is focusing on women, and therefore kinship, lineage, and the core of their society. More than the West's celebrity culture and the Vortex's Taliban culture misunderstanding each other, the whole premise of romantic love, or even "choice" on the part of the participants, calls into question the validity of the potential marriages the Taliban's clients might seek to arrange for their children or enjoy themselves, especially if they had gained status through their service to the cause and were cementing this with familial ties via an arranged marriage. Romantic love, as practiced in the West, has no place or meaning in the insurgents' world, however much individual insurgents may love their wives and children.

Harder to identify, but no less significant, a cause to the gender issue in Afghanistan are psychosexual fears and insecurity. Islamic ideology, expressed by Al Qaeda-generated propaganda and used post-2001 by groups such as both the Afghan and Pakistani Taliban, has been able to make use of the insecurity in the face of what is seen as a world dominated by infidel culture that does not respect or understand the importance of honor valued in patrilineal Pushtun societies. With satellite television, radio, cassettes, and the DVD providing increased familiarity with—

but not increased understanding of—an outside culture that is at once attractive and existentially threatening: even those without sophisticated psychological insights can still use this disconnect and fear to extract support. If you do not take arms to fight the foreigners in Kabul, your women may become like those in the bootleg Bollywood movies the Taliban have taken such pleasure in burning. Or even worse, your women might become like those you imagine exist in the infidel world, which would render it impossible to live as a Muslim and as a man of honor and so bring shame to your kin. "The most common Pushtun feeling is that there is a war on our culture," is the sentiment according to Massoud Kharokhail of the Kabul-based Tribal Liaison Office, which is a developmental NGO. Afghans of other ethnicities are more likely to agree with these Pushtuns than elites of their own groups. While no group is as conservative as rural Pushtuns, Afghan cultural conservatism cuts across ethnolinguistic divisions. They share an emphasis on Islam and kinship, even if they lack the Pushtuns' tribal divisions.

Westerners have tended to view the complexities of Afghan gender relationships in a way that reflects the gender-consciousness of their own societies. This led to the 2009 Shia personal status law, signed by President Karzai on 27 July only after international protests over restrictive provisions, including those that limited married women's rights to travel without a spouse's consent and attempted to give the force of law to a husband's sexual access.[345] The Afghans considered that providing the Shia with their own personal status law rather than one based under Sunni Hanafi-based jurisprudence was a multicultural and good thing. While many of the more offensive provisions were removed, the incident showed Karzai as submitting to outsiders in the eyes of conservative Afghans; and it alienated foreign donors, who considered allowing Afghan politics to stand in the way of achieving international human-rights standards unacceptable. But this incident revealed more than the disconnect in the worldviews between the Afghans that sit in the parliament and the Westerners that advocate human rights in Afghanistan. Westerners have no problem with using the state's rule of law to regulate gender relations, whereas to many Afghans this is not an inherently obvious solution. Murder is normally not a crime but a tort under Pakistan's FCR or the customary law of Afghanistan's Pushtuns (under Pushtunwali). This means that if someone is killed, many Afghans do not want the state to come in and try and punish the murderer: they want the murderer's kin to make them whole for the loss of a family member by turning over as compensation valuables such as money, weapons, livestock, or, in some cases, unmarried women to become the wives of aggrieved family members. This is a traditional justice mechanism and, as such, is opposed by the Taliban, who insist that their brand of state justice, using Sharia law, must prevail. The Taliban banned the exchange of women between kinship groups to settle feuds and blood debts, claiming it has no status under Sharia law.

Westerners see the injustice, frustration, sheer waste of human potential, and barriers to development inherent in much of Afghanistan's gender relations. Yet to change these social constructs, there is a risk that even the most well-intentioned of efforts, however legitimate according to international norms (and Afghans do want to be recognized as a country like any other) and Islamic theology, can still lead to widespread opposition because of how it is implemented. Afghanistan is a conservative country, and the harder change is pushed, the more the Afghans will either cling to tradition or, more often, grasp at change but in a way that they believe makes them more Islamic. Gender can be an issue where, in order to maintain the proper relationships they see as required by religion, a particular code of honor or to avoid shaming their kin, Afghans will feel compelled to make common cause with the insurgents, largely because of the alternative approach to gender relations they represent.

Despite this, both the Kabul government and the international community committed to mainstreaming gender issues. But in reality, the Ministry of Woman's Affairs has often proved to be the only political advocate for women, and its relation with parliament, which often tends to cut its funding, has often limited its effectiveness. To compound this, the deteriorating security situation in Kabul in recent years made even fewer Afghan women willing to do anything that would make them vulnerable. The Taliban view on the appropriate role of women—that they need to be absent from the public sphere—is shared by many who oppose the Taliban (Karzai's wife, though a medical doctor, does not appear in public). Despite the government's accession to international agreements, the set-aside representation for women at multiple levels of government, and the foreign-supported gender-mainstreaming policies, women's role in the public sphere remains limited and contested, not only politically but by threats of intimidation and violence. According to one educated Afghan woman in Kabul in 2008, "Women will be attacked if we go too fast, not by the Taliban but by our own groups."

Kinship is all-important. An American woman with many years of experience in Afghanistan said "Kinship precludes choice." This collectivist orientation applies to politics as well as life; in 2009, 59 percent of the Afghans polled agreed with the statement that a person should vote how his or her community votes, not according to individual preference.[346] Afghan women can rely on few other links outside of kinship. This reduces options for women through fear of alienating valued male relatives. What a woman wears outside the family compound, the scarf-like chador or the enveloping burqa, is seen as a reflection on the entire family. There is a reason why the word *purdah* comes from veil or curtain: a veil not only hides women, it literally saves face (of her kin). Many of Afghanistan's powerful and influential women are so because they have access, through kinship ties, to resources and networks.

Attitudes on gender-based power cut across political, religious, and cultural lines. Yet it remains in Afghanistan that many of the "good guys"—especially but not limited to Pushtuns—remain highly conservative in their views on the place of women in society. What differentiates these attitudes from those of the Taliban is that the pre-2001 Afghan Taliban used state power to enforce them. This hurt their legitimacy and support even among conservative Pushtuns. Having the religious police beat women in Kabul with car radio aerials for dress-code violations was something deeply alien to the Afghan conscience. It was one of the many blows to the old Afghanistan from which it has not recovered.

Elites that do not object to women's rights on Islamic grounds may subordinate these concerns to the reality of Afghan politics. In the future, the desire to bring at least some Afghan insurgents into the political process may be difficult to reconcile with their insistence that religion indicates women be kept remote from the public sector. Similarly, neither embracing modernization nor opposing political Islam will necessarily safeguard women's rights. Some religious Muslims, secular Muslims, and anti-religious Khalqis alike have considered it justified and even righteous to kill a daughter who would disregard an arranged marriage and elope, while others within these same socio-religious groups would treat the same woman with compassion or even support. But it takes only a vanguard of those willing to attack girl high school students or burn clinics where women are treated by healthcare workers to prevent education or healthcare from reaching many Afghan women.

Gender issues have been highlighted by Western popular culture more than any other subject in Afghanistan, in novels, memoirs, and motion pictures dealing with Afghanistan. Despite the media access accorded to individual Afghan female exiles and groups such as the Revolutionary Afghan Women's Association (RAWA), Afghanistan's women do not largely perceive themselves as an oppressed group looking for outside aid. Even though many outsiders still insist that the reluctance of many women to accept aid is really a symptom of oppression, this insistence will not change the fact that painting women as the social group in greatest need will incur great hostility from the majority of Afghans and will not solve the problems that are actually tearing the nation apart.

Not surprisingly, in a country of great economic underdevelopment and little income, polling suggests that security, employment at above subsistence level, and education are the primary concerns of women in Afghanistan and that men's concerns are similar, with women being concerned about their rights.[347] Women's networks, some operating clandestinely, that were established under the Taliban largely aimed at achieving these goals when state power blocked them pre-2001. Women's progress is reflected by their inclusion in those areas where life has been made better for all Afghans, especially education (expanding girls' schools) and development of the health system (although infant and maternal mortality rates in rural Afghanistan still remain among the world's highest). To succeed in these areas means that social and economic progress is being achieved across the board, because to have better schools and healthcare means there is security as well as resources available. The widespread availability of cell phones has meant that relationships between women and their access to outside information can no longer be effectively controlled by husbands or a father (which leads to a view that the cell phone can be a tool of immorality in women's hands).[348] Institutions where women can participate outside of kinship and patronage networks, such as government employment, NGOs, and political parties remain, however, relatively beyond their reach. In the words of one educated Afghan woman in 2008, "We need to fight for things. But it is we who need to decide what it is we will fight for."

Security, jobs, and education at basic levels are still the aspirations of many Afghan women. None of this means that there are not powerful or influential women in Afghanistan. They have included a few women who have been cabinet ministers or provincial governors, and more are found in parliament, in councils, government ministries, Afghan or foreign NGOs, or working with those that they have access to, which includes Afghan leaders (to whom they may be related by kinship) or Western journalists or aid workers. Afghan women, facing a difficult struggle, participate in existing Afghan patronage networks more often than they participate in support systems formed by outside foreign supporters. This is why many women participating in CDCs are those with patronage or familial ties to their male counterparts, rather than with the goal of representing women's rights as a specific group. Kinship and patronage can trump gender in Afghanistan. But women can also access kinship and patronage and use them as tools. Those who instead access foreign supporters can use that to influence Afghanistan through that source. The Afghan Taliban targets all these sources, not only because they believe that female participation in the public sector is religiously unsupportable, but because, as totalitarians, they oppose all networks and loyalties they do not control.

It is difficult to generalize about Afghan attitudes to gender. In many ways, these are like ethnic and linguistic divisions, multiple and flexible. That "modest dress" and a black or white headscarf are required is a widespread belief; most everything else is negotiable. In some areas, such as support for girls' education, its legitimacy has largely been accepted by the majority of Afghans, although many conservatives and Taliban

supporters remain opposed.[349] Female representatives in parliament and
CDCs often appear to have been as accepted as Afghan female doctors in
medicine, even among conservative rural Pushtuns. Afghanistan's gender-
specific set-asides—mandating a greater level of female participation in
representational politics than has been achieved in the West (except,
perhaps, Norway)—have not alleviated either the conservative's resistance
to change in gender relationships nor the insurgent's ability to use it as a
rallying cry of Islam and women's honor in danger. Yet the use of gender
set-asides is not always popular. In 2009 polling, 50 percent of the men
and 45 percent of the women polled opposed women representing them
at the national or provincial level.[350] Similarly, while Afghans tend to be
aware of the Ministry of Women's Affairs, its function often appears
opaque to them, outside of providing patronage in Kabul by allocating
resources received from foreign donors.

Gender relationships vary greatly between regions. The Hazaras,
though in many ways the poorest and least developed of Afghanistan's
ethnic groups and still socially conservative, demonstrated by the controversy in the west over the 2009 Shia law affecting domestic relations
that passed the Afghan parliament, have been the most accepting of
women in the public sector. In 2008–10, the Hazara-majority Bamiyan
province had Afghanistan's only female governor and had active female
participation in provincial government and councils. The predominantly
Hazara Hezb-e-Wahdat party has seats reserved for women in its central
council and a committee for women's issues. The Hazaras' experience is
a beacon for what could potentially be a reality for much of Afghanistan. Societal attitudes are often more important than modernization or
development.

Women's political participation is still part of a male-centric system.
When a female member of parliament, Malalai Joya, gave a speech in May
2007 attacking many of the male members as no better than beasts and
accusing many that had fought the Soviets and Taliban as war criminals,
she gained support abroad but ended up being suspended from the parliament and deterring potential allies for women's issues among the male
majority.[351] Women elected for set-aside seats in parliament and provincial councils (about ten percent of the 3,400 candidates running in 2009

were women) have tended to be those with links to the most significant patronage networks. They are as much a part of the system as they would otherwise be without Western involvement. This is why, in Afghanistan, gender issues cannot be presented as a woman-friendly center against a backward periphery. Women do better among the "backward" Hazaras or where they can join patronage networks due to local, kinship, or political links. Groups such as RAWA, whose patronage links are not with other Afghans but with the foreign groups that provide funding, have little impact inside Afghanistan. This is not surprising. Afghan institutions today tend to be weak, especially those that are amenable to incorporating women while cutting across ethnolinguistic divisions, political allegiance, and essentially a highly entrenched cultural norm in doing so. In a country where even political radicals can be social conservatives, the Western view of women's rights literally is hard to translate into Afghan concepts. Acceptance of girls' education and female healthcare suggests that most of the conservative grassroots can be brought along with such policies if they see it as leading to a collective benefit. The same applies to women working outside the family. While more men than women remain opposed to this, the economic necessity is often irrefutable. In rural Afghanistan, without women's work, no one eats.

Outsiders

In an Afghanistan context, "outsider" does not simply apply to foreigners. In many Pushtun areas, anyone from outside the immediate family, clan, or tribe is a potential "outsider." Afghan hospitality and xenophobia exist in parallel; both are strong forces that have the potential to enact change, for better or worse.

Muslims are often considered outsiders in Afghanistan. Afghans often consider that non-Afghans are not "proper" Muslims. Non-Pushtun Pakistanis and Arabs are often unpopular and resented. Many of these showed scant respect for Afghan customs and religious practices. The influence Al Qaeda had over the pre-2001 Taliban undercut their support even among Pushtuns, one of the reason few Afghans would fight for them.

For the insurgents to be successful, they need to avoid the perception that they are outsiders, coming from Pakistan or from elsewhere in

Afghanistan. They have also effectively used the Al Qaeda-generated narrative that the foreign presence in Afghanistan is not to help Afghans but is part of the global war against Islam. Resentment of foreigners has only increased in Afghanistan since 2001. In 2008–09, polling showed that for the first time more Afghans had a negative view of foreigners than a positive one, although a majority of Afghans still saw the foreign presence as a way of assuring that the country will not again be plunged into a more-intense war. Afghans holding a favorable view of the US declined from 83 percent in 2005 to 43 percent in 2010, while those holding an unfavorable view increased from 14 percent to 50 percent.[352] While the foreign presence is becoming less popular than it was, Afghans still recognize that without it, their economic and security situation would be even more dire. In 2009, some 70 percent of Afghans polled still saw the country as needing foreign support (not the same thing as *wanting* foreign support).[353]

Demographics

Afghanistan's demographics pose both short- and long-term obstacles to development and reconstruction.[354] In 2008–10, Afghanistan was estimated to have some 40–55 percent unemployment and that more than half the population was living below the poverty line. Finding meaningful jobs in Afghanistan for the estimated 66–80 percent of the population that is rural or depends on the agricultural sector remains a challenge. Polling in 2009 showed that Afghans identified the lack of jobs as what Afghans see as the most important problem facing their country and the cause of instability.[355]

Unemployment reflects demographic as well as economic factors. There is a high rate of Afghan population growth, starting in the refugee camps in Pakistan during the 1980s and continuing to the present. This growth has created a lop-sided age spread; the "youth bulge" is highly pronounced in Afghanistan. In the words of GEN David Petraeus, "a huge youth population faces a situation where there are inadequate opportunities."[356]

Many Afghans today grew up under wartime conditions or in the refugee camps with no education, no skills, and no prospects for an independent future. These Afghans often had no chance to learn traditional Afghan community standards. Additionally, the "brain drain" from Afghanistan in this period was extensive. The exile and limited return rate of the educated professional and intellectual classes removed the social constituency required for a secular state.

Post-2001, the rate of population growth continued to increase. Afghanistan is one of the few Asian countries where this has been the case, because it has not shared much of the increase in quality of life seen in other countries. The annual rate of growth is 2.629 percent, according to a 2009 estimate. The average Afghan woman is likely to have five or more children in her lifetime, reflecting prevalence of patriarchal societal attitudes (the number of sons is all-important both for status and as a labor force) and the lack of educational or economic opportunities. Improvements in access to basic health care mean that more of these children will survive infancy.

Even the successes of development created additional demographic challenges. Educational opportunities have increased. By 2008–10, there were some seven million Afghan children in primary school, which means that, in a few years, one million Afghans a year will graduate from the school system with limited prospects for jobs or entry into vocational or higher education.

The Afghan youth demographic influences many of Afghanistan's current problems, including filling the ranks of insurgents and narcotics traffickers for lack of alternative direction and employment. The youth bulge has been touched by globalization, reflected in their embrace of cell phones throughout Afghanistan and the popularity of computer and English-language courses in Kabul. Yet what brought stability to pre-1978 Afghanistan—legitimate and effective tribal or local authorities and traditional Islamic practices—is likely to be history without relevance to the young. While to an older generation of Afghans of all ethnicities and classes there was a reflexive nostalgia for the Golden Age, the young know it not. They have no framework through which to imagine a prosperous Afghanistan, no shared vision to fight or work toward. A young population like that of Afghanistan is likely to be less prone to stability and more susceptible to revolution or violence.[357] Despite high rates of economic growth in recent years, the combination of the youth bulge and high unemployment means that many young men are unlikely to earn enough money to marry in the traditional Afghan way except through taking part in Afghanistan's conflicts, either for the government or the insurgents and narcotics traffickers. They are thus unlikely to have a personal stake in peace and stability.

The political counselor at the Afghanistan embassy in Washington, Mohammed Ashraf Hadiri, set out the importance of this youth bulge: "The voting age is 18, and if you recall from the 2004 presidential elections, there were 10.5 million eligible voters, 80 percent of whom turned out to cast their votes. By the following year for the parliamentary elections, the number of eligible voters at 18 years of age rose to 12.5 million. So, if we add two million eligible voters to the electorate each year since 2005, we will have at least another five million young voters. This means that the majority of the electorate in 2009 and 2010 will be between 18 and 40 years of age."[358]

Any approach aimed at winning over the youth runs the risk of alienating those of the older generation currently in power. The current violence will also have a direct impact on the future; the attacks that target schools throughout the south and east mean that rural Pushtuns are less likely to be educated, continuing the downward spiral of uneducated young Pushtun men, who are susceptible to insurgent recruitment. "We need to win the insurgency by offering new things to the young men who fight," said BG Richard Blanchette, ISAF spokesman in 2008.[359] The steady flow of new recruits will have to be stemmed, not just for the short-term goal of slowing insurgent replacements but for the long-term future of Afghanistan.

Looking for Afghan Solutions

In 2001, Afghanistan was a nation desperate for a better future. Today, only desperation remains. The Afghans wanted to be part of the solution, but through a series of failures by Afghanistan's political class, aid donors, and coalition partners, this did not happen, and now the future is not of their own making, much to everyone's detriment. "The gap between the people and government of Afghanistan is getting bigger," said Dr. George Varughese, former director of the Asia Foundation in Kabul.[360] The policies by the Afghan government and US alike have not slowed the growth of this gap. It often seems that any action whatsoever will have the potential to only widen it more.

In a conservative, Islamic country where authority depends on legitimacy in Islamic and national terms, governance has been undercut by corruption as much as incapacity to govern. Too many of the Afghan political actors "forgot" that stealing was wrong. Donors refused to provide aid where it was most needed and met their objectives by spending their resources in such a way that only a fraction of every dollar pledged actually made it into the hands of Afghans. Only in 2009–10 were these issues really first addressed. Afghanistan never achieve a functional private sector economy, without which peace and stability are unlikely, but the threat of state failure, division, and civil war is all too likely without reform.

The story of the military and developmental policies since 2001 has been one of missed opportunities. Years of failing to perceive emerging threats—whether from Pakistan or corruption and narcotics money—meant that the US and the coalition supporters were acting reactively.

Decision-makers, in Washington, London, Brussels, and elsewhere, insisted that the hard Afghan realities of conflict and corruption reported to them by soldiers, diplomats, or aid workers not be allowed to interfere with their preferred agenda. It takes a long time for sophisticated institutions to learn, identify changes, secure needed funding, implement changes, and then put in place adaptive processes. All the while, an entirely new group of crises have emerged. Then everyone rotates out from Afghanistan, tour of duty expired, and the process begins again. Even the US Army—an organization that has made a point of being open to learning and adaptation—found that at the sharp end, each new relief brought a new battalion trained with outdated tactics and led by a new lieutenant colonel eager to make his reputation in combat, and the cycle began again with too little progress.

There is great concern in Afghanistan that since the current government and ANA arrived with US and coalition forces, it will depart with them as well, starting with the reduction in US force levels in

2011 President Obama announced in his 1 December 2009 speech. The Afghans—government and electorate alike—are as conscious of their current weakness and limitations as they are proud of their achievements. In any event, the extent to which the long-term future of Afghanistan can be put in Afghan hands, for fighting at first and then for governance, then outside commitments will finally have a chance of being meaningful and the government and organizations built in Afghanistan since 2001 may actually prove enduring.

"Afghanize—let Afghans lead" is the recommendation of Jim Drummond, South Asia Division Director of the UK's DfID.[361] "Afghanize and the incentive to oppose the US will die out," said Saleh Registani, Member of Parliament from Panjshir province.[362] Change—even if initiated from outside—can be accepted if approached in this manner. "We're not out to create New Zealand. We will use the local structures, appropriate for Afghanistan's history, culture, and background," said GEN David Petraeus. The US and its coalition partners have amassed a generally poor track record in picking Afghan winners. Afghan political and social forces—or even institutions—have the potential to be better at addressing these issues than outsiders that have tended to both manipulate and be manipulated by competing Afghan groups. Yet there have been few examples of where Afghan approaches have been given the chance to succeed. Doing things the Afghan way means finding a place for traditional justice, traditional and tribal decision-making and justice, and armed groups outside the ANA and ANP. The current government limits the power of local leaders in the provinces, who may lack education but are accepted by the locals and have access to local patronage networks. Their clout lies in traditional authority. Changes that may contribute to enhancing the legitimacy of Afghan democracy would include amending some of the centralization in the current Afghan constitution. Elected provincial governors would still be limited if they lacked an independent taxing authority. Real political parties could add to stability. Ways of working with traditional authority and judicial systems until the state systems are viable need to be identified and implemented.

Yet there is no agreement as to what the Afghan solution should be. To many Pushtuns, it requires that their ethnolinguistic group retain state power despite their tribal divisions and Pakistani influence; to non-Pushtuns, this is unacceptable and no way to repair Afghanistan or enter modernity. An Afghan solution may not be one outside supporters are willing to live with. Negotiations with Taliban figures in 2008–10 made it seem to many that Kabul was being asked by the Pakistanis and Saudis who acted as interlocutors to negotiate away issues such as its commitment to a multiethnic democracy and women's rights. More significantly, it was seen by non-Pushtuns as an ethnic Pushtun power grab to be resisted and a backward step toward conflict.

There are also real limitations as to what an Afghan solution can realistically provide, especially in the absence of US and coalition support. The Afghans cannot solve all the conflicts in Afghanistan, because they are not all of their own making. Al Qaeda's strategy is to use Afghanistan as one of many fronts in a conflict to win the support of the world's Muslims, one of these looming issues that has worldwide implications. Pakistani strife is being fought out in Afghanistan, demonstrated by the series of ceasefire agreements with insurgents that encouraged them to take political and cultural violence over the Durand Line to Afghanistan. The Afghan insurgency reflects issues originating in both Afghanistan and Pakistan. Narcotics and their suppression have their origins in the demand for illicit drugs in distant wealthy countries.

Making Governance Work

The government in Kabul still has a degree of residual legitimacy, but the hope and trust that many Afghans had in it in 2001 have eroded, wasting the good feelings, the spirit of optimism, and the political momentum over years that were instead dominated by corruption, incompetence, and violence. Until they see tangible results in their day-to-day lives, Afghans will not buy in to change and will resist taking responsibility for it. The good work that has been accomplished has largely been the result of change the Afghans did buy into. By 2009, Kabul had more reliable power and there were 600,000 reported connections to Afghanistan's electrical power grid, a 178 percent increase since 2003. It was seen in the successful constitutional and electoral processes, improvements in areas such as communications and healthcare, or in the better-trained units of the ANA. These successes all have the potential to point the way for improvement in other areas. If the investment in training, equipping, and enabling the ANA had been repeated in other areas—the ANP, the judicial system, civil administration, government at the provincial and local level, education, even religion—Afghanistan would be in better shape today than it is. Many Afghans expected this kind of reconstruction effort.

They did not get it. The ANA has worked out better than other Afghan institutions because it is being created and mentored by the US military, which has substantial experience in training foreign military forces and lots of trainers and resources to put behind this effort in Afghanistan. There is no comparable force, in the US or elsewhere, that has the capability, resources, and numbers to create and train the other people Afghanistan needs, such as teachers and civil administrators willing to get out and live among the people to make their life better, non-corrupt judges, agricultural engineers to rebuild irrigation systems and help the farmers, or ulema more interested in preaching the faith of their fathers than radical politics.

They also have not received security. Security more than any single issue determines legitimacy; the insurgent's claim to legitimacy is that they can provide it. Rising crime in Kabul, Herat, and other areas hurts the Afghan government and the foreign presence. The dramatic rise in food and energy prices in 2008 further strained the Afghan economy. The government's legitimacy has suffered through demonstrating their inability to do anything about it.[363]

By 2008–10, the government was also seeing its legitimacy hurt by failing to get outside Kabul and interact with the population, to be seen in the act of exercising authority versus nominally delegating it to corrupt officials or ineffective ministries that have no presence outside Kabul and provincial capitals. "Is the government able to talk to the people? Many uneducated people are able to do excellent things. . . . The state is not engaging people on the ground," is how Massoud Kharokhail saw the situation in 2008.[364] Eshan Zia, Minister of Rural Rehabilitation and Development, agreed that there was a "total disconnect between state institutions and citizens of Afghanistan."[365] Again, we come back to the impossibility to instituting effective governance in a "top-down" manner in Afghanistan.

Currently, democracy, for all its failings to date in Afghanistan, may be the only alternative to renewed civil war and increased proxy involvement by the neighbors. The unpopularity of the Karzai government, the culture of corruption, the failure to provide effective governance and the widespread perception of fraud in the 2009 presidential election have all challenged democracy's appeal for Afghans. There has, however, been no perceptible groundswell of support, either among elites or the grassroots, for a non-democratic alternative, either Islamic or otherwise authoritarian. War-weary though the vast majority of Afghans are, they are unlikely to accept authoritarian rule by a ruler or a group in Kabul that is not their own, even though instability, crime, and corruption have led many Afghans to wish for a strongman. There may be no alternative to a democratic Afghanistan except a war-torn Afghanistan. No single strong figure, whether dictator or president, is likely to be able to pull Afghanistan together, due to the ethnolinguistic divisions. Looking for a new "iron *amir*" is not likely to be a success. Yet a successful Afghan democracy may not resemble those in the West.

The problem with democracy, however, is that the foreign supporters have packaged it in a way that includes much cultural baggage that Afghans may not accept or will find alien. Rapid modernization, without establishing support and getting buy-in, can destroy legitimacy in Afghanistan. The West has not aimed to present democracy in the forms that the Afghans have found it appealing, either by linking it to development and schools or by showing its Afghan roots in the institution of the *jirga* and its Islamic roots in *majlis-e-shura*. Elections, while important, are a tool for democratization, not a substitute for it.

The 2010 parliamentary elections were perceived as less corrupt than those in 2009, with access to financial resources often being decisive rather than overt fraud. The 2010 parliamentary elections raised issues not so much of widespread fraud (as did the 2009 presidential election) but the reduction of Pushtun representation due to the security situation in areas where they were a majority.

CHAPTER EIGHT

PAKISTAN'S INSURGENCY

"There is a great deal of ruin in a nation."

—Adam Smith, 1782

In recent years, effective governance in Pakistan has eluded both military and civilian governments. The current civilian government has engaged in political infighting rather than building up their credibility or addressing Pakistan's economic and security crises. Governmental and economic power remains largely in the hands of the military, elites, and bureaucracy in a system frequently described as feudal. The Pakistani military continues to view itself as the insurer of independence, distrusting civilian rule. It is willing to run the country as well as defend it. The continuing security competition with India has provided the rationale for the Pakistani military to maintain effective control over their country's national security policy, including that in Afghanistan. The military's increased entrenchment in the economy and government has led to them taking on the feudal characteristics of the civilian leadership. Different elites seek to maintain their power and hold over patronage networks with what often appears to be scant regard for the national interest or for the bulk of the population.

Pakistan's civil society, as a whole, remains weak. Institutions and practices that could enable civil society have been largely ignored by elites and underfunded throughout the history of Pakistan, resulting in state schools that do not function and taxes that are not collected. With the state school system plagued by absent unpaid teachers, Pakistanis have turned largely to religious-based education. The madrassa system increased from 900 schools in 1971 to, by 1988, 8,000 official and 25,000 unregistered madrassas, an estimated two-thirds of them connected to the Deobandi movement.[366] Only an estimated one percent of the entire population pays income tax.[367] Yet continued support for democracy still endures, despite widespread disillusionment with the current elected civilian government. A desire for the revival of civil society has been demonstrated in protests led by lawyers and young people in recent years.[368]

The Baluchistan Insurgency

The current fighting in Baluchistan has been essentially ongoing since 1973–77, and no resolution is in sight.[369] It pre-existed and is distinct from the insurgency and terrorism that have emerged elsewhere in Pakistan since the defeat of the Afghan Taliban in 2001.[370] Pakistan has long ascribed the Baluch insurgency as well as secular Pushtun and Sindhi nationalism to Indian-led actions. Indeed, the Pakistan military sees these problems primarily in terms of Indian aggression, rather than a symptom of problems at home.[371]

Conversely, it is widely believed in both Pakistan and Afghanistan that the Pakistani military has been responsible for the increased presence of the Afghan Taliban and their Pakistani allies in Baluchistan. They believe that the Pakistani military is aiming to use insurgents that it believes it could control as a counterweight to the nationalist Baluch insurgents. This sentiment led to Pakistani escalation of the Baluchistan conflict starting in 2005, while at the same time they were concluding truces with the Pushtun insurgents in the FATA that were to become the Pakistani Taliban.[372] In 2006, the Pakistani military used tactical aircraft and attack helicopters against Baluchi villages, incurring international and domestic condemnation. The ISI targeted Baluchi leadership in airstrikes that killed Nawab Akbar Shabaz Khan Bugti in August 2006. He was a distinguished elder statesman, a former governor and chief minister of Baluchistan province. His death was seen by many Baluch as a declaration of war against them by the Pakistani government, with whom there had not been peace since the 1970s. In response, the Baluch insurgents have looked to the Gulf for financial support and to Afghanistan and elsewhere in Pakistan for weapons to put together a more militant nationalist movement, though the Baluch insurgents, with their roots in a secular nationalism and their own strong tribal system, have not used their shared Sunni Islam to make common cause across ethnolinguistic lines with either the Afghan or Pakistani Pushtun insurgents, motivated largely by Islamic radicalism.

The Baluchistan insurgency has an impact far beyond that remote province and is important for the future of Pakistan. It is important because it shows what forces Pakistan, especially the military, considers an internal threat and what it believes it can control or use to its advantage, either in the security competition with India that dominates its national security concerns or in internal politics. Former US Ambassador Teresita Shaefer said at a talk in Washington: "Baluchistan is important for its internal insurgency and its impact on Afghanistan. It has a different dynamic from the NWFP: Islamabad sees Baluchi nationalism as anti-Pakistan, while the threat in the FATA is seen as simply misdirected Pushtuns who want to kill infidels."[373] The distinctions between the insurgency in Baluchistan and that being waged elsewhere in the country was clear to a retired Pakistani officer who had served with ISI: "Baluchistan was an anti-national insurgency with outside support, while what we are seeing in the FATA is the US insisting Pakistan do militarily, regardless of the cost to its national security, what the US itself cannot do, defeat the Afghan Taliban."

These two opinions highlight a major divergence in the Pakistani military worldview. Insurgents who threaten the national integrity of Pakistan, in Baluchistan since the 1970s or in Swat since mid-2009, are opposed with military force, while other terrorist and insurgent groups—Afghan and Pakistani alike—are tolerated, some to a high degree. Only in late spring 2009, as the Pakistani insurgents showed every sign of expanding their holdings after their success in Swat, did the Pakistan military decide that at least some of the Pushtun insurgents and their allies from elsewhere in Pakistan had shifted to the first category as threats against national integrity. In 2007, the army had also shown its willingness to consider some Islamic radicals in this category as well, with the storming of their Lal Masjid (Red Mosque) stronghold in Islamabad. This represented a shift in policy from the years immediately following the expulsion of the Taliban and Al Qaeda from Afghanistan, when "foreign" terrorists were the priority target.

The Rise of the Pakistani Insurgents, 2001—04

The Pushtun society in the FATA, Baluchistan, and North West Frontier Provinces had been strongly influenced by the "Taliban culture" that had appeared in Pakistan since the 1970s. Indeed, the Taliban culture has had an impact beyond the Pushtun borderlands. Taliban principles have meshed with the long-standing desire of Pakistani governments, civilian and military alike, to ally themselves with elements of Islamic practice that allow them to demonstrate piety without imperiling their control. It was the secular president Zulfiqar Ali Bhutto who banned alcohol in the 1970s. The secular General Nasrullah Babur, Benazir Bhutto's interior minister in 1994, helped create the Afghan Taliban, providing funding and weapons and coordinating their support with Pakistan's Pushtun transport mafia to open up the roads to central Asia for trade from Karachi, and convinced the Pakistani leadership that "our boys," the Afghan Taliban, could be controlled by Pakistan and its military.[374] The cosmopolitan and primarily ethnically Punjabi city of Lahore followed the widely publicized actions of the Afghan Taliban and also banned kite-flying.[375]

The current Pakistani incarnation of the Taliban and other Pushtun insurgent movements emerged in the Vortex as a result of the intermingling of radicalized Pakistani Pushtuns with the original Afghan Taliban. Once the main "circuit cable" of international Islamic terrorism was plugged in to the FATA, enough money could be brought in to change power in the region. The Pakistani insurgents are also heavily influenced by Al Qaeda and their foreign allies, possibly even more so than their Afghan counterparts. Uzbeks, Uighurs, and Chechens brought their own brand of desperation and ruthlessness after being expelled from Afghanistan. The Uzbeks alone are estimated at 1,000 strong, many of them veterans of fighting with the Afghan Taliban in that country's civil wars. Arabs in the region both manage and use the network of "safe houses" that extend throughout Pakistan, houses that provide hiding places, weapons caches, and secure planning and organizing. Kashmiri groups have trained in the border area for decades, and their members also joined forces with the different Pakistani insurgent groups. Large numbers of Punjabis and Sindhis were carrying Kalashnikovs in this new conflict. Many of these Pakistani insurgents had fought in Afghanistan or in Kashmir against India, and they had contacts with the Pakistani security services, were well-versed in guerrilla warfare, and had worked with a broad range of criminal groups. They had access to the networks established by the ISI and other Pakistani security services, as well as links to Pakistani religious groups. Many Pakistani insurgent groups have benefited from the support of Punjabi groups, such as the anti-Shia Sipah-e-Sahaba, who have been fighting in Afghanistan alongside the original Afghan Taliban since the 1990s, where together they had committed numerous atrocities against Hazaras and other Afghan Shias. Other recruits to the insurgency came from the ranks of groups that had been concentrating on the insurgency in Kashmir, which continued until the Musharraf government initiated talks with India and agreed to stop invasive violence and other offensive action by 2003.

Pakistan helped enable the US and coalition intervention in Afghanistan. Musharraf broke relations with the Afghan Taliban government and withdrew its ISI officers and other Pakistani supporters that had been taking part in supporting their war against Afghanistan's Northern Alliance. Pakistan provided the coalition with bases and permitted overflights and shared some intelligence. It moved additional forces to the Afghanistan-Pakistan border to backstop fleeing Taliban and Al Qaeda members, although those of Afghan or Pakistani nationality were not usually taken into custody.[376]

The years following the US intervention in Afghanistan saw the rise of insurgent leader Nek Mohammed, a Pakistani Wazir who had fought in Afghanistan with the Afghan Taliban and had close contact with Al

Qaeda leaders in Waziristan. When Al Qaeda fled over the border in 2001–02, Nek Mohammed welcomed them into Waziristan. The links with the Afghan Taliban and the foreigners provided Nek Mohammed with the ability to start consolidating political power in Waziristan. He was soon joined by other insurgent leaders among South Waziristan's Wazir and Mehsud tribesmen. Among these was Abdullah Mehsud, a one-legged veteran of Afghanistan's civil wars who had been held prisoner by the US. He rose to command a large force of insurgents before killing himself during a Pakistani police raid in July 2007. Another figure to emerge was Behtullah Mehsud, who had good contacts with Al Qaeda while fighting in Afghanistan and made a fortune running a mule taxi service over the mountains for fugitive terrorists.

These emerging insurgent leaders' willingness to use violence against secular Pushtun authority in Pakistan started in the FATA's South Waziristan agency, but spread throughout the FATA and then into Baluchistan and to the NWFP. Throughout Waziristan, tribal *maliks* were murdered in large numbers, especially by Al Qaeda's Uzbek allies. By targeting the tribal leadership, the insurgents gained support of current tribal leaderships' internal rivals, the "tribal entrepreneurs" who could offer influence (if mullahs) or money (if traders) and the members of the trading mafias. For all the previous decades of political unrest and undercutting of traditional authority by Pakistan's policies, the widespread campaign of the murder of Pushtun leaders was previously unheard of since the Khalqis attempted the same thing on the Afghan side of the Durand Line in 1978–79 and provoked large-scale armed resistance. By killing these men, the insurgents expanded the vacuum in authority in the FATA that had already been increasing for decades.

Pakistan's initial attempts to deal with this terrorism in the FATA relied on lightly armed *khassadar* tribal police and, only after they failed, by the Frontier Corps. On a number of occasions, when the Pakistani authorities tried to form traditional tribal *lashkars* (armed groups) to oppose Pakistani insurgents in the FATA, they deserted while hanging on to their weapons. The political agents that represented the government in the FATA paid subsidies to maliks and other local leaders to try to keep the peace. Outside the FATA, the 2002 local government reforms have made it hard to act quickly and decisively against any terrorist challenges to state authority. The paramilitary Frontier Constabulary and the Frontier Police, the NWFP's provincial police, were inadequately armed and poorly trained to confront murderous veterans of Afghanistan's wars.[377] Applying any sort of force against insurgent groups operating in the NWFP required the cooperation of the provincial government, which was usually not forthcoming, especially after the MMA took control of the provincial government in the 2002 election. And so, governmental authority quickly eroded in much of the FATA and NWFP within a few short years after the Afghan Taliban's retreat into Pakistan.

The Frontier Corps, intended to keep the peace on the frontier, consists of Pushtuns serving outside their home areas led by seconded army officers, often non-Pushtuns. Some 80,000 strong, it is divided into separate forces for the NWFP and Baluchistan. Equipped only with light weapons, they were outgunned by the insurgents, who had access to world markets. The Pakistani insurgents, through their alliance with Al Qaeda, had access to worldwide sources of funding that allowed them to out-buy the government of Pakistan for local allegiances. The Frontier Corps, under the command of the Ministry of the Interior, is a "limited liability" political force, intended for an "economy of force" presence in the FATA.[378] The politicization and then the radicalization of the Frontier Corps had started in the 1980s. Involving this force in Pakistan's strategy toward Afghanistan was beyond its capability and an invitation for a blowback effect of unanticipated results.[379] The Frontier Corps had been asked to provide support to the ISI and other Pakistani security services' Afghan proxies, initially HiH but later the "Afghan Arabs" and the Afghan Taliban. This put them in contact with the Islamic radical support infrastructure in the Vortex. Throughout the course of fighting with Pakistan's insurgents, the Frontier Corps has often proved more willing to turn over its arms to them than fight pitched battles against them, and has sometimes joined with them to fire on US troops in Afghanistan.[380]

After 2001, the idea of a Pakistani Taliban became more than a general expression of radicalized Pushtun solidarity. The pre-existing group, called Tehrik-e-Nafaz-e-Shariat-e-Mohammed (TNSM), was

inspired by Al Qaeda escapees from Afghanistan, the consolidation of
Islamic radical power in South Waziristan, and aimed to achieve similar
results in the Bajaur Agency, which was their stronghold, adjacent to
Afghanistan's war-torn Kunar valley.[381] The TNSM had been formed in
the 1990s as an offshoot of JI and had spent years recruiting Pakistanis to
go fight with the Afghan Taliban in the civil war and, later, to fight the
Americans. In 2001, the TNSM sent large numbers of madrassa students
to defend the Taliban regime in what became known as "The Children's
Crusade." Few returned alive. The result contributed to the radicalization of Pakistani Pushtun tribes that had provided these new "martyrs."
Other insurgent groups appeared in the NWFP, taking advantage of
the weak governmental authority and aimed to spread the radicalization
already controlling South Waziristan. Mangal Bagh Afridi organized the
Lashkar-e-Islam, a radical insurgent group espousing violent opposition
to the Sufic religious practices of many Pushtuns. This group has links to
narcotics trafficking and operates throughout the NWFP. Qazi Mahbubul Haq organized the Ansar-ul-Islam in the NWFP's Tirah district. This
group set up Sharia courts in the areas it controlled. It soon became a rival
of Lashkar-e-Islam, opposing their anti-Sufic violence.[382] Plans to overthrow Pakistan's government were reportedly drafted as early as 2003,
with the seizure of Swat intended to provide an interim headquarters on
their way to Islamabad.[383]

The Insurgency Spreads, 2004–07

The Pakistani military did not move against the Pakistani insurgents in
their formative stages. Rather, the Pakistani Army saw them, much like
they had seen the Afghan Taliban, as a controllable strategic asset. The
Pakistani military hoped that these groups would join the Afghan Taliban fighting in Afghanistan and not threaten Pakistan. Even after large
numbers of maliks had been murdered, the army hesitated to act. They
were focused on the primacy of the military threat from India, especially
in the wake of the 2001 terrorist attack on the Indian parliament that
raised tensions.

It was not until March 2004 that the Pakistan Army, at US urging,
moved into South Waziristan to help quell the growing insurgency. Yet

by the time the army arrived in South Waziristan for this "coercive deployment," it was evident that the initial Pakistani government response was inadequate. While fighting in Waziristan, the Pakistani army, trained and equipped for conventional conflict with India, demonstrated a profound lack of capacity for counter-insurgency warfare. Counter-insurgency was not taught at Pakistani staff colleges. The army leadership, predominantly Punjabi, lacked an understanding of the culture and politics of South Waziristan. The land was remote and foreign even to most of the ethnic Pushtun officers in the army, who may have known the language but not the area's complexities (the British Indian Army would not recruit Wazir Pushtuns back in the days of the Empire because they were too independent, and to this day the tribe lacks the traditions of government service that have been important to Pushtuns elsewhere, but not there). In 2004, Musharraf introduced local representative assemblies to the FATA, which had already been set up in the rest of the country four years earlier, but with more restricted powers and fewer seats reserved for women as concessions to the conservatism of the Pushtun population. Rather than acting as a stabilizing force, these assemblies were seen as an attempt to further undercut the preexisting system of governance and impose institutions alien to local customs and traditions. The attitude of many Pakistan Army officers was that the campaign in Waziristan was taking Musharraf's promise to cooperate with the US "Global War on Terrorism" too far.[384]

The March 2004 Pakistani military offensive in South Waziristan did not succeed in reestablishing governmental control. All the elements of the old control system—the maliks, political agents, khassadars, tribal levies, the Frontier Corps—had been uprooted. Many Pushtuns had become radicalized and sympathized with the insurgents.[385] Pakistani religious parties urged negotiations, especially the JUI, with links to both the insurgents and the national and NWFP and Baluchistan provincial governments through their participation in the MMA political coalition.[386] The continued military setbacks led to a truce and subsequent peace agreement between the insurgents in Waziristan and Pakistani authorities in April 2004. Nek Mohammed said "I did not surrender, they came to me." His view was widely accepted in Pakistan: it was the army that had given in.

The April 2004 South Waziristan peace agreement was the first in the cycle of localized cease-fires and attempts to co-opt insurgents which really has only allowed them to run even more rampant. The truces with the army provided the insurgents with a degree of legitimacy in the eyes of the people. If the army would negotiate with them, they were obviously not outlaws and could be accepted as part of Pakistani society. Most Afghans were convinced the Waziristan deal would not work from the start and would only cause them more grief. Rather, they saw this agreement as an attempt to secure peace in Pakistan by focusing the insurgents on fighting in Afghanistan. In the words of Pakistani journalist Ahmed Rashid, it was perceived that "The Army is willing to pull back, surrender sovereignty to the Pakistani Taliban. The agreements say, do not fight us, fight the US in Afghanistan, and fight NATO."[387] That was something the insurgents proceeded to do. Infiltration of guerrillas into Afghanistan reportedly increased 300 percent after the first South Waziristan agreement.[388]

Since its original negotiations with the insurgents in Waziristan, the army has mostly kept their part of their bargains. Pakistan did not block US Predator UAV attacks against the insurgent leadership. When the Pakistani army moved back into South Waziristan in June 2004, it was to target Chechens, Uzbeks, and Arabs operating in the Shakani valley. This was followed by a further peace agreement with the Pakistani insurgents in South Waziristan in November 2004, although this proved short-lived.[389] Following these truces with the army, however, the insurgency in Pakistan acquired a momentum of its own. The insurgents set up a de facto parallel government that ruled South Waziristan, imposing their version of Sharia law, beheading "spies" and imposing strict Taliban-style social controls, requiring beards and banning music and DVDs. This was copied by other insurgents throughout the FATA, starting in 2004 and spreading to Bannu and Tank by 2007, and Sharia courts followed insurgents into Swat in 2008–09. By 2004, the insurgent movement was no longer limited to the FATA, but was targeting parts of NWFP, especially the Swat valley. Despite the lack of a central command, the insurgency in Pakistan was able to use the pre-existing contacts and networks between different tribes and agencies to their advantage, acquiring and moving money, weapons, and supplies. The TNSM, operating in Bajaur and Swat, was motivated to more openly challenge the Pakistani authorities by the insurgent success in Waziristan.

All these insurgent actions gave an aura of success to the Waziristan insurgency's new leader, Behtullah Mehsud, then in his transition from mule driver to charismatic commander following the death of Nek Muhammed in a US Predator UAV attack in June 2004, just a week after his ceasefire with the government went into effect. With the vacuum caused by the death of Nek Mohammed and with the erosion of Pakistan's state control over the FATA, Behtullah Mehsud was able to extend his authority across tribal lines. There was also an increasing tempo of insurgent activity in the FATA, as shown by the kidnapping of Chinese telecommunications engineers by Abdullah Mehsud in October 2004.[390]

Behtullah Mehsud led the insurgents in an offensive against established leadership in the FATA, unimpeded by the 2004 truces. His leadership of South Waziristan's insurgents appeared acknowledged by a further peace agreement with the army in February 2004. In 2005–06 alone, some 200 Pushtun secular leaders were murdered.[391] In 2006, Behtullah Mehsud opened an expanded terrorist campaign in Pakistan, using suicide bombers, which an expanded recruitment and training effort allowed him to sustain for years.[392] In 2007, a jirga of tribal leaders in NWFP were attacked by one of the seemingly limitless number of largely non-Pushtun teenage suicide bombers collected from Pakistan's madrassas and controlled by Behtullah Mehsud. In other areas, the insurgents were able to offer money and guns to support local allies. The insurgent-established Sharia courts offered a rough frontier justice, mainly targeting common criminals and informers, but also resolving property disputes. Local governance through jirgas was banned, and the Pakistani government was kept out by roadblocks.

The October 2005 earthquake in northern Pakistan created much damage and demonstrated the inability of the government to help the victims. Islamic non-governmental organizations, some of them associated with radical groups, provided the most effective relief work. The insurgents were able to take advantage of some of the good will among the population that this created.

All of the insurgent groups shared links to radical parties elsewhere in Pakistan, often providing greater access to communications and media. Behtullah Mehsud's well-known DVDs of executions helped solidify his control over South Waziristan by adding to his already formidable reputation for ruthlessness. The strength of the Taliban culture in the FATA was demonstrated by Mullah Fazlullah, the TNSM "Radio Mullah," who made effective use of FM radio broadcasts in 2007 to almost completely halt polio vaccinations in Swat and the Bajaur agency by reporting that vaccines were an impotency serum created by the West intended to wipe out Muslims. The Pakistani insurgents, as with the Afghan Taliban and Pakistani extremist groups, have benefited from new advances in media technology, by using propaganda DVDs, both legal and illegal FM radio stations, and, more recently, satellite television broadcasting.

In 2007, there were reportedly 14 to 16 Taliban groups operating in Pakistan with no cohesive unity or command structure, but they did share common objectives of defeating the foreign coalition presence in Afghanistan and overthrowing the government in Pakistan. One of the major shared objectives of these groups was blocking (or extracting funds by not blocking) Pakistan-Afghanistan trade routes. Some groups aimed at the main route from Karachi to Kabul, on which the US-led military coalition presence in Afghanistan depends as the only major port available to them. Some 14 of these groups—divided by tribe or region in the FATA and NWFP—were pulled together into the Tehrik-e-Taliban-Pakistan (TTP), the umbrella organization for Pakistan's Taliban, formed in December 2007.[393] The TNSM was among these but kept its operational independence. Behtullah Mehsud was acknowledged as the TTP's leader. Hafiz Gul Bahadur, a Wazir insurgent leader from North Waziristan, was appointed as his deputy. A governing shura was established. The TTP followed this up with battlefield success, storming and capturing Sararogha Fort in South Waziristan in January 2008.[394] The military responded with a renewed offensive into South Waziristan, aiming to target the TTP leadership. Failing to capture them, the military instead destroyed large numbers of villages, creating over 200,000 internal refugees who were then recruited as supporters by the insurgents.[395] But when the offensive ended in May 2008, the army again withdrew from

South Waziristan. The government of Pakistan banned the TTP in August 2008, but this had little effect on its operations.[396]

As the TTP emerged, other Pakistani insurgent groups also became better organized. The "Punjabi Taliban"—a descriptive term for a loose network of Punjabis from radical organization with strong links to TTP rather than a formal organization—has emerged as a separate insurgent force and has been associated with terrorism inside Pakistan.[397] It originally drew its members from insurgent groups such as Lashkar-e-Taiba and Jaish-e-Mohammed who had fought in Kashmir and pre-2001 Afghanistan. Sipah-e-Sahaba, another building block of the Punjabi Taliban, had its origins in anti-Shia terrorism inside Pakistan, especially against Shia landlords in the southern Punjab. The members of the Punjabi Taliban went from Kashmir and Afghanistan to fighting alongside the predecessors of the TTP and TNSM in the FATA and then brought the struggle back to their home province.[398] Punjabis were an important part of the insurgent forces that fought the Pakistan military in areas such as Swat and Waziristan.

By 2007, the TNSM leadership was in a strong position. Maulavi Fazlullah propaganda radio broadcasts continued without government interference, all while weapons and resources were being sent up from Waziristan by Behtullah Mehsud, helping to consolidate his position of power. He linked insurgent forces coming out of Waziristan with those in Bajaur and Swat, including his father-in-law Sufi Mohammed, who had fought in Afghanistan for the Afghan Taliban in 2001 and Fakir Mohammed, a Bajaur-based member of the Mohmand tribe. The TNSM eventually displaced government authority and held sway over the population through armed gunmen, first in the Bajaur Agency of the FATA and then in the Swat valley, part of the NWFP, in 2007. This provoked an army response, but as the troops advanced, the TNSM insurgents largely sidestepped the blow and withdrew back to Bajaur, threatening any of the local inhabitants that cooperated with the government with retribution when they returned. The army soon withdrew its troops and, without a capability to establish effective civil governance in Swat, the population was soon again threatened by the TNSM. The TNSM also made significant inroads into the Malakand and Dir districts of the NWFP in 2007, as the MMA-dominated provincial government in Peshawar was reluctant to move against them.

Responding to the Insurgency, 2007—10

By 2007, the Pakistani insurgents and their allies had become a sophisticated political insurgency operation.[399] Linked to the anti-democratic religious forces growing throughout Pakistan, these groups shared what amounted to a sanctuary as well as the support system of paymasters, networks, and material support infrastructure with the Afghan Taliban, Al Qaeda, and its transnational terrorist allies, not to mention narcotics traffickers and criminal enterprises. By 2007, the Pakistani insurgents were affecting all of Pakistan, not just the FATA and NWFP. They had shown signs of entering the political mainstream. Maulavi Omar, the TTP spokesman, was a regular commentator on Pakistan television until his arrest by the government in August 2009.[400]

But the decisive event in showing that the insurgents were having a nationwide impact was the July 2007 siege of the Lal Masjid (the Red Mosque) in Islamabad.[401] It had been founded by two veteran Pakistani religious radicals with strong links to Al Qaeda, for which they had been imprisoned in 2004, Maulana Abdul Aziz and his brother Mullah Abdul Rashid Ghazi. The mosque was built in the 1960s but started operating as a challenge to the government in January 2006 with what was at first just a handful of radicals; but within a year, it had been reinforced by radicalized Pushtuns, Punjabis, Kahsmiris, and Al Qaeda supporters. He organized a brigade of female activists that ransacked businesses and kidnapped women accused of immoral behavior.

The Musharraf government first supported the radicals at the Lal Masjid, as previous Pakistani governments had done since the 1970s, and funded them to buy them off, then ignored them until they were entrenched at the mosque and had taken hostages. The government's first move was to negotiate, but this failed to free the hostages. When Pakistan finally sent in the army, there was a pitched battle resulting in hundreds of casualties, many of them the hostages who had been taken by these radicals. Mullah Abdul Rashid Ghazi, instead of fighting to the end, gave cell phone interviews to the Pakistani news media until stopped by an army bullet. Many of the radicals were able to escape to the FATA at the close of the siege. The Lal Masjid reopened in October 2007, and an unrepentant Maulana Abdul Aziz was released from prison.[402] The incident demonstrated that the military could not control radical groups that it had previously supported. It also demonstrated that the military would eventually move against Pakistan's religious radicals if their challenge was too blatant. Whether their actions would be effective was another matter. The Lal Masjid incident meant that the insurgency was no longer literally "peripheral" to Pakistan, but was affecting the core and could pose a real threat to its future as a cohesive state.

The Pakistani army commanders in the FATA became more important than the political agents who had been the representatives of state power there since these positions were established by the British. With the continued rise of insurgent power in 2007, the ISI therefore took the lead and sought to counter them by backing Pushtun rivals to Behtullah Mehsud and other leadership figures. In 2007, as Pakistan attempted to restore the authority of the maliks of the Wazir tribe in Waziristan, the ISI allied itself with South Waziristan militia leader Maulavi Nazir, a Pakistan Taliban leader, despite his armed strength overshadowing the power of the Wazir maliks.[403] As a result, Maulavi Nazir rallied support for both his own personal position in the local power structure and a Pakistani nationalist approach. He advocated fighting not against the Pakistani government but rather in Afghanistan. He also urged his followers to fight transnational terrorist organizations, especially the Uzbeks of the Waziristan-based transnational Islamic Movement of Turkistan (IMT).[404] To encourage Maulavi Nazir to fight in Afghanistan and counter the terrorist Uzbeks, ISI reportedly provided him with 150,000 dollars, truckloads of ammunition, and a guarantee of free movement into and out of Afghanistan. In January 2007, Maulavi Nazir and his men fought the Uzbeks, killing at least 250 of them. By working with Maulavi Nazir, the ISI was able to strengthen an alternative leader to Behtullah Mehsud, counter the Uzbeks who had helped enable the rise of the insurgency in Waziristan, and directed his fighting against targets in Afghanistan rather than Pakistan. The ISI also worked with Haji Namdar, the biggest recruiter of warriors in the FATA's Khyber Agency, to fuel the Taliban-led insurgency in Afghanistan.[405] As a result of ISI support, he helped, through a mixture of persuasion, bribery, and force, to keep open in 2007 the coalition supply lines from Karachi to Kabul that ran through the Khyber Pass.

The army also moved, unsuccessfully, against TNSM insurgents in Swat in 2007. In its February 2008 offensive into Southern Waziristan, the army learned from its 2004 experience and demonstrated better tactics, killing over 1,000 TTP and Uzbek fighting men, but still failed to dislodge Behtullah Mehsud's control of the area through military action.[406]

The spread of the insurgency through the FATA made the NWFP appear the next target in 2008.[407] A secular ANP government was elected in the NWFP in the February 2008 elections, replacing one controlled by the MMA. The election was marked by a low level of voter turnout reflecting the security threat and disenchantment with Pakistan's politicians. Led by ethnic Pushtuns and elected by popular vote, the ANP could challenge the insurgents' nationalist appeal in NWFP. The ANP government, unlike the national government and the military, was pro-Karzai, pro-Kabul, pan-Pushtun, anti-Durand Line. The unanswered question was whether the NWFP government has suffered the same delegitimation as has most Pushtun-related secular authority in Afghanistan and throughout Pakistan. With access to the media, the ANP could counter the "battle of ideas" that the insurgents and their supporters had waged so successfully over the years. Instead, the NWFP government limited these tactics to the areas that were already "secure." Despite widespread popular dislike of the insurgents, their brutality and the lack of effective engagement by the ethnic Pushtuns opposed to them prevented the emergence of an effective grassroots movement against the insurgents in most of the NWFP.

The insurgent offensive in the NWFP opened with the ambush and murder in the Khyber Agency in May 2008 of a major tribal elder with strong links to the ANP, Ahmad Khan Kukikhel.[408] Within months, insurgents were able to threaten Peshawar, the provincial capital of the NWFP. Insurgent roadblocks were in place within an hour's drive of the city, controlling access to the countryside. The ANP-led government in

Peshawar received little support from the Pakistani national government or the military, which had long-standing hostility toward the ANP as potentially divisive ethnic nationalists.

Most of the Pakistani military action in NWFP was in Swat.[409] There had been a ceasefire agreement with the insurgents in Swat negotiated in April 2007, but this had effectively broken down by July, when Pakistani troops started to be deployed in the area.[410] When the Pakistani military moved against the TNSM insurgents in the Swat valley in November 2007, they avoided the army's firepower not by fleeing over the Durand Line into "lawless" Afghanistan, but rather deeper into Pakistan, where they were able to regroup.[411] This resulted in negotiations with the TNSM by the NWFP government. It appears that the initial goal was, as in the peace deals negotiated by the military in previous years, that the insurgents would get a free hand in the direction of Afghanistan in return for peace in Pakistan. This mindset had been explicitly stated by NWFP governor Owari Ghani in talks with US military officials in May 2008: "Pakistan will take care of its own problems. You take care of Afghanistan on your side."[412] But as the negotiations went through several stages in 2007–08, it became apparent that the TNSM was less interested in fighting in Afghanistan than consolidating its position to support a decisive expansion of its power in Pakistan.

The military next targeted the TNSM's new foothold in the Bajaur agency of the FATA, between Swat and Afghanistan. Insurgents under Qazi Zia Rahman had displaced pro-government local tribesmen in 2008. In August 2008, the military launched a major offensive with a reinforced division-sized force that was supported by heavy artillery and F-16 fighters using precision-guided munitions. It was uncertain whether this firepower killed many insurgents, but there was no doubt that over 500,000 internal refugees were created by the offensive, and the army's inability to help them further weakened the already fragile social fabric. But the inability to replace the insurgent control of Bajaur with effective governance led to the TNSM returning to much of that agency as early as spring 2009.[413]

The strength of the insurgents allowed them to turn their attention on the supply lines for the US-led coalition that runs from the port of

Karachi in Pakistan into Afghanistan. In June 2008 alone, 44 trucks with 220,000 gallons of fuel were lost on that route in Pakistan to attacks or other events.[414] The insurgents let most of the supply trucks pass, enriching themselves by bribes and protection payments. To many in Pakistan, that the insurgents were funding themselves through money originating with the US and coalition seemed proof that the Western presence in Afghanistan was not about reconstructing and stabilizing that country but had its real goal as destabilizing Pakistan, which threatened the "Global War on Islam" seen as being waged by the US, India, and Israel.

The 2008 food and energy crises further increased the pressure on the state, in the wake of the fighting and the huge numbers of internal refugees. In the 2008 election, economic issues proved to be a higher concern among the voters than even security concerns. The insurgents took advantage of this to supply basic needs, such as cooking oil, to the local population.

Within months, the insurgents returned to Swat and some 12,000 troops were unable to prevail over 3,000 insurgents in fighting that resumed in July 2008.[415] The military began to play an increasing role in non-military action. In 2008, the army claimed to have built some 2,000 km of roads, plus schools and wells to reduce the insurgents' appeal. But there was still widespread hardship and disruption to the local population that the insurgents were often quick to identify.

Pakistan Fights, 2008–09

Even after the Lal Masjid incident, the civilian government elected in Pakistan in 2008 was still slow to treat the insurgency on its territory as an existential threat. The Pakistani military was slower still to take appropriate action. In 2009, the military pulled troops from counter-insurgency missions over to the Indian border after the Mumbai terrorist attacks raised fears of a retaliatory strike. Pakistani elites and grassroots alike were unwilling to accept Islamic radicals as a threat to Pakistan, as shown by widespread sentiment blaming India for the terrorist attack on the Sri Lanka cricket team in Lahore. As late as April 2009, Pakistan's Prime Minister Yousaf Raza Gilani had told the parliament that the insurgents posed no threat to the nation's integrity, while Interior Minister Rahman Malik identified the real threat to Pakistan as aggression from Afghanistan, India, and Russia.[416] This was stated despite the fact that the insurgents, by that time, controlled an estimated ten percent of Pakistan's entire surface area, including most of the FATA, and were gaining ground.

Nor was there an immediate response to the de facto insurgent seizure of Swat by the resurgent TNSM that led to the ceasefire agreement on 16 February 2009 with the NWFP provincial government.[417] In the months before the cease-fire, the TNSM had increased their control over much of Swat, ending girls' education and polio vaccinations.[418] The ceasefire agreement, providing for Swat to be governed under Sharia rather than the laws of Pakistan, effectively left the insurgents in control. This ceasefire agreement was endorsed by the parliament. President Asif Ali Zardari signed the Nizam-e-Adl Regulation (NAR), which allowed Swat to be governed under Sharia law and called for the creation of a new Islamic appeals court. The NWFP government failed to disarm the insurgents, who then spread into surrounding districts, threatening them. After the army had withdrawn again, as in 2007, without reestablishing effective civil governance, TNSM radio broadcasts threatened any who resisted their reassertion of authority over Swat with dire punishments. As a result, some 700 of the 1,700 Frontier Constabulary and Frontier Police in Swat deserted, and the others were reluctant to oppose the TNSM's return to power.[419] By April 2009, the insurgents has re-occupied much of Swat.

What finally spurred the military to action in 2009 was that after the TNSM-led insurgents established their control over much of Swat, they advanced on Buner, Dir, and other districts of the NWFP, failed to disarm, and continued inflammatory FM radio broadcasts, all in express violation of the ceasefire terms. They also insisted that decisions of their Sharia courts established in Swat could not be appealed to Pakistani courts, as provided for under the ceasefire agreement. Beatings, floggings, and beheadings were widespread in the insurgent-controlled areas. The insurgent advance raised inter-ethnic tensions in Karachi and threatened the Punjab. Their leader, Sufi Shah Mahmoud, denounced all "infidel institutions" in Pakistan that he intended to sweep away with his Islamic revolution. This included civil society, the legal system, and, of course, the military.

A two-division army operation to reoccupy Swat started in May 2009, opposing up to 70–80,000 insurgents. Hundreds of thousands of refugees were displaced by the fighting and received little effective aid from the national or NWFP governments and were essentially fodder for the insurgents.[420] But the insurgents' brutal reign in Swat and their threat to Pakistan's existence prevented them from receiving additional support from the local population. An estimated 2,000 insurgents and over 300 Pakistani military personnel were killed. In 2009, the military put a greater emphasis on the non-military actions of counter-insurgency. The Pakistan military, as it took back control over Swat in 2009, emphasized that it was there to hold the area and not just clear away the insurgents temporarily. It demonstrated this new policy by implementing relief efforts for the refugees that the civilian government was unable to organize due to lack of resources and capability. Restoring effective governance to replace the rough Sharia-based justice administered by the Pakistani insurgents has not yet occurred in those areas where the military has taken back territory, in effect leaving the same political vacuum that hurt them before. Once the army reoccupied Swat, they demonstrated the change in the Pakistani military's perception of the insurgents in Swat by their increased use of death-squad extrajudicial killings to remove the clandestine network of insurgent sympathizers.[421] The Pakistani military, convinced of the weakness of their country's justice system, sees these murderous methods as part of effective counter-insurgency.[422]

Countering the Insurgency in Waziristan, 2009–10

The army, while it had tried to negotiate with insurgents to provide an improved security situation in the run-up to the Pakistani election in February 2008, has been reluctant to carry out such negotiations since then, following the insurgents' repeated reneging on agreements. By 2009, negotiations were no longer the Pakistan government's tactics of choice in dealing with the Pakistani insurgency. Rather, they would support rivals to the insurgent leaders and launch military offensives against those leaders whose actions threatened Pakistan outside Pushtun areas. Part of the Pakistani military approach in 2009 was apparently to focus the Pakistani insurgents' efforts inside Afghanistan. Following their reoccupation of Swat, the Pakistan military turned their focus toward North and South Waziristan where the TTP controlled the two agencies. The TTP based there had, like the TNSM, threatened Pakistani state power outside their own area. Behtullah Mehsud's claims of responsibility for the terrorist attack on a police training facility near Lahore in April 2009 underlined this.

In 2009, the Pakistani military initially looked to counter the TTP through the ISI, building on its successful record of cooperation, and was reportedly working with local rivals to Behtullah Mehsud, including Turkistan Bhittani and Qari Zaihuddin, insurgent leaders and former TTP allies.[423] The ISI provided weapons to Turkistan Bhittani in order to create a militia of men from his Bhittani tribe that would keep the TTP from advancing into the Tank district of NWFP. Hafiz Gul Bahadur,[424] an insurgent leader from North Waziristan, was also seen as a potential counter to Behtullah Mehsud.[425] Both Maulavi Nazir and Hafiz Gul Bahadur demonstrated that their alliances with the Haqqani Afghan insurgent network did not imperil their relationship with the ISI.[426] But the Pakistani military proved unsuccessful in its attempts to put together an anti-TTP Mehsud tribal militia in 2009, although similar efforts in North Waziristan and in the Orakzai Agency were successful.[427]

In response, in February 2009, Behtullah Mehsud and the TTP[428] formed the United Mujahideen Council, an alliance reportedly created at the urgings of Al Qaeda and the Afghan Taliban to resist Pakistan's efforts to divide the Pakistani insurgent leadership in North and South Waziristan.[429] Hafiz Gul Bahadur's militiamen killed at least 23 Pakistani soldiers in an ambush in June 2009, a direct betrayal of the aid given him by the ISI and thought to be a result of his role in this alliance. Behtullah Mehsud continued to murder potential rivals. Khalil Rehman, a Mehsud leader who raised a pro-Pakistan and anti-TTP lashkar in South Waziristan, was assassinated in June 2009, and his fighting men, facing a similar fate, had to be evacuated by the army along with their families to Dera Ismail Khan, outside the FATA. Qari Zaihuddin, another ISI collaborator, was assassinated by one of his own bodyguards, reportedly at the orders of Behtullah Mehsud, in June 2009.[430]

The death of Behtullah Mehsud in a US UAV attack in August 2009 fractured the United Mujahideen Council alliance, creating a resurgence of old rivalries. There has been extensive infighting within North and South Waziristan and in TTP groups throughout Pakistan. Hakimullah Mehsud eventually succeeded as the head of the TTP after an internal power struggle in which he overcame his major competitor, Rehman Mehsud.[431] While Hakimullah lacks his predecessors' political skills and multi-tribal appeal among Pushtuns, he has stronger links to Punjabi radical groups, including the "Punjabi Taliban" and anti-Shia groups residing outside the FATA.[432] Qari Hussein Raess Mehsud, Behtullah's suicide bomber recruiting and training specialist, Hakimullah's cousin and a member of the anti-Shia Sipah-e-Sahaba, has become Hakimullah's deputy. Wali Mohammed led the TTP in South Waziristan in 2010.

This tumult provided an opportunity for the Pakistani military to launch an offensive into South Waziristan in October 2009.[433] Afrasiab Khattak, general secretary of the ANP, said: "dismantling militant sanctuaries in FATA and taking short-term and long-term measures to open up the area and integrate it with the rest of the country needs urgent national attention if we are to avoid the impending catastrophe."[434] The Pakistani military for the first time received reconnaissance provided by US Predator UAVs.[435] Defending their strongholds along with the TTP were some one to two thousand Uzbeks. The offensive was unable to capture or kill the TTP leadership. The Pakistani insurgents responded to the October 2009 offensive asymmetrically, with a terrorist offensive throughout the country.

After years of urging greater Pakistani military action against the insurgents, the US supported the new policies. Large-scale security assistance, over two billion dollars since 9/11, provided encouragement.[436] COL Patrick McNiece, USA, deputy intelligence director of ISAF, said in 2008: "Pakistan's leadership knows the FATA problem is their problem, not India or the US."[437] In October 2009, US Central Command combatant commander GEN David Petraeus paid tribute to what he called "heartening work by the Pakistan military and Frontier Corps in the past six months. . . . Following a two-division operation, the Frontier Corps cleared the majority of the Swat valley. Some 80–85 percent of internally displaced persons have returned. Pakistan is determined to hold and build, not clear and leave."[438] The US contributed to Pakistan's increased capabilities through intelligence sharing and aid, including an expanded training program. US special operations forces, through a "train the trainers" program, started to retrain the Frontier Corps as a counterinsurgency force. US aid provided them and the army with equipment they had previously lacked, such as lightweight body armor. The army benefited from the provision of helicopters and air assault training. The police and the civilian institutions required to restore governance after the insurgents have been forced from an area, in contrast, have made less improvement, although some US aid funding is being channeled to the Frontier Police.[439] The $750,000,000 US aid program targeted at the FATA, suspended in January 2009 due to the insurgency, has had uncertain results in helping assure local stability and has not been matched by Pakistani political reforms that could reduce the appeal of the insurgency.[440]

In November-December 2009, the Pakistani military started a buildup for potential military action against insurgents in the Khyber and Orakzai areas.[441] However, Afghan insurgent groups based in Pakistan still have an effective sanctuary and are not being targeted by Pakistani military actions.[442] Pakistan responded to repeated US urging to move against these groups with increasing hostility.[443] Nor have the groups in Pakistan that had their origins in the Kashmir insurgency been targeted.[444] This policy shows that to the ISI, the military, and many Pakistani elites, including those on the left that have no love for either the army or Islamists, the Afghan insurgents and even some Pakistani insurgents are not seen as the enemy. They believe that the threat to Pakistan stems from the fact that the 2001 US-led intervention in Afghanistan displaced Al Qaeda but also the pro-Pakistan Afghan Taliban regime in Kabul and so preempted the emergence of a "moderate Taliban" that would have provided, in their view, peace for Afghanistan and thus security for Pakistan. Few Pakistanis want to cooperate with the US-led actions against the Afghan insurgents that are not seen as threatening the future of their own country and may help Afghanistan being used by countries hostile to Pakistan to encircle it when the US again inevitably disengages from the region.[445] Former US Ambassador Teresita Shaefer said at a talk in Washington: "To many in Pakistan, the conflict on the western border is the 'American War,' forced upon them by Musharraf's cooperation with the US war on terror."[446]

In the final analysis, the Pakistani military's goals reflect their internal political concerns rather than ending insurgencies. General Ashfaq Kiyani, army chief of staff since 2007, has repeatedly stated that the military's focus remains the threat from India, not the insurgencies.[447] Despite the changes seen in 2009, Pakistan has demonstrated a limited capability to clear and hold areas and follow this up with effective efforts to win over the local population to the side of the government. Despite US aid and the hard-bought lessons of campaigns since 2004, the Pakistani military (and intelligence) are still far from waging an effective counter-insurgency campaign. The army's use of firepower and creation of internal refugees has led to widespread hardship. They are conscious of the cost to legitimacy in killing or displacing Pakistani civilians and appearing to be the tools of the US in a global war against Muslims and yet are powerless to avoid this collateral damage. The military remains reluctant to take offensive action because if they again fail as they did in South Waziristan in 2004–05, it will look even weaker, both in terms of domestic politics and in its competition with India. Political concerns over the military losing popularity by being seen to be fighting the Americans' war against their fellow Pakistani citizens have also limited their willingness to use force against the insurgents. Along with collateral-damage concerns from the UAV attacks, the Pakistani military was able to use nationalist concerns to rally support against US oversight provisions in the Kerry-Lugar aid package passed in October 2009.[448] In 2009, as Pakistan's civilian government showed itself unable to solve the problems affected the lives of Pakistanis, the military's political prestige began to increase again. Pakistan faces the prospect of the cycle of political instability continuing.

The Ongoing Insurgency

Since the 2008 election, the Pakistani government has wanted to distance itself from the policies of former president Musharraf, seen as siding too much with the US and Pakistan's insurgents and religious radicals, all highly unpopular. President Asif Ali Zardari, the widower of Benazir Bhutto, and the Pakistan Peoples Party (PPP) government have resumed moves toward reconciliation with India, improving ties with the US, rapprochement with Kabul (he attended Karzai's second inauguration in November 2009), and ending the Afghan insurgents' sanctuary in Pakistan. New Prime Minister Yousuf Raza Gilani announced that it would be a "problem" if Pakistan concluded any negotiations with insurgent groups that was not also fair and advantageous to Kabul.

But Zardari's lack of support within his own PPP and from the nation as a whole has limited his ability to govern. This began when he had to go against his post-inaugural pledge and seek aid from the International Monetary Fund (IMF) in the wake of the 2008 financial crisis. His main political rival, Nawaz Sharif, and the military have voiced disapproval in the form of a resentful nationalism. Continued military control of Pakistan's national security policy and its Afghanistan policy has appeared beyond Zardari's capability to change. However, his first year in office did see some changes. In Quetta, Taliban leadership figures adopted a low profile. The improved intelligence flow within the military also suggests that there are still people in the FATA who will provide intelligence that can be used against the TTP and other insurgent groups. It shows that the FATA has not been overrun just yet. Soon after Zardari's election, the new army chief, General Ashfaq Pervez Kiyani, stated that he wanted to take the army out of politics, at least at the visible level, giving them more freedom to operate and less limited by the political costs of counter-insurgency operations.

As a result of this limited headway, there was no halting of US Predator UAV operations against Al Qaeda and Pakistani insurgent targets in the FATA upon Zardari's election. According to unconfirmed reports, there were more armed Predator UAV attacks in Pakistan in the first nine months of the Obama administration than the entire Bush administration, although the base for the Predator operations was moved from Pakistan, at Shamsi in Baluchistan, to Afghanistan after protests from the Pakistani government.[449]

According to unconfirmed reports, improved targeting information based on HUMINT supplied from Pakistan has reduced the occurrence of collateral damage incidents that have been the source of much tension in the past. According to unconfirmed reports, the UAV campaign that eventually succeeded in killing TTP leader Behtullah Massoud in 2009 required 14 months, 16 missile attacks, and up to 207–323 collateral casualties.

Pakistan has reportedly insisted on policies limiting the Predator attacks to the FATA and has blocked US proposals for attacks on targets in Baluchistan and the NWFP. The Predator attacks are politically highly unpopular in Pakistan, and limiting them to the FATA, where the laws of Pakistan do not apply, appears a way to reduce the stigma of collaborating with a foreign country in attacks on its own citizens. Pakistan only permits Predator attacks on Pakistani insurgents and "foreign" Al Qaeda leadership, restricting their operations. Attacks on Afghan insurgents in Pakistan, including the Taliban's Quetta shura with headquarters in Baluchistan or the Haqqanis whose headquarters are in the FATA, were apparently forbidden. Despite its improved cooperation with the US and Afghanistan in 2008–10, the Pakistan military has never moved against or tried to prevent the functioning of the Afghan Taliban leadership or its support network, and this includes preventing Predator strikes on them. US demands that Pakistan change this policy were seen as part of an assault on Pakistan's national sovereignty and were resisted by the military. The Pakistani military are unwilling to pay the costs in turning against policy tools that they continue to believe are valuable to their national security policy in Afghanistan and elsewhere. All of these policies suggest that in 2009, the Pakistani military saw the Pakistani Taliban and at least some of the insurgents in Pakistan as a threat while they continued to see the Afghan Taliban and insurgents as strategic assets.

Pakistani insurgent groups that had their origins in the cross-border insurgency in Kashmir, despite their more recent ties to transnational terror attacks outside Pakistan as well as internal terrorism, also seem to be tolerated. This includes groups such as Lashkar-e-Taiba, accused of having carried out the terrorist attack in Mumbai in 2008. Shabaz Sharif, who ran the Punjab provincial government, and his brother, the former prime minister and current leader of the opposition, Nawaz Sharif, both have refused to crack down on radical groups in the Punjab and have maintained links with some of their leaders such as Hafiz Saeed of Lashkar-e-Taiba.[450] In this case, it reflects their long-standing relationship with Islamic radicals and parties that have functioned, in many cases, as political allies. The Pakistan military may still believe that they can be controlled or at least put aside for a proxy.

Pakistan and Afghanistan: The Influence from the US, China, Saudi Arabia, Iran, and India

In 2009, the incoming Obama administration, seeking to differentiate its policies from those of its predecessor, started referring to "AfPak" as a conjoined entity, reflected in the appointment of Ambassador Richard Holbrooke as the special representative to both countries. The Obama administration would, rightly or wrongly, view Afghanistan and Pakistan as representing a single conflict, militarily and diplomatically. But while the US has troops on the ground in Afghanistan and a great deal of leverage with the government in Kabul, the US cannot fight the war in Pakistan, and its ability to affect governmental actions is limited. For Pakistan, whose relations with Afghanistan have usually emphasized hostility or conflict, this was an unfamiliar context. Relations with the US, China, and Saudi Arabia have been traditionally been what geopolitically mattered most to Pakistan, with India and, to a lesser extent, Iran as competitors for what is seen as the vital issue of political control and influence in Pakistan's neighbor Afghanistan.

US policy regarding Pakistan after 2001 concentrated on assuring mutual cooperation in capturing foreign Al Qaeda members. In this matter, Pakistan did cooperate, as reflected by the arrests of several terrorist leaders. But in so doing, the displaced Afghan and emerging Pakistani Talibans were largely ignored by the Pakistani security services or, indeed, were encouraged by the Pakistani government, military, and civilian political parties, especially the pro-Musharraf MMA and religious organizations. They were perceived as potentially being valuable tools of Pakistani strategy as their predecessors, the Afghan and Kashmiri insurgents, had been in the 1980s and '90s. The US concentration on capturing "foreign," non-Afghan or Pakistani, Al Qaeda terrorists (in which Pakistan acquiesced) allowed Al Qaeda to replace their losses with skilled Pakistanis who had access to both the support networks created by the ISI to support the conflicts in Afghanistan and Kashmir and those running through Pakistani ethnic communities worldwide, especially in the UK and US, plus they had the added advantage of effective "immunity" in Pakistan through their links with the security services, who were not interested in sending their countrymen to Guantanamo. The post-9/11 rhetoric by Musharraf inspired Washington by raising expectations of a restoration of effective civil governance and the hopes of a regional peace that would mean the end of state support for the Kashmir insurgency. These hopes were instead eclipsed by the reality of Pakistan's Afghanistan policy firmly in military control, who continued to tolerate if not support the Afghan and Pakistan Talibans, the Taliban culture, and their infrastructure of support, effectively circumventing any headway gained by the apprehension of Al Qaeda members.

China, on the other hand, has been distant from supporting the current government in Kabul, instead focusing on supporting Pakistan, a long-standing friend. China is Pakistan's third-largest foreign direct investor, exceeding the US. Trade between China and Pakistan more than tripled in 2001–06. A free-trade agreement came into force in 2007. In 2008, both Musharraf and Zardari went to Beijing, appealing for help with Pakistan's economic crisis. That both came away with little to show for their efforts did not undercut China's continuing importance to Pakistan.

Chinese policies toward both Afghanistan and Pakistan are shaped by its interests in security and economic access in central Asia, as has been seen by the creation and operation of the Shanghai Cooperation Organization (SCO), which both countries have participated in, Afghanistan as a guest and Pakistan as an observer.[451] In 2009, the Obama administration sought additional involvement from China in Afghanistan as well as in

Pakistan on security issues.[452] While China has not opposed the coalition effort in Afghanistan and has, from its position on the Security Council, enabled UN actions there, it has tended to see Afghanistan's stability undercut by the West's insistence on creating a new Afghanistan in their own alien image and sidelining those Afghans that have the potential to provide peace; while these have not been explicitly identified, Chinese diplomats have seen the conflict in Afghanistan as a result of neo-imperialist attitudes.[453] China's Afghanistan policy appears largely to follow their Pakistani friends' goals in Afghanistan, although China has been willing to cooperate with Russia and India on Afghanistan rather than attempt to exclude them.[454] While China would ideally prefer that the US have a limited role in central Asia, ensuring its own access to the region's energy, resources, and markets, a stable Afghanistan would also feed into China's economic interest, even if it meant allowing a US foothold. US Secretary of Defense Robert Gates expressed concern over China's voracious demand for new sources of energy and willingness to employ "coercive diplomacy."[455] This has the potential to affect future Chinese policy toward Afghanistan.

However, for all their economic interests, China is concerned about terrorism and the rise of Islamic-based threats. Since the 1990s, non-Han ethnic groups including Uighurs, Kirghiz, and others farther to the east in China's Xinjiang province have been unsettled by radical Islamic influences emanating from Pakistan and Afghanistan.[456] Uighurs have been a presence in Pakistani terror training camps since the 1990s and fought alongside the Afghan Taliban in 2001, although they were far outnumbered by other foreign groups such as the Uzbeks and Chechens.[457] China has relied on Pakistan as a bulwark against these threats, although this has been strained by the growing radicalization and internal instability there.[458]

China's relations with Afghanistan have so far been reflected primarily by their investment, including the three billion dollars associated with their development of the Ainaq copper deposits.[459] Prior to this, China had been largely disengaged from the security situation in Afghanistan, though it has benefited from the coalition efforts.[460] Increased Chinese involvement has the potential to benefit Afghanistan.

Saudi Arabia is, along with the US and China, one of the long-standing pillars of foreign support for the government of Pakistan. Saudi Arabia conversely has long aimed to increase its influence in both Pakistan and Afghanistan, with donations, often by non-state actors or through NGOs, being the preferred means. Saudi funding of Wahabi education and activities in Afghanistan and Pakistan flourished during the 1980s. Saudi Arabia was also an initial enabler of the Taliban culture, helping fund the madrassas of the FATA and the "rupee mullahs" and Islamic NGOs operating in the refugee camps. Saudi Arabia was one of the three governments (along with Pakistan and the UAE) to recognize the Taliban regime of 1996–2001 and was a strong ally of Mullah Omar until the Taliban's links with Al Qaeda and Osama bin Laden soured the relationship even before the 9/11 attacks. The Saudi government tolerated the US-led coalition intervention in Afghanistan in 2001.

Saudi Arabia's Afghanistan policies reflect its own security concerns. It sees Iranian influence in Afghanistan as hostile, intended to gain an advantage against them and their friends in Pakistan and Afghanistan's Persian-speakers as basically suspect as a potential Iranian fifth column. The Saudis viewed the power of the Northern Alliance in the initial post-Taliban Afghan government with concern. This put their views in alignment with those of Pakistan. After the fall of the Taliban, Kabul viewed Saudi aid and investment as suspect, due to its previous support of Mullah Omar. Dr. Abdurrab Rasul Sayyaf, the only Pushtun leader of the "Peshawar Seven" parties to be part of the Northern Alliance and hence in a good position in Kabul following the US intervention, used his connections to bring in this "tainted" Saudi money that he used to develop real estate and, less successfully, secure his political position.

The post-2001 tensions between the Saudis and Kabul has extended to the institution of the Organization of the Islamic Conference (OIC). There are few Muslims, including those from Turkey and Egypt included, and still fewer Arabs, including those from the UAE, among the countries contributing to the coalition in Afghanistan. Despite the obvious utility of an increased Muslim coalition presence in Afghanistan, with the ability to counter the hostile propaganda of an infidel invasion and help with areas where non-Muslims lack credibility, such as in the training of ulema, they have largely declined to increase their commitments to Afghanistan, despite the urgings of both the Bush and Obama administrations. This is often seen in Kabul as reflecting Saudi suspicion toward the US-led coalition and sympathy to Pakistan's desire to exert influence in Afghanistan. These Saudi attitudes have affected the policies of other Arab states toward Afghanistan. In 2008–10, it was widely perceived in Kabul that Saudi aid was going to rebuild, if not the Afghan Taliban, then the "Taliban culture" it had previously encouraged, especially by funding fundamentalist religious figures and activities, who, on the whole, have not been supportive of new social and economic development in the region and have been hostile toward the non-Islamic foreign presence.

To further this breach, the Saudis also have strong ties with the ISI, dating back to their aid for the Afghan resistance fighting the Soviets in the 1980s and their shared suspicion of transnational Islamic movements that they themselves do not control, such as Al Qaeda. Prince Turki, the head of the Saudi Central Intelligence Department, built personal relations with successive ISI directors. The ISI also introduced the Saudis to the Taliban in the 1990s and helped ensure that the Saudis became, along with Pakistan and the UAE, the only foreign governments to actually recognize them as the legitimate government in Afghanistan. The Saudis provided aid to the Taliban while they were in power and helped train their religious police, who became the most hated instrument of repression in Kabul. It is no wonder, then, that many Afghans are suspicious; yet without Saudi support, Afghanistan will have limited access to outside support from the Arab world.

Saudi Arabia has also been a long-standing participant in Pakistan's internal politics, providing funding for religious parties and the madrassa system as well as many mosques, an even deeper level of involvement than what they displayed in Taliban-ruled Afghanistan. The Sharif family and religious parties have links with Saudi Arabia dating back to the 1980s and have used this to access funding. The Saudi distrust of the PPP, the political rivals of these Pakistani political friends, was reflected in their refusal of Zardari's request to defer oil payments in the wake of the financial crisis in November 2008.

Iran provided limited support to the anti-Soviet Afghan resistance in 1978–92, and their attempts to gain control of Afghanistan's Shias during that time contributed to a civil war in the Hazara Jat, where they supported revolutionaries who drove out or killed most of the pre-war Hazara elites.[461] Since then, Iranian political interference remains resented among the Hazaras, despite extensive post-1992 Iranian aid efforts such as expanding Bamiyan airport and a shared respect for Shia religious authorities. Nor has Iran been able to make strong political inroads among Sunni Dari-speakers in Afghanistan despite their cultural links to Iran due to their shared Persian language, culture, and gratitude for Iranian support against the Taliban prior to 2001.

Since 1992, Iran has opposed Pakistan's desire for control over Kabul and access through Afghanistan to central Asia to provide links to the sea competitive with those offered by Iran. Iran is worried about Sunni extremism in Afghanistan and central Asia and its hostility to Shias. Iran was an opponent of the rise of the Taliban pre-2001 and blamed Pakistan for sponsorship of the Taliban and Islamabad's inability or unwillingness to curb Taliban excesses. This led Iran to provide limited financial and humanitarian aid, as well as military supplies, to the 1992–96 ISA regime in Kabul, and they continued this during their continued resistance to the Taliban in 1996–2001. Iran developed good relations with Ismail Khan, the leading Sunni resistance commander in Herat, during the anti-Soviet war. Iran saw him as a balance to the Panjsheri leadership of the Northern Alliance's military forces, and paid to get him out of a Taliban prison after he was captured in 1996. Relations between Iran and Pakistan declined precipitously over Afghanistan. In 1998, Iran sent 200,000 troops to their border with Afghanistan after the murder of Iranian diplomats in Mazar-e-Sharif by Pakistani extremists fighting with the Taliban, leading to a further deterioration of relations.

Accompanied by US and coalition special operations and intelligence advisors, the Northern Alliance forces that entered Kabul in 2001 did so while riding Iranian-supplied armored vehicles and wearing Iranian-supplied uniforms. Iran was the largest single pre-2001 aid donor to the Northern Alliance, giving it increased leverage at the Bonn conference later that year. US Ambassador James Dobbins described the Iranian role at Bonn as "quite constructive."[462] At Bonn, the Iranians pushed for mention of democracy and commitment to counter-narcotics and counter-terrorism as Afghan goals in the final document. Iran helped prevent the political leaders of the Northern Alliance's constituent parties from functioning as spoilers and has remained a supporter of the Kabul government.

Afghanistan was seen by Iran as the most significant issue where they could potentially work with the US. This made Afghanistan part of the conservative-vs.-reform struggle that has dominated Iranian politics in recent years. When it became apparent that the US was not interested in working with Iran in Afghanistan, reflecting concerns over Iran's commitment to developing nuclear weapons, Iranian policy shifted drastically, causing them to reach out to their 1990s enemies, the Taliban, despite their many differences and continued hostility. Iran has provided the Afghan Taliban with a few high-value weapons, such as explosively formed warheads for use in IEDs and Chinese-made HN-5 man-portable SAMs, suggesting more would follow in the event of US or Israeli military action against Iran, and the Taliban has already made limited use of these weapons in Afghanistan. Iran is now hedging its bets, providing support to insurgent groups and sending a signal to Washington not to escalate its pressure over the nuclear issue or face increased aid to insurgents in Afghanistan and Iraq and creating "dual-track under-the-table support for Taliban," in the words of COL McNiece.[463] But the level of assistance the insurgents receive from Iran still pales next to that they receive through Pakistan. However, it is far from negligible. Iranians cooperate with Al Qaeda, allowing them transit without stamping passports to avoid alerting Western security services if they later try to enter their countries.[464] The Iranian Revolutionary Guards Corps (IRGC) and its Al-Quds (Jerusalem) political warfare force (or its predecessors) have been involved in Afghanistan since the 1980s, either at the direction of the central government in Tehran or as an example of an independent policy initiated and implemented by the IRGC. The Al-Quds force is still reportedly training Afghan insurgents.[465] Despite their willingness to aid the insurgents and seeing Kabul as a US puppet, Iran still sees it as a preferable option to a new Pakistan-backed regime based on Sunni insurgents.

Aid has allowed Iran to entrench its influence in Afghanistan with both the Karzai government and officials and grassroots Afghans alike in western Afghanistan, which remains economically dependent on Iran.[466] The most significant program is a railroad that will link Herat to Iran's national rail system. In 2010, Hamid Karzai stated that Iran "gives us bags of money." Iran serves as a source of jobs for Afghan expatriate workers. In 2008, in the words of COL McNiece, "Iran is the second biggest investor in Afghanistan behind the US and has good political influence."[467] Despite US hostility toward Iran, the Karzai government has a public policy of maintaining good relations.

Iran has a long-standing commitment to stemming the narcotics trade, especially that concentrated in the area of the Afghanistan-Iran-Pakistan border tri-junction.[468] Dating back to the 1980s, Iranian paramilitary counter-narcotics operations have led to pitched battles with well-armed traffickers. However, there have also recently been unconfirmed signs of cooperation with select Afghan narcotics traffickers, with some Iranians, possibly including the IRGC, letting them transit Iranian territory for a share of the proceeds.[469] Iran's counter-narcotics forces are reportedly suffering from increasing levels of corruption and cooperate with traffickers.[470] The rectitude of Iran's drug interdiction operation may also have been a casualty of war.

Pakistan resents any and all Iranian involvement in Afghanistan, which Pakistan believes should be in their sphere of influence. Pakistan continues to see Afghan Persian-speakers as a natural fifth column for Iran and any non-Pushtun government in Kabul as a potential Iranian puppet. Pakistan has thus been suspicious of Iran's energy-based dealings in the region and has blocked Iran's ambitions for energy pipelines running to India. By 2008, Iran was concerned about the anti-Shia objectives of the insurgency in Pakistan as well as the TTP's links to Iran's rivals in Saudi Arabia and throughout the Gulf. Iran feels loyalty toward Pakistan's Shias that go back to the 1980s, including Shia Pushtun tribes such as the Touray, which have faced violence from both Pakistani religious groups and Afghan Islamists such as HiH that had strong relations with the Pakistani security services. This has been reflected in providing access to funding that was used to acquire, in the case of Shia Pushtuns, weapons for self-defense.

For Pakistan, the conflict in Afghanistan has traditionally been viewed through two prisms: domestic as involving Pushtuns and religion; and international, first opposing the Soviet Union and then India. The Pakistani military and many elites believe that India is trying to use Pakistan's disparate groups and weak civil society to destroy the entire country and annex its territory or, at best, reduce it to a compliant client state. The actions of the US and its coalition partners are perceived in Pakistan to weaken their influence in Afghanistan, making it less of a barrier against Indian encirclement. The US is seen as having become increasingly pro-India since the 1990s or worse, according to some Pakistanis, as part of an alliance with Israel and India to destroy or subjugate Islam.

Indo-Pakistani tensions have been playing out in Afghanistan since 1947 when New Delhi took over the British policy of supporting King Zahir's government in Kabul, albeit at a greatly reduced level of resources. Afghanistan voted against Pakistan's admission to the UN over its opposition to the Durand Line as the international border. India encouraged Afghanistan to raise its territorial claims to Pakistan up to the Indus as Pushtunistan, following King Zahir's calling a Loya Jirga in 1949 that repudiated the Durand Line, insisting it was not what Pakistan and the world community saw it as, the international border. During Afghanistan's Golden Age, Pakistan saw Soviet and Indian support for this Afghan border policy as being much more important than the minimal amount of cross-border violence that resulted from Kabul's Pushtunistan claims. Indian influence in Kabul encouraged Afghanistan to create and use the Pushtunistan issue as a lever to dismember Pakistan; and Pakistan, in return, became committed to excluding Indian influence from Afghanistan. But Afghanistan never took advantage of Pakistan's conflicts with India to take action; there has never been a "stab in the back."

Before 1978, India maintained a significant presence in Afghanistan, keeping consulates and listening posts at Kandahar and Jalalabad, in addition to its large embassy in Kabul. These outposts provided New Delhi with the means to assist the then-thriving local Hindu and Sikh communities, which today have been reduced to a few hundred. The Indians kept contact with the Pushtunistan Movement in Afghanistan and Pakistan, some of whose Pushtun leaders, including Khan Abdul

Ghaffar Khan, the "Frontier Gandhi," had been close to Jawaharlal Nehru and the Indian National Congress pre-partition.[471] This contributed to the Pakistani military's suspicion of secular Pushtun nationalists as potential secessionists.

Improved relations between India and the Soviet Union in the 1970s increased Pakistan's fears of encirclement. India had refused to vote in the UN to condemn the 1979 Soviet invasion of Afghanistan and maintained a small military assistance mission in Kabul during the period of the Soviet occupation. With the end of the Soviet Union over a decade later, increased Indian involvement in Afghanistan reflected concern over Islamism and its potential impact on Indian Muslims as well as Pakistan's attempts to use Afghanistan-trained guerrillas and insurgent networks in Kashmir, fueling a cross-border insurgency there starting in the late 1980s. After 1992, India developed contacts with Ahmad Shah Massoud and the other leaders of the Northern Alliance in an effort to oppose Pakistan's proxy war in Afghanistan through HiH and the Taliban and counter militant Islam.

Since the collapse of the Taliban in 2001, Indian diplomatic and economic involvement in Afghanistan has increased. From Kabul's perspective, Indian involvement in Afghanistan appears benign—four consulates (the same number as Pakistan); 750 million dollars in Indian aid in 2001–09 and a further 1.6 billion dollars pledged—making it Afghanistan's sixth largest bilateral aid donor.[472] But when the Indian consulates that had operated until 1989 re-opened in Jalalabad and Kandahar in 2003, it was seen as an act of offensive political warfare by Pakistani officials. Pakistan has repeatedly claimed that these consulates have been used to support the secular nationalist insurgency in Baluchistan and to collect intelligence against Pakistan. By mid-2008 there were an estimated 4,000 Indian civilian and security personnel working in Afghanistan, which further raised Pakistani fears. Pakistan also perceives India's involvement in reconstruction programs as a threat, especially the program of road building, some carried out by India's Border Roads Organization (especially the Zanaj-Dilarm highway), believing it is a cover for establishing an Indian military and intelligence presence in Afghanistan. The BRO's paramilitary nature and roots in India's long-standing internal counter-insurgency campaigns are widely perceived in Pakistan as a harbinger of greater Indian military involvement. The Indian government's access to the Farkhor airbase in Tajikistan, granted by that government with Moscow's apparent approval, fed Pakistani perceptions of a threatening encirclement.

Musharraf's back-channel diplomacy on Kashmir that led to the end of cross-border support for the insurgency in Kashmir in 2003–04 was matched by India's unwillingness to make meaningful concessions to improve relations with Pakistan or soften its control of Kashmir, widely resented by Pakistanis across the political spectrum. India has offered Pakistan little reconciliation and no concessions for its ending the cross-border insurgency in Kashmir and threatened military retaliation for attacks by terrorist groups tolerated by the Pakistani security services. Insurgents in Pakistan desperately needed to prevent any India-Pakistan rapprochement in order to sustain the momentum of their conflict. The 2002 attack on the Indian parliament and the 2008 Mumbai attack are examples of the terrorist need to preserve India-Pakistan hostility. India, like Israel and the US, is seen in Pakistan as providing terrorists more fodder for recruits and attacks by appearing to be waging a global war against Islam. That the Mumbai attack also targeted a Jewish community center shows that solidarity with Islamic violence worldwide has an important motivational factor.[473]

No More Frontiers

Radical religious groups are no longer a fringe threat on the outskirts of Pakistan's society or the margins of its national territory. Years of low electoral turnout for religious parties—usually less than ten percent—does not accurately reflect their influence on Pakistan's society and politics. Mainstream politicians now make major policy decisions to gain their support, such as Nawaz Sharif's unimplemented plans, announced in 1999, to introduce Sharia law nationwide. In addition to support for the religious parties by many of Pakistan's political leadership, religious radicalization has been fed by the economic downturn that reversed much of Pakistan's growth experienced in the decade prior to 2008, increased urbanization, the impact of terrorism, and the insurgencies and the propaganda. While some 87 percent of Pakistanis polled in 2009 described themselves as religious, 83 percent believed Sharia permitted girls' education and 75 percent believed it permitted women working; the radicalization has more turned opinion against the US than in favor of fundamentalism or insurgency.[474] The polarization of Pakistani popular opinion against the US and what has been portrayed as its "Global War on Islam" greatly increased in the last two years of the Musharraf government, and this has not decreased.[475] Yet the unpopularity of the US does not mean that the Pakistani insurgents are necessarily popular. The Pakistani insurgents have demonstrated little interest in taking part in democratic politics. In 2009, polling suggested than only about 10 percent of Pakistanis actually support the insurgents or radical ideology.[476] Yet this is a vocal and politically mobilized 10 percent, and their links with the religious parties mean that even the military, which sees itself as the guardians of Pakistan's future, must treat them with caution even as they oppose their attempts to gain greater political and societal power.

The 2008 elections, which were apparently less corrupt that those in 2002, created a democratic opening in Pakistan; but as this has appeared to erode away in subsequent years, as have other such openings in past decades, it may concede the rest of Pakistan's future to democracy's enemies and beyond the point of no return. The economic downturn of 2008, unresolved structural problems, the ongoing ethnic and regional divisions, the absence of any likelihood of internally directed reform, the low quality of political leadership, and the continued focus on opposing India are all contributing to trends that have undercut the civilian government and reversed any real headway to create a functional civil society. After the optimism that greeted Zardari's election in 2008, within a year deep despair and cynicism over the failures of civilian politicians have led many Pakistanis to look at rule by the military as a preferable to the current politics. But the military rule option may well not yield another Musharraf-like government, acceptable to Pakistani elites and foreign supporters. Rather, it may be a "colonel's coup" of radicalized anti-Western officers as a violent reaction against a dysfunctional political system. A less explosive alternative was seen in the military's pressure against Zadiri, seen as too pro-US and soft on opposing India and supporting the Afghan insurgents, in late 2009.[477] "The economy is trashed and law and order is approaching a crisis, but the military is reluctant to come back into power as it knows the public is fed up with them," in the words of a veteran journalist.

The first years under Pakistan's post-2008 new democracy did not augur well for success. National-level politics remained deadlocked between the Pakistan Peoples Party (PPP) and the Pakistan Muslim League-Nawaz (PML-N), with the pro-Musharraf Pakistan Muslim League-Quaid-e-Azam (PML-Q) watching from the sidelines. The highly personalized competition between their leaders and their families for national leadership and the personal and economic benefits power brings with it has limited opportunities for effective political cooperation. Even without the effect of the military, it is the vocal religious parties, the entrenched power sources of large landowners or other elite family organizations, and powerful retired military officers and government officials that have actually limited democracy in Pakistan, coupled with the fact that the political parties themselves have not yet made the internal transition from personal patronage networks to modern political institutions and are thus stuck in the highly personal "feudal" ways. The parties, like society, are still fixed on traditional lines, making the move into a modern democracy all the more difficult. The insurgency and the economic crisis have made it more difficult for Pakistan's leaders—both elected officials and unelected elites—to put aside their essentially feudal battles. Expecting the civilian government to alter the military control of national security policy, including Afghanistan, is not reasonable in the short term in light of these continued disputes. In the longer term, the transition to a democratic Pakistan will require outside aid—financial and providing expertise—and assistance in strengthening the institutions of governance. This is required for the first steps toward a Pakistan where state schools teach, income taxes are collected, and politics is a matrix for reconciling differences, not maximizing the wealth and power of those in office.

No elected government in Pakistan has ever served out its full term. Pakistan's civilian political leaders have had limited influence on any Afghanistan-related policy since the 1970s. Until that fact changes, there is unlikely to be a break in the tightening cycles of policy failures, with the military fearing Indian encirclement through Afghanistan. The only way the Pakistan military has been able to feel secure from this threat has been to continue their decades-old policies of using Afghan proxies to put a government in Kabul that will exclude India and further Pakistan's security interests.

The Pakistan Dimension

"It is impossible to sustain Afghanistan if we lose Pakistan" is how former House of Representatives speaker Newt Gingrich sees it, and he is correct.[478] Pakistan's historical relationship with Afghanistan has been, despite improvements in recent years, largely hostile. Pakistan's relationship with the US is marked by low levels of transparency and trust, despite having been allies in the Cold War years. From Kabul, it appears that Pakistan is at the root of many of Afghanistan's intractable problems, even those that to others may be seen to have indigenous origins.[479] Unless Pakistan is stabilized and its downward spiral is turned around, Afghanistan's war will be fueled by Pakistan's perceptions of insecurity and waged from a sanctuary on its territory.

Pakistan's foreign policy is still dominated by the security competition with India and Pakistan's internal strife. The Pakistan military has spent years trying to reconcile its need for a security relationship with the US—along with China and Saudi Arabia, Pakistan's traditional allies—with its belief that the Afghan insurgents and the Pakistani groups that supported the insurgency in Kashmir are still, despite all recent occurrences to the contrary, controllable and a vital asset to Pakistan's national security, especially with regard to India.[480] The military and the security services owe much of their preeminence in the political and, increasingly, economic sphere to the perception that the nation is under an imminent external threat—mostly from India—that is aiming to use internal divisions to tear Pakistan apart; and, given the intense internal strife, it is easy for many citizens to believe this claim.

If Pakistan is not to drag down Afghanistan in this quest to assure their own security interests there and keep India out, the US and the international community need to work for better relations between the two countries. While Afghan recognition of the Durand Line as the legitimate international border would contribute to a renewed relationship, it is not likely under the current Afghan government. It would be hard for an ethnic Pushtun Afghan head of state to be seen to have given away Afghanistan's claims to the lost patrimony of the lands between the Durand Line and the Indus.

In its relations with Pakistan, the US needs to insist on action against the insurgency that threatens Afghanistan, not just the ones being waged at home. Until there is evidence that Pakistan is actually moving against the sanctuaries of the Afghan insurgency, how much its relations with the US can be improved is limited. Similarly, as long as the international presence in Afghanistan is dependent on bulk cargo and fuel being delivered to Karachi and trucked to Afghanistan over a tenuous 1,250-mile supply route—although some cargoes can be airlifted in and there is an effort to bring cargoes in by rail through central Asia—the pressure the US can put on Pakistan to change its policies will also be limited.[481] Pakistan does not have to threaten to close the supply route. It can effectively close it at any time by deciding to tolerate insurgent action against it unless concessions are made. Pakistan in 2010 displayed tremendous leverage over US policy through the fact that, in the words of US undersecretary of defense Ashton Carter, "Next to Antarctica, Afghanistan is probably the most incommodious place, from a logistics point of view, to be trying to fight a war."[482]

The US relationship with Pakistan is especially challenging in this situation. The US needs to keep Pakistan's nuclear capability secure and safe and prevent additional proliferation to more dangerous potential threats. In the longer term, it is to everyone's advantage for a future that sees Pakistan living in peace with India; and if this is ever to be achieved, it is likely that the US will have to be a facilitator. Until then, the US must work to counter Pakistan's policies in Afghanistan, to make it clear to Pakistan that its national security will be better served by relying on its economic strength in Afghanistan and participating in the international effort there than continuing failed policies. The US also needs to continue to work with Pakistan's military and security services to build a counter-insurgency capability that does more than encourage home-grown insurgents to instead take their battle over the Durand Line.

US aid and support to Pakistan will have to, first, address the weakened state and, second, to give the US a degree of contact and leverage with Pakistan outside the military, which is something it has lacked in recent decades. American unpopularity in Pakistan makes conditions and milestones in such aid politically unpalatable, as the controversy over the Kerry-Lugar foreign aid bill in 2009 demonstrated, with the accountability provisions of the law subjected to criticism, initiated by the military, that they are an insult to Pakistan's sovereignty. Yet US political realities require accountability, as much as this is resented by Pakistanis, if the aid flow is going to be of a size and scope that is going to have a real impact in Pakistan. The US needs assurance that its aid is being used as agreed, and verification should be done on a government-to-government basis as much as possible to meet the requirements for careful oversight and accounting and to ensure that the money is not going to the pockets of the ruling elites, as much appeared to do in the past.[483]

Despite all they have done to keep Afghanistan in a state of conflict, it remains that the Pakistan military is not the real enemy of the US and should be viewed as a genuine if reluctant ally, as the military, like it or not, remains the most important single institution in a country where civil society remains weak and politics has hardly exceeded the lowest expectations. American policymakers also need to make clear to their own electorate why there is a need to engage with Pakistan so closely, as Pakistan has not been presented in a favorable light by either the media or its own actions. Otherwise, withdrawal or escalation, disengaging or sending in troops to resolve Pakistan's security problems, may appear appealing even if both are likely to prove disastrous. Barack Obama, as a presidential candidate, backed direct US military action against targets in Pakistan.[484] It is not realistic to expect that the Pakistani military will believe that the US has the capability to succeed in Afghanistan if the US electorate does not also believe it. The continued cost in lives and money and the difficulty in identifying meaningful progress has made this later goal problematic.

The elections of 2008 and the series of crises leading up to them offer a potential for a turning point for what may be the best—or possibly the last—chance for democracy to flower in Pakistan. The insurgents, seemingly poised to march on Islamabad, were put on the defensive by the military, an indication that they were willing to fight when pressed. US UAV strikes are benefiting from Pakistani intelligence targeting, indicating a renewed cooperation despite recent hostility to the campaign. Leaders willing to oppose the TTP, TNSM, and terrorists have been able to hold on to power in the NWFP and FATA and are not being pushed out.

In the long term, dealing with these threats requires the rebuilding of civil society in Pakistan. The years of military rule worsened Pakistan's crisis of governance, weakening civil officials to the point of impotence and leading to the increasing politicization and corruption of what the average Pakistani sees as "the face" of government. Civil courts are slow and frustrating, making Sharia courts, with their cachet of Islamic social justice, often appear to be appealing alternatives. The insurgents in Swat won approval from many for their goal of putting a Sharia legal system in place in 2009, but what resulted was nothing an alim would have recognized as Sharia. Social justice elements of Islam, often neglected in recent years, have been appropriated by the insurgents to gain a degree of mass support where people cannot rely on ties of ethnicity or religious practice in the absence of a civil system. Taxation power has been used almost exclusively against those who lack the political connections to avoid it. Many have not seen the benefits of recent economic growth, but did of course feel the impact of the downturn that followed them. Rebuilding Pakistan's state educational system, the failure of which has led to the rise of the madrassas, is often seen as the most important element of rebuilding civil society, an effort that has unfortunately received limited amounts of recent US aid; the post-2001 aid effort had focused on security-related funding, especially for military hardware. If Pakistan can do these things, then it may be easier to reconcile its policy interests with that of the Afghans and other regional players. The prospects for a better relationship with India, which, in the waning years of the Musharraf regime, seemed to only await a stronger government with greater legitimacy in Islamabad to proceed, but have since been frozen, could be a real possibility.

The threat posed by the Pakistan insurgency is not simply radical Pushtun lashkars entering Peshawar. Some action by the insurgents may be the trigger that tips Pakistan over the edge into ungovernability, but the insurgency is not the root cause of the chaos. The military remains cohesive enough to prevent the insurgents from seizing power by force of arms. The problem is that the military's action could then turn out to be more damaging that anything the insurgents could do directly. The insurgents may be unlikely to take control with a small well-directed minority. They may become a catalyst for wider concerns and polarization, pushing Pakistan from its current decades-long crisis of governance into ungovernability.[485] In the words of Pakistani journalist Ahmed Rashid, "we can expect a slow, insidious long-burning fuse of fear, terror and paralysis that the Taliban have lit and that the state is unable, and partially unwilling, to douse."[486]

"In Pakistan, all the solutions are long term but all the risks are short term," said Dr. Marvin Weinbaum, a former State Department official.[487] Pakistan's structural and historical crises are such that a major transformation of the country and its institutions will be needed if the country is to endure. Such a transformation can only be brought about by the Pakistanis themselves, but the US can help Pakistan with its internal struggles and address the need to recreate a strong civil society. The US should aim to expand and empower democratic policies and institutions. Economic aid and security aid are both important. There is a need to rally the economic community to realize that the future of Pakistan is important to both democracy and stability. China and Saudi Arabia certainly have an interest in its stability. Convincing them that it is worth it for them to invest in this long-term process will be a challenge. Winning or losing the conflicts in Afghanistan against terrorism, insurgency, and narcotics will all be affected by Pakistan's evolution or devolution in the next 5–10 years.

The 2010 flooding demonstrated the weakness of civil governance and contributed to rising rural poverty. In 2010, Pakistan's continued political weakness, exacerbated by the impact of flood damage, prevented effective military action against either Pakistani or Afghan insurgent strongholds. The flooding will have a negative impact on the economy and development for years to come.

PART THREE
WINNING THE CONFLICTS

CHAPTER NINE

COUNTERING AFGHANISTAN'S INSURGENCY

"Prestige is everything in this kind of warfare."
—C.E. Callwell (of insurgency)

"NATO's future is on the line here."
Ambassador Richard C. Holbrooke (of Afghanistan)

"Afghanistan is not a graveyard. It is my home. People do not live in a graveyard. You cannot equate the presence of the US and the coalition in Afghanistan today, who came to help, with those of the past, empires or otherwise, that tried to conquer or control" are the words of Afghanistan's defense minister Rahim Wardak.[488] However, to those Afghans fighting against Wardak's soldiers and their coalition allies, the continuity between them and the would-be conquerors of the past is obvious. For them, fighting with the aid of Pakistani security services and Arab supporters is what they started against the Soviets and Communist Afghans in 1978, continued against the Islamic State of Afghanistan government in the 1990s, and have revived after 2001. There has been little incentive for them to change, and most of them apparently think that they, eventually, will defeat the coalition and the Kabul government as they defeated the Soviets and their Afghan allies.

If history has shown that "empires" do poorly in Afghanistan, it is not because Afghans are intrinsically destructive to them. Nor, despite what Al Qaeda and the Taliban may claim, should the Afghan reaction to the US presence be equated to that which has led Afghanistan to be called "the graveyard of empires." Empires are proud, big and slow to learn, and interested in their own power and politics much more than those of the countries in which they are involved. When empires apply templates developed elsewhere to Afghanistan, they do not realize they are making bad policy decisions by default until it is too late. Empires tend to rely on armed force, which is less effective in Afghanistan in the absence of a visible center of gravity and where overthrowing and seizing state power is all too easy and consolidating and retaining power very difficult. Empires also discover that when things go bad in Afghanistan, they do so rapidly and with few potential ways to reverse a deteriorating situation. At this point, the empires tend to find that they have better things to do than invest further resources in Afghanistan and thus abandon the conflict, leaving the Afghans to face the economic and political damage. But this defeat and failure tends to follow the empires home from Afghanistan, because it was there, not Afghanistan, that defeat had its roots. The conditions that cause the empire to withdraw, whether lack of resources, will, or failure to adapt to challenging conditions, can become fatal flaws when faced with less peripheral threats. Afghanistan itself does not defeat the empires. The empires defeat themselves.[489]

A Divided Counter-Insurgency

The absence of a unitary strategy has meant that hard-won successes on the part of the US, coalition, Afghans, NGOs and others in each area—military, development, reconstruction, governance, the economy—have not been pulled together to build a secure nation-state. There is no US strategy that cuts across these spheres of conflicts and can reach across the borders. Coalition members impose their own restrictions on participation. Pakistan has to counter the same threats, but cooperation with integrated grand strategy that involves the US appears an unrealistic goal as long as the primacy of the Indian threat and the willingness to tolerate sanctuaries for Afghan insurgents are the most visible manifestation of a highly nationalistic strategy that treats the US and its Afghan allies with continued wariness, ranging into covert hostility.

Organization has been a weakness of the US, coalition, and Kabul efforts to counter Afghanistan's conflicts from the outset. Unity of command and unity of effort have been difficult to achieve, both on a purely military basis and between military and non-military efforts. The International Security Assistance Force (ISAF) was created in 2002 in an attempt to facilitate UN and NGO participation in Afghan security, as these groups did not want to interact with the US Operation Enduring Freedom (OEF) headquarters that had led the initial 2001–02 invasion and overthrew the Taliban.[490] UN Security Council Resolution 1386 on 20 December 2001 authorized the establishment of ISAF. The different origins of the two headquarters, ISAF under Europeans and intended to keep the peace and OEF under Americans (although with coalition participation) and intended to capture terrorists, made it hard for them to pull together. When it became apparent that the US was not going to put in place a single headquarters that would be able to handle security throughout Afghanistan, ISAF expanded its headquarters' reach starting in 2003–04, again authorized by the UN Security Council, bringing in higher ranking generals and more capable staffs to manage their operations. The US headquarters in Afghanistan were correspondingly increased, but by then the effective and unified operations of 2001–02 were gone and the US and ISAF were on the paths to separate strategies. US special operations under SOCOM operational command were not integrated with other elements of the overall strategy or with the government of Afghanistan.[491] Development was more divided and divorced from the efforts to hold back the insurgent activities that could potentially negate any gains or benefit to the Afghan people realized from humanitarian efforts. When NATO took over responsibility for ISAF in August 2003, it could then access US personnel and support; by the end of 2008 about a quarter of ISAF's 52,000 personnel were US military and civilians, removing some of the gaps between the US and ISAF efforts. Throughout this period, there was no unitary command plan, let alone strategy, for both US and ISAF forces. Each organization had differing priorities, rules of engagements, and operational methods. Terrorists, insurgents, and narcotics traffickers alike were perceptive enough to identify the gaps between the two and exploit them: for example, often operating in close proximity to ISAF forces that were considered unlikely to attack them to reduce vulnerability to US airstrikes.

Progress in addressing these problems was made in 2008–10. GEN David Petraeus said: "We need a comprehensive whole-of-government counter-insurgency approach. The legitimacy of government is the key ingredient in any counter-insurgency."[492] This approach was announced by NATO in 2008 and stressed that military operations needed to be carried out in coordination with developing Afghan institutions and capabilities while enabling reconstruction and development.[493] 2008 saw the previously distinct US and ISAF/NATO chains of command inside Afghanistan brought together under US GEN David McKiernan, which made the parallel chains of higher-level command that continued, running separately to the two coalition commands from Brussels (NATO) and Florida (CENTCOM HQ), more palatable. McKiernan also ordered the drafting of the 2008 ISAF Joint Campaign Plan (JCP) that clearly stated objectives and approaches that would be shared throughout the coalition effort. Although McKiernan was sacked in May 2009[494] as too much of a conventional coalition warrior, out of touch with the new command structure, and replaced by US GEN Stanley McChrystal, the unified command arrangement was retained. McChrystal wearing two hats, worked as both a US and NATO commander. However, NATO retained its Senior Civilian Representative (SCR) position in Kabul, outside of ISAF, a position held in 2010 by UK Ambassador Mark Sedwill. This means that there is still no single "NATO voice" in interactions with the US and the Afghan government. In January 2010, UN Secretary General Ban Ki-Moon called for such a capability.[495]

In mid-2009 McChrystal used his dual command authority to implement unity by revising the tactics, techniques, and procedures of both US and ISAF forces in Afghanistan. His successor GEN Petraeus, retained both the command authority and the TTPS. A revised ISAF tactical directive has been, according to Petraeus, "All about taking lessons learned with a very nuanced and granular appreciation of the situation on the ground. It emphasized the imperative of avoiding civilian casualties and the numbers have been reduced by rigorous implementation."[496]

ISAF Joint Command (IJC), an intermediate US/ISAF headquarters for Afghanistan, was created using assets from the Germany-based US V Corps headquarters under US LTG David Rodriguez. Operational in November 2009, IJC provided a joint level of command responsible for the full range of daily tactical operations and providing the interface between the high level commands of US Forces-Afghanistan and ISAF and the six contiguous regional commands (RC) (Regional-Commands, East, West, South, Southwest, North and Center) that have the primary responsibility for operations.[497] US and ISAF forces are integrated under these five regional commands. In late 2010, RC-Center was under Turkish Command, RC-East and Southwest were under US command, RC-West was under Italian command, RC-South command under the UK, and RC-North was under German command. US Special Operations Command is a supporting rather than supported command in these operations, thus working under CENTCOM and not functioning as an independent command, although it can operate as such for operations such as high-priority raids where operational security is especially important.[498] CENTCOM continues to operate special operations forces and has a counter-terrorism special operational task force under its command.

Afghanistan already has a complex set of internal divisions, but the coalition military effort has added a new set of competing tribes: the military forces of ISAF's 71,000 personnel from 49-plus countries, each with their own way of operating and each with unique national goals and objectives.[499] The impacts on the multiple intertwined conflicts have been dire. GEN Bantz Craddock said that "Political leadership in NATO is AWOL."[500]

Tactical interoperability among NATO members reflects a high level of professionalism. But the operational effect of this is undercut by the explicit national caveats, issued by 20 nations' governments, that restrict the orders that ISAF may give to their troops.[501] National caveats can include prohibitions on night operations, proactive patrolling, or in taking part in the disarmament of Afghan groups and counter-narcotics operations. Germany's large coalition troop presence in Afghanistan has had its actions limited by restrictive national caveats and rules of engagement. German troops can use deadly force only in self-defense and have their ability to move or operate at night limited.[502] German training and advisory teams cannot conduct combined offensive operations with ANA units. The highly capable German special operations forces were effectively confined to their forward operating base. Other coalition members have taken other limited-liability approaches to their Afghanistan commitments, rendering the coalition militarily weaker than it should be, given the breadth of international participation. France has restricted the number of troops deployed, although its combat units have few restrictive caveats limiting their operations. Norway, Sweden, Italy, and Spain have made widespread use of national caveats and have restricted the areas in Afghanistan where their troops can deploy and operate, while Denmark, with fewer limitations, has allowed its troops to operate integrated with the UK contingent. In some cases, countries have committed only forces suitable for non-combat tasks, such as operating the civil-military Provincial Reconstruction Teams (PRTs) that provide much of the coalition's development work in rural Afghanistan. Other countries that have deployed combat units continue to make force protection, rather than the effective low-level tactics normally associated with successful counter-insurgency warfare, their priority.

The US has pushed its coalition partners to reduce the impact of national caveats, and several countries have removed or reduced them. NATO has moved toward interoperability and shared operational capabilities in more conventional operations and learned the nuances of international peace operations the hard way in the Balkans, but it had no framework at all with regards to counter-insurgency warfare. Some NATO members still do not officially recognize the term. Many of the coalition armed forces committed to Afghanistan are neither trained nor equipped to take part in the full range of military operations required and have lacked the resources or capability to adapt.

But the overall NATO effort has been undercut by the withdrawal of two of the alliance's most effective members, Canada and the Netherlands, from ground combat operations (although not necessarily training and development) that started to take place in 2010–11. Other coalition members have the potential to find that their commitment may become even more politically unpopular at home if they suffer more than minimal casualties.[503]

Collateral Damage

The unwillingness by many coalition members to commit large numbers of troops and to allow them to take part in effective counter-insurgency operations has actually contributed to collateral damage. When there are too few troops on the ground, they have to redress their lack of numbers by calling in indirect fire or airstrikes, which are especially frequent in southern Afghanistan where there are relatively few troops and insurgents can come together quickly. Many coalition troops remain in their protective positions due to lack of numbers, with force protection being seen as a higher priority than offensive action. Yet moving in rural Afghanistan with large forces is what will strengthen the appearance of an army of occupation that is not comfortable with the Afghan people.

This underlines the fundamental tension collateral damage concerns are placing on coalition operations. More troops are needed to reduce the need for collateral damage, which creates resentment for the coalition and sympathy for the insurgents. While more troops will, in turn, have the potential of appearing as an army of occupation and also creating such resentment, they also have the potential to provide enhanced security for the Afghans that can enable reconstruction and win over support. These contradictory requirements have given additional importance to the use of smaller, special operations forces that will strike using accurate and timely intelligence targeting. But here again, when they are perceived to target the wrong Afghans, regardless of the underlying reality, their actions can undercut overall coalition strategy.

With regards to collateral damage issue, US Chairman of the Joint Chiefs of Staff ADM Mike Mullen said that "I believe each time we do that [kill civilians] puts our strategy in jeopardy. . . . We cannot succeed in Afghanistan—or anywhere else, but let's talk specifically about Afghanistan—by killing Afghan civilians. The center of gravity in Afghanistan is the people of Afghanistan."[504] A poll published in 2009 shows that 77 percent of Afghans considered such collateral damage unacceptable.[505] By 2007, President Karzai was acting as a spokesman for these concerns.[506] In 2008, Rahim Wardak, Afghanistan's defense minister, said "Civilian casualties and collateral damage hurts the support of the people for the government and the international presence. Better intelligence, integrated planning, cohesion, the use of Afghan forces for house searches, avoiding the use of air forces or indirect fires in populated areas can be achieved by use of ground forces and ensure that reaction is proportionate to the target."[507] The importance of the issue was emphasized by the 22 August 2008 incident where an airstrike killed 95 Afghan civilians in the village of Azizabad in Herat province, which led to strong concerns being voiced by Karzai and UN authorities.[508]

But collateral damage remains a potential cost inherent in the number of troops required for security against the insurgency, requiring effective mitigation and limitation approaches to be put in place.[509] In 2009 polling, among Afghans that report bombing or shelling by US or NATO/ISAF forces in their area, support for the presence of US forces in Afghanistan drops to 46 percent, as opposed to 70 percent among those that report no such activity.[510] In 2010, collateral damage decreased with UN estimates that coalition firepower was creating 12 percent of Afghan casualties.[511]

The impact of civilian casualties has been increased by the Afghan's expectation as to the precision of US military action. The highly responsive capabilities of US military firepower were clear to the Afghans from the battles of 2001–02. A precise target could be destroyed in just minutes. House searches, non-precision tactics potentially affecting any rural Afghans, special forces raids which take people away in the middle of the night, and road accidents caused by foreign forces, were among the coalition tactics that created not necessarily a mass movement, but large numbers of individual Afghans with grievances that their culture told them could not be easily ignored or explained away without a blow to their self-image.[512] The widespread searching of houses by coalition forces after 2001 presented a challenge to traditional Afghan values. As with collateral damage, there is no avoiding the fact that house searches are required in effective counter-insurgency operations although they create resentment. The increased use of Afghan forces, especially the Afghan National Police (ANP), is part of the required mitigation, but this will require reform and better training of this force. The Afghans will need to see for themselves that the searches help result in the increased security they desire.

Insurgency and Response

In 2001–02, the bearded long-haired snake-eating special operations forces and intelligence operators from the US, UK, Australia, New Zealand, and other allies that had been on the ground during the actual fighting against the Taliban and Al Qaeda had interacted effectively with the Afghans, both the more established forces of the Northern Alliance and other improvised anti-Taliban groups in Pushtu-speaking Afghanistan, of which future president Karzai was one of the leaders. When the special operators withdrew and were replaced by regular soldiers, and the optimism of 2001–02 and the political momentum of the initial successes were allowed to dissipate, the cultural shock became very real and dysfunctional. The zero-defect US military encountered total-defect Afghanistan in 2002 and there was a mutual lack of understanding and a failure to adapt.[513] In Operation Anaconda, which took place in early 2002, heroic US military actions could not prevent Al Qaeda and Afghan Taliban fighting men withdrawing across the border from Afghanistan into Pakistan.[514] The Afghan forces under Northern Alliance commanders and others (ethnic Pushtuns) recently recruited to their cause against the defeated Taliban were more interested in securing their position for postwar access to power and patronage. Pakistan rounded up some "foreign" Al Qaeda leaders but had no interest in moving against the Afghan and Pakistani fighting men who soon settled into the Vortex and sat around drinking tea unmolested while plotting revenge on Kabul and Islamabad alike.

The post-2001 US strategy was initially to "get" Al Qaeda and Taliban leadership and was shaped by the insistence that the US "did not do nation-building." The US military, preoccupied with Iraq, having demonstrated its ability to help rapidly collapse the Taliban regime, believed that the reconstruction and institutional replacement could best be left to non-governmental organizations and the troops of willing allies. This coincided with the George W. Bush administration's political goals; in the 2000 campaign, he had claimed he would "absolutely not" do "nation building," unlike his predecessor, and he announced in his 2003 State of the Union Address that the US exercises "power without conquest."[515] In Afghanistan and Pakistan, it was widely interpreted as a strategy that precluded a long-term commitment to the region but rather was part of a greater global objective. The US policy was seen by those favorable to it as a "global war on terrorism," while many of those opposing it saw it as part of a "global war on Islam," which were all attributed to US-enabled action, including the long-running crises in Kashmir and the Middle East.

The resulting 2002–03 US policy in Afghanistan stressed limiting the number of foreign troops and declining the participation of their combat units, especially from Muslim countries. The US was opposed to expanding the ISAF presence outside of Kabul. In both of these decisions the US was supported by Afghanistan's Northern Alliance, then controlling many of the key ministries in Kabul, who saw ISAF troops as limitations on their power and Arab troops as a potential tool of pro-Taliban Saudi policies. The US policy was intended to minimize the number of troops and money required and opportunities for collateral damage and Afghan resentment. During the Bonn process, few thought that Afghanistan would be free of political violence. Karzai claimed to have warned the US that the main threat was not Al Qaeda but rather an undefeated Taliban currently regrouping in Pakistan.[516] But, instead, most threats to Kabul or US and coalition goals were presented in terms of warlords or the Northern Alliance. In 2001–04, conflicts between regional commanders in the north and provincial and local leaders in the east, all nominally loyal to Kabul, drew attention of the outside powers. The Afghans, perceptive of such things, explained the failure to defeat the enemies of 2001 away with conspiracy theories—the US was not interested in capturing Al Qaeda and Taliban leaders, the UK was bank-rolling the Pakistan Taliban through protection money for truck convoys from Karachi—and turned increasingly toward narcotics and other forms of corruption. If they could not save their country, they would, at least, save themselves.

The failure to prepare for Afghanistan's next war, a Pushtun insurgency supported from sanctuaries in Pakistan, limited investment by aid donors—Afghanistan itself was generating minimal internal revenue—in Kabul's security and law enforcement capabilities.[517] Few foreigners, their attention fixed on Kabul and warlords, focused on southern Afghanistan before the insurgency opened, and did not perceive the mixture of ineffective rule by local nominally pro-Kabul Pushtuns and the ability of the insurgents to fill the power vacuum this created as potentially explosive. The US and coalition military presence in the south, before ISAF arrived, was limited to a few battalions and some special operations forces. In 2001–04, the US approach to Afghan security depended on eliminating foreign support for a renewed insurgency (especially from Pakistan) and the Musharraf government following up on its commitments as a major ally in the "Global War on Terror." Instead there was the continuation of the policies ISI had backed for decades, with their continued reliance that they could control terrorists and insurgents on their territory and use them in Afghanistan for their own ends.

In 2005–06, the realization slowly came over US and Afghans alike that the lack of a unified command with a coherent strategy had created an unsustainable situation. 2006 was a pivotal year for Afghanistan's insurgency. Only then was the situation in southern Afghanistan—a well-resourced insurgency with sanctuaries in Pakistan—taken seriously. The migration of terrorist tactics, techniques and procedures (TTPs) to the Afghan insurgents was shown by the rise of suicide bombings from 21 in 2005 to 118 in 2006. All suicide attacks increased from 27 to 139, IEDs from 783 to 1677, and armed attacks from 1,300 to 4,542. In August 2006, NATO took over operations in southern Afghanistan. The war expanded in size and scope: an estimated 8–9,000 insurgents in the field, 1,250 Afghans killed in the three months of summer 2006. While signs of instability emerged outside the south and east, those areas remained the focus of the insurgency.

In 2007, more troops were deployed, leading to less dependency on airstrikes, thus mitigating collateral damage. However, there was still a 27 percent rise in insurgent-initiated violence, mostly in the hotbed south. In the south, the Canadians and Netherlands forces bore the brunt of these attacks, demonstrating a sophisticated insurgent strategy aimed at fracturing the alliance. The increase in the number of insurgent actions was some 30 percent higher in the first quarter of 2008 than the comparable period in 2007. Cross-border attacks increased from 20 a month in March 2007 to 53 in April 2008. By 2008, it was increasingly apparent that in addition to the areas in the south and east where the insurgents had established control or at least had an internal presence, more areas in central and eastern provinces including Wardak, Laghman, and Logar saw increased levels of violence, making the limited headway gained by troop increases starting in 2007 unable to turn around a deteriorating security situation in 2008. In May 2008, US Deputy Secretary of State John Negroponte described the continued influx from Pakistan as "unacceptable," the strongest public language directed at that country since 2001.

The US military, though it had the bulk of its attention focused on Iraq until 2008, again proved to be an institution that can learn and evolve. It shifted to aiming to do what ADM Eric Olson, SOCOM combatant commander, described as "change what is currently a habitat conducive to terrorism."[518] The evolution in US COIN doctrine reversed the 2001–04 failure to engage with grassroots Afghanistan and has been described as emphasizing "the protection of the population and recognized that the only way to secure people is to live among them."[519]

This led to the operational approach described as "shape, clear, hold and build," implemented starting in 2008.[520] It attempted to apply lessons from Iraq and set out in a new US counter-insurgency military field manual.[521] It starts with *shaping* an area through information operations and non-military action that run concurrently through the entire campaign, followed by military action to *clear* the insurgents from the area and separate them from the population that is the objective of this approach; *holding* is provided by creating a capability for governance and *building* through enabling reconstruction and development. The new operational approach demonstrated an increased awareness that counter-insurgency was primarily a non-military process and required increased coordination with political and developmental efforts.[522] The "shape, clear, hold and build" operational approach was demonstrated first by US and Polish troops moving into Wardak and Logar provinces in autumn 2008.

Making this new approach possible is an increased emphasis on "shaping" an area before coalition forces go in. In addition to the psychological operations and information warfare that will both precede troop presence and run concurrently with it, this "shaping" will aim to identify what the local population wants and see that what follows the coalition forces—the restoration of Afghan government authority—is effective, meets local needs, and does not leave a power vacuum for the insurgents to refill after only a few months. Yet the weakness of the Afghan government has meant that, even when coalition forces succeed in clearing the insurgents from an area, it is difficult to establish rule of law, provide governance and economic development to the locals, and help them realize their aspirations. "You can make a difference by making them safe but how can you have better governance?" asked BG Blanchette.[523] This is where the final element of this new operational approach—"build"—will really come into play, the building of an effective civil society as well as providing physical reconstruction.

The insurgents responded to the new operational approach not by fighting for the population but by mounting increased asymmetric offensive operations. In January through April 2009, compared with the year before, there was a 64 percent increase in insurgent attacks,[524] an 80 percent increase in the IED attacks that caused sixty percent of coalition and Afghan government casualities,[525] and a 90 percent increase in attacks on Afghan officials and district centers.[526] These attacks, coupled by the increased exposure resulting from getting out among the population, has led to increased casualties, with coalition deaths up by 55 percent and ANSF deaths by 25 percent in April 2009 from the year before. Rather than try to stop coalition and Afghan actions, the insurgents have instead aimed at making their presence outside their fortified forward area bases (FOBs) and among the Afghan population too costly to sustain. While seeking to protect the population, this new operational approach put more coalition forces into harm's way. At the same time, the coalition has withdrawn many smaller outposts in remote and border areas that appeared to be offering the insurgents targets rather than protecting Afghans. Part of the rationale is also to demonstrate to the Afghan people that military operations can help their security; in 2010 polling, the percentage of Afghans saying that US/NATO/ISAF forces had a strong local presence declined to 36 percent from 57 percent in 2006, while those saying that they provide effective security declined to 36 percent from 67 percent in 2010.[527]

In 2009–10, the "shape, clear, hold and build" operational concept was applied to the Helmand River valley. There was success when US and coalition forces were "living amongst them," but insurgents retained use the ties of kinship, tribe, or the threat of future, violent retribution. Repeatedly when coalition forces have cleared insurgents from an area, there was no Afghan government capability able to backfill behind them. This led to a 2010 priority, coalition forces providing the locals with a better alternative to allegiance, or at least cooperation, with the insurgents. It was also apparent that there would be a long way to go before the Afghan National Security Forces had either the numbers or the training to take over the "hold" or the Afghan government could provide the "build." Thus, the numbers of Afghan National Army (ANA) and ANP personnel, minimized in the early years of the coalition presence, needed to be increased and increased again to aid the in last two elements of this operational approach. The Obama administration's Afghanistan policy review in March 2009 led to a prolonged consideration of increased troops levels requested by US Army GEN Stanley McChrystal, which was approved in December 2009. "Shape, clear, hold and build" as an operational approach—not a strategy—provides a potentially effective way to use military and non-military assets to combat the insurgency. It does not answer the question of how best to achieve the desired end-state in Afghanistan.

Special Operations and Intelligence, Surveillance and Reconnaissance

Coalition special operation forces (SOF) were a success in 2001, but when the direction of the war shifted and was seen as demanding more conventional warfare, SOF assumed a secondary role, although, since then, they have still been heavily involved throughout Afghanistan. In addition to targeting insurgent commanders by direct action and using their reconnaissance missions to call in firepower, special operations forces have proved effective when they acted as "hammer" while larger forces were the "anvil" to defeat an insurgent presence. Using intelligence developed by the "anvil" presence in an area, the "hammer" provided maneuver, often driving insurgents out of secure areas and into the firepower of the "anvil." This was effectively done with coalition special operations in Uruzgan before the Dutch moved in during 2005–06.[528] Effective cooperation between the Dutch and SOF—especially the Australian SAS—continued until 2010. For example, SOF targeted the local Taliban commander Baz Mohammed in 2007, which led to divisions within the insurgents as there were disputes over who would succeed him, making insurgent operations less effective for months thereafter.[529] In 2009–10, increased US Special Operations Command (SOCOM) and coalition operations in Afghanistan targeted insurgent leaders.[530]

MG Mark Milley described coalition SOF as "critical to our overall effort of full-spectrum counter-insurgency operations. Special operations target leaders of the insurgency and target networks, whose cellular structure otherwise makes them hard to locate and defeat. Their use must complement conventional forces. Conventional force operations set the conditions for special operations. . . . Interdicting the enemy on the ratlines is fundamental to what we do."[531] He stated that the existence of a separate chain of command for SOF did not undercut their coordination: "Every special operation in Regional Command-East must be coordinated and approved. We do not command the forces, but RC-E owns the battlespace." With SOCOM functioning as a supporting commander in Afghanistan, special operations must be coordinated with CENTCOM, and, through it, the regional commands in Afghanistan and their tactical units. CENTCOM also controls its own special operations forces, and these must be coordinated in a similar way.

Special operations have been an important part of coalition intelligence surveillance and reconnaissance (ISR) efforts, gathering intelligence through contact with Afghans in areas away from conventional forces or with covert observation posts. MG Mark Milley described coalition ISR as having greatly improved since 2008. "ISR incorporates patrols, human intelligence, space-based platforms, UAVs, signals intelligence, and full-motion video. We see improvements every 90 days. The intelligence community is on a steep upwards slope of improvement."

Others, however, had a less optimistic view; one Afghan official said: "The coalition is good at seeing, less good at understanding." Despite improved technology such as the use of UAVs, providing the close integration of intelligence and operational commands that is vital in counter-insurgency conflicts has often proven difficult to achieve by US and coalition forces. Counter-insurgency warfare puts the emphasis on providing operational intelligence, and this continued to be lacking in many cases. Battalions often do not have their own UAV capability. In April 2008, US Secretary of Defense Robert Gates, expressing a concern that the US services were not moving fast enough to provide needed ISR capabilities, formed an ISR task force to assess requirements and meet operational needs. CENTCOM formed its own ISR Task Force. US airborne ISR increased 500 percent in 2009–10.

Indeed, understanding has often been far behind collection capability, but efforts have been made to provide military leaders with more in-depth knowledge on the Afghan and human dimension of the situation, for example, by the US investment in deployed human terrain teams (HTTs) able to bring expertise about the local population and their customs and behavior to support forces in the field, who otherwise would lack specialist insights to assist their task of knowing and "understanding."

ISR is currently in the hands of the coalition. Coalition HUMINT, vital in other counter-insurgency situations, has been more limited, reflecting language and cultural barriers and their deployment in forward operating bases rather than right in the villages.[532] Afghan defense minister Rahim Wardak greatly regrets the Afghan National Army's (ANA's) lack of an independent ISR capability.[533] The Afghan National Police (ANP) still lacks an intelligence capability that can build on its contacts within the population and thus make this information available to their coalition allies where it is needed the most.[534]

However, Afghanistan's intelligence service, the "Amaniyat," the National Directorate of Security (NDS), is generally considered a success by coalition and Afghan observers alike. Its former director, Amrullah Saleh, had a reputation for competence and rectitude and was considered (along with Atmar, the former interior minister both fired by Karzai in 2010) to be one of the brightest and sharpest of a new generation of

Afghan leaders. Pakistani observers have claimed that this organization is heavily influenced by India and that it has carried out political warfare and terrorism inside Pakistan, but this dissenting view should not undercut their importance.[535] However, the Pakistani perceptions of the NDS as an adversary reportedly led to the assassination of the deputy director of the NDS, Dr. Abdullah Laghmani, in September 2009; he had reportedly been targeted by ISI for a decade, and his death has been a loss to security efforts in Afghanistan.[536] The NDS is a large service, runs multiple networks of informers, and has had success infiltrating terrorist and insurgent groups as well as narcotics traffickers, making the continued coalition support and engagement with this Afghan agency important for any future successes.[537]

Shift to a Broader Insurgency

In 2008–10, insurgent groups in Afghanistan were made up of only a minority of one of Afghanistan's ethnolinguistic groups, the Pushtuns. But tensions between the current government in Kabul, with its Pushtun leaders but significant non-Pushtun power, and Afghans of other ethnolinguistic groups have caused instability to spread beyond the Pushtun districts that have been the hotbed of the insurgency. The widespread dissatisfaction of non-Pushtuns with the Karzai government became too virulent to be ignored on 29 May 2006, when a road accident with a coalition convoy in Kabul led to large-scale rioting, started by Panjsheris, which soon spread to other groups as the government's weakness and inability to deal with the situation made resentment toward foreigners a magnet for broader disaffection.[538]

In the north of Afghanistan, the security threat is from Pushtun insurgents, mainly from the population that has lived in these majority Dari and Turkic-speaking provinces since King Abdur Rahman resettled them in the nineteenth century. These provinces also have suffered from the local culture of corruption and criminal activity, neither limited to Pushtuns. In 2008–10, it was apparent that weapons from the more secure northern and western areas of Afghanistan were ending up in the hands of the insurgents in the south and east. These weapons originated in areas where opium production has been cut back, which included almost all of the non-Pushtun areas of Afghanistan, and therefore illicit trading in other valued commodities had the opportunity to thrive. The weapons were sold to traders and resold to the insurgents, largely in Pakistan's border bazaars such as Wana and Parachinar.

In 2008–10, criminality in northern Afghanistan was increasing, although it was not as severe as in southern and eastern Afghanistan.[539] Some criminals in otherwise secure areas have made common cause with those in authority with whom they share ethnolinguistic or other links, often by being former comrades in arms from previous conflicts. Criminals in the south and east are often effectively protected by insurgents who prevent government action against them. Many of these criminals claim to be Afghan Taliban, but really it is the actual Afghan Taliban to whom they owe protection for the very ability to function. This practice has led the Afghan Taliban to create an "ombudsman" function to resolve complaints against them by grassroots Afghans.

In 2008–10, the German forces stationed in the north reported a sizable increase in violence by other non-Pushtun ethnolinguistic groups, reflecting increased resentment toward the Kabul regime and its coalition allies. The security situation in the north deteriorated soon thereafter. The Afghan Taliban had made a deliberate effort to increase their activities in the north in response to pre-election counter-insurgent offensives by coalition forces in the south during 2008–10. Kunduz, a Pushtun city in a largely Tajik province, became the flashpoint for the increasing insurgency in the north.[540] Kunduz has been the focus of the German military commitment for a number of years. The Germans' restrictive national caveats and rules of engagement (RoE) have been seen as contributing to increased insurgent control, especially in the districts around Kunduz city and northward to the border with Tajikistan. Insurgency has also increased in Badghis province, where the Spanish coalition forces stationed there are similarly restricted by their national command authorities.[541]

2008–10 saw "insurgency creep," reflecting political dissatisfaction, cultural opposition, and lack of economic opportunity even in areas where there has not been insurgent action in the past. There is widespread disaffection in the north and west over the preponderance of aid flowing to the

Pushtun south and east, which are also the two regions where violence is the worst. Mark Ward, a UNAMA official working on aid issues, said: "If you look at the security map, it does not stay the same. The bad guys are going where we are not. We cannot afford another front."[542] The challenge is to allocate enough resources to create a stable enough civil infrastructure throughout all Afghanistan so that the "bad guys" are not able to move into areas where they had not previously operated and undo the progress that the coalition and Afghans have worked to achieve. The insurgency is spreading.

The Afghan Security Forces

By 2002, the Taliban and Al Qaeda fighting forces had fled across the border to Pakistan, and the future of Afghanistan's armed forces became an issue. The Northern Alliance initially envisioned their forces, the nominal army of the Islamic State of Afghanistan, transforming into the actual army of the new post-Bonn Islamic Republic of Afghanistan. But when all the armed forces of the anti-Taliban Afghan forces were added together—designated the Afghan Military Forces (AMF)—they proved too large, too unwieldy, and totally unreformed. They retained their basic characteristics of either retaining loyalty to one of the three major groups of the Northern Alliance—Tajiks, Uzbeks, and Hazaras—and their limited number of pre-2001 ethnic Pusthnun allies, or were anti-Taliban Pushtun militias that had been improvised in the south and east. In addition, the defense ministry, then under the former Northern Alliance battlefield commander Mohammed Qassam Fahim, along with the interior ministry, had only nominal control over a number of provincial and district level militia and police forces. In Pushtun areas, this control was even more minimal. As part of the AMF, these forces were meant to be designated as military units and their commanders commissioned as formal officers. The fighting men were to receive military salaries, small as they were. These men were mainly recruited by local warlords or strongmen to whom they remained loyal. In addition, separate from these, there were other Afghan militia forces, organized and led by coalition troops in many cases.[543] Using the Northern Alliance as the cadre for the new Afghan army proved unacceptable to other Afghan groups, especially among Kabulis and returning exiles, all of whom lacked comparable forces and were concerned that this would give the Northern Alliance's strength of arms effective sway over the national government, regardless of the results of the constitutional and electoral processes.

In 2002–03 there were already extensive problems with the AMF. Fahim had established 40 divisions that were concentrated in—but by no means limited to—the south, even though many had only a few hundred fighting men. There were so many "ghost" soldiers, kept on the rolls so their commanders could pocket their pay, that no one knew the size of the AMF. Many of the AMF unit commanders in the south were Pushtuns who had turned against the Taliban in 2001. However, they were still often identified with repression under pre-Taliban regimes or else shared the Taliban's loss of legitimacy. Conflicts involving local AMF units resulted when factions of nominally pro-Kabul Pushtuns clashed in Kandahar, Paktia, Khost, and Nangarhar provinces in 2002–04. In addition to the tension caused by the coalition supporting AMF commanders who effectively were local Pushtun warlords, many Pushtuns resented the Kabul-based control of the AMF by non-Pushtuns, especially Panjsheris.

In 2003, the US decided not to invest resources in reforming the AMF and those militia forces that were under US or coalition control. Instead, they focused on demobilizing them and instead forming two new organizations, the ANA and ANP. The ANA was first created in 2002, with the goal of giving the Kabul government a politically reliable force as a counterweight to the AMF with its links to the Northern Alliance. But these old forces were disbanded before the ANA and ANP were ready to take their place, giving the insurgency a chance to re-emerge. This was especially notable in areas such as Khost, where the local 25th Division of the AMF and militias together had worked with the provincial governor and the local population. When they were disbanded, the insurgent activity in the Khost area increased rapidly. Fahim was replaced as minister of defense in December 2004 by Rahim Wardak, a US-trained professional solider and returning exile who had served as military chairman of one of the Peshawar parties in the anti-Soviet conflict and as chief of staff of the ISA's army in 1992. The Northern Alliance leaders saw this as a move to deny them participation in the post-Taliban government. This marked the transition to the emphasis on the new ANA rather than continuing the forces that had fought the Taliban in 2001. Because the aid donors were providing the resources, they directed the process and set priorities. This included setting age limits for enlistment that kept many veterans of the anti-Soviet war out of the ANA enlisted ranks, making them available for service with the insurgents or narcotics traffickers.

The disbandment of the AMF meant that Disarmament, Demobilization and Reintegration (DDR) of its forces became a coalition priority. Former interior minister Ali Jalali stressed the importance of disarming and demobilizing both the AMF and local armed groups and relying on the uniformed forces of the ANA and ANP to keep the peace: "In DDR, we had to demobilize militias to create a safe environment. To fill the vacuum, we had to create the ANA."[544]

The Japanese-funded UNAMA Disarmament, Demobilization and Rehabilitation (DDR) program started with good intentions, but ended up being perceived by non-Pushtuns as a way of disarming them while building up the forces of a new Pushtun-dominated government in Kabul. To these Afghans, the DDR program was seen as being intent on preventing any future self-defense against foreign invasion while leaving the Pakistan-based insurgency, where most of the conflict originated, unaffected. Historically, especially against the British and Soviets in past centuries, the defense of Afghanistan against foreign invaders has relied on the local people of Afghanistan in arms rather than the uniformed Afghan military. Saleh Registani, member of parliament from Panjshir province, said that the re-emergence of the Taliban was encouraged by "Disarmament of the United Front/Northern Alliance and the mujahideen in general, the only groups that were capable of fighting the Taliban and the groups that would never accept the Taliban's ideology."[545] The desire, especially by the coalition and the Kabul government, to see Afghanistan rely on the ANA and ANP, which they controlled, for defense against the insurgents has had to be compromised with the reality that effective counter-insurgency warfare includes armed villagers acting in self-defense. Yet the potential for armed groups of Afghans fighting their own private conflicts was very real. Reconciling these two requirements in a country where there are lots of weapons and a tradition of individuals being armed even in peacetime has been a challenge that the formation of the ANA and ANP has not yet resolved.

The Afghan National Army

Today, the Afghan National Security Forces (ANSF) comprises the Afghan National Army (ANA), which includes the Air Force and the Afghan National Police (ANP).[546] The ANA was created by the coalition, who guided it throughout its formation and now its operations. The ANA is intended to be the national army of Afghanistan, with ethnic quotas being applied to both the force structure as a whole and to individual *kandaks* (battalions) to ensure that it accurately reflects the demographic makeup of the country as a whole.[547] The ANA has emerged far ahead of any other Afghan government institution in terms of capability, competence, minimized corruption, and its ability to operate with ethnolinguistically diverse personnel. Since its organization, the ANA has seldom been defeated in action by insurgents and has been in few battles where it has not prevailed. It has become something for Afghans to take pride in as well as a successful example of what can be accomplished for other Afghan governmental institutions through a complete overhaul. Only in the most heavily insurgent-controlled areas of the south are the ANA considered an outside, foreign, and therefore hostile force. "It is the most respected institution in the country. That it went from zero to that in five to six years is significant," said MG Mark Milley, US Army, deputy commander of Regional Command-East in 2008.[548] While the ANA's progress has been great, further challenges remain, especially as the coalition pushes for it to quickly expand and take over the burden of ground combat operations.

In the initial years of its existence, ANA infrastructure was limited. Many of their barracks even lacked running water. A rapid buildup was not a priority; rather, the overall approach was aimed at minimizing US aid expenditure. By not anticipating that there would be another insurgency coming about any time soon, the US and its coalition partners "wasted so many years," in the words of Rahim Wardak, Afghanistan's defense minister.[549] It was only in 2007 that the US provided greater funding for a faster buildup of the ANA. The decision to disband the Afghan Military Forces and recreate the ANA from scratch meant that there was no opportunity to build on an existing foundation, making the buildup process even lengthier. But such a clean slate was seen by the coalition and Kabul government alike as required to break down the links with pre-2001 forces, limit ethnolinguistic divisions, and weed out corruption.

The ANA is now committed to a program of rapid expansion. In November 2008 the ANA was 79,000 strong (plus five thousand absent without leave personnel) with 78 infantry and five commando kandaks.[550] By January 2009, 56 of these kandaks were assessed by ISAF as being capable of battalion-level operations. A specialist counter-narcotics infantry kandak is also being formed. In January–April 2009, an average of 83 ANA deliberate operations per week were being mounted, compared with 37 the year before.[551] Five corps headquarters provided the ANA's operational leadership: the 201st Corps in Kabul, 203rd Corps in Gardez, 205th Corps in Kandahar, 207th Corps in Herat, and 209th Corps in Mazar-e-Sharif. The ANA expanded to 138,000 in October 2010 and plan for 216,000 in 2014, as well as for the acquisition of additional helicopters and transport aircraft. New equipment is being provided; artillery and armored vehicles will be delivered though US and other coalition security assistance programs. The ANA's Kalashnikov rifles are being replaced by US-designed M16 series weapons, and Soviet-era tanks will be replaced by US-designed wheeled armored vehicles. The ANA will retain some of its Soviet-designed equipment, including its helicopters.

In 2009–10, the deteriorating security situation in Afghanistan led to further initiatives to expand the ANA and ANP. A total end-strength of 400,000 ANSF personnel was being considered in Washington. GEN Petraeus said: "I'm not going to get into numbers, but there is a pretty general assessment that number is in the ballpark, whatever you do, in facing an industrial-strength insurgency in Afghanistan."[552] He added "there are limits to how fast you can accelerate growth, especially the development of officer and non-commissioned officer leaders. . . . The ANA has gone up from under 20,000 in 2005 to over 85,000 in 2008. We need a lot more, now 90 battalions or so. . . . They will fight but have a long way to go before they can take over security responsibility in any systematic fashion." By the time even the 134,000 force level is reached, the ANA would have 20 brigade headquarters throughout the nation, plus a division headquarters in Kabul, alongside artillery, engineer, and Quick Reaction Force (QRF) assets. Because of the limited pool of trained and competent Afghan military leaders, this expansion remains problematic. "I don't know how we are going to get there," said COL Jeff Haynes, USMC, former chief advisor to the 201st Corps.[553] The expansion of the ANSF is likely to have to be throttled back to meet Afghan realities rather than coalition political goals. New leaders will have to be identified among those that have proven themselves in combat without weakening those units already in the force structure.

Even developed countries have found that the rapid expansion of armed forces is difficult to accomplish, even given practically unlimited resources. For the Afghans, with too few literates willing to fight and with the ANSF dependent on foreign security assistance for training, equipment, and funding, they may have to look again at other measures, such as militia or self-defense groups. Conscription may have to be considered as an alternative to the current all-volunteer forces, although this would potentially have negative political and stability impacts if Pushtuns were conscripted to fight fellow Pushtuns or educated Afghans were unwilling to serve in uniform.

ANA expansion plans to date do not include forces, weapons, or capabilities that would be able to take on Pakistan's army. Under current plans, Afghanistan will not receive weapons such as surface-to-air missiles or anti-tank weapons from the US or any other source. This expansion has also stretched available training resources, which were strained to begin with. While ANA expansion is a coalition-wide effort, ISAF forces have often failed to provide required resources. As of November 2010, they had provided 87 out of 103 ISAF OMLTs (operational mentor and liaison teams) that, along with the comparable 12–20 man US Embedded Training Teams (ETTs), are integral to ANA units, training them in garrison and operating as part of them in the field. Many OMLTs are limited by national caveats and so cannot accompany ANA units on some missions, while the smaller armed forces providing OMLTs lack the US military's depth of resources. There has also been a long-standing shortage of Afghanistan-trained advisors and trainers that can operate in the field alongside ANA officers. The Combined Security Training Command-Afghanistan (CSTC-A) has an ANSF-wide training function, and in November 2009 this was consolidated as part of the NATO Training Mission-Afghanistan (NTM-A). This action was intended to encourage other coalition members to increase their participation in the training mission.[554] The shortage of advisors and trainers has been exacerbated by Canadian and Dutch withdrawl. GEN McChrystal requested reinforcements in 2009 to provide additional advisors and trainers, but shortfalls remain.

The ANSF took over security in Kabul starting in August 2008. This shift in responsibility away from the coalition has been relatively successful. Even with the increase in insurgency-related violence, "the security services are doing better, and discover more threats," according to Dominic Medley, UNAMA spokesman.[555] The ANSF operations have not been limited to Kabul. In 2008, BG James C. McGonville, deputy commander of Regional Command-East, confirmed that: "Most operations in Regional Command-East are being lead by the ANA."[556] While Afghans are willing to watch others fight the insurgency for them, when made to take responsibility and when trustworthy Afghan commanders can be promoted and retained regardless of patronage, the ANSF has been effective in specific areas, not yet provinces or nationally.

To facilitate coordination with coalition forces, the ANSF has established Operations Coordination Commands (OCCs), six regional (OCC-Rs) co-located with the ISAF Regional Commands and in Kabul and 34 provincial (OCC-Ps), located in each provincial capital. These are coordination rather than command centers. There is no ANSF national command post, and the separate ANA, ANP and intelligence chains of command remain intact.

In recent years, expansion of the ANSF has been seen as the most important investment toward reversing the trends of a more powerful and widespread insurgency. While much is expected from the ANA, it still faces substantial limitations as demands for rapid expansion have stretched its limited trained cadres thin and it must rely on foreign resources to sustain a rapid buildup. Indeed, the ANA is not sustainable without foreign assistance before 2024, even given optimistic economic projections.[557] In 2008–10 the ANA was still heavily dependent on foreign forces for funding, fuel, air support, casualty evacuation, and indirect fire support. Technical arms, artillery, and the Air Force have all lagged behind in development. Widespread absence without leave and desertion remains a problem. In some areas of Afghanistan, especially in the south, ANA units are seen as outsiders by many Pushtuns who have not embraced the army's multiethnic composition. Having an army better developed than civilian government has, in other countries, most notably Pakistan, led to the military seizing power. While the ANA's American and coalition creators have tried to mold it as a non-political force, this might not endure a reduction in the aid it depends on to function. In 2010, the ANSF consumed five times GIRoA's revenues.

The culture of corruption that affects all Afghanistan has not spared the ANA, although it is probably the least corrupt Afghan government institution. This is due in large part to its financial autonomy, being largely funded by US and other coalition donors with funds that go directly to it.[558] Afghan politics and patronage relations continue to shape high-level command appointments, keeping the incompetent employed and frustrating their more-competent subordinates. Throughout the ANA's command structure, the importance of traditional Afghan patronage relationships is often at odds with the need for a functioning chain of command that does not always line up with old loyalties. At senior levels, many ANA officers have achieved commands due to patronage rather than competence, making the entire organization at risk for continued nepotism. "It took me nine months to get an incompetent and criminal ANA brigade commander fired, and it would not have happened if I had not threatened to pull out the advisory teams," COL Haynes recalled. The lack of willingness to accept individual accountability, encouraged by both traditional Afghan practices and lingering Soviet training, remains strong. One experienced Afghan journalist believed that, under pressure, it would dissolve and that it could fracture along ethnolinguistic lines: "It is a myth that the ANA is professional and competent." Yet it remains that the ANA is doing better than most Afghan governmental institutions.

Progress has been made, but is likely, in the future, to be as slow and frustrating as all progress is in Afghanistan. Relying on the ANSF for too much or speeding its expansion puts at risk what has been gained so far and has the potential to undercut the chance to fix its limitations.

Historically, Afghan armies have fragmented under pressure, their soldiers deserting with their weapons to defend their homes alongside their kin. Afghan soldiers fought, but not as an army, against the British in the Second Afghanistan War and against the Soviets after their 1979 invasion, but rather as part of a people in arms, with little or no national or central command or direction. The challenge for the ANA is to quickly create a force that will not fragment if faced with the challenge of assuming the primary security responsibility for Afghanistan. This is likely to require more competent Afghan leaders, more coalition trainers, more resources, and more time than current US and coalition plans project.

Rapid expansion has the potential to undermine ANA capability and so it must be done with care. Counter-insurgency is a war of low-level command, not a few highly professional generals. The Soviets found that, in Afghanistan, the professionalism of their generals mattered less than the inadequacies of their captains, lieutenants, and NCOs. Rapid ANA expansion has stretched the limited supply of these critical Afghan leaders thin indeed. Insistence on ethnic quotas, while important in many other ways, and age limits that keep out most veterans of the war against the Soviets and even the civil wars in ground combat units (the Air Force was originally primarily of Soviet-trained aircrew), have reduced the combat leadership pool still further. A reliance on a professional NCO corps on the model of the US and UK armed forces has been difficult to introduce. As in so many other areas, competent Afghans tend to be hired away by NGOs or contractors that can pay much higher salaries and gives them employment away from insurgent landmines and ambushes.

At the unit level, the combination of the Soviet-era distrust of initiative and the traditional Afghan reluctance to accept individual responsibility has hindered the emergence of functional leadership. These same factors undercut all Afghan organizations and the ANSF, with the help of its coalition trainers and advisors, has done more than any other to overcome them, but they still remain strong. This has prevented them from having true "ownership" of the security situation even when they have taken the military responsibility, as in Kabul, and allowed them to continue to avoid accepting responsibility for the circumstances in their own country. This last especially applies to the ANA's leaders. Only if their honor (and that of their kin) is at stake will they not be fighting a "limited liability" war against an enemy that respects no such limits. Threatening to disengage and leave them to face the enemy alone is no answer—it did not work for the Soviets—but a long-term commitment to Afghanistan is only going to be credible if it becomes apparent that the Afghans rather than foreigners can and will be able to handle the bulk of the conflict.

But there is no substitute for the ANA, despite its many problems and lack of readily implementable solutions. The Afghan people will engage with and support the ANA in a way they will never do with coalition forces. Villages turn out to welcome ANA patrols. Just the proximity of the ANA to many villages—that there is an outpost flying the national flag and that Afghan-led reinforcements are nearby—has encouraged Afghans and given them hope to resist the insurgents in many areas. The ANA's progress, however limited, provides Afghans with an example that other government institutions may be able to follow, showing the potential for Afghans to achieve the capability to provide security in a stable, independent nation.

The Afghan National Police

In decades before Afghanistan was plunged into conflict in 1978, the average rural Afghan did not interact with the police. The police force was only there to safeguard state power, government officials, and tax collectors, rather than involve itself in the lives of Afghans or maintain security. Tribal decision-making could be enforced by a temporary *arbaki*, a posse of armed tribesmen embodied to enforce a specific judgment. The major cities had small well-disciplined police forces, many trained by Europeans. A national gendarmerie provided paramilitary security. The Afghan Communists, following the lead of similar regimes worldwide, created large security police forces, which were trained and supported by the Soviets. When they held state power, the Taliban had nominal police forces, especially in cities where their legitimacy was weakest. This force was resented, even by the Taliban supporters, discouraging an already weak tradition of civil policing now tainted by an association with state repression.

After the defeat of the Taliban, police reform was not a high priority. The Bonn agreement made the Afghans responsible for maintaining security. The UN "light footprint" approach to reconstruction meant there that it was not involved in police reform. In 2002, Germany assumed the role of "lead nation" in law enforcement training, but they concentrated on thoroughly training a few officers for civilian police duties, on their pre-1978 model, rather than creating a force able to deal with insurgents and narcotics. This led to the US Department of Defense to start providing its own police training in 2003. By this time, the police had emerged as a major problem in Afghanistan's security. The rise of narcotics cultivation provided ample scope for bribery. Kabul's inability to pay local police led to widespread desertions and the practice of extorting payments from local inhabitants. Many policemen were illiterate and untrained, appointed by local officials or warlords to whom they owed loyalty. Then, the emerging insurgency thrust this force into the front lines of a conflict it was never intended to fight.

Today, the Afghan National Police (ANP) is subordinate to the Ministry of the Interior and includes the Afghan Uniformed Police (AUP) which constitutes the bulk of its personnel, Afghan National Civil Order Police (ANCOP), Afghan Border Police (ABP), and the Counter Narcotics Police of Afghanistan (CNPA). There are also smaller specialized ANP organizations including the Criminal Investigation Division (CID) and Counter Terrorism Police (CTP).[559] The Afghanistan Special Narcotics Force is a paramilitary organization that reports directly to the Minister of the Interior. Operationally, the ANP are organized in six regions—Kabul, North, Central, South, West, and East—and are centrally commanded, so provincial and district police chiefs report up the chain of command to the Minister of the Interior rather than being responsible to their local provincial or district governor or to ANA commands.

Policing was one of the largest failures of the security effort post-2001. In much of Afghanistan, the police failed to provide security but carried out repressive and extractive behavior, especially but not exclusively in the south. The formation of the ANP has been aimed to address these failings. "The ANP is the face of government, still corrupt, a few years back from the ANA" said BG Marquis Hainse, CF, in 2008.[560] "The ANP needs a significant amount of work. It is the front line of government with the people" said US MG Mark Milley in 2008.[561] Mohammed Hanif Atmar, former minister of the interior, agreed, in 2009, "The ANP is supposed to get to grips with terrorism, criminality, and narcotics, but is not up to the job."[562] Since the ANA cannot be everywhere, a responsible, honest, and respected police force is needed to achieve domestic peace. In 2009, increasing narcotics use in the ANP led to a coalition-imposed campaign of testing and identity checks.

The ANP was 76,000 strong in November 2008, and by 2010 there were 120,000 ANP personnel divided into approximately 500 units. This personnel ceiling represents an arbitrary limit; Iran has some four times the number of police per capita. The ANP's personnel strength includes an estimated 20 percent that are absentees or are "ghost" policemen who are paid but never report for duty, according to Atmar.[563] In 2009, GEN McChrystal urged that the target strength of the ANP be raised to 160,000, although recruiting new officers was likely to prove difficult given the forces' low pay and poor equipment and the intensity of the combat they are often committed to.[564]

Training and reform have been slow, making growth difficult. Because they are in the front lines of the insurgency, "the ANP spends lots of time fighting, not providing police functions," according to Ben Rowswell, former DCM of the Canadian embassy in Kabul.[565] This also does little to encourage more young men, and a few young women, to join the force.

The US has implemented the Focused District Development (FDD) program in which the AUP is moved out of an entire district for two months of intensive collective training by US military and civilian personnel while ANCOP units move into their district to provide law enforcement in their absence. The FDD takes the AUP out of their home environment to identify and disrupt corrupt preexisting networks and subjects them to the scrutiny of their trainers, who can dismiss policemen that are incompetent. The district's judicial and legal personnel also receive intense training by US civilian personnel at the same time, with the objective of creating a functional civil justice system. After this training, the AUP are returned to their home district, with an embedded US training team. The program started in January 2008, with a target of 48 districts' AUP going through the program each year. By April 2009, 52 districts' AUP had received FDD. The initial districts selected were ones that had experienced problems with the AUP, followed by those near main roads in the south and east. Success has been mixed but limited, especially in the south, while there have been observable improvements in districts where the ANP has gone through FDD, the amount of training has often proved inadequate to compensate for initial shortfalls, and the scarce training resources available have constrained needed follow-up training.[566]

ANP morale remains problematic. They operate alongside the better equipped and paid ANA and do not receive the same respect from the population. The burden of ANP training has fallen on the US military's Police Mentoring Teams (PMTs), supplemented by P-OMLTS (shortfall of 243 in 2011). Other countries, such as the UK, conduct police training through their PRTs or bilateral programs. PMTs originally were not intended to deploy on operations with the ANP, but have been doing so, in order to function as advisors. Atmar said: "In terms of training aid to the ANP, we have received only 30 percent of what we have planned for. With additional support, we can do training in two to three years, not five to ten."[567] The ANP's training program has not been as thorough or as well funded as that of the ANA. This is an area where additional commitments of trainers and resources can make a difference, but insisting that Afghans rely on the police rather than their kin and neighbors in arms for security is likely to continue to be a difficult goal to implement.

The European Community EUPOL police training effort, undercut by a shortage of trainers and resources, concentrates on providing the additional training ANCOP will require for their more difficult missions.[568] Some ISAF members, including Canada (using the Royal Canadian Mounted Police) and the Netherlands (using the Marechaussee), had separate bilateral police training programs, as police training, like counter-terrorism, is not within ISAF's mission statement and so is done by its members outside of ISAF. NATO has plans to implement a police training program in Afghanistan, financed by the US, in 2010. But these programs together did not amount to what Atmar identified as required to meet the needs of the ANP.

The ANP's Afghan National Civil Order Police (ANCOP) are "like the [Italian] Carabineri," according to MG Milley.[569] They had 14 operational battalions in April 2009 and 5,400 police in 20 battalions in 2011. It was formed after the ANP proved ineffective in dealing with rioting in Kabul in May 2006. Its urban battalions have an anti-riot mission as well as special weapons and tactics (SWAT) teams. Other ANCOP battalions serve in rural areas as a backup for the AUP, including filling in when they leave their home districts for FDD. ANCOP units receive more extensive training than the AUP. They were the first ANP units to receive US-provided body armor and uparmored HMMWV light trucks.

The Afghan Border Police (ABP), according to MG Milley, was, in 2008, "in bad shape and need[ed] radical improvement," especially as insurgent infiltration and narcotics trafficking alike make border security important.[570] In Kandahar province, the local Border Police were formed from an Achakzai tribal militia and for years had been more interested in armed tribal politics and extracting revenue at checkpoints than dealing with the insurgents.[571] As a result, in 2007, CSTC-A allocated more resources to ABP training, but the shortage of PMT resources has limited improvement. An upgraded US-run Focused Border Development (FBD) training program for the ABP was put in place in 2008. Two cycles, producing 20 trained companies, were completed by April 2009, and by autumn its graduates were operating in the field alongside US forces.[572] The ABP have also received additional weapons, vehicles, and equipment.

Yet for all its failings, the ANP is still the front line force against the insurgency. Unlike the ANA, the police do not operate in tactical units but in small groups, from a handful to a few dozen, often based in unfortified police stations. Not only do they suffer higher casualties due to their proximity and vulnerability to the insurgents, but they have less equipment and funding to start with. The police are armed with old Kalashnikovs and receive little ammunition. Their vehicles, when they have them, are US aid–provided pickup trucks, not tactical vehicles, and they are often unable to use what vehicles they do have due to lack of fuel. Unlike the ANA, the ANP does not receive body armor or even basic field equipment such as stretchers.

Yet even the old, unreformed police, too often corrupt or extractive, unpaid and underarmed, would often behave heroically. The police were driven from Maiwand District in Kandahar Province in 2006 only after prolonged unsupported resistance against guerrilla groups. A quarter of this 60-man force was killed in action all while the local district leadership cut a deal with the Taliban in the end.[573] In the first six months of 2008 alone, the ANP had 700 personnel killed in action. LTCOL Malalai Kakar, one of the highest ranking of the nine hundred female personnel in the ANP, was assassinated by the Taliban in Kandahar in September 2008.[574] From January 2007 to April 2009, the ANP suffered more than 180 percent of the combat deaths of ISAF and the ANA combined.[575] Atmar said, of ANP casualties, "Corruption and lack of training in the ANP is a liability, but they are willing to die for Afghanistan every day, four to six people. That is their greatest asset."[576]

Atmar has pointed to several instances of success by his police forces: "The 13 February 2009 terror attack on the Ministry of Justice was a failure. The ANP handled the attack in three hours where a similar situation lasted two days in Mumbai."[577] The "shape-clear-hold-build" operational approach of US forces in 2008–09 made additional use of the ANP as the interface between the military and the civilian population they were supposed to protect from the insurgents.

Afghan Self-Defense

By 2008, it was apparent that there was a need to enlist local Afghans to defend themselves and their homes against the insurgency. The local population is a strength of Afghanistan, while the central government has proven ineffective. Foreign military presence is costly and is going to be reduced by 2014. To counter an insurgent threat that can potentially endure indefinitely requires a force that is able to operate just as long. Local Afghans may carry with them local rivalries and resentments, but they know the territory and the people, speak the language and respect the customs, as former Assistant Secretary of Defense Tom Mahnken noted that "[local] Partners understand more than we could—no rotation."[578] US GEN David Petraeus said that effective action in the coming years "will require local defense initiatives and community defense initiatives. We have a keen interest in fostering this."[579] Yet despite the reality that Afghans have been defending themselves for centuries, Kabul and the coalition have had problems with employing this strength effectively in Afghanistan's conflicts.

Previous attempts to create self-defense forces by enlisting former anti-Taliban fighting men, who were often, especially in Pushtun areas, pro-Taliban militia members until just before the end, had some success, especially when partnered by US Special Forces units. But these forces often ended up badly, disintegrating or turning against neighboring groups or the local population. These "private militias" had no claim on state money and had to fund themselves locally, and thus were extremely vulnerable to corruption or carrying out crimes. These groups were seen as being more concerned with extracting revenue for themselves and doing their local patrons' bidding (which often included land grabs) than effectively combating the insurgents or protecting the local populations. In non-Pushtun areas, without the threat by insurgents, the Taliban background, and the tribal divisions, such groups had less opportunity or motivation to create their own security problems and so were more likely to keep the local Afghans, with whom they shared ties of loyalty or kinship, secure.

A plan developed in 2006 to deploy the Afghan National Auxiliary Police (ANAP), a force of 11,000 formed from village militias, was a failure. "The auxiliary police asked local strongmen to form a force, paid them, and gave them weapons," Atmar explained, but neither Kabul nor the coalition wished to create a force independent of the central government that would undercut the highly centralized constitutional order that emerged from the Bonn process. Many were concerned that the ANAP reversed the effects of the DDR program with its potential human-rights abuses.[580] Some non-Pushtun observers thought what Kabul really feared was the creation of local armed forces in non-Pushtun areas that would serve as a counterweight to Pushtun power.[581] The ANAP members received only a few days' training but received a monthly stipend, envied by ANP members whose pay was often in arrears. ANAP personnel, in practice, still gave their primary loyalty to local officials or warlords. In Pushtun areas, ANAP ranks included many insurgent infiltrators. The ANAP was disbanded in May 2008.

After the failure of the ANAP program, among the alternatives proposed have been the formation of expanded and regularized *arbaki* (tribal deputies, normally temporary) and the creation of *lashkars* (traditional Pushtun tribal armies). GEN Petraeus said "There exists tribal elements in some areas that can be built on. . . . Local or tribal elders or mullahs have said, we want to protect our territory."[582] The need to have local Afghans do this was once again apparent. People in arms, rather than regular militaries, have been effective counter-insurgency forces worldwide, most recently in Iraq, but also in previous conflicts including Malaya, Algeria, Kenya, and Guatemala. In the words of Massoud Kharokhail, "Community policing is possible with less money, more commitment, and better governance. We need arbaki in the east; we may need lashkars in the south."[583]

The result was the organization of the Afghan Public Protection Force (APPF). In the words of Atmar, "These are not militia but a state force, regular, full-time, uniformed; they will be US and ANA trained and not report to their commander. The local community will have a chance to nominate and vet candidates for this force as well as the government."[584] British retired LTG Graham Lamb in 2009, studied how the force would be organized. Previous failures have limited the scope of the program, which in 2009 aimed to arm some 6,000 Afghans in groups of 100–200 in 40 districts, mainly along major roads. APPF personnel go through a three-week training process.

In early 2009, as a pilot project, APPF-like units were formed in Wardak, with mixed results. There, the provincial governor, Mohammed Halim Fidai, was quoted as saying "We don't have enough police to keep the Taliban out of these villages and we don't have time to train more police—we have to fill the gap now."[585] Corruption has slowed and undercut their formation and, in Pushtun areas, many who would be willing to serve alongside their kinsmen are reluctant to join a force that could be seen as anti-Pushtun and pro-Kabul, fighting not to defend their families from outsider insurgents but defending an unpopular government. In Wardak in 2009, the strongest recruitment was among non-Pushtun groups, Tajik and Hazara, which organized units in conjunction with the US Army's TF Spartan, based on the 3rd Brigade, 10th Mountain Division.

While Atmar saw the limited number of APPF that were operational in 2009–10 as doing good work, he was concerned that there was still opposition to the force among Afghans, especially in the parliament, that saw the APPF as really just a separate Pushtun force. However, he believed that, looking ahead to a time when Kabul will have to take over a greater security role and foreign forces pull back, armed Afghans will have to play a role: "The ANA is a strike force to shape and clear areas. The ANP and APPF will then have to hold."[586] In response, the US and other coalition forces have helped organize other Afghan militia forces; while the foreigners do not provide arms, the Afghans have access to them from Afghan government sources. This has included Uzbek and Turkmen groups in Kunduz province, although Pushtuns have proven more difficult to recruit.[587] The 2009–10 experience in Wardak did not demonstrate how this could be done successfully.

Yet the reality of Afghan politics, especially in Pushtun areas, is that if one group gets money and weapons from the government and another does not, the local balance of power will shift and there will be a strong impetus for extractive behavior. Given the lack of predictable non-narcotics sources of income in much of rural Afghanistan, the motivation for a tribe or local group armed by the government to resolve its fiscal crisis through violence and extracting resources from less well-armed neighbors is significant if neither the government nor a local or regional warlord has the potential to prevent such behavior. The insurgents will be able to use that situation to their own advantage by preying on those who feel oppressed by these forces. There is also concern among non-Pushtuns that local protection forces, being concentrated in the Pushtun areas where they are needed to defend their villages against insurgents, would make these local Pushtuns more willing to join with the Taliban to fight for Pushtun power, tipping the political balance in Afghanistan in favor of Pushtuns even more. Saleh Registani, member of parliament from Panjshir, said: "Arming Pushtun tribes on this or the other side of the border will backfire. If the ultimate goal is modernization, security, and democratic government, they are not an appropriate instrument. Tribal militias would certainly use guns against each other."[588] The strong Ministry of Interior involvement in the formation of the ANPP is an attempt to mitigate these concerns.

The Afghan Local Police (ALP) was established in 2010. Local Defense Initiative (LDI) programs also started in 2010. GEN Petraeus said "You have to have local solutions to local problems, not just secure but mobilize Afghan civilians."[589] LTC Cavoli saw that the role of foreign forces must be in "providing security and benefits in a way that does not impose religious or cultural costs."[590] This includes countering the "culture of dependency" that the fallout from decades of conflict and reconstruction together has fostered. Afghans may have few resources, but they can still invest themselves and stand up, with their kin, for their own security. BG Hainse observed that "local Afghans can provide security better than allowing foreign forces to take responsibility for it."[591]

But many issues, political, material, and cultural, continue to stand in the way of Afghan self-defense. The foreign military presence has been costly; a million dollars buys four to eight infantrymen deployed in Afghanistan for a year, depending on nationality. Rahim Wardak claims he can deploy 70 ANA solders for the cost of one of their coalition counterparts, and these Afghan soldiers are "politically less complex; we will not run into the international politics of foreign countries."[592] Former US Ambassador James Dobbins noted that in Afghanistan, "indigenous forces are more likely to have trust and access to the population."[593] There will never be enough foreign troops in Afghanistan to live among the people—the key "human terrain" in an insurgency—and to provide a presence at the district and local level. GEN McChrystal wrote: "Pre-occupied with the protection of our own forces, we have operated in a manner that distances us—physically and psychologically—from the people we seek to protect."[594] The combination of coalition lack of understanding and will, along with Kabul's emphasis on centralized power, has too often meshed with grassroots Afghans' desire to avoid responsibility and let others fight for them. Yet these are the same Afghans that, a generation ago, fighting the Soviets, became a people in arms, carrying out the greatest national rising of the twentieth century. Tapping into the spirit and motivation that made that possible and enlisting it into building the future for Afghanistan is required to turn the situation around.

Ending the Insurgency

If the battle in Afghanistan is to be won, a critical mass of insurgents have to be won over and allowed to profit from their decision to reenter Afghan life and politics. The way is dangerous, as multiple contacts between the US, Kabul and insurgent leaders in 2008–10, direct and through Saudi Arabia and Pakistan, showed. Mediated attempts have generally proven unsuccessful.[595] The way these were conducted seemed to hint at Kabul's reaching out to insurgent Pushtuns through a deal that would reduce the political and economic power of non-Pushtuns. Even though Kabul has little autonomous capability as of yet, Afghan leaders, in and out of government, may be better able than any other interlocutor to deal with the Afghan Taliban's central leadership, the Haqqanis, Hekmatyar, or even individual insurgent leaders scattered throughout the countryside. The insurgents' ideology, which includes an implicit demand that state power in Kabul be in the hands of Pushtuns, is one that would be difficult to reconcile with Afghanistan's other ethnic groups, who are already convinced that the Pushtun insurgency has been met by too much appeasement and excessive allocation of resources to Pushtun areas. But Kabul cannot turn off Pakistan's sanctuary for the insurgency in Afghanistan. Nor can Kabul prevent anyone who crosses over from becoming a target for assassination.

Similarly, reconciliation with insurgent groups that have brutal human-rights records and leaders with blood on their hands will be hard for the US and its coalition partners to accept. Kabul cannot deal at all without the support of its foreign backers, as it depends on foreign aid for its income and foreign troops for its security. This foreign dependence hurts legitimacy in a country where nationalism and suspicion of outsiders, including Muslims, is as strong as the tradition of hospitality than welcomes and shelters them. It allows the insurgents to portray themselves as defenders of Afghanistan's culture and values, and makes reconciliation difficult.

Limiting the insurgents' willingness to negotiate is their perception that they are winning the conflict, that the US will withdraw and that their Afghan supporters will go into exile or switch sides when insurgent victory appears inevitable. The Taliban's goal is restoration of their emirate and its associated totalitarian regime, not participation in elections or compromise with other groups. Their connections to Al Qaeda and radical Islamic groups in Pakistan and worldwide push them toward a continued struggle even if Kabul uses Afghan-to-Afghan links to look for peace. The large number of Afghans that depend on narcotics, which, in turn, depends on the lack of security and the reach of the state, is a potentially powerful force against any successful settlement of the insurgency. The Taliban has portrayed itself as the avenger of the rights of Pushtuns against usurpers in Kabul, as defenders of the national integrity, protectors of those that depend on the poppy crop, and bulwark of all Islam against a worldwide war of aggression by the infidels; it will be hard for it to reach an agreement that compromises these principles. The Taliban has demanded first the pullback of all US and coalition forces to garrison and, within 18 months, their complete withdrawal from Afghanistan as the first step in any negotiations they might participate in. Other demands for negotiations include the immunity of Taliban leaders from the ANSF and being allowed to retain their weapons. These demands have proven impossible to reconcile with Afghan government and US insistence that renouncing violence and accepting the constitution is required for any negotiations.

Success on the ground in Afghanistan is, almost by definition, the sum total of local successes, understandings, and truces, all enabled by a flow of money and resources, capped by the creation and maintenance of patronage relationships. But this locally based approach to countering the insurgency will still not solve the larger threat emanating from Pakistan. Current Afghan Taliban fighters and their allies from other insurgent groups are largely directed from sanctuaries in Pakistan, which makes it hard to deal with their leaders on an Afghan-to-Afghan basis.[596] In most areas, local insurgent leaders are less important than those from across the border in Pakistan, and removing them from the conflict through negotiation will not slow the insurgency too much and may instead lead to their assassination or replacement.

While the remote insurgent leadership in Pakistan may lack an interface with Afghan constituents that could persuade them to create a ceasefire, they do care about grassroot Afghan opinion and their own reputations. However, the insurgency has metastasized into an indigenous conflict in a number of areas in recent years, including districts throughout the south, east, and, increasingly, northern provinces including Badghis and Kunduz. What this means is that the insurgents were able to fill the vacuum in governance, either already nonexistent or filled by extractive police and officials that had existed since 2001. The insurgents may not have gained ideological allegiance in these areas, but are in a position to offer employment where there would otherwise be none. They can use money, tribal, personal kinship, or family connections to sway local Afghans. It does not necessarily means that the locals like or approve the Taliban—indeed, many in these areas resent or fear them and consider them outsiders—but to the extent that they can provide work and security for the local population, they have the opportunity to legitimate their control and garner a modicum of loyalty in the absence of any real alternative. This situation makes local negotiations difficult, for the insurgents are unlikely to agree to terms that do not leave them in control of the governmental functions in an area: otherwise they would find themselves competing with Kabul, with its greater access to outside support and resources.

In 2009, GEN McChrystal identified as a current need "ISAF requires a credible program to offer eligible insurgents reasonable incentives to stop fighting and return to normalcy, possibly including the provision of employment and protection."[597] Yet while some insurgents are fighting for money and because there are no other jobs available, simply providing more money and better jobs is not going to be sufficient to win over sizable numbers unless they enable Afghans to legitimate their decision to switch sides in national and Islamic terms. The Soviets offered money and jobs to Afghans willing to switch sides and found few takers. Kabul has created programs to try to create a way to help insurgents switch sides while still appearing good Afghans and Muslims. The National Reconciliation Program (NRP) has aimed to bring former Taliban into alliance with Kabul through the Program Takhim-e-Sohl (PTS, strengthening peace), directed by Dr. Sibghatullah Mojadidi, the respected Naqshabandi Sufic figure and first ISA president. Reflecting a lack of resources, it was estimated that perhaps only one in ten of those eligible to participate in the NRP have taken advantage of it. Lack of resources, along with the insurgents' belief in ultimate victory, made the NRP's task difficult. By 2009, the US planned to reenergize this program.[598] This led to Karzai establishing the High Peace Council in September 2010. This is led by former President Burhaddin Rabbani.

Other times when significant numbers of the insurgents might have come over to join with the government, either at the time of the Bonn conference in 2001 or in 2003–04, they were either not invited in or there was no agreement within the Afghan government and with the coalition as to who would receive amnesty.[599] It is possible that at those times, insurgent leaders such as the Haqqanis and Hekmatyar could have been persuaded to come over to the side of Kabul if they were suitably rewarded and treated as heroes. Neither the Afghans who had experienced their violence nor the US and its allies who would have to pay the bills for bringing them over saw this as an attractive option, nor did they wish to have to justify it to their constituents.

So these men continue doing what has been their life since 1978: fighting against other Afghans and foreigners with the support of Pakistani intelligence services and outside Arab allies. To these Afghans, they are waging jihad, just as they did against the infidel Soviets and the *takfir* Islamic State of Afghanistan. It will require strong actions to alter this powerful and well-financed continuity.

Former interior minister Ali Jalali asked fundamental questions about negotiations: "What is the end state? Will the opposition accept the constitution? Denounce violence? They will do so only when they can see they cannot win through violence."[600] But the insurgents are unlikely to come to this conclusion in the absence of a long-term US security commitment or trends showing that their Afghan opponents are becoming more effective and united in preventing their return to power. In 2010, insurgent anticipation of victory has continued to prevent effective negotiations.

Ending the insurgency is likely to require having to deal with the attitude of potential spoilers in both Afghanistan and Pakistan. The government of Pakistan has acted as a spoiler in the past, preventing Afghans reaching possible agreements in the 1980s and 1990s that might have ended or limited Afghanistan's conflicts yet did not satisfy Pakistan's strategic objectives. Therefore, they encouraged and funded rivals and proxy conflicts to spoil such agreements. This applied both to local agreements, such as when Pakistan acted to prevent the Afghan resistance from dealing with the Kabul regime in Kandahar province in 1988, or at a national level, as when they enabled HiH to attack rather than join a coalition with the ISA government in Kabul in August 1992, providing the rockets that eventually leveled much of the city. However, Pakistan declined to play the spoiler role in the 2001 Bonn agreement or throughout the political process in Afghanistan that followed, and so there is hope that Islamabad will help and not spoil any potential progress.

Since Bonn, the regional consensus when all Afghanistan's neighbors could talk together on how best to move forward has been lost, but other processes—perhaps a new conference like Bonn—could aim to identify common grounds for cooperation. If Pakistan sees peace is needed, it may not block an agreement between Afghans. Getting Pakistan to act affirmatively to stop harboring the Afghan insurgency would be a difficult but not impossible requirement and one that would alleviate so many current problems. But in 2008–10, despite an increasing willingness to treat Pakistan's own insurgents as a threat to the future of the country, there still remains a perception that the Afghan insurgents are less a threat to Pakistan than are the US and the government in Kabul.

CHAPTER TEN

AID AND DEVELOPMENT

"Above all, it behooves us Americans, in this connection, to repress, and if possible to extinguish once and for all, our inveterate tendency to judge others by the extent to which they contrive to be like ourselves."
—George Kennan, 1951

"Just as the US military is reinventing itself through a counterinsurgency strategy, US civilian actors need new instruments, practices and thinking."
—Clare Lockhart, 2009

Afghanistan is unique in many ways, but its needs are similar to those of other countries and thus the lessons of history are applicable. Aid has helped devastated countries recover from conflicts, Mozambique being a prime example in the 1990s; or at least provide incentives for the population not falling back to conflict, as is the case with Bosnia and Kosovo. In the Cold War, aid and a strong international commitment helped devastated countries in Europe and Asia eventually become stable and prosper. Compared with these countries, Afghanistan has a less developed political system and deeper divisions in the population, and lacks infrastructure, institutions, sizable resident educated elites, and residual state capabilities. Better aid programs that aim to build up these lacking components of civil society could have had better results and inflicted less collateral damage on society.[601]

Much of the aid that has been devoted to Afghanistan has been absorbed by the aid efforts themselves and only a relatively small percentage has been effective in making life better for Afghans. In addition to the aid effort absorbing resources being devoted to it and allocation often reflecting donor rather than Afghan priorities, the amount of aid has been inadequate. Afghanistan has received much less aid on a per-capita or per-area basis than other post-conflict aid efforts, despite Afghanistan's more widespread devastation and lower level of pre-war development. One 2006 overview of the aid process summed up as follows: "While aid has undoubtedly contributed to progress in Afghanistan, a large proportion of aid has been prescriptive and supply-driven, rather than indigenous and responding to Afghan needs. It has been heavily influenced by the political and military objectives of donors, especially the imperative to win so-called 'hearts and minds.' It has tended to reflect expectations in donor countries, and what Western electorates would consider reconstruction and development achievements, rather than what Afghan communities want and need. Projects have too often sought to impose a preconceived idea of progress, rather than nurture, support and otherwise expand capabilities, according to Afghan preferences."[602] Aid efforts, along with the military action by the coalition in Afghanistan, demonstrate that their ability to do good is inherently limited by the difficulty of changing Afghanistan for the better, while their ability to do harm suffers no such constraint. The result has been, in the words of Ashraf Ghani: "International technical assistance is considered to be largely wasted. . . . Hundreds of millions of dollars have gone into technical assistance only to increase corruption and misgovernance."[603]

Aid to Afghanistan

Afghanistan has been dependent on outside aid since its emergence as a buffer state between the British and Russian empires in the nineteenth century, with some of the aid going to development of a national government, mostly going to the state running and supporting elites who were part of various high-level patronage networks in order to ensure their support for, or at least non-resistance to, Kabul policies. The high point of this approach by donors and Kabul alike was the Golden Age: foreign aid provided the Afghans with actual gold. In terms of creating a stable state post-2001, Afghanistan was, in effect, starting from where the former king began, when his 1933 coronation offered peace after years of civil war, not like when he was overthrown in 1973. The way the monarchy established itself starting in the 1930s was to convince the Afghan people that it was in their personal (and financial) interest to be associated with the state, including supporting and participating in state-established institutions, such as education. With the benefit of hindsight, the former king's policies, of building a centralized state with limited capabilities, appear to have often been the wrong choice for achieving stability, as the growth of the Communist opposition, with foreign support, demonstrated. The growth of a private sector economy was neglected in favor of state-controlled and -directed investments. Making the life of the average Afghan better was not a high priority even in the nation's supposed Golden Age, and making the life of the average Afghan woman better was more remote still.

Because previous Western governmental aid efforts with Afghanistan were largely cut off in the 1990s, many of the lessons learned by the nations supporting the Afghans during their war against the Soviets had to be re-learned, especially the pitfalls: widespread corruption and diversion, minimal accountability, and the collateral damage caused by the creation of the culture of dependency. Programs were too often judged by how many resources were allocated rather than their effects in reaching Afghan grassroots.

Outside aid for the Afghans did tremendous things in the 1980s. Covert aid enabled the Afghan resistance to endure and eventually prevail against the Soviets. Humanitarian aid kept the worlds' largest population of refugees from starving in Pakistan. Cross-border aid kept many Afghans on their land inside Afghanistan. But parts of the aid flow contributed to Afghanistan's continuing problems. Pakistan's ISI allocated the covert aid and favored the Islamist HiH and other Pushtun parties it believed it could control. Arab money and the Pakistani security services enabled the rise of the Taliban Culture in Pakistan in the 1980s.

In 2009, Eshan Zia, Minister of Rural Rehabilitation and Development, said "to strengthen legitimacy we must enable government to serve the people"; this has not been a self-evident fact through Afghanistan's history, but this historical precedent seemed to have been swept away by the assurance that pervaded the population that the US-led intervention in 2001 was going to make life better for everyone.[604] The international aid effort effectively preceded the emergence of a functioning Afghan national government or a national economy, and the current divisions and direction of international aid in Afghanistan flow from the fact that in 2001–02 there was no government to engage with when the programs started to help unify its flow in the most effective manner.

Since 2001, Afghan governance has depended heavily on aid in the absence of a functioning national economy and still lacks the ability to fund itself. In 2008, 90 percent of all Afghan public expenditures depended on international assistance. The 750 million dollars that the Afghan government raised from duties and taxation itself was equivalent to what Afghanistan received from just one aid program, the US Department of Defense's CERP (commander's emergency response) program. Afghanistan has one of the lowest domestic revenue-to-GDP ratios in the world, around seven percent. This by itself helps create a culture of dependency, as nothing can function without outside assistance. Experience has shown that reliance on an aid flow creates rent-seeking behavior that undercuts democratic institutions; the "curse of aid" is worse than the "curse of oil." Both aid and oil provide money in a way that counters the establishment of an effective independent government and a functional civil society alike.[605] While the flow of aid has been insufficient to rebuild or stabilize Afghanistan, it has been enough to fuel the growth of the culture of corruption and dependency, and, through that, the Taliban culture that promises both Islamic rectitude and an end to the cultural chaos caused by these outside influences, be they well-meant or not. But the importance of aid means that, for all its drawbacks in Afghanistan, there is no alternative except for the Afghan government to rely on it until a functional national economy emerges.

The post-Bonn government was the first to make improving the daily life of the average Afghan a state priority; but where they have done this, as in the provision of opportunities in education and basic health care, it was overshadowed by the raised expectations that were created by the 2001 US intervention and new frustrations with the continued corruption, lack of jobs, violence, and narcotics trade. Aid resources went to implementing the provisions of the Bonn agreement, such as the *Loya Jirgas* and presidential and parliamentary elections, not to creating a stable, legal economy, restoring agriculture or local governments and a civil society free from corruption.

At the time of the Bonn conference, the US resistance to a commitment of open-ended "nation-building" led to a donor-driven approach, where nations pledged what they wished, coordinated at international conferences, and provided criteria for Afghans as to how this aid was to be used. With a donor-centric aid approach, the Afghans have tended to get what the donor or Kabul believes they want, rather than what they are actually willing to take ownership of. Like most of Afghanistan's problems, there is no easy solution. Each option has real costs and limitations that can only be mitigated rather than prevented.

This amorphous policy reflected the political reality in the US and other donor nations. The US Congress was simply not going to authorize funds for nation-building and institutional creation in Afghanistan when it was competing with the commitment to Iraq and other priorities and there was no way to guarantee that the money would not go to line the pockets of a corrupt few. The US approach of emphasizing donor priorities meshed with and encouraged the UN "light footprint" concept that the then-Special Representative of the Secretary General (SRSG) Lakhdar Brahimi had put forward. Security Council Resolution 1401, which passed on 28 March 2002 (since renewed annually), established the United Nations Assistance Mission in Afghanistan (UNAMA), which is led by the SRSG. This was also not intended to create a strong top-down UN direction to the aid effort. Brahimi said that his priorities were "security, security and security," recognizing that without providing Afghans with security, both the Kabul government and its foreign supporters would have their claims to legitimacy severely undercut, and their ability to carry out real social and economic reconstruction would be limited. The UN wanted to ensure that the Bonn process was seen as an

Afghan-run process so that cultural resistance and suspicion of outsiders would be mitigated and the growth of Afghan capabilities enabled. It was not going to repeat its direct hands-on involvement seen in post-conflict situations such as East Timor, despite its relative success there.

The US wanted only a limited UN presence in post-2001 Afghanistan, and it was unlikely that the UN could have taken a larger role even had this been their goal.[606] The US instead encouraged the "lead nation" concept which eschewed a unified aid effort. The "lead nation" approach was adopted internationally at the January 2002 Tokyo donor conference. Five different nations would each have "lead" responsibility for a high-priority aid area: the UK was responsible for narcotics, the Italians in the judicial sector, the Japanese (through funding UNAMA as the lead agency) in disarmament, demilitarization and rehabilitation (DDR), and the Germans in police training.

In reality, much of the implementation of this approach proved counterproductive, as the discrete assignments were, in reality, all interconnected on the ground and required a unified approach that was difficult to achieve without a mechanism for coordination, planning, and resource allocation between the five "lead nation" donors.[607] Despite the pledges made in Tokyo, the "lead nation" aid approach ended up woefully underfinanced. This disjointed approach was distrusted by the Afghans and proved inadequate in scope and funding. "We are to have German cops, Italian judges, and British drugs," lamented an official in the Afghan government at the time, wishing instead for a Afghan-led unitary effort. Shortfalls in the lead nations' programs, such as the German failure to train meaningful numbers of non-corrupt police, the Italian failure to create a judicial system, the British failure to reduce narcotics cultivation, and the Japanese-funded UNAMA efforts that made DDR appear not as a confidence-building measure between Afghans but rather an attempt to impose centralized power on pro-Kabul non-Pushtun Afghans and make them unable to resist the emerging insurgency by well-armed ethnic Pushtuns, all together had an impact long after this approach had come to an incremental end in 2003–06, before it was officially replaced by the Afghanistan Compact and subsequently the Afghanistan National Development Strategy (ANDS).

The impact of outside aid on Afghanistan in the past decade has, iron-ically, not all been positive. After the fall of the Taliban, it was assumed by Afghans that an aid effort would have the same scope and efficacy as the military effort that defeated the Taliban and chased Al Qaeda and would now solve all of Afghanistan's vast problems. No Afghan leaders emerged to dampen this view and put realistic goals in place, and so this tremendous amount of hope started to turn into bitter cynicism and mistrust of the coalition and the Afghan government alike for failing to bring about this better life when it appeared within their reach. Rather, each Afghan leader or elite looked to get as much as he could from the fledgling nation, either in terms of acquiring governmental or local power or, more often, self-enrichment. Instead, what Afghans saw as the pre-ponderance of the money went to foreign consultants or else never really left the donor country, and that which made it to Afghanistan often van-ished. Afghans, elites and grassroots alike, cut out from the process, saw this as yet another form of corruption by the donors and responded to it with their own, Afghan, corruption, because they felt it was essential to their survival in the absence again of any real alternative.[608] "A collection of haphazard, fragmented, and short-term responses" was former finance minister Ashraf Ghani's bottom-line view regarding the aid effort.[609] The Afghan response to it was similarly short-term–oriented.

"All supply-driven, never demand-driven" has been the widespread characterization of the aid process. The donor-centric aid process, in repeated international conferences since 2001—Tokyo, London, Paris, and The Hague—has put down many markers for the Afghans but few for themselves. The Afghanistan Compact that emerged from the London Conference in February 2006 had 77 benchmarks for the Kabul government but none for donors, which could have covered controversial issues like how quickly commitments would be converted to cash and how much of each dollar pledged would benefit Afghans.

The aid effort—from contractors to donors, international organiza-tions, and NGOs—often appeared to Afghans as a foreign intrusion on their way of life without the obvious benefit of preventing renewed civil war which they have continued to ascribe to the foreign military presence. Some 40 percent of aid never leaves the donor country, as it is turned into corporate profits and consultant salaries; when in-kind transfers of aid to Afghanistan are counted, the percentage of many aid-for-Afghanistan programs that end up going to the donor country is nearly double.[610] The US was one of the worst donor nations in terms of how many cents of every aid dollar had a direct benefit on the lives of Afghans.[611] Again, this reflects political realities and a strong rationale. The Congress would not authorize funds without US operational control and has long insisted that US contractors be used in aid programs; the widespread corruption and incapacity associated with the Afghan government has made them reluctant to make aid on a government-to-government basis, at least until it can be demonstrated that progress has been achieved in achieving transparency and removing corrupt officials.

Developmental aid has often been so filtered through a series of subcontractors that little is reaching Afghans. This is especially true with regard to the US-sponsored road-building and other infrastructure programs. The quality of the Kabul-Kandahar highway, built with US funding, was so poor that stretches had deteriorated after two years' use as the multiple layers of contractors had undercut accountability. At each level, protection payments to the insurgents by contractors contributed to the deterioration of the security situation. It is unlikely that a unitary Afghan-directed aid program could have avoided these problems, but at least it had the potential to use aid to create loyalty toward Kabul as King Zahir had done.

In 2009 GEN McChrystal recognized that aid contracting was part of the security problem: "ISAF must pay particular attention to how development projects are contracted and to whom. Too often these projects enrich power-brokers, corrupt officials or international contractors and serve only limited segments of the population."[612] Whether an aid program will benefit the local Afghan population, corrupt Afghans, or outside contractors depends on project-specific details.

As of March 2008, only 15 billion dollars of the 39 billion originally pledged in aid to Afghanistan had been spent, with the remainder still in the donors' pockets or amounting to no more than promises. In May 2008, the Kabul government estimated the total cost of reconstruction at 30 billion dollars, with a further 50 billion being required for a five-year development program aimed at creating effective governance, a functioning state, and a national economy. At the fourth donor conference for Afghanistan that was held in June 2008 in Paris, the Afghan government presented the Afghan National Development Strategy (ANDS) as a roadmap document and received pledges for an additional 20 billion dollars over the next five years. The creation of such a roadmap was considered a needed first step for increased Afghan government participation in the aid effort and has been an improvement in the quality and direction of donor action (and not necessarily just providing more money) and has made an effort to incorporate grassroots consultation. The ANDS provides transparency, showing what the Afghans intend to do if they are given the needed resources. The Hague conference in March 2009 continued this approach.

A Divided Aid Effort

Aid, however well-meaning by the donors, has been slow to adapt to Afghan realities. Many Afghans tend to disregard this altruistic meaning or explain it away cynically as expressions of self-interest by the donors and instead see only the disappointing results, which many see as proof that neither Kabul nor the coalition is really interested in their having a better life. Aid to Afghanistan is, despite recent improvement, delivered in a splintered and fragmented way. The lack of a single aid effort, an effective Afghan central government, and needed infrastructure and institutions have all contributed to this result. Major aid donors, such as the US and UN, divided their programs among multiple agencies that often did not coordinate with each other, let alone other donors.

Ashraf Ghani said: "In Afghanistan, every agency has a separate set of priorities and we do not know how capable they are because they are unaccountable. Even within single international organizations, there is no coordination. When I was Minister of Finance, I found that UN agencies are not coherent; they are not co-coordinated. Under one UN program, six of the UN agencies in Afghanistan are not even willing to disclose their audits to their own board of governors. Then I went to the EU, and found that the member nations did not coordinate or share their aid allocations and priorities. As for the US, the Department of Defense was spending money separate from that of AID."[613] Ghani's experience underlines that the lack of capacity of the Afghan government is not solely the result of the lack of public administration skills or widespread corruption, but because it has to deal with a divided and often dysfunctional aid process to provide needed resources and has encouraged Afghans to compete for foreign money rather than work together.

With no one in charge of the aid effort, it was almost a guarantee that resources could not be effectively allocated. No one person had authority to change aid priorities and address changing situations as Afghanistan encountered emerging problems. When the insurgency escalated in 2005–06, it took almost four years afterward for resources to move through the budget cycle, be authorized, appropriated, and finally spent on the ground in Afghanistan where they were needed to be integrated with military efforts as part of an effective counter-insurgency strategy.[614] Those aid efforts, such as those run by the US Department of Defense, that proved more responsive to urgent needs helped Afghanistan beyond their dollar value. Here again, the Afghan government, plagued by incapacity and corruption, has a limited ability to provide this unity of effort and direction, but minimizing its participation has often made a bad situation worse. The Afghans need to do more, while the donors need to insist on needed transparency more than micromanaging programs.

Prioritizing where aid should be allocated has been part of the problem. The things the average Afghan most looked to receive from outside aid in 2001 failed to materialize: security, non-corrupt law enforcement, effective governance, dispute resolution, economically viable agriculture, and religion that is not a tool of the Taliban and their allies. Western aid programs often focused on agendas generated by donors and ignored the inputs of those on the ground who better understand and accept the disparate nature of Afghan society.

Division in the aid effort has fed into Afghan factionalism and division, as each different donor has acquired its own Afghan clients and sources of information. This fractured system has encouraged Afghans to compete for outside resources rather than force them to make hard compromises and work together for a shared reward. This current climate has also done nothing to alleviate the culture of dependency, previously discussed, as endemic to modern Afghan society, from local farmers to Karzai and Kabul. Each separate aid program has created a new set of dependencies, with the different donors as patrons. A more unified aid effort would both provide more to Afghans and enable the Afghan government to work better.

Aid Successes

Despite this misdirection and underallocation of aid resources, many of the successes that Afghanistan has experienced since 2001 have their roots in either aid or outside investment. Some five to six million Afghan refugees returned from Pakistan, Iran, and internal displacement, and the educational and public health systems were able to cope with these because the Afghans were able to devise programs and set priorities for the international donors that provided resources to deal with this massive influx. Communications and the spread of cell phones has proven a great success, funded almost exclusively by the private sector, and has managed to avoid corruption. This was largely carried out by Afghans working in the private sector, borrowing money and acquiring technology from outside as required, rather than relying on donor nations.

Education has been one of the ways life has become better for Afghans, and aid has made this possible. On *Nawroz*, the Afghan New Year of 2002, the state school system reopened nationwide, and it was the first act by a Kabul government since 1978 to be heartily accepted and willingly implemented nationwide. By 2008–10, there were over six million Afghan children in school (up from 750,000 in 2001), with a third of these primary schoolchildren being girls who were denied access to education by the previous Taliban regime.

Public health is another area where Afghans are today better off, with over 80 percent of the population having access to health care. This was made possible by aid, with the Afghan government playing a strong, positive role. After the Ministry of Public Health found it had no idea what facilities were being built, personnel trained, or standards achieved, it insisted that all donors in the public health field follow the Afghan guidelines, reflecting the Afghan National Development Strategy (ANDS). The Ministry of Public Health provided Afghan-created guidelines and priorities for donors that produced two new nationwide baseline healthcare capabilities: the Basic Package of Health Services (BPHS) and the Essential Package of Hospital Services (EPHS). By having donor healthcare efforts meet Afghan-generated priorities as to their location and capabilities, the Ministry of Public Health was able to almost triple the number of health-care facilities, from 496 in 2003 to 1468 in 2008.[615]

These significant successes were abetted by functional and competent Afghan ministers who were able to implement a unitary Afghan approach rather than the multiple nation-specific approaches that are frequently a factor when aid comes from multiple donors. Even after these ministers have left office, these successful examples of Afghan-directed aid have been sustained by their successors. They provide an example of how aid can succeed and the Afghans can play a better role in directing its effects.

"When Afghans lead, we have greater impact," said Mark Ward, a UNAMA official working on aid issues.[616] Other ministries have provided examples of other approaches where the Afghan government can make a positive contribution to aid effectiveness. The Ministry of Rural Reconstruction and Development was licensed by the Ministry of Finance to have the freedom to put together its own funding packages from donors. This proved important because it has enabled Afghans to shift funding to meet changing needs on a more responsive basis than would be possible from relying on multiple programs carried out by outside donors bypassing the Afghan government. There have even been recent successes in the areas of the Ministries of Agriculture, Irrigation, and Livestock; and Energy and Water, historically two of the most incapable ministries. For example, 2009 saw Kabul suffering fewer of the unscheduled power blackouts than it had in previous years and more Afghans having access to electric power. Despite the continuing problems of pervasive corruption, the Afghan government can still, if enabled rather than worked-around by its outside supporters, provide part of Afghanistan's needed solutions. Mark Ward said: "Donor coordination needs strong government leadership and willing donors."[617] These examples show that the two can be brought together. The challenge is to apply these lessons to other sectors in Afghanistan.

There have been some improvements. The Afghan National Development Strategy (ANDS) provides a shared vision and direction, which has helped Afghan government ministries unify the aid flow in some areas, though the gap between it and Afghan realities remains large. Following the expansion of UNAMA's mandate by the Security Council in 2008, Kai Eide, then UN Special Representative of the Secretary General (SRSG), retained the focus of Lakhdar Brahimi's original approach—that the UN should increase Afghan capacity, governmental and non-governmental, with a limited presence of international staff—by enabling the Government of Afghanistan to take over functions from donors and their foreign contractors. UNAMA has acted to coordinate donor programs, although it has no authority to move around money even between UN programs, let alone that of other donors. The Joint Coordination and Monitoring Board (JCMB) in Kabul has had successes in reconciling Afghan government participation and donor programs, ensuring that Afghan priorities are heard, if not always heeded, and acting to ensure that aid has a positive impact at the local level. The Afghan government's Independent Directorate for Local Governance (IDLG) is also aiming to coordinate aid for local development out in the provinces, where it is often needed most, yet this is also where the Afghan government has the least capability. This is being countered on a slow, ministry-by-ministry basis in recent years, using the ANDS for guidance. The US is providing direct aid to some Afghan ministries that have developed effective internal controls. Another step forward has been the creation of the Afghan Reconstruction Trust Fund (ARTF), managed by UNAMA, the International Monetary Fund (IMF), the World Bank, and other donors. This has provided greater Afghan involvement and flexibility in aid programs, by pulling together multiple donors' contributions into a single ARTF account that can, with oversight, be used to meet what the Afghan government considers the most pressing needs.

Ashraf Ghani has pointed out that successes in some sectors does not necessarily carry over into areas where failing to secure Afghan support and participation has created alienation and undercut legitimacy. "You cannot have ownership of the country unless they are at the forefront of assuming responsibility."[618] Successes in areas such as education and public health have been difficult to apply to other ministries, each with ministers and bureaucracies jealous of their prerogatives and each having a different set of outside donors.

Achieving Afghan Ownership

The importance of having Afghan buy-in and ultimate insistence on ownership and responsibility for the results of the aid effort applies both at the national level and at the grassroots. Too often, donors saw the recipients in rural Afghanistan as passive, waiting for top-down benefits, rather than recognizing that the highly politicized society was engaged and, indeed, competitive. The donors failed to provide the believable vision of a reward for cooperation across local, political, or ethnolinguistic lines, but rather encouraged an intense competition for aid resources that has become the "real" Afghan politics today. By 2008–10, this competition for aid resources had emerged in Kabul as central to politics in Afghanistan, with policy issues (those not associated with an aid flow from a foreign donor) pushed to one side or limited to the parliament (with their goal of advancing their own or their clients' interests). The "winners" used the resources, too often, to fuel corruption. Little of this aid reached the rural Afghan population. The lack of capability in Kabul and governance outside Kabul, especially in rural areas, means that donors (whose programs' templates are aimed at working with governmental bodies) often lack effective Afghan partners. Effective Afghan partners can enable donors to achieve the sort of concrete successes that have been seen in these areas. Creating them remains a challenge. Donors (including international organizations and NGOs) created competition between different Afghan groups in Kabul, too often supporting "their" Afghans rather than either donor or recipient taking part in an integrated process, although actions by the US government working directly with some Afghan ministries, the UN SRSG, and the JCMB have improved this situation in recent years.

Even in a developed country, political power and influence follow money. In the absence of a viable national economy and an ability to collect revenue domestically, Afghans must look to receive money for their ministries, home provinces, and NGOs from foreign donors. Even when it is passed through the Kabul government, which the US and other donors will generally not do, reflecting the perceptions of its corruption and lack of capacity, the Afghan involvement is too often seen as irrelevant, imposing only another layer of those taking their cuts without an evident value-added to the process. Yet, while oversight of aid is required, increased Afghan government involvement is required if there are ever to be more sectors where, like education and public health, aid has made the life of the average Afghan better. Afghans who wanted the benefits of aid went to the donors directly (or their Afghan clients and intermediaries who had influence with the donors) rather than the Afghan government. The donors provided the resources but failed to insist on effective oversight from the Afghan government, who they did not let distribute the aid. This has prevented Kabul from building its legitimacy and capability the way King Zahir did, who used aid money to reward those who did Kabul's bidding in the provinces and withholding it from those that did not. In 2007–08, some two thirds of assistance, including almost all that provided by the US government, bypassed the Kabul government; 70 percent of US funds went to security and narcotics.

Only since 2008 has this practice slowly changed. In 2009, there were also attempts by the Afghan government and donors alike to break down the various "stovepipes" in aid program created between ministerial-level fiefdoms and their outside donor patrons. Instead, the intention is to require the government to work and distribute funds across ministries, creating four multi-departmental clusters of ministries, which prevents the least competent and capable ministries from blocking this long-overdue move towards cohesiveness, until Afghan politics allow their ministers to be replaced and a new generation of Afghans comes forward to run effective government. It has also brought Afghan ministers together for a common cause, something they have seldom been willing to do since 2001, each jealous of each other's position and divided by politics, ethnicity, and, too often, the short-term interests of themselves and their families.

An increased Afghan role in the aid effort cannot wait on rooting out corruption from the Afghan government, a process that will take a decade even if all goes well, but needs to be implemented concurrently with it, with measures put in place to mitigate corruption. Otherwise, the current US goal for the ANSF to take over the burden of ground combat operations in Afghanistan will be undercut by the lack of an effective government.

It is not only the Afghans that compete for aid. Major coalition members have used their aid programs to push donors to make their areas of responsibility a priority; the British pushed for aid to Helmand province, when their troops were deployed there, while the Canadians want these same resources devoted to Kandahar, which is their responsibility.

For much of the past decade, Afghanistan has seen its reconstruction "contracted out" to those selected by the donors, much as it saw its fighting similarly "contracted out" to the coalition forces that were keeping the insurgents at bay. Many Afghans are certainly willing to let the outsiders do these things for them and not take responsibility, but instead focus on short-term gain, enriching themselves and their clients and cutting out rivals. The skill in creating and implementing effective policies in Afghanistan is to require the Afghans to buy in to the process so that they have everything at stake in the ultimate outcome. This is going to mean an increasing Afghan role in both development and fighting.

Missing the Grassroots

When international aid began to flow into Afghanistan after 2001, with the intent to help the country rebuild after the fall of the Taliban, it was primarily directed toward the state, even though the state had never been a pillar of strength in Afghanistan's society under any government throughout its history. Afghanistan has always been very different from the Afghan state. Even in the Golden Age of a centralized but limited state, Afghanistan's strength has been its peoples, their faith, their qawms; and how society functioned on a local level. All this defeated the Soviets, though at terrible cost to each of them. The Afghan state did not defeat the Soviets; that was effectively in hostile hands in 1978–92.

While there was acknowledgement of how important it was for aid to reach the grassroots, the view of donors and Afghan elites alike still tended to focus on Kabul, even though the bulk of aid flowed from outside donors to contractors without touching the Afghan government. In an Afghan context, national does not mean the same as central. This underlines a fundamental policy dilemma facing the US and other aid donors. They need a strong and non-corrupt Afghan government, but the needs aid is intended to answer cannot wait until the Afghans achieve that goal, which will likely take a generation. While the US and the coalition need to rebuild the Afghan government, waiting for it to become more functional and less corrupt before engaging with the Afghan grassroots is not a valid policy option. The insurgents are taking advantage of this vacuum on a daily basis. US and coalition policy needs to help Afghans have a better life. When the Afghan state can do this, it needs to be supported. Where the Afghan state is not doing this, effective aid policy requires alternative means, such as the Provincial Reconstruction Teams (PRTs), to do this.

The donors—international, governments, and NGOs—have demonstrated too often a willingness to embrace quick-fix solutions and imported templates, with the context and true nature of Afghan society largely ignored. Reconciling the near-term needs of counter-insurgency, with its need to protect the population of Afghanistan with the long-term needs of effective development, is a challenge. Coalition military forces represent the bulk of each country's presence on the ground in Afghanistan, and their efforts include much more than fighting. These military personnel are deployed on short-term tours, a year for the US, six months for the British and many other coalition partners. This has led to an emphasis on shortterm programs that, over the years, have failed to accumulate into lasting benefits. Fresh troops have had to keep learning over and over how to effectively interface with the locals. In many areas, involving both military and development, the coalition does not have ten years of experience in Afghanistan to draw upon, but rather ten one-years' experience, which is a very different thing. International development programs are normally planned to run for 20–25 years, but in Afghanistan there has not been the long-term commitment to funding from the international community that would make such actions more than rhetoric. The military effort needs to beat back the insurgency in the next few years. The aid effort will take a generation to reach its objectives. Carrying out the near-term surge to prevent collapse while at the same time enabling the generation-long process of rebuilding that may, some day, provide Afghanistan with stability is going to be difficult, but it is a task that must be undertaken.

Part of supporting Afghan is prioritizing aid sectors that are important for the grassroots. Agriculture aid has been identified by Afghan officials and aid donors alike as an overall failure.[619] While there have been successes, aid to the agricultural sector, the source of employment for the majority of Afghans, lags due to being underfunded pre-2009. This helped create the vacuum that was filled by opium cultivation and trafficking. After the Taliban fell in 2001, there was never enough aid provided from abroad to create meaningful employment for many of Afghanistan's former fighting men in carrying out reconstruction or learning to read, among other needed tasks for the society to deal with the damage caused by decades of conflict. The conflicts resulted in a "lost generation" that continues to provide manpower for warlords, narcotics cultivators, and terrorists and insurgents in the absence of a viable alternative. It demonstrated that outsiders were not willing to invest in making the average Afghan's life better, only in backing a self-interested leadership and unresponsive but centralized state power in Kabul. This has led not to the grassroots support that Kabul needs to make any effective use of aid to benefit the average Afghan, but instead to increased corruption that benefits a few elites. A tribal elder in Paktia said about this: "Paktia has lots of problems, but the issue of lack of clinics, schools, and roads is not the problem. The main problem is we don't have a good government. . . . Without a clean government, millions of dollars are stolen. If you increase the amount of money it will also be useless because the government will simply steal more. There's a growing distance between the people and the government and this is the main cause of the deteriorating security situation."[620] Increased oversight and transparency is an important step in achieving this, but the fundamental disconnect between the grassroots and the Afghan government that this statement addresses is going to require direct involvement by aid donors while the government is reformed and made more capable, which is likely to take longer than the current crisis in Afghanistan will permit.

One of the reasons why aid efforts need to directly help the Afghan grassroots at the same time they try to build government capability is because most post-2001 aid efforts originally ignored rebuilding of key non-governmental groups, institutions, and networks, such as those of the *ulema*, crucial to conflict resolution, a source of local leadership and vital to keeping local society stable and making conditions less hospitable to insurgents and narcotics.

Aid was thought to speak for itself in those early years, and there was little effort made to get grassroots Afghans to support the program or achieve the vital "buy-in" that is a prerequisite to their taking ownership and, ultimately, responsibility. Too often, hard as they may have competed to receive it, the aid appeared to the grassroots Afghans to have come from "out there"; and when they were not made to take responsibility for it, they did not care about it. If something is important to Afghans, they will fight to the death for it, as they fought the Soviets when they saw their country invaded and their religion threatened. Fewer Afghans are willing to fight this way for a paved road or a school. This has led to the scene, repeated multiple times throughout Afghanistan, of schools being built for which there were no teachers (because the foreigners are only funding building the physical plant rather than paying money to recruit and retain the educated Afghans who normally do not wish to be village schoolteachers in remote rural areas) and so were turned into storehouses, or new mosques where no one will preach because it was a creation of infidels. In southern and eastern Afghanistan, the insurgents burn these schools or mosques down first thing, and the local people often look the other way, indifferent. Afghans will not fight insurgents for a school or a mosque when they are the results of an aid process that they were not part of from the start. Afghans *will* fight anyone—Soviets, Americans, or insurgents—who appears to threaten what they value. Where there is ownership of an institution, a policy, or an object, Afghans will defend it, as they defended old Afghanistan from the Soviets or as some insurgents think they are defending Islam from invading "Crusaders and Zionists" who seek to destroy it. The challenge is to get the Afghans to transcend the culture of dependency and the continued pervasiveness of corruption—both in large part the results of collateral damage from outside aid efforts—and enlist them to work for reconstruction and against the insurgency; otherwise no progress will ever be made.

The most competent Western soldiers and the most caring Western aid workers are no substitute for the Afghans that need to be trained to do these jobs. Afghans want to be trained for jobs that are going to provide more than a subsistence living. The roadside signs in every Afghan city and town advertising computer skills and English-language tutoring are evidence of this. But making this training available, and ensuring that the Afghans selected for training are those best suited to it rather than those with the best patronage connections, has proven to be a challenge. The international community cannot substitute for Afghans even where they can substitute for a lack of capability by Kabul. Training is important because it gives grassroot Afghans a stake in a system that, if presented to them in terms of country and faith, they may be willing to fight to preserve.

Even though no foreigner should do a job an Afghan is capable of doing, Afghans will often disperse resources to secure patronage relationships and fob off responsibility, so their "job" actually never gets done. Then, when things do not get done, Afghan collective society can diffuse any personal responsibility for this failing. Avoiding this vicious cycle of passivity and failure requires that patronage and social collectivism be used to enforce performance rather than reinforce failure. If an Afghan group has bought into a project and they expect it to be done, failure becomes less acceptable, for then the Afghans involved will lose face by letting others down. The first step in doing this is, despite the inherent frustrations, by committing to having Afghans doing any jobs that they can be trained for, so they are the ones that have their reputations and those of their kin at stake in its success. The problem will be in ensuring that trained Afghans remain in Afghanistan to work. During the war against the Soviets, while many Afghan medical doctors operated in resistance-controlled territory, many more went into exile, some finding driving taxis in the West more appealing than undergoing hardship in a hostile environment in Afghanistan.

Aid to Grassroots Governance

"The unit of reconstruction of Afghanistan should be the district; unless you build there, you cannot build the nation," said former Afghan interior minister Ali Jalali.[621] In 2005, Afghanistan had 398 districts in its 34 provinces, the number changing slightly over the years due to administrative reorganizations. The district level is where the crisis of governance in Afghanistan is most intense. Most provinces are too large and diverse to permit a nuanced approach to local realities, and provincial capitals are remote from the villages. Militarily, "district and below is where the fight will be won or lost. We have 130 combat outposts, pushing troops out. We have to live with people, have to get out there," was how BG James C. McGonville, deputy commander of RC-East, saw the situation in 2008.[622] Most of these outposts were co-located with ANSF forces, although a few were US-only. Some 40 of these outposts were platoon-sized or smaller. In late 2009, a number of these outposts were abandoned or consolidated, giving up a US presence in areas where they were seen as not being effective or vulnerable to insurgent attacks. Just as there is a military rationale to deploy troops down to this level, even if it makes them more vulnerable, aid needs to take risks to fill the governance power vacuum at the district level and below.

Yet Afghanistan has limited governmental capability at district level: an appointed governor, an elected council (elections scheduled for the summer of 2010) in those areas where they are functioning, and teachers and health personnel. In districts with a strong insurgent presence, as in much of Helmand province, this may amount to only a few dozen Afghans; in more secure districts in the north, a few hundreds. District Development Assemblies (DDAs) include two representatives from each CDC. In provinces such as Helmand, these are not currently functioning. Many DDAs were not formed until 2008–09, so it is too early to assess their value, but they have started to prove effective in districts throughout Afghanistan, especially when provincial reconstruction teams (PRTs) have worked closely with them as in Panjshir and Parwan provinces.[623] In some areas, non-elected district shuras have been set up and these have been successful, as they are able to provide services to the population and protect economic resources from insurgent destruction (as has been the case in eight of nine districts in Wardak province) by using traditional collective decision making and dispute resolution. As a result, the insurgents have targeted the shuras and the Afghans that take part in them, claiming that any competing approach to their own administration of Sharia law as unIslamic.

Development at the level below district—the villages where rural

Afghans live—is primarily the responsibility of the PRTs and the United Nations Development Program (UNDP) Afghan Subnational Government Policy program. It is far from adequate as a critical element of a successful counter-insurgent strategy in the rural Pushtun areas of the south and east where the insurgent pull is strongest. Another capability, introduced first in Wardak and Helmand provinces and which may be applied elsewhere, is the Afghan Social Outreach program in which the government identifies local leaders and has them form local shuras, which then help produce plans and direction for development on a village-by-village basis, allowing for local concerns, specifics, and leadership to be reflected.

Provincial Reconstruction Teams and Their Security Impact

Post-2001, the US initiated the organization of PRTs (Provincial Reconstruction Teams), which is a military force that includes government civilians, who are supposed to spearhead reconstruction projects throughout Afghanistan. As of late 2009, there were 26 PRTs in Afghanistan, 12 of them provided by the US. US PRTs include some 80–150 personnel; coalition PRTs may be smaller, reflecting the smaller pool of resources available to providing countries such as Lithuania, or larger, in the case of the UK. Military PRT members carry weapons, but only for their own safety, not to defend the local Afghans. The PRTs are capable of self-defense but not of securing the areas in which they work and are dependent on other coalition military forces for this as well as their logistics support. The PRTs in the most hotly contested provinces, notably the Canadian-led PRT in Kandahar and the UK-led PRT in Helmand, greatly expanded; they were among the most reliable sources of development in those provinces.

Many of the US PRTs have limited non-military participation, usually with only a single AID (Agency for International Development) officer, a State Department officer, a Department of Agriculture representative, and a few civilian specialists, if lucky. The bulk of US PRTs are made up of non-specialist military personnel. "PRTs are essential for aid delivery in insecure areas," said Jim Drummond, director of the South Asia division of the UK's DfID.[624] The main role of the PRT is working with local Afghans at the provincial and district levels. The Afghans help identify needed reconstruction projects. The PRTs, to the extent that their funding permits and the programs fit coalition priorities, will then pay for these projects to be carried out, creating jobs and needed capabilities. The PRT then provides oversight of the bidding process for the project and its implementation. In addition to building, PRTs administer a range of other programs, including agriculture and institution building.

Many different coalition members are responsible for PRTs. This has resulted in highly disparate approaches to distributing aid to Afghans. PRTs have also been interpreted differently by multiple nations.[625] Most of the countries providing PRTs are NATO members (including the UK, Italy, Lithuania, Germany, Turkey, Spain, and others), while some (Sweden, New Zealand) are not. Non-US forces all still require backup from the US military. The US provides much of the logistics support and intelligence that enables coalition PRTs to operate. Few of the PRTs managed by non-US coalition forces have the resources available to American PRTs in terms of quick-reaction funding and so are less effective. Many countries, with personnel only on six-month tours, lack the continuity of Afghanistan experience necessary to work amidst the complexities of the culture with regards to soldiers, diplomats, and aid workers alike. They need to know who to trust, how to gain local buy-in for projects, and when oversight is best carried out by one Afghan with a bodyguard and when it requires a show of force. All of this requires a degree of local knowledge that is not easy to acquire or retain once personnel rotate.

Working with Afghans is the PRTs' primary mission. Some PRTs spend a lot of time in the field, cooperating with district councils and supervising projects. Some coalition members keep their PRTs largely behind barbed wire in their compounds, signing contracts for building reconstruction projects with local Afghan firms. They rely on Afghan contractors for oversight. Some PRTs tend instead to direct their funding to Afghan NGOs. Others are building "hearts and minds" or, in the case of New Zealand's PRT in Bamiyan province, they are much loved by the Shia Hazara inhabitants, demonstrating a link to international acceptance and support from the coalition that transcends the local suspicion of Sunni-dominated rule from Kabul.[626] Some PRTs have been innovative. The Netherlands PRT in Uruzgan province was one of the first to integrate social scientists among its personnel to better understand the "human terrain" in which they had to work.

All PRT missions, regardless of their national affiliation, include monitoring aid programs. But reconciling the need to protect the PRT personnel with retaining flexibility to interact with local Afghans in an effective way is problematic. "How do you send a convoy of 15 HMMWVs to monitor a ten thousand dollar project? Will the locals protect it? The Taliban will beat the locals for giving the PRT tea and destroy the project," according to Massoud Kharokhail.[627] This essentially sums up one of the key reasons why it is hard to carry out development work, even through PRTs, in the provinces in Afghanistan threatened by the insurgency. GEN McChrystal saw the problem as not just limited to the PRTs. "When ISAF forces travel through even the most secure areas of Afghanistan firmly ensconced in armored vehicles with body armor and turrets manned, they convey a sense of high risk and fear to the population."[628] Mark Ward agreed: "We need to get out more. Leave some armor behind. Get out with the people."[629] Effective counter-insurgency operations mean getting out among the "human terrain," it means that force protection, staying in fortified locations, cannot be the prime objective of either infantry units or PRTs.

To make the PRTs more effective, in November 2008 ISAF restructured its oversight procedures, intended to provide analytical feedback and share lessons learned. In December 2008, the Executive Steering Committee, including ISAF, Afghan, and UNAMA representatives, was reconstituted to coordinate PRT operations with other reconstruction efforts. Elsewhere, in more secure provinces, PRTs are sometimes duplicating Afghan government functions or competing with local officials. In November 2008, President Karzai complained that PRTs were creating a "parallel government" to his own in the countryside, and other Afghans perceived that many of the resources devoted to some PRTs were absorbed by multiple layers of contractors and sub-contractors, foreign and Afghan, so that little actually reached the grassroots.[630] There is concern that in secure areas "where the Afghan government has created local institutions, PRTs delivering services are doing harm. Where the government is there and has the capacity to deliver services, Afghans should go to the government," said Mark Ward.[631] Zoran Milovic, a public opinion researcher, believed that having the Afghan government provide reconstruction rather than the PRTs, once this stage of stability is reached, is important. "The face on reconstruction is important. It is important to show the government gaining strength. The image must not be that of foreigners, but that *my* government is doing *this*."[632] The coalition countries that run PRTs in provinces where Afghan governmental capabilities to carry out reconstruction and administration do exist, however, are unenthusiastic about redeploying their assets to the conflicts in the south and east, where the danger is considerably higher. Yet with Afghan government capability still limited, the PRTs effectively have to stay around in most provinces to ensure the continuity of their projects for the foreseeable future.

The US has supplemented the PRTs with other military development efforts. In 2009, as US forces started to move into the Task Force Kandahar area of responsibility, they supplemented the Canadian Kandahar PRT with three District Support Teams (DSTs). The DSTs are intended to carry out PRT-type missions but are smaller and focused on an individual district. More have since been formed.

The US military has recognized the importance of agricultural aid to their goal of a "comprehensive counter-insurgency strategy." Agribusiness Development Teams (ADTs) are largely drawn from National Guard units from farming states and include agricultural experts. The first two deployed in 2008, followed by a further five in 2009. GEN Petraeus said he was "very grateful for them, they play an important role."[633] BG James C. McGonville, deputy commander of RC-E in 2008, said: "Some 80 percent of Afghanistan's people know how to farm, but they are not efficient. Their value chain lacks cold storage and potentially valuable costs are often wasted. In addition, they have to rely on Pakistan for food processing and getting to markets."[634] The ADTs supplement civilian and NGO development efforts to aid the Afghan agricultural sector and have the capability to work in districts where unarmed personnel would be vulnerable.

The US military also has its own developmental funding through the CERP. US commanders consider the CERP "one of their most critical weapons" in counter-insurgency, because it puts funding in the hands of the same commanders that carry out combat operations, ensuring that development and kinetic operations are fully integrated.[635] The CERP is considered one of the most responsive aid programs in Afghanistan. CERP funds are also used to pay local Afghans for collateral damage. British officers in Afghanistan regret the lack of a similar responsive military-directed aid funding capability in their forces.[636] CERP funding started at 40 million dollars in fiscal year 2003 and has expanded to 683 million dollars in fiscal year 2009. To provide jobs and reduce insurgent recruiting opportunity, some 70 percent of CERP funding goes to paying local Afghans for work, which includes tasks such as helping to create and maintain coalition forward operating bases.[637] Because of the importance of jobs to Afghan perceptions of security and the insurgents' recruitment of those without them, this is likely to provide the most effective use of CERP funds. There is a general consensus that the US military needs to allocate more personnel to administer the CERP, because the combat units that give out the funding have to rely on non-specialists for aid allocation and oversight.[638]

Aid and Corruption

Poorly targeted and directed aid programs have hurt the legitimacy of the entire international effort over the past 10 years. They have also helped feed corruption, albeit unwittingly. When Afghans have seen foreigners either dividing aid money pledged to Afghanistan up among themselves or spending it unwisely, it appeared an open invitation to have some of it themselves as soon as they are given the opportunity. This has led to a crisis situation where corruption threatens the legitimacy of the Afghan government and the steps being taken to counter it by donors also have the potential to do more harm than good.

The Afghans saw that the aid system was siphoning off most of the money before it even reached Afghanistan. Adjusting to the rules of the new game, Afghans started to take off their share as well as soon as they could. The result, however, of this new game has been to make losers of the vast majority of the Afghan people and those elites that have not benefited from it. In 2009, the US had three inspector general organizations watching how aid flows through to Afghanistan. Yet reducing corruption in Afghanistan is going to take a long time, and Afghanistan needs well-directed aid to avoid a short term crisis. "Spending money in Afghanistan and avoiding corruption is hard to reconcile. You have to accept some risk," said Mark Ward, a UNAMA official working on aid issues.[639] The risk is not a trivial one, considering the importance aid has had in creating the culture of corruption that threatens Afghanistan, yet it is probably better to accept policies that give the Afghans more authority and insist that they assume more responsibility, even if this means a higher risk of diversion of resources.

The perception of corruption helps ensure the reluctance by donors, especially the US, to relinquish their control over the aid process and allow the Afghan government a larger role in both determining priorities and implementing programs. Aid has also contributed to the rise of the culture of corruption by hiring many of Afghanistan's competent former civil servants and technocrats away from the Kabul government and into their international or donor organizations. In addition, too often the aid process has demonstrated a lack of transparency and accountability by both the donors and recipients.

Aid and the Afghan Economy

Afghanistan needs a functioning private-sector national economy for long-term peace and stability. Afghans identify unemployment and the lack of a way to legally prosper as the most important single threat to national security. The insurgency is ethnolinguistically largely limited to the Pushtuns, while unemployment is a nationwide crisis that gives insurgents, warlords, and narcotics traffickers alike more power through their ability to offer jobs where there otherwise would be none. If Afghanistan's economic situation in recent years was perceived internationally as not as critical as its security situation, this is due to the influx of aid and the money from opium cultivation. Real legal GDP growth has not reached the 14 percent experienced in 2005, but has still remained relatively high, at an estimated 13.5 percent in 2009. Inflation was reduced from ten percent in 2008 to seven percent in 2009. However, food and energy costs increased in 2008 and the impact of the world economic downturn in 2009 created real hardship among the poor even if it did not undo many of the post-2001 gains reflected in development in Kabul and the availability of work on development programs.[640] While this did not lead to food riots or hunger, even after neighboring countries restricted their exports, it became harder for the average Afghan to live. The hope for a better life that all Afghans shared after the ouster of the Taliban receded.

Despite busy bazaars, a trading tradition, and a history of free exchange and silk-route merchants, Afghanistan's economic development before the 1978 Communist putsch was dominated by the state. Since the 1980s, the part of the economy outside Kabul's control has been dominated by regional markets and an economy based on illegal extraction: opium, smuggling, clear-cutting forests, and weapons trade during the Tajikistan Civil War. Much of the recent development since 2001 has been dominated by foreign donors and investors or those Afghans who have access to money and connections abroad, sometimes illegal: the trans-border transport and lumber mafias, narcotics traffickers, and the Kabul real-estate developers. Other Afghans used connections with Saudi Arabia and the Gulf, dating back to the war against the Soviets, to access investments from there. The creation of an entrepreneurial Afghan diaspora since 1978 has made possible much of the recent legal economic growth. Those who did not return to Afghanistan have often provided investment and access to international markets and investment. But the global Afghan community does not have the human and natural resources nor access to capital like China or India.

As with aid, there are examples in Afghanistan of economic success that can potentially serve as a model that can be applied to other sectors. The communications sector provided an example of a success through private investment that has avoided corruption. Media growth, also privately funded, means that even remote Afghan villages can now share Internet access and satellite television or listen to a broad range of news sources. Banking and finance, writing on an almost blank slate since 2001, have grown effectively, linking Afghanistan to the world economy and providing Afghans with a way to transfer funds other than the *hawala* system. This means ANSF personnel no longer have to leave their posts to deliver their pay to their home villages. Afghanistan now has a thriving privately owned transportation sector, ranging from international airlines to single truck operators. The high rates of economic growth created by the development of Kabul provided employment to a large number of Afghans. If this can be recreated on a national basis, it would directly attack the economic insecurity that clouds Afghan life today. Investment in the agricultural sector to enable exports also has the attraction of being able to potentially provide employment in areas where today poppy cultivation is the only alternative. Resource development, such as the Chinese investment in copper deposits, is another potential source of economic growth. However, Afghanistan is unlikely to achieve a functioning national economy until it can offer Afghans and investors alike security and rule of law. While these remain out of reach in the areas dominated by the insurgency in the south, instability has not blocked economic growth throughout Afghanistan. Nangarhar province continues to be the location of a strong cross-border trade with Pakistan despite the insurgency. Kabul and the more secure provinces in the north and west have better economies, and these offer potential for investment and growth.

Nothing is more important for Afghanistan than creating a viable private-sector–based national economy. It can provide more resources than aid and, more than any number of troops, offers the potential for a more stable future. The problem is that the troops are required to prevent the threat of terrorism, insurgency, and narcotics from sweeping away this future in the near term. The Kabul government and foreign donors alike have recognized the importance of the private sector, but nurturing it has often proven problematic. Applying the successes in communications, media, transportation, and other sectors throughout the economy has been difficult. The impact of decades of state domination of the economy is still being felt, but privatization efforts have often been undercut by corruption and favoritism and have failed to take advantage of the collectivist nature of traditional Afghan society to give grassroots Afghanistan a stake in the process and, through that, a feeling of belonging in the future of the national economy. "Public ownership should have been through letting the locals buy shares and collect dividends," was the view of a veteran journalist in October 2008. Instead, it has been marked by widespread accusations of corruption, most notably in the leasing of copper mining rights to China and in the sale of state assets, such as cement plants, to foreigners working in partnership with Afghans with family connections to the Kabul government.

Creating the New Afghanistan

The ability of aid, like foreign armed forces, to produce desired results in an Afghan context is, and will continue to be, limited. Merely throwing troops or money at the situation in Afghanistan will not be effective unless it is part of an overall strategy integrated to meet Afghan realities and encourage Afghan participation, decision-making, and responsibility, all vital if the country is to be viable with a reduced foreign troop presence and aid flow in the future. The deteriorating security situation in recent years has limited the ability for aid to reach into the areas where there is, arguably, the most need for it, especially in southern and eastern Afghanistan. Even though the situation in Afghanistan mandates more troops and more aid, neither is sufficient, individually or together, to ultimately create stability that will enable Afghans to live and grow their economy in peace and not revert to being a source for global terrorism, regional instability, and narcotics. More nuanced and responsive policies must be employed, aimed at enabling the Afghan ability to rule themselves and withstand the effects of terrorism, insurgency, narcotics, corruption, warlords, and all that would return the country to the decades of conflict that came close to destroying it.

The need to have Afghans act on behalf of Afghanistan applies to allocating aid resources as well as carrying rifles in the ANSF. Mark Ward, special advisor on development to UNAMA, said "We have got to train Afghans, not have more Pakistanis, Indians, or Iranians doing skilled jobs."[641] This course of action will ensure that local Afghans will be involved and have a direct stake in the future development while still empowering Kabul as the national government to use incentives for cooperation that only a central state could provide: roads, health, and the educational system, including universities and scholarships.

Development that is inserted, top-down, by Kabul, foreign military forces, or NGOs, without consulting local Afghans whom it will personally affect and without insisting that there be an opportunity for buy-in and a corresponding expenditure of resources—however limited—by the local population, will remain alien and undervalued and thus the target for insurgent attack. This is the only way to create sustainable solutions that the Afghans will agree to and take ownership of and, eventually, pay for and maintain themselves. This is reflected in the Afghan government's Nationality Solidarity Program (NSP) having a "requirement of a ten percent community contribution toward the cost of projects" to give them a stake, according to Eshan Zia, former Minister of Rural Rehabilitation and Development.[642] Contributions can be cash, labor, or donation of resources, but are vital to give the locals and their kin a stake. Other local contributions have come as a result of grass roots initiatives. Local shuras or jirgas that want development in their home area will often levy such contributions to show support and attract potential donors or patrons. Projects done by Afghans are also cheaper than those done through foreign contracting. The cost per Afghan-contracted classroom in a school comes to 13,000 dollars, which is less than a third of the cost associated with foreign contracting for the same job, according to Jim Drummond, director of the South Asia division of the UK's DfID.[643]

Effective development will have to reach agriculture and religion, two areas of great importance to the average Afghan. Agricultural development will have to be tailored to each district. The Afghan state supported the emergence of cotton cultivation in the Golden Age, and there have been proposals to revive this. Afghan high-end produce, the raisins and pomegranates it has grown for centuries, have ready potential markets in the subcontinent and central Asia. Expanding such markets requires reconstructing Afghanistan's agricultural infrastructure and removing political barriers to international trade. Friendly Islamic countries have been used as intermediaries to work with developing Afghan religion as a social force so as not to concede its role in Afghan life to those aligned with the insurgents.[644] Such aid from Islamic donors can help provide mosques and maintain mullahs, while creating a system of Afghan religious education aimed at keeping radicalized pro-Taliban mullahs from holding political power or mobilizing public opinion in sermons against the Afghan government and constitution. Other foreign supporters need to be approached to mobilize their religious establishments to counter the claims that the coalition presence in Afghanistan has become part of the international "war on Islam" that is at the heart of efforts to enlist support for terrorists and insurgents.

Afghanistan will require a strong aid effort, the "pot of gold" that rewards cooperation rather than conflict. This same philosophy should apply too when trying to shore up a much more developed but troubled Pakistan, whose impact on Afghanistan, for better or worse, is undeniable. Any aid effort is a hard sell, considering the financial downturn among the rest of the world. Years of aid have not led to a secure Afghanistan, but there is no substitute for an influx of aid as a way of helping to stabilize the region and prevent more costly wars in the future. Aid is more effective in the long term than troops in bringing security to Afghanistan, but without troops there will not be the security that aid programs require and that allows Afghans to better their own lives. Aid needs to create a non-corrupt government to enable a functional private-sector economy that offers Afghans a chance for a life above subsistence levels that will not force them into siding with the insurgents or growing poppy for lack of alternatives.

Aid and Pakistan

Aid to Pakistan, like much of the US policy in the region since 2001, has reflected good intentions but has not been effective.[645] It is not unexpected that President Zardari has made requests for aid a central part of his relations with the US, telling a reporter "We have many plans including dealing with the 18,000 madrassas that are brainwashing our youth, but we have no money to arm the police or fund development, give jobs or revive the economy."[646] Yet Zardari's political weakness, the military-led nationalist opposition to the US oversight provisions in the Kerry-Lugar aid bill, and the poor track record of Pakistani governments, civilian or military, in dealing with such fundamental problems, show that it will be difficult for aid to Pakistan to create tangible improvement. Despite this, aid to Pakistan remains an important tool to help create change in Pakistan that will contribute to reducing the security threat to Afghanistan.

Aid has become even more important with the impact of the economic downturn in Pakistan. Before then, the growth in Pakistan's economy provided the resources for constructive change even if political insecurity and the Musharraf government's lack of legitimacy limited widespread application. Pakistan's more established economy allows the US to work with international financial institutions such as the International Monetary Fund, World Bank, and Asia Development Bank to a greater extent than in Afghanistan. Pakistan has a well-established banking system and a governmental infrastructure, including a still-independent if flawed judicial system.

US aid to support Musharraf's rhetoric of reviving civil society and strengthening state institutions, such as the school system, proved inadequate in scope and limited in reach. About eighty percent of the 11.8 billion dollars in aid to Pakistan provided under the Bush administration went just to the military in order to rebuild conventional forces to balance India rather than to create a counter-insurgency capability. Little went to military efforts to aid internal refugees from Pakistan's insurgency or natural disasters. US development aid to Pakistan, targeted at the FATA, had limited effectiveness due to violence undercutting any capability for hands-on direction on the part of the US.[647] There was widespread concern in the US, especially the Congress, that there was insufficient accountability for how aid funds were being spent in Pakistan. This led to the inclusion of oversight and transparency requirements being included in the 2009 Kerry-Lugar aid bill.

Pakistan needs to receive priority in stabilization efforts because the stakes are higher and the potential for collapse is not a graceful bankruptcy but the emergence of a long-feared "nuclear Somalia." In the short term, the population's vulnerability to increased energy and food costs must be combined with balance-of-payment and budgetary support in determining aid priorities. In the longer term, the best aid approach to Pakistan would be to remove constraints imposed by the US or European Union (EU), such as lifting textile quotas or freeing up funds for investment in regional energy pipelines. Additional funding—perhaps as much as fifty billion dollars over ten years—is required for Pakistan to start to rebuild its civil society and build up governmental and non-governmental organizations that will contribute to stability and help combat the political incapacity and internal violence that threaten its future.

In 2009, a renewed aid approach was implemented by the Obama administration, aiming to create greater leverage for the US in Pakistan. This started with the 19 May 2009 commitment of 110 million dollars in relief aid. The Kerry-Lugar aid bill passed the US Senate in October, described as "very heartening" by GEN Petraeus.[648] The Kerry-Lugar bill provided Pakistan with 1.5 billion dollars a year over the course of five years with a separate provision for military aid worth over 1 billion dollars and was considered to be a necessary complement for the further 5 billion dollars in international loans pledged at Tokyo in April 2009. Yet Kerry-Lugar became an explosive issue in Pakistani politics during October 2009.[649] The Pakistani military used this issue to rally nationalist sentiment against the civilian government, using the unpopularity of the US among elites and grassroots alike in Pakistan, saying that the oversight provisions were imperialist interference in Pakistan's sovereignty and that the certification provisions were an attempt to undercut the position of the Pakistani military in domestic politics. Public dissatisfaction with US UAV attacks, despite the fact that the Pakistani military cooperates with them, also fed into this opposition.[650] This reaction to the Kerry-Lugar bill also served as a public statement that the Pakistani military, even if they were forced to reluctantly take military action against domestic Islamic radicals and insurgents, were not going to be leveraged by the US to take open and public action (intelligence sharing and targeting excepted) against Afghan insurgents in their sanctuaries in Pakistan. The military objected to the bill setting conditions for the aid, which required that the US secretary of state certify that Pakistan is dismantling nuclear-proliferation networks, that Pakistan remain a democracy, that civilian control be maintained over the military and the defense budget, and that the government of Pakistan is not supporting militant groups on its territory. Even though there were provisions for the US president to waive these conditions, the precedent for questioning the military or putting it under democratic supervision was at the heart of opposition to it in Pakistan. The Pakistani military saw that accepting the provisions in the Kerry-Lugar bill called into question their self-appointed role as the guardians and definers of the country's national security interests, which includes allocating aid received, and as attempting to empower a civilian political system they increasingly saw as corrupt and dysfunctional. Aid will continue to prove a critical issue in the difficult US relationship with Pakistan's military.

US policy has stressed that the crisis in Pakistan is not purely a bilateral issue. The US has encouraged the EU and other countries to make a strong commitment to support Pakistan. In 2008, the International Monetary Fund pledged a standby loan, and the April 2009 Tokyo conference brought together additional international supporters of Pakistan. The total pledges were 5.3 billion dollars. While this has the potential to help with Pakistan's near-term economic problems, its history of using such resources to reward internal support of the government rather than address Pakistan's more long-term and intractable problems remains worrying.

In 2010, Afghan and coalition civil and governance efforts achieved less success than the military. Corruption remained extensive. Rule of law is limited. The Karzai government was working on political consolidation on the lines of traditional Durrani overlordship. He has acted to control outreach to insurgents through the peace jirgas and talks through Pakistan and Saudi Arabia. He sacked foreign-supported interior minister Atmar, intelligence chief, Saleh, and Fazel Ahmed Fariqyar, assistant attorney general handling anti-corruption. Karzai will not act against his clients, even when involved in corrupt or criminal activity, as long as he can build political leverage on their loyalty. The 2010–11 efforts to take over private security concerns and women's shelters were to nationalize on behalf of Karzai clients the patronage networks of these institutions, then running to foreign patrons. Karzai has reached out to Pakistan, Iran and China. The goal is to create a regime that can endure post-2014. Though there are increasing numbers of encouraging exceptions, overall Afghan leaders of all types at all levels still fail at everything other than rewarding clients. Aid efforts have generally improved, including in areas such as agriculture, often ignored pre-2008, encouraging 2009–10 economic growth rates of over 20 percent.

CHAPTER ELEVEN

CONCLUSION: THE FUTURE

"The world ain't going to be saved by nobody's scheme. It's fellows with schemes that got us into this mess. Plans can get you into things, but you got to work your way out."

—American humorist Will Rogers (1879–1935)

I n recent years, most of Afghanistan's trends were not heading in the right direction. Afghanistan was plagued by a regionalized yet still bitter and violent insurgency, a crisis of legitimacy based in corruption and ethnolinguistically polarized populations that share, along with their commitments to Islam and Afghanistan, increasing disillusionment, resentment, and rage all tinged with despair over the future. Yet this amalgam of crises began before the security situations deteriorated in recent years.

There is still cause for hope and prospect for success in Afghanistan. Most of non-Pushtun Afghanistan remains largely peaceful despite increasing crime with roots in government corruption, narcotics, and lack of alternative livelihoods. Afghan cities such as Mazar-e-Sharif, Herat, Balkh, Bamiyan, and elsewhere, have all shared some of the economic growth experienced in Kabul. Development programs are progressing, and the foreign presence that makes them possible is still largely accepted. 2010 saw battlefield success in the south. Some districts in the east and center, including some in Nangarhar and Paktia provinces, that were previously the site of extensive insurgent activities have seen improved security situations as well as a marked fall in opium cultivation. In the first five months of 2009, there were 0.6 and 0.4 average daily insurgent attacks in those two provinces, compared to 10.7 in Helmand and 4.6 in Kandahar.[651] In the spring of 2009, civilian deaths were down by 44 percent and kidnappings and assassinations were down by 17 percent.[652] Polling in March 2009 reported that 35 percent of Afghans thought that the security situation had improved over the past six months while only 13 percent thought it was worse, improvements over 28 percent and 17 percent respectively answering the two questions the same way in the previous quarter.[653] The Afghan National Security Forces (ANSF) are larger today and more effective than in previous years, though the ANA is still not capable of independent operations and the ANP requires continued reforms to cure widespread corruption and enhance their capability to defend the population from the insurgency. Some government ministries in Kabul—such as Finance, Education, and Rural Reconstruction and Development—have demonstrated an ability to work effectively and contain corruption. Other ministries, such as Interior, have made progress in increasing effectiveness even if they have not yet cured internal corruption. Ministries previously seen as ineffective, such as Agriculture and Energy and Water, have demonstrated progress.

In Afghanistan's least secure districts, in the heart of the insurgency in the south, the situation is nowhere past redemption. What the insurgents rapidly gained there, they just as rapidly lost in 2010. The insurgents' approach to Islamic practice, their lack of regard for the welfare of much of the population, and their continued attacks that bring death and destruction rather than the longed-for security have prevented them from seizing the high ground of Afghan nationalism and Islamic faith, even among most Pushtuns. There are still many legitimate nationalist and religious leaders who can be brought into the process of building stability in Afghanistan. In the first four months of 2009, some 80 percent of insurgent attacks were concentrated in 13 percent of Afghanistan's districts;[654] only 11 districts were then under insurgent control (with 119 more where governance was problematic).

If Afghanistan is to have a peaceful, viable future, it will be achieved through building on those peaceful cities, competent government ministries, and other Afghan successes that benefit the population, such as the creation of a cell phone network and the emergence of new, independent media. This future is, to many, no more apparent in today's conflict-defined Afghanistan than today's prosperous Republic of Korea was necessarily visible in the poor, devastated land that many saw in 1953. The outside world tends to see Afghanistan through a Kabul-centric view, as that is where the diplomats and reporters are based. This view served Afghanistan poorly after the fall of the Taliban, as the focus was taken away from the gathering storm of a renewed insurgency reentering Afghanistan from Pakistan. More recently, with Kabul afflicted by an expanded insurgency and increasing corruption, this view has shifted to one of impending collapse and dysfunctional Afghans both in and out of government. But Afghanistan is much more than Kabul, and neglecting this wider view is misleading. Afghanistan will have to draw on the strengths that are found elsewhere that have aided it throughout its history, its qawms and its faith, the determination and commitment of its people that prevailed against the Soviet invader, if it is ever again to be a peaceful nation, not requiring a large-scale foreign military presence just to see it through from one day to the next. Afghanistan will never be like the West or even other countries. It may never contain its insurgencies or interethnic rivalries even to the extent that India does, or limit corruption in its government and legal system as well as that which still afflicts Brazil, or, certainly, have the gender relations of Norway. But Afghanistan can be what it once was, governed the way most Afghans wished it to be.

What Afghanistan needs to achieve this, more than anything else, is time. This includes time to train and equip security forces. Even more time will be required to create a constituency for effective non-corrupt governance and to train those that will take part in it. It will be years before the last of the current warlords pass from the scene. A new generation of Pushtun leaders that are neither fanatics, radicals, nor tools of foreigners needs to emerge. Time is needed for Pakistan to change too, so that it no longer sees its current strategy of tolerating Afghan insurgency and aiming for proxy control in Kabul as necessary for national security. In Afghanistan, outsiders need to temper ambition with realism, including an understanding of the counterproductive nature of imposing top-down reform without first securing local ownership and an awareness of the limitations of anyone, including Kabul governments, to create change in Afghanistan. Afghans remain wary of reforms that are in reality heavy-handed attempts to impose control; such actions are often resented as attacks on national and Islamic legitimacy, and outsiders need to avoid having their involvement associated with them.

But only the outsiders can give Afghanistan time. The outsiders need to provide the security and required aid so that the Afghans can identify and put in place Afghan-led solutions. Even with the best intentions, outsiders' solutions create Afghan problems; the differing "small footprint" approaches to both the foreign troop presence and the UN role did not yield reduced resentment of outsiders and increased Afghan governmental responsibility, as had been planned, but rather failed to prevent insurgency and corruption. Outsiders can help enable Afghans to work together and remove negative incentives that encourage corruption. The problem is that there are competing outsiders: Washington, Islamabad, not to mention the terrorists, insurgents, and narcotics traffickers. All have competing visions for the future of Afghanistan.

Amongst the US and its coalition allies, there is widespread frustration over the situation in Afghanistan, be it regarding costs, casualties, or political unpopularity. The fact that there is no end in sight only heightens the frustration. Understanding Afghanistan's realities and what is needed to succeed on both the international and Afghan levels remains elusive. Even at its best, progress in Afghanistan involves one step back for every two forward, and in recent years things have been far from the best. The temptation to mitigate costs, limit liabilities, scrap the entire commitment, and consider Afghanistan outside the sphere of interest of lands that need to be defended (as the Republic of Korea was, briefly, in the years between the withdrawal of US occupation forces in 1948 and the invasion in 1950) has an appeal across the political spectrum in many countries including the US, UK, Germany, Italy, Canada, and other coalition partners. A Pew Global Attitudes survey of June 2007 reported majorities of NATO countries except the US and UK said troops should be withdrawn as soon as possible.[655] Since, commitments to Afghanistan have become even less popular; casualties have increased and the political situation in Afghanistan remains problematic despite military successes.

Afghanistan is not the only country that needs time, always a difficult commodity to provide, and outside support. By 2009, in Pakistan, the civilian government survived many of the crises it inherited from Musharraf's era. The military was taking action against Pakistan's insurgents in Swat and South Waziristan and throughout the borderlands, in a change from its previous policies. Pakistan continued to provide targeting intelligence for US UAV attacks against the terrorist and Pakistani insurgent leadership and is reportedly cooperating in on-the-ground activity by US intelligence in Pakistan,[656] even if the Afghan insurgents retain the benefits of sanctuary. But despite this progress within Pakistan's own borders, the political system remains in crisis. The threat of state failure remains, if not imminent, very real. It is of vital geopolitical interest that Pakistan remains viable. US security and aid policies alike need to try and help assure this.

Afghanistan's Conflicts

The five conflicts taking place in Afghanistan today are not primarily military. In combating insurgency, military forces must play an important role. Against other threats, military force is of a lower order of importance than many other factors, such as intelligence or effective politics. The first conflict is against international terrorism, primarily at the hands of Al Qaeda. These were the people that masterminded the 2006 plot to destroy transatlantic airliners and the 2008 attack on Mumbai, but it also has a wide range of targets throughout Afghanistan and Pakistan that do not necessarily register on international consciousness. The second conflict is the conjoined insurgencies in Afghanistan and Pakistan, including the Taliban forces in both countries, a unitary conflict divided only by the international border and Pakistan's policies which offered sanctuary to Afghan insurgents and urged its own insurgents to target their offensive against Kabul rather than Islamabad. The third conflict is narcotics and, therefore, counter-narcotics. Opium needs instability and an absence of state authority and, so far, Afghanistan is still chaotic enough for cultivation and trafficking to thrive. The fourth conflict is the multi-faceted internal strife within Afghanistan itself, resulting from ethnolinguistic divisions, religious practice, warlords and power brokers, political relationships, gender relationships, and land and water rights, to name only a few. The fifth conflict is within Pakistan, going beyond the insurgency and including the crisis of governance in that country that has been internationalized to such an extent that it has directly affected its neighbor Afghanistan.

These conflicts are all winnable. Afghanistan became a failed state not because of the Afghans, but because it became the primary battleground for fighting Soviet imperialism and, later, transnational Islamic terrorism. It is not true that Afghanistan was "never a real nation" and so does not merit international concern or support. It used to be a relatively peaceful country with a centralized but weak government. It lacked the emphasis on security and the imperial infrastructure of its neighbors like Pakistan, former Soviet central Asia, or Iran. Nor has the concept of Afghan nationhood been made impossible by the extensive societal divisions. The current government in Kabul has not had its legitimacy fatally compromised *ab initio* by its alliance with the US and the coalition, which the vast majority of Afghans of all ethnolinguistic groups welcomed in 2001. Rather, it needs to take more steps to base its strength on that of the Afghan people and not appear to be so heavily bound to the West. The corruption that permeates so much of Afghan government is a more serious challenge, but the potential for establishing legitimate governance still exists. Even widespread fraud in the 2009 election did not defeat Kabul's legitimacy. Afghans are not uniquely prone to internal and international conflict. For all the cultural conservatism of Afghanistan, there is widespread support for governance and rule of law, even if there has never been support for highly centralized rule from Kabul among grassroots Afghans. There is a deep desire for peace and security. Much of the insurgents' strength has been in their ability to promise these things, even though what they deliver has usually turned out to be much grimmer indeed.

Though each is winnable, victory in none of these conflicts is assured.[657] Al Qaeda continues to enable terrorism throughout the world as well as

Afghanistan and Pakistan. The Afghan insurgency is resilient and well funded with outside support, with sanctuary across the border in Pakistan. Afghans may not have the resources to make up for wartime devastation or the capabilities to outgrow internal divisions on their own, and so need foreign aid that, if misapplied, can instead worsen these problems and create new ones, such as corruption. In recent years, patience with the government in Kabul was largely exhausted throughout Afghanistan. But in all of these options, the constraints that may prevent victory are less the results of the adversary's strengths than the inability or unwillingness of the international community, including the US, and the Afghans to pay the price to counter them.

The US and Afghanistan

Many coalition leaders have demonstrated an inability to deal with Afghanistan's complex realities. Their electorates are too disordered and preoccupied with pressing domestic issues to deal with or even to recognize the threat of transnational terrorism; in Europe there remains a widespread perception that the threat would be reduced by an end to the coalition support for Afghanistan. The US leadership, military and civilian, has tended to assume that problems facing the coalition's policies originate from outside the US, and that America provides solutions, with little thought given to the potential that Afghan efforts could actually be smarter and better implemented or at least better suited to their native conditions. Despite large US and coalition involvement over the past several years and the certainty that policy decisions made in Washington *will* affect Afghanistan for better or worse, this remains an Afghan story, and therefore Afghan solutions must be part of the ultimate resolution. To the extent that Afghanistan is seen as an outsider's conflict, with foreign troops, costs, casualties, and political realities determining what happens, it undermines the future, which will require Afghans making hard political decisions. This future will be difficult to achieve but has succeeded in the past, as the Bonn agreement and the *Loya Jirgas* that followed it demonstrated. The most important thing the outsiders could have done for Afghanistan was to have kept Pakistan from providing a sanctuary for the insurgency; this they have been unable to do. Military force, predominantly provided by the US, only became increasingly important in Afghanistan after the US was unable, through diplomacy, persuasion, aid, and any of the other available policy tools, to sustain security after 2002–03. Before that, the "small footprint" of a limited US troop commitment appeared not only required by the emphasis on Iraq but also the approach best suited to Afghanistan; the fault was in staying with this concept when it became apparent that Afghan realities did not fit Washington's plans. The focus needs to remain on Afghanistan, not the US, regardless of the importance of US policies to Afghanistan's future.

On 27 March 2009, the new Obama administration announced a new "AfPak" strategy for Afghanistan and Pakistan, to differentiate what it intended to do from what it had described as the pre-2008 lack of resources and priority by the previous administration. The Obama administration, despite the unpopularity of its predecessor, had taken over a bipartisan consensus that Afghanistan was a necessary war and one that must be won to prevent serious international consequences for years to come. In his inaugural address, President Obama committed to "forge a hard-earned peace in Afghanistan."[658]

Ambassador Richard Holbrooke was appointed special envoy to "AfPak." The new administration's policies included the deployment of an additional 21,000 US military personnel and hundreds of non-military personnel, government, and contractors to work in the military and aid efforts, an expansion of the Afghan National Security Forces (ANSF), and the sacking of US GEN David Kiernan and his replacement by GEN Stanley McChrystal to head coalition military (though not aid or diplomatic) operations. He, in turn, was replaced by GEN Petraeus in 2010. In Pakistan, the military operations and the expanded US UAV campaign gained some success against Pakistani insurgents (the US carried out a reported total of 110 UAV attacks in Pakistan in 2010 compared with 53 in 2009), though the Afghan insurgents' sanctuary in Pakistan remained effective.

Defense Secretary Robert Gates said in a May 2009 interview that public support for the Afghan war will dissipate in less than a year unless the Obama administration achieves "a perceptible shift in momentum."[659] In Afghanistan, the increased troop presence, prior to the 2009 election, intended to prevent insurgent control of a sizable percentage of the Pushtun population, led to increased casualties by US and coalition forces. This, along with widespread accusations of fraud in Afghanistan's August 2009 presidential elections, contributed to a widespread deterioration of support for US presence in Afghanistan by the electorate in September 2009.[660] Within nine months, the previous consensus view on Afghanistan had collapsed and Obama faced strong opposition over Afghanistan even within his own party, leaving him with the necessity of working with a Republican opposition that neither likes nor trusts him. In many other coalition countries, Afghanistan was already deeply unpopular, and the events of 2009 only heightened the dissatisfaction. When GEN McChrystal completed his strategic review in September 2009, it was widely felt that the political consensus was rapidly eroding.

In October 2009, the Obama administration agonized over GEN McChrystal's request for additional troops, conscious of the considerable political and financial costs. By autumn 2009, estimated US costs in Afghanistan totaled 227 billion dollars, including nearly 16 billion dollars in foreign aid and diplomatic operations, with an additional 73 billion dollars projected to be spent during fiscal year 2010 alone.[661] In October 2009, there were press reports that "White House officials . . . have concluded that McChrystal's approach could be doomed by election fraud, corruption and other problems in Afghanistan, by continued Pakistani covert support for the insurgency, by the strains on the Army, Marine Corps and the federal budget; and by a lack of political and public support at home, which they fear could also undermine the president's domestic priorities."[662] If these reports prove to be correct, they have the potential to undercut any US policies in Afghanistan and send that country back into more decades of conflict. If an effective Afghanistan policy is precluded by a preoccupation with the US domestic policy concerns of the administration, it may prove to be even more counterproductive to national security than did the US disengagement from Afghanistan that followed the Soviet withdrawal in 1989.

When Afghanistan rose to the top of the US national agenda in 2009, it brought with it the attention of official Washington and the mainstream media that saw it as reflecting polarized US politics and priorities, rather than reflecting an understanding of Afghan realities, much as Pakistan has seen its own Afghanistan policy as an extension of domestic politics for decades. Those in Washington remember that no one lost their jobs when the US disengaged from Afghanistan and distanced itself from newly nuclear Pakistan. The US seemed to care little about Afghanistan after that until Al Qaeda served notice with their attacks on US embassies in 1998. To many Americans, Afghanistan is seen through the prism of Vietnam, another unpopular and costly war that threatens to devour an ambitious domestic political agenda.[663] This is likely to be as misguided as seeing Vietnam through the prism of the 1930s and Munich was in the 1960s. Afghanistan is not about the unsolvable problems of political and cultural divisions in America but rather those of Afghanistan, which are highly disparate but largely solvable. Afghanistan's conflicts are all winnable. The US concern for an "exit strategy" rather than a unitary strategy to prevail in each of Afghanistan's five conflicts and playing out US politics in Afghanistan has the potential to prove disastrous for the Afghans. The emergence of the perception in the region, however inaccurate, that the US is more concerned with limiting its liability in Afghanistan rather than achieving success has the potential to undercut all that has been achieved by American action there since 2001.

The Obama administration aimed to address these concerns with the president's 1 December 2009 speech, announcing the deployment of additional US troops. The Obama speech emphasized the need for additional manpower—some 30,000 additional military personnel—as well as setting out what they are needed to achieve once deployed.[664] Coalition members are expected to provide a further 7,000 personnel. These reinforcements cannot change the situation in Afghanistan; what they *can* do is provide time and a suitable level of security for the US, coalition allies, and the Afghans to make these needed changes, in the Afghan governance and in diplomatic relations with Pakistan.

This Obama speech laid out three elements for an effective strategy: "a military effort to create the conditions for a transition [exit]," a civilian surge, and effective partnership with Pakistan. Within these constraints, GEN McChrystal's efforts were given a green light to create the effective integrated strategy that the coalition and Kabul has lacked up to this point, and although his authority only extends over the first of the three elements Obama identified, it can provide the security for the other two steps to consolidate. McChrystal said "Success is achievable but it will not be attained simply by trying harder or 'doubling down' on the previous strategy. Additional resources are required, but focusing on force or resource requirements misses the point entirely."[665] This reflects that while these resources, in troops and dollars, are needed in the short-term future to prevent disaster, only the long-term strategy of rebuilding Afghanistan, physically and politically, with responsibility for its own security enabled and underlined by a security commitment from the US, is likely to lead to success in all five of Afghanistan's conflicts.

Obama placed great emphasis on an exit strategy and a date set for the start of withdrawal of US forces from a combat role, and so the speech unfortunately had the impact of undercutting what Afghanistan needs most, a sense of long-term commitment to enable it to rebuild itself and prevail against internal enemies and neighbors alike. In the past, no exit date was set for other security relationships where the US support for a local partner has been important to deter adversaries, such as with Germany, the Republic of Korea, or Israel. Supporting these countries has cost the US lives and money over the years, but it has been critical in creating international stability. With these countries, the US commitment is that strong and believable that *it*, rather than the number of US troops or the dollar amount of US aid, is important. A commitment of foreign troops to Afghanistan is less important, or desirable, than the knowledge by the Afghans that they can count on US support. The speech did not provide assurance that Afghanistan has a long-term relationship with the US. Rather, it reinforced the perception that, at the end of the day, the US is going home and the Afghans will have to deal on their own. The message the speech sent to Afghan insurgents and Pakistani generals alike was that the US was going to disengage, starting with the 30,000 reinforcements that would withdraw in 2011, and was starting to limit its liability, and those adversaries that had the time and the patience to wait them out would be in a good position to prevail in the end, especially if many of the Afghans the US had relied on decide to disengage along with them. What Afghanistan really needed from the US, and has not received, was the knowledge that the insurgents and the ISI will not be able to wait out the US commitment.

Nor will these US and coalition troops implement an integrated strategy in Afghanistan. While Petraeus and McChrystal were clear as to how these resources will be effectively used, the same cannot be said about the other two elements of Obama's strategy, the surge of US civilian personnel (including those that will help train Afghans for more effective governance) and better cooperation with Pakistan. Effective plans to achieve both goals are not evident.

The focus of friends and adversaries alike was shifted to the 30,000 troops that will withdraw in 2011, not to the US relationship with Afghanistan that needs to remain even if troop numbers or aid dollars are reduced. "We're not interested in staying in Afghanistan. We have no long-term stake there. We want that to be made very clear," Hillary Clinton, the Secretary of State, had previously said on 15 November 2009.[666] Secretary of Defense Robert Gates, while stating that the US aim is to "signal resolve," also cautioned "this is not an open-ended commitment."[667] While these statements themselves are true, and apparently intended to counter the local perception that the US interest in Afghanistan is to have a base for its "global war on Islam," their effect has been to underline the limitations in the US commitment.

The 2009 Obama approach dispirited Afghans, clinging to the remains of the hope created in 2001, afraid that once again the US will disengage with even more disastrous results than in the 1990s. Addressing corruption will become more difficult as Afghans have a motivation to earn enough to allow them to go into exile if things fall apart. Others may look to deal with the enemy, looking toward a settlement that cuts out other Afghans. US and NATO commitments made in 2010 to keep combat troops deployed through 2014 has not reversed this impact.

What the US can do for Afghanistan, in the final analysis, is limited. The most important changes needed in Afghanistan can only be carried out by the Afghans themselves. This includes turning away from the culture of corruption and polarizing politics and taking responsibility for their own future. This will likely take a generation to accomplish, and the West may not like how the Afghans end up doing this or approve of some of the people that will take part in this process, but the alternative is disengagement and more decades of conflict. The US commitment gives time, among other things, for Pakistan to change its strategy and the Afghans to change their politics. But this is going to require a perception that the US commitment, regardless of troop levels and aid payments, will remain, just as the commitment has remained to the Republic of Korea. Demanding an exit strategy from Afghanistan in 2010 may be as counterproductive as insisting on an exit strategy from Korea would have been in 1952, or making disengagement a priority in other US security relationships.

Afghans can and will work and fight for themselves, even if some will gladly evade responsibility and let outsiders shoulder these burdens in their stead or will accept their aid money when this is offered. A few will even pocket this money if they see others getting rich. The pro-Soviet Kabul regime endured successfully in 1989–92 after Moscow had withdrawn its combat forces but kept up a strong commitment in the form of money, support, and advisors. They were able to survive an offensive by the Afghan resistance forces based in Pakistan, well armed by the US and other donors. The 1989–92 Kabul regime could survive the withdrawal of Soviet troops; what it could not survive was the end of the Soviet Union, which removed the source of committed outside support that had enabled them to hold things together. But if the Afghans must fight for themselves, they will do it their way, and outsiders may not like what happens.

Afghanistan needs security for any progress in its conflicts. Long-term commitments from the US are important for that security. Foreign troops in the field and foreign aid programs and advisors are short-term tools needed to turn around trend lines and rebuild confidence. Troops and aid are important both for what they do and, perhaps more important, because they are evidence of this commitment. Troops and aid can be reduced, if the situation on the ground permits, if there is a perception that the commitment remains. The long-term solutions will require the Afghans to rebuild security and resolve conflicts for themselves, which will take a generation. But without the short-term actions by the US and coalition, requiring troops and aid, Afghanistan's long term may belong not to the Afghans, but to the terrorists, insurgents, and narcotics traffickers. In the longer term, restoring the consensus for a US commitment will be difficult, but showing the importance of Afghanistan's conflicts on a global basis, while not whitewashing its limitations and problems, is a necessary first step. Efforts to bring the voice of the Afghan people to Western audiences, as took place during the conflict with the Soviet Union, would also help remind them of the lives and futures that are at stake there.

Last Chance for Afghanistan?

"They are not doing what it takes to win," one long-time observer of Afghanistan said in Kabul in October 2008. The "they" in the statement refers to Afghans and their US and coalition supporters alike. This situation has not been turned around by actions by the Obama administration, nor have Kabul and the larger but divided Afghan population changed their ways that have contributed to the crisis. Afghanistan needs to change before it becomes likely that, rather than gradual disintegration, some unforeseen event, even a relatively minor one, may lead to a widespread collapse.

Providing Afghanistan with just the minimum resources it needs to stay afloat when it needs to achieve stability to enable development sets it up for eventual disaster from terrorist attacks, insurgent success, or natural causes such as drought, the population growing faster than employment, or even simple entropy. By 2013, or at least 2018, if significant advances in stabilizing the country are not made, Afghanistan as a nation could be so incapacitated that any gains since 2001 will be at risk and Pakistan-backed insurgents could conceivably be back in power in Kabul while waging a civil war against non-Pushtun Afghans. It took mistakes and failures by all the participants, Western, Pakistani, and Afghan, to create the troubled Afghanistan that replaced the hopeful one of 2001.

Even if success is achieved in Afghanistan, transnational terrorism is likely to continue to be a threat worldwide, with Al Qaeda as a participant or an inspiration. In the event of a foreign disengagement from Afghanistan, NATO Secretary-General Anders Fogh Rasmussen said "Al Qaeda would be back in a flash,"[668] and yet the threat is not so much from an Al Qaeda able to operate freely in Afghanistan as it is to the encouragement and example its success would provide to other groups and individuals that share its fundamentalist goals and destructive methods. Al Qaeda, for all its protean resilience, has limited appeal, both in Afghanistan and Pakistan as well as worldwide. Al Qaeda has worked around this through links with groups that had their origins in the Pakistan-supported conflicts in Kashmir and Afghanistan that have made them transnational threats as well; the next follow-on to the Mumbai terror attack may be further abroad than India. Al Qaeda operates from Pakistan and could feasibly operate from other bases, in places such as Yemen or Somalia. But the cachet of returning to Afghanistan, a liberated part of the *umma*, would be irresistible as a major theme foreshadowing eventual success in the global battle of ideas. It would light the beacon of Al Qaeda as the leader of transnational terrorism.

Some Westerners focus their attention only on international terrorism, putting aside the insurgencies in Afghanistan and Pakistan because they do not directly affect their national security. However, the average American or European has an interest in preventing the reemergence of transnational terrorism that would potentially be fueled by an insurgent-controlled Afghanistan. Seeing the defeat of democracy in Afghanistan would encourage terrorism's supporters, both in the regions surrounding Afghanistan and among the disaffected in the US and Europe. But while victory in Afghanistan will not prevent terrorism in the West, especially attacks that rely on recruits from the local population, as has been the case in the UK and throughout Europe, a Western defeat—which is how disengagement will be perceived—will likely embolden and encourage such terrorists to an even higher degree, providing an example of how a few hard men overcame great powers. The terrorist threat did not begin with the intervention in Afghanistan and is unlikely to end with it. Nor are the divisions between terrorists and insurgents in Afghanistan and Pakistan likely to prevent cooperation. Both groups have, in recent years, demonstrated a willingness to cooperate toward a "common goal" as they are linked by ideology, shared networks, and through even the ties of blood and marriage. Al Qaeda, for all its limitations, may have shown the way to the next generation of networked and internationally aligned terrorists.

Success in the insurgencies means prevailing over or incorporating in the political system the Afghan and Pakistani Talibans that are also deeply flawed yet strong contenders for power—political, social, and cultural—in Pushtun Afghanistan and Pakistan. The Afghan insurgents are even more deeply divided than those Afghans supporting the government, yet the Taliban's apparent absence of corruption has been touted in both Afghanistan and Pakistan as a way to contrast themselves with unpopular governments. This "lack" of corruption, however, is likely due to the fact that no one has been able to report on their inner workings and survive. The problem really lies with the future of one ethnolinguistic group—the Pushtuns—and they are superimposed on the future of the two countries. Effective Pushtun leaders need time to emerge in Afghanistan, where they have been limited by conflict, affiliation with the Taliban, and Pakistani influence, and Pakistan where they have been limited by military rule and feudal national politics. Such leaders would provide an alternative to the Pushtun insurgent leadership in both countries. Additionally, narcotics will continue to fund terror and insurgency alike so long as southern Afghanistan grows it in the absence of governance that eliminating the crop would require.

Currently, Kabul is still seen as Afghanistan's legitimate government, but it has been slowly undercut by perceptions of corruption and its failure to improve the quality of life (power, roads) for the average Afghan. The lack of economic success throughout much of Afghanistan, the failure to create a viable national economy and the jobs that would go with it has proven as critical, if not more so, as the challenges posed by the insurgency, narcotics, and corruption. There is deep ambivalence toward cultural issues and the foreign presence, though attitudes on the whole remain favorable, especially as the perception remains widespread that the foreigners are preventing another round of Afghan civil war enabled by Pakistan and other regional powers. This means that any solution has to be seen as an Afghan solution; whether the foreigners are happy with it must be subordinated to what will work between Afghans. But the Afghans are going to have to rely on the foreigners to provide security until their own forces are ready and provide aid until they have achieved a national economy. In the longer term, any Afghan solution will have the potential to be disrupted by Pakistan or other neighbors. A US security commitment will be required post-2014. In the final analysis, the US needs to help bring about a future where Pakistan is stable, democratic, and at peace with its neighbors and where its national security is not defined by the military. That is truly a long-term objective, but both the nuclear security issue and the security of Afghanistan mean it is one worth pursuing.

The Afghans had hoped for a better life in the wake of 2001 and bitterly resent it being available only to a few. There emerged few Afghan leaders or institutions that were willing to moderate these desires and convey the fact that it would not happen overnight, reminding elites and grassroots alike that while defeating the Al Qaeda and the Taliban militarily may have taken weeks, rebuilding Afghanistan would take decades. Fewer still Afghans were willing to take responsibility for the condition of their country, instead focusing on their own ethnolinguistic group or benefiting themselves and their kin. The over-centralized Kabul government created by the 2004 constitution has proven to be an unwieldy vehicle. Changes—through constitutional amendment or, once a consensus exists, a *Loya Jirga*—are needed to give the Afghan people more control over their government at the lowest possible level, in order to get them to take personal ownership and responsibility for their future. A more parliamentary and less centralized government in Kabul could possibly have something like a British-style war cabinet that meaningfully engages major opposition figures. This would prevent Karzai's previous policies of aiming to sideline the opposition, denying them access to resources and so choke off their ability to provide patronage. There is a need to reduce the size of the Afghanistan cabinet, enlarged previously to provide patronage opportunities for Karzai. Decision making should be decentralized, increasing district and local authority and, through that, responsibility. There is a need to speed up reconstruction in stable provinces. Major drug traffickers and some senior corrupt officials need to receive high-profile trials and exemplary sentences. All the while, Afghanistan needs to give more power to the provinces, district, and villages. The Afghan people, above all, need to be made responsible for their own future, which must include empowering (and arming) them to defend it. Just as government cannot be limited to Kabul, security cannot be limited to the ANSF alone. In the short term, this policy will require village-based forces with their own weapons. It has to involve the

Afghan people, the same ones that defeated the Soviets and endured the 1992–2001 civil wars. They are tremendously tired and war-weary, but they can do it, if allowed to do it in their own way.

Enabling change in Afghanistan requires a form of policy "judo." Rather than resisting with sheer force, pull with the strength of those parts of Afghanistan derived from its social structure and culture and then try and direct it in the desired direction. This works better than opposing what is strong and trying to build up what is weak. But change in Afghanistan will not result from top-down foreign-directed initiatives. It will require a generation to build Afghanistan's institutions and create constituencies, and what foreigners can do best is help provide security and aid to see this needed generational change completely through.

Afghans, when they are not being polarized by foreign supporters, have been capable of working things out themselves, and this can be capitalized on today. The best of Afghanistan—a mixture of anti-Soviet guerillas, former Najibullah supporters, returning exiles, and educated Kabulis with roots in state service—together present a formidable group that cuts across ethnolinguistic lines and has real potential. Outside of Kabul, those Afghans willing to provide a bulwark against collapse, at least in the short term, may not have the qualifications and skills of those in Kabul, but they demonstrate that the strengths of the old Afghanistan still exist and they need to be on the "team" as well. The challenge will be to pull together these divided Afghans in both Kabul and the grassroots and cut out those that are there for their own power or enrichment (much of the government).

Without any doubt, there is a substantial price tag on a sustainable Afghanistan, in terms of money, commitment, and troops. But not paying this price now will likely lead to failure, exacting an even higher price in the future, be it a renewed terrorist haven for new attacks on US soil, threats to shaky neighbors, or something else we dare not dream of. The insurgency in Afghanistan will not be won by foreign troops or aid, but they are needed to build up and reform Afghanistan's governance and enable the ANSF to hold the line until there is a chance for a modicum of peace and economic growth.

The likely 2011–14 security situation in Afghanistan will require outside troops to prevent further deterioration or even compensate for earlier actions not taken, be it actions to build an unitary security and development campaign, have an effective strategy for military operations, development and reconstruction; or help create legitimate Afghan governance for both the government and the grassroots. There was no alternative to increased reliance on foreign troops and money by the time of Obama's December 2009 speech. Unless effective and legitimate Afghan governance can follow in 2011–14, especially in the rural areas where the majority of the population lives, troops will provide only a temporary solution. Troops from additional coalition partners, especially from Muslim countries, are part of this requirement. While Turkey has been reluctant to commit additional ground forces,[669] those countries that originally offered troops to ISAF, such as Jordan and Oman, may be willing to reconsider following the US withdrawal from the unpopular conflict in Iraq. An increased role for Islamic coalition members would be diplomatically difficult to achieve, but would also help with the cultural dimensions of the conflict.

In 2010, the increased number of US and coalition ground troops was able to defeat and clear insurgent forces in Helmand and Kandahar. The weakness in 2010 was the capability to fill the power vacuum in the wake of the troops and create governance that will negate the insurgents' lingering threat that they will eventually return to kill all who collaborated. The Afghan government was, as in the past, not been able to perform this vital, final act. When Musa Qala in Helmand province was reoccupied by coalition forces late in 2007, the Afghan government personnel that moved into the heavily fortified district headquarters reportedly spent most of their time in the basement waiting for a helicopter back to the provincial capital at Lashkar Gar, hardly confidence-inspiring. In 2010, the ANSF moved to protect the population in the south, but effective governance was harder to achieve. Building up the ANSF will be only part of increasing Afghan security responsibility. In places like Helmand in 2010, respected Afghans resolved land and water disputes and mullahs preached peace and not jihad in the mosques. These proved harder to win over than competent Afghan security forces, but are no less important. In 2010, the US tried to make sure that they, and the Afghan civil society they represent, were reestablished where security permits. In the words of one veteran observer of Afghanistan, "More soldiers are not the solution without good governance to fill in behind them," even when the soldiers are Afghans.

In addition to strengthening Afghan civil society, the coalition and Kabul need to de-legitimate—through the battle of ideas—what the insurgents have to offer: the suicide bombs, the rough justice of the Qazi courts applying a brand of Sharia unlikely to be recognized by genuine ulema, the maximalist practice of Islam, and the continued alliance with narcotics traffickers. All these things are unpopular with the Afghan people. What has been lacking is a way to leverage this unpopularity so that the population will resist the insurgents. The negative message against all these things is important, but it will lack credibility unless it is matched by a positive message, of demonstrating to the people that the Afghan government is competent, effective, and able to make their life better and not make them targets for insurgents or coalition collateral damage alike. Any insurgency is more a political than a military conflict, and in democracies people daily have evidence of the importance of effective communications to political success. Yet it remains that the coalition and Afghans alike have often been less successful in getting their message out to the Afghan people than the terrorists and insurgents.

"The Taliban is fighting for their ideology, even one not acceptable to Afghans. What is our ideology?" asked Engineer Mohammed Es'haq, comrade-in-arms of Ahmad Shah Massoud and a veteran of Afghanistan's conflicts since the Panjshir Revolt of 1975.[670] His question highlights the disturbing fact that Afghanistan and its allies have been losing the battle of ideas to their enemies since 2001. Just as those standing against the terrorists, insurgents, and narcotics traffickers in Kabul and throughout Afghanistan could become a strong world-class team, so too is there a potential to pull together an ideology to unify them. An Afghan national vision (embraced by Ahmad Shah Massoud), Afghan Islam, a willingness to embrace democracy down to its roots in the Afghan jirga and Islamic requirement for *majlis-e-shura*, and a commitment to better the quality of life could, together, offer a future more appealing than any the insurgents could envision. It is here that the battle for hearts and minds can be won.

Afghans have earned the right to live as a nation, in peace and freedom, the same way Americans did, by fighting for it and voting for it. The Afghans remain independent in their thinking and committed to freedom. For all their many shortfalls, Afghans of all political allegiances remain proud of what they have successfully accomplished since 2001, from holding the *Loya Jirgas*, creating the constitution, and providing free elections, even if the most recent of these was tainted by corruption. The Afghans define nation, peace, and freedom differently from the Americans, seeing true freedom as only partly a secular concept. "Freedom" lacks meaning without also including submission to Islam and living life in accordance with Sharia law and the "Afghan way."

Pakistan and the Future

The future of Afghanistan is also being shaped by decisions made over the border in Pakistan, be it by the government, the military, or the insurgents. The February 2008 Pakistani elections and the peaceful demonstrations against Zardari and even Musharraf before him show that there is widespread support for rational, competent, and effective civil society in Pakistan. In the past, when the military has stepped in to take power, rationality and competence was what they offered, but the latter years of the Musharraf government discredited them, especially when the economy declined, and Pakistan experienced the rise of insurgency, and terrorism appeared to be a response to cooperation with US policies. Even though, by 2009, the concern over the insurgency and dissatisfaction with the civilian government and the economy made the military look better in comparison, they have been reluctant to take over again. There are too many intractable problems for which the military has no solution, and neither Pakistan's electorate nor its foreign friends want to see them back in power.

Pakistan's radical Islamic parties and the insurgents offer another alternative to Pakistan's often-dysfunctional politics, but through the path of Sharia law, which they claim would bring about long-denied social justice for all Pakistanis, not simply the "feudal" political leaders and their patrons. But in the FATA, Swat, and elsewhere, it is becoming obvious that they offer beheadings and beatings rather than a better life.[671] There has been no groundswell of popular support for the radicals, despite the widespread disillusionment and dissatisfaction.

The insurgent takeover in Swat was eventually met by military action in 2009 only when the TNSM's Maulana Sufi Mohammed used this success to challenge the legitimacy of Pakistan's constitution and to condemn democracy as a way of life counter to Islam.[672] This energized Pakistan and persuaded the military that the insurgency was actually a threat to the future of the country. The need is for policies that will show Pakistanis that there *is* a way to achieve a better life. South Waziristan remains no one's model of a good life, and the Pakistani state needs to build on that hard truth to deny the appeal of the radicals and insurgents, especially in the FATA, where they were able to use the "Taliban culture" to become entrenched.

In Pakistan, countering the insurgency needs to work on a number of levels. The bottom line is strengthening civil society. Until then, foreign aid will be required. All the armed Predator UAVs in the world would not be able to prevent the reestablishment of terrorist infrastructure nor, more to the point, can they enable the establishment of a legitimate Pakistani authority, one that can gain popular support, run a school system, or collect taxes. Pakistan-India rapprochement would make the needed internal changes in Pakistan easier, as with everything else in the subcontinent. Peace would undercut the Pakistani military's current claim to determine national security policy and government spending priorities. But India has shown itself unwilling to effectively compromise on issues such as Kashmir, and the US has been unable to raise any benefits to Pakistan accruing from its better security relationship with India. So while such action remains a long-term goal, meanwhile steps to strengthen Pakistani civil society such as aid to education, or development and political integration in the FATA, must help stem the long-running crisis of governance in Pakistan that neither military nor civilian governments have succeeded in addressing.

Pakistan's military and elites fear India and distrust the US, the perceived leader of a world in which their country is increasingly unable to cope with mounting challenges. The Pakistan military does indeed oppose terrorists that set off bombs in their cities or insurgents that occupy their territory, but Al Qaeda, other terrorists, and the Afghan insurgents are not among those whom they perceive to be the true enemy, which remains India and, to an extent, the US, now seen as India's supporter in its quest for regional power. Pakistan's strategy of supporting Afghan insurgents and tolerating Pakistani terrorist groups stems from its belief that it can use these groups, despite the fact that blowback from their actions could cause national disaster, as when India threatened military action after high-profile attacks there in 2001 and 2008 were linked back to Pakistan-based groups. But in attempting to persuade the government of Pakistan of this fact, the US is effectively asking them to turn away from their primary policy tool in Afghanistan, namely a proxy war through Pushtun insurgents, while, at the same time, demonstrating that these polices may lead the US (and its coalition partners) to withdraw from Afghanistan. Pakistan needs US cooperation to prevent Afghan civil war.

Pakistan's objective of putting a "moderate" Pushtun-dominated government that would be responsive to its security into power in Kabul cannot be achieved by tolerating insurgent sanctuaries. If Afghan insurgents are ever able to regain power in Kabul, the impact on Pakistan will be devastating. Pakistan will be less able to control such a regime than it was pre-2001. The blowback, in terms of refugees and radicalization, will likely outstrip anything seen in previous decades, and so the rational choice for Pakistan is to align with Kabul and the coalition and look at Afghanistan as a potential site for economic growth. While Pakistan has done this in the past, as when it refused to act as a spoiler to the Bonn agreement in 2001, persuading them to do this as a fundamental part of their national security policy, however, is still a task that remains, and will be difficult as long as Afghanistan is perceived in terms either of India-Pakistan competition or Pakistan's internal politics, especially the role in them of the military, ethnic Pushtuns, and Islamic radicals.

Future US and Coalition Actions

Unless current trends are turned around, the future for Afghanistan may turn out to be worse than its already grim past. If the US and other foreign supporters disengage from Afghanistan or withdraw their troops in the near future, it will not bring peace. Nor will it remove the motivation for continued violent attacks by the insurgents. Disengagement from Afghanistan is likely to seem an attractive option as casualties and expenses mount. If those Afghans working for the government in Kabul or those standing against the insurgents in their home districts see that they are going to be triaged away again by the same foreign countries that supported them against the Soviets and then walked away in the 1990s, many will end up fleeing or cutting a deal with the enemy. Some will stay and fight another round in Afghanistan's civil wars. The foreign supporters will have then ended up undercutting rather than enabling Afghan self-determination.

The US and the West have tried disengagement (effectively giving Pakistan a free hand) as their Afghanistan policy before, starting in 1989, and results were 11 September 2001 for the US, misery and destruction for Afghans, blowback and insurgency for Pakistan. Even today's Afghanistan is much preferable to leaving the future to a new, more brutal, Afghan Taliban and their allies. That would mean another generation of conflict in Afghanistan and, instead of a beacon, a torch to the dry tinder of the surrounding regions of central Asia, the subcontinent, and Iran and the Gulf. The rise of the Pakistani and Punjabi Talibans are an indication that the Taliban brand name remains a beacon to increasingly radicalized Muslims frustrated by current regimes and looking for the answer in fundamentalist religious politics.

Walking away is simply not going to work. It will not even make people in the West feel good about themselves. It will instead bring things back to the 1990s, with regional powers—especially Pakistan— backing Afghans in a proxy war, creating a huge humanitarian crisis among other disasters. It will not make today's networked terrorists focus their activities on a different set of target countries. It *will* mean that those in Pakistan's security services who bet on the Taliban will have succeeded. But that is unlikely to be good news for Pakistan. The consequences of their previous policies created the current insurgency, and more such policy implementation may prove fatal to the future of the country. As it is, violence is eroding away what Pakistan actually needs: strengthened civil society, revitalization of the economy, and development. This is especially the case in the FATA, which needs these things more than even the remainder of Pakistan. The Pakistani Taliban did not create the four percent female literacy that currently cripples the FATA, but they surely have taken advantage of it and the lack of development, political isolation, and economic marginalization that goes along with it.

People in the US and the West need to care about Afghanistan and the regions it borders because the threats there have still not been defeated and thus have the potential either to strike at them directly, as on 9/11, or create a crisis by turning Afghanistan back into an international anarchic battleground and Pakistan into Somalia with nuclear weapons. Just as Afghanistan is not a graveyard[673]—people do not live in graveyards—neither the US nor NATO is an empire. Empires used to be able to triage away places like Afghanistan, full of independent-minded people with many weapons and few exploitable natural resources. The Romans built Hadrian's Wall. The British drew the Durand line. Neither was a viable long-term solution. They could keep out invading warbands or lashkars, but not the movement of individuals or ideas. The West found this out when transnational terrorism planned in Afghanistan led to the 11 September 2001 attacks. Pakistan found this out when their Afghanistan policies, supported by military and civilian governments alike since the 1970s, incubated the Pakistani insurgency that was threatening Islamabad in 2009. The impact of any failure in Afghanistan cannot be limited to Afghanistan. Failure will come home from Afghanistan.

Neither the globalized world economy nor the globalized security system that sent NATO troops to the battlefields of Afghanistan can build a new frontier to protect themselves from terrorists and insurgents. An effective frontier is a flexible economy-of-force approach that allows those manning it to decide which outsiders are a threat and which can be incorporated into the system. The world of the frontier is a far cry from the world of the Bush administration's Global War on Terror, where "you are either with us or against us." Pakistan remains the friend of the US, yet has been both "with us *and* against us" with regard to its Afghanistan policy.[674] The money that enables terrorist and insurgent action comes heavily from friendly countries, including Saudi Arabia and the Gulf. Even Al Qaeda, a group that thinks in moral absolutes and acts with bloodshed, has been successful because it has been able to deal with those that are both with it and against it, including the Pakistani security services and Afghan and Pakistani Pushtuns who do not share their worldview, religious practices, or focus against a primary enemy that is also a distant one.

With the coalition's limited sense of the history of Afghanistan and why it is the way it is today, there has been too strong an emphasis on the short-term goals of the coalition partners. There have been too many outsiders who sought to reverse the whole course of Afghanistan history since 1973 during a unit's tour of duty, or before the next donor conference or before the next election. Not all these frustrated outsiders are Westerners. They include the Pakistanis who have seen their strategy backfire and Arabs who have seen their religious proselytizing resisted and their clients proven unreliable. Similarly, there are enough negative examples of policy failures in Afghanistan to warn future decision-makers. The US in the 1990s tried disengagement. The Soviets in the 1980s tried massive firepower, bribery, and political consolidation. The Afghan Khalqi Communists in 1978–79 were willing to murder everyone who opposed them. King Zahir started in the 1930s to build centralized state power but failed to check the growing power of the Communist opposition that was receiving Soviet support. None of these policies worked. There is no alternative to an incremental, trial-and-error approach, stressing effective feedback that reflects the nuances of Afghan realities rather than what the decision-makers want to hear.

Success in Afghanistan means creating a country that is viable in security and economic terms. With aid, the Afghans were able to have a Golden Age and defeat the Soviets. In recent years, there have been enough Afghan successes among the larger picture of disappointment and frustration to suggest how they might once again accomplish great things. Policies need to leverage the proven dedication and courage of the Afghan people rather than their divisions and polarization, emphasizing the strengths of society rather than the reluctance to take individual responsibility or avoid corruption that stems from its collectivist nature. Faith needs to be embraced as a foundation of society rather than a tool of fundamentalist politics. Insisting on Afghan responsibility and backing Afghan solutions is important; but those who seek to have the Afghans responsible for their own security or economy in a finite, single-digit number of years so that the foreign combat troops can go home and aid can be reduced are sending the message that the Western commitment will be a transient one. This is the message that has inspired Pakistan to view the Afghan Taliban as a policy tool rather than a threat and Afghans to view any access to money and power as an opportunity to get what they can while they can, making the cycles of dependency and corruption harder to break. Only a long-term commitment by the US and the coalition can make fundamental changes in these perceptions.

For a long-term commitment to be potentially sustainable by the US and its allies, Afghan forces will have to be able to carry the burden of combat operations, but in a controlled manner, as the rapid expansion of the ANSF offers many potential pitfalls, stretching the limited pool of competent and literate Afghan leaders and creating a force that will be dependent on foreign aid for its funding. Afghanistan will need to offer legitimate governance throughout the countryside and be able to point out that their enemies offer neither peace nor Islam, despite their claims. The US should commit itself to enable Afghans to build a future for the same reasons it defended West Germany in the Cold War and South Korea after the Korean War. In Germany, when the threat was internal Communist penetration, the US and its allies countered with building democratic institutions. When the threat was Soviet tanks through the Fulda Gap, the US and NATO countered that by committing large forces to Europe's central front. Today, unlike the Cold War, there is no peer competitor to the US. There are individual adversaries, each requiring a different set of actions to counter them. Some of the most persistent adversaries—including the Pakistani military—are, in many ways, also friends. As with the Cold War, there will likely be no substitute for US engagement. Afghanistan, like Israel, may never be at peace, may have tensions with its neighbors (even those that are US friends), have a percentage of the internal population more or less permanently alienated from the state, deal with lingering corruption, and endure adversary relations between elites. But to survive this way requires a commitment from the US that will be more important than the number of troops, and to get to this relatively stable situation requires a near-term military commitment to stabilize the situation, so that a new generation of Afghan leaders and elites of all ethnolinguistic groups can move in and demand and work for effective governance, a functional private sector economy, and a civil society.

Winnable Conflicts

In 2001, Afghanistan was a country without hope. It experienced the Taliban, a civil war, poverty, and misery. Then, in the wake of the US-led coalition intervention, hope arrived. Hope for functional politics, effective development, and a better life. When the schools reopened on 21 March 2002, it was the first time in decades that an Afghan government had done something embraced by its entire people. It was a good day.

This book has been about what has happened to this hope since then and why it has dried up but not yet all turned to dust. Hope was not a stupid illusion in 2001. It was stupid for the Soviets in 1979 to have thought that the combination of massive firepower and local political clients would allow them to achieve their policy goals in Afghanistan. In 2001 it was all going to be different. Since 2001, Pakistan's policies, US and coalition failures in policy formulation and implementation, and the self-serving and short-sighted actions of Afghanistan's political elites all soaked up Afghanistan's hope like so many sponges.

Afghanistan is still a winnable situation. The US and coalition partners know how to defeat terrorism and insurgencies, as well as creating governments that have at least a change for internal legitimacy and international acceptance, and have the means to do it again. There is no pathology unique to Afghanistan that kills empires that touch it or means that actions that succeeded elsewhere are doomed to failure there. Even in the most developed countries, it is widely said that the main cause of problems is solutions, and each solution identified for Afghanistan has the potential to create further problems. The question is thus not so much whether the US can prevail, but whether it is willing to pay the considerable costs associated with so doing. This will not be easy. Afghanistan is a country where actions tend to have high transaction costs and yield low returns. In the short term, the Afghans are either going to have to have the transaction costs paid for them (such as aid funding the creation of the ANSF), or they are going to have to do things their own way, which could open the door to other, less ideal, options, such as extractive state practices or looking to competing regional players such as Iran for support.

The US and its coalition partners are tired of the cost and casualties. There is no arguing that the returning dead and the financial drain are even more difficult to accept when the rationale for all of it was largely undiscussed or not understood. Even those who supported the heroism of their own country's forces were shown it outside of its larger context. The conflict has become unpopular. To the electorates, Afghanistan remains a distant and alien country and the Afghans a little-known or understood people. The 2009 debate in the US was over troop levels. In the region, it was seen as being about commitment. The 2010 increase in US force levels, in return for its costs, bought time to turn trend lines around and identify lasting solutions. But none of this is likely to succeed if friends or adversaries alike discern a lack of US commitment and a preoccupation with an exit strategy.

If the US disengages—in terms of commitment more so than the actual number of military personnel on the ground—Afghanistan's remaining hope will turn to dust. The US troops, the humanitarian NGOs, the Afghan expatriate investors, and all who have helped build on Afghanistan's hope since 2001 will go home. The hard men from the Vortex will yell themselves hoarse with triumph and, with the help of their supporters in Pakistan, will go back to waging a civil war in Afghanistan. Pakistan, hard pressed to survive the blowback of its previous Afghanistan policies that came home in 2001, will find it harder still to hold on in a world where Islamic radicalism has a new stronghold over the Durand Line and their goal of controlling Kabul is likely to prove as elusive as it was pre-2001. If the Pakistani military's perception of inevitable US disengagement is realized, there is no reason to believe Pakistan will be able to control what may emerge in Afghanistan, or, indeed, if anyone can. Those looking to create a clash of civilizations will tell the disaffected from Morocco to Mindanao that they have beaten the Americans as they beat the Soviets, and those governments that stand between them and an Islamic future cannot stand.

It is not simply prestige that is at issue, but the confidence and perceptions of billions of people as to who will control their future. If the infidel foreigners are forced from Afghanistan—not just their troops, but their culture and their global economy—where can they not be defeated? In the Middle East? The territory of the long-lost Kingdom of Grenada (identified as unredeemed by Al Qaeda)? The terrorists will find a new place to plan their schemes of burning buildings and bodies everywhere. Most Afghan elites will go into exile. Some Afghans will go on fighting the terrorists and insurgents, going back the mountains where the fighting started in the 1970s, and they will weep bitterly for Afghanistan and its lost hope. And a few foreigners will come to see them and write it down.

The US-led coalition, in 2010, succeeded in waging a successful counter-insurgency campaign, reflected in the weakening of the insurgent hold throughout much of Kandahar and Helmand provinces. The insurgents have responded with increasing targeted killing of Afghans. Around Pushtun and in the east, security improved. Increased special operations and UAV attacks took a toll of mid-level insurgent leaders. The insurgent's momentum demonstrated in 2008–09 was halted and, in some areas, reversed. Yet in 2010 the insurgents still increased the number of kinetic actions, up 70 percent since 2009 and 300 percent since 2007. Over 90 percent of these events took place in RCs South, Southwest and East in 2010.

The 2008-10 period has been highly dynamic. Looking at any issue in terms of a few snapshots is misleading. Militarily, both the insurgents and the counter-insurgency demonstrated increased proficiency. Policies in areas such as aid and governance that have been restructured and improved. In 2010, the decision to make ANSF responsible for security from 2014 did not address how effective governance could be achieved to backfill behind withdrawing coalition forces. "Government in a box" remains but a coalition catchphrase. Yet the potential for a post-2014 collapse, especially if aid spending is cut, remains real if the transition is mishandled.

AFTERWORD

O sama bin Laden died on 1 May 2011, killed in a US special operations forces raid on the compound in the city of Abbottabad, Pakistan, where he had lived, concealed, for several years. There has been no more significant kinetic event in the multiple conflicts in Afghanistan and Pakistan since the collapse of the Afghan Taliban in 2001.

His death appeared to many to be the culmination of the long and frustrating US commitment to Afghanistan, a "mission accomplished" moment that will require a strong rationale for a continued presence. The raid that killed bin Laden was part of the US targeting of terrorist and insurgent leaders, a key part of the operational approach put in place in 2009. Whether it will yield lasting strategic advantage remains uncertain.

For Pakistan, the death of bin Laden is problematic. While Al Qaeda has carried out terrorist attacks in Pakistan, the circumstances raise questions about Pakistan's complicity. Since bin Laden was living concealed very near a major Pakistani military installation, it is unlikely that the ISI, with its large networks of informers, was ignorant of his presence. Pakistani sanctuary is not limited to Afghan insurgents. By directly striking at bin Laden, the US fueled Pakistani resentment, as have continued UAV attacks and the transparency provisions of the Kerry-Lugar aid bill (which meant that little of the money had actually reached Pakistan by mid-2011, as it is seen as furthering the goals of neither the military nor political elites).

The death of bin Laden is not likely to have an immediate impact on the conflicts in Afghanistan. While the leadership of all the major insurgent groups fighting in Afghanistan had significant links to bin Laden, some of them tied by personal relationships or through marriage, these have been less important in recent years than their support infrastructure in Pakistan. It is uncertain how the loss of bin Laden's ability to reach out to and coordinate transnational assets will affect either the Afghan insurgents or transnational terrorists, especially the rise of Pakistan-based threats.

Al Qaeda, and the Salafist-inspired approach to transnational Islamic terrorism with which bin Laden was identified, has lost their one instantly identifiable leader, adding him to their long list of martyrs. The 1 May raid reportedly resulted in an intelligence haul of computers and papers. With bin Laden gone, the different global elements of Al Qaeda—the franchises, the sympathizers, the money sources—will have to assume that anything that he had received is now in US hands. Even if they are able to continue operations, they will have to re-establish contacts, increasing their vulnerability. Al Qaeda was already under pressure from a number of sources, including the 2011 political changes in the Arab world that embraced neither Salfism nor terrorism.

The death of bin Laden removed a powerful figure from the conflicts in Afghanistan and Pakistan, and from terrorism worldwide. But it has neither ended these conflicts nor reduced what is at stake in them.

ACKNOWLEDGMENTS

I n recent years, I have often been asked to talk about Afghanistan on television, to the media, to governmental and non-governmental groups. This book is what I wish I had time to say.

I started out talking about Afghanistan, but I have realized that I cannot explain what is happening in Afghanistan without reference to the situation in Pakistan. Conversely, it is hard to set out a way to attain a relatively peaceful Afghanistan—one where development and reconstruction can take place throughout the country—without first having solved the crises and pathologies that threaten Pakistan. Even if this should happen, other crises and tensions—Kashmir, Palestine, political, economic, and demographic problems—will continue to have an impact in Afghanistan.

This book is about Afghanistan and the borderlands of Pakistan: countries, people, conflicts, and importance. The bottom line is that the book is written for non-specialists to explain what is happening there and how it might turn out better. While it refers to past events (and includes a chronology and glossary), this book does not set out to review the post-2001 history of the Vortex—and those who live or are operating in it—the inadequacies, failures, and limitations of all the participants—US, coalition partners, international organization, non-governmental organizations, Pakistani and Afghan alike—since 2001 would require a book much longer than this one. Despite the heroic and selfless acts of many, progress has been slow and frustrating but has been nonetheless real.

This book is a survey and an introduction to a complex and highly nuanced current situation, intended to provide insights beyond that of news accounts and to provide commentary at greater depth than is provided by opinion pieces. Many aspects of the conflict deserve whole book-length treatments to themselves. I have had to go over programs or events that need in-depth treatment in a sentence and, in a country of great diversity and complexity, have had to generalize with a top-down view, although I have tried to avoid the Kabul-centric approach that so often afflicts outsiders, meaning that there is no problem when Kabul is secure, but if Kabul is unsecure they shift to crisis mode. This is not primarily a work of military analysis. It would be possible to fill a whole book on each of the US, UK, and other NATO and coalition diplomatic and aid capabilities, armed forces or intelligence services in the current conflict. The conflicts in the Vortex are not primarily military. The insurgency in Afghanistan—the conflict that NATO has deployed its troops to win—is of a type of war where accepted wisdom limits the military dimension to providing at most a fifth to a quarter of any ultimate solution. This is reflected in the emphasis on these aspects of the conflict in this book rather than my preference for the strategy, tactics, and technology of military action that I have focused on in my three previous books on Afghanistan (and those I wrote on the Soviet military, NATO armed forces, and other subjects). Rather, this book attempts to explain why these events came out the way they did, usually with reference to realities in Afghanistan or Pakistan that pre-existed 2001. Indeed, some of them pre-existed just about everything.

Afghanistan can kill you; it *will* make you sick; but it will never bore you. I am often asked why I picked Afghanistan to write about; my response "You don't pick Afghanistan, Afghanistan picks you" is a cliché but actually true. Afghanistan and the Afghans deserve better. In the wake of the victory of 2001, Afghanistan was, for once, full of hope. What happened to that hope and how it can be revived before it disappears entirely into smoke, leaving more years of conflict and heartbreak, is the subject of this book.

I would like to thank Anne Marie Shackleton for all her help and support. I am particularly grateful to Ian Drury, editor and comrade-in-arms for many years, and to Claiborne Hancock and Jessica Case at Pegasus Books in New York, for making this book a reality. Those that read the manuscript to help prevent me from making errors (which are, of course, all my own) include: John Jennings, Prof. Thomas Johnson, Prof. Charles Kamps, Dr. Sean Maloney, Julie Sirrs, Esq., and Andrew Smith, Esq.

I am also grateful to many press offices, government relations and spokespeople from Afghanistan, Pakistan, and the US and coalition governments and military forces. I would also like to thank the US and ISAF military units with which I have been embedded for their help and support. Their provision of information, interviews, transportation, accommodation and, when required, protection in the field made this book possible.

One of the benefits about having been writing about Afghanistan and Pakistan since the early 1980s and traveling often to the region is the benefit of continuity. This has also put me in the debt of a tremendous number of people, in Afghanistan, Pakistan, Europe, and the US over the years who have provided information or helped me out. Because security concerns and retribution fears are very real, I have not identified many sources in Afghanistan and Pakistan. Many interviews were on a not-for-attribution basis and much wisdom was received preceded by "don't quote me on this." Where violence and political retribution are daily events, this is understandable. Many of the people I spoke with in Afghanistan and Pakistan I did not seek to identify, but my gratitude toward them is nonetheless real. These over the years have included but are certainly not limited to: Dr. Abdullah, Dr. Khalid Akram, Dr. Hedayat Amin Arsala, Dr. Joseph J. Collins, Anthony Davis, Hadji Daoud, Otilie English, Engineer Mohammed Es'haq, Anders Fange, Massoud Farivar, Benedict FitzGerald, Sayid Hassan Gailani, Dr. Ashraf Ghani, Dr. Thomas Gouttiere, Dr. Max Gross, Nasrine Gross, Hadji Abdul Haq *shaheed*, Prof. Ali Ahmad Jalali, Dr. Thomas Johnson, Dr. Philip Jones, Peter Jouvenal, Hekmat Karzai, Kenneth Katzman, Ambassador Massoud Khalili, Dr. Elie Krakowski, Jonathan Landay, Jolyon Leslie, Dr. Nancy Lubin, Ambassador Ahmad Zia Massoud, Ambassador Walid Massoud, Haroun Mir, Fawad Muslim, James Phillips, Gay-Leclerc Qaderi, Ahmed Rashid, Dr. Olivier Roy, Dr. Barnett Rubin, General

Rahmatullah Safi, Mrs. Sara Safi, Dr. Ziba Shorish-Shamley, Dr. Tom Tulenko, and General Abdul Rahim Wardak. For many others, who provided knowledge, interviews, support, source material, encouragement, and so much more, I can simply say thank you.

Seen through the prism of the US and the West, Afghanistan's cost, in terms of lives and money, appears real and immediate. The potential results appear distant and highly contingent. In the US, it is frequently asserted that there is no reason to believe that US failure and disengagement in Afghanistan, while admittedly disastrous to those living there, would prove no more disastrous to the national interest than were earlier failures and disengagements from Southeast Asia in the 1970s, Lebanon in the 1980s, or Somalia in the 1990s. This relies on an assumption that subsequent conflicts in Afghanistan will prove peripheral to the US and will not repeat the 1990s experience where disengagement helped bring about a disastrous security environment. Failure to bring a degree of stability to Afghanistan and a better life to the Afghan people that welcomed intervention in 2001 is a likely significant result. Failure in Afghanistan is likely to have impacts in the regions it borders and, through transnational terrorism, worldwide. Those that fail in Afghanistan do so not because the Afghans are unique, but because it is they that cannot cope with its challenges. They then fail again, first closer to home, then at home.

This book began with a quote from one twentieth century poet. In conclusion, looking to what is possible in Afghanistan, it bears remembering the words of another: *"Success is relative: it is what we can make of the mess we have made of things"*. —*T.S. Eliot*

DAVID ISBY
http://www.DavidIsby.com
Washington, 2011

Sources

Introduction

1. Richard A. Oppel Jr. and Archie Tse, "One in 4 Afghan Ballots Face Check for Potential Fraud," *The New York Times*, 21 September 2009.
2. Charles Bremner and Michael Evans, "British Envoy Says Mission in Afghanistan Is Doomed, According to Leaked Memo," *The Times* (London), 2 October 2008.
3. Gary Langer, *Public Opinion Trends in Afghanistan*, ABC News, 11 February 2009 and 6 December 2010. While polling methodologies in Afghanistan are often problematic, due to societal tendencies to give a polite response and the diversity within provinces (provincial capitals are often unlike rural areas) among other issues, they are valuable to point out trends (especially when asked in the same way over a period of years).
4. Carlotta Gall, "Leadership Void Seen in Pakistan," *The New York Times*, 24 June 2008, pp. A1, A12.
5. Anthony H. Cordesman, *The Afghan-Pakistan War: The Rising Threat: 2002–08*. Washington, 11 February 2009, CSIS, p. 57.
6. Kate Clark, "Taliban's 100M Dollar Opium Takings," *BBC News*, 24 June 2008.
7. Talk at the Atlantic Council, Washington, 22 April 2009.
8. Ali Ahmad Jalali provided this reference.
9. See generally: Antony Arnold, *The Fateful Pebble*. Novato, CA: Presidio, 1993.
10. Louis Dupree, "Afghan and British Military Tactics in the First Anglo-Afghan War." *Army Quarterly*, v. 107, n. 3, 1977, pp. 214–221.
11. Amnesty International, *Afghanistan: All Who Are Not Friends are Enemies. Taliban Abuses Against Civilians*, April 2007.

Chapter One

12. Sources: Louis Dupree, *Afghanistan* (Princeton: Princeton University Press, 1980); Richard F. Nyrop and Donald Seeking, *Afghanistan: A Country Study* (Baton Rouge, LA: Claitor's, 1991; http://memory.loc.gov/frd/cs/aftoc.html).
13. ABC polling, 6 December 2010.
14. Keith Bradsher and Andrew Martin, "Hoarding Nations Drive Food Costs Even Higher," *The New York Times*, 30 June 2008.
15. Olivier Roy provided this regional division.
16. *Afghanistan Human Development Report*, 2007, executive summary.
17. The concept and definition of jihad as it has applied to Afghanistan is a critical issue. Much of the extensive literature on radical Islam does not come to grips with the tension between the multiple theological and operational approaches to jihad. Sources include: Ayesa Jalal, *Partisans of Allah, Jihad in South Asia* (Cambridge: Harvard University Press, 2008); Laurent Murawiec, *The Mind of Jihad* (Cambridge: Cambridge University Press, 2008); Laurent Murawiec, *Pandora's Boxes. The Mind of Jihad, Volume II* (Washington: Hudson Institute, 2007).

18. Gary Langer, *Public Opinion Trends in Afghanistan*, ABC News, 11 February 2009.

19. Ali Wardak, *Jirga—A Traditional Mechanism of Conflict Resolution in Afghanistan*, University of Glamorgan, 2005; http://unpan1.un.org/intradoc/groups/public/documents/apcity/unpan017434.pdf.

20. Talk given at CSIS, Washington, 28 May 2009.

21. Richard A. Oppel and Sangar Rahim, "Afghan Lawmakers Accuse a Governor of Graft," *The New York Times*, 15 April 2009.

22. Talk given at CSIS, Washington, 26 February 2009.

23. Interview following talk at Brookings Institution, Washington, 25 February 2009.

24. For the emergence of Afghanistan as a *rentier* state: Barnett Rubin, *The Fragmentation of Afghanistan: State Formation and Collapse in the International System*, 2 ed. New Haven: Yale University Press, 2002.

25. Talk given at CSIS, Washington, 26 February 2009.

26. Nabi Misdaq, "Traditional Leadership in Afghan Society and the Issue of National Unity," *Central Asian Survey*, v. 9, n. 4, 1990, pp. 98–115.

27. C. J. Chivers, "Arms Sent by US May Be Falling into Taliban Hands," *The New York Times*, 20 May 2008.

28. Arthur Keller, "Propaganda and Peace Deals: The Taliban's Information War," *CTC Sentinel*, v. 1, n. 8, July 2008, pp. 15–18.

29. The role of the qawm in Afghan life and warfare is set out in: Oliver Roy, *Islam and Resistance in Afghanistan* (second edition). Cambridge: Cambridge University Press, 1990.

30. On Islamism in Afghanistan, see: Olivier Roy, "Has Islamism a Future in Afghanistan?" in William Maley, ed. *Fundamentalism Reborn? Afghanistan and the Taliban*. New York: New York University, 1999, pp. 199–211.

31. Formally the United Islamic Front for the Salvation of Afghanistan. In addition to JIA, it included the Shura-i-Nazr (council of the north, the cross-party organization Massoud had formed in 1985), Hizb-i-Wahdat (predominantly Hazara), and Junbish Milli-i-Islami (predominantly Uzbek). It also included two predominantly Pushtun parties, Dr. Abdul Rasoul Sayeff's Ittehad-i-Islami (one of the Peshawar Seven) and the Nangarhar shura of Haji Qadir (previously part of HiK).

32. Talk at American University, Kabul, 1 November 2008.

33. Ibid.

34. In 2010, polling results were that only nine percent of Afghans preferred the Taliban rule, up from one percent in 2005. Gary Langer, *Afghanistan: Where Things Stand*, ABC News, 6 December 2010.

35. Again, the lack of anything like an Afghanistan census on a national basis, let alone by province or district, is one of the challenges faced by effective polling.

Chapter Two

36. On the relationship between crime and insurgency: John Mueller, *Hatred, Violence and Warfare: Thugs as Residual Combatants*. Paper delivered at the 2001 meeting of the American Political Science Association.

37. The current international boundary differs from the 1893 line, especially in the Chen-

nai Hills area of Baluchistan, and has done so for decades. Afghan usage still terms it the Durand Line, Pakistani usage the international border.

38. See generally: James W. Spain, *The Way of the Pathan, the Pathan Borderlands* (Oxford: Oxford University Press, 1972); James W. Spain, *The People of the Khyber, the Pathans of Pakistan* (New York: Praeger, 1962, pp. 46–47).

39. Sources on the Pushtuns and their world include: Akbar Ahmed, *Pakhtun Economy and Society* (London: Routledge and Kegan Paul, 1980); Sir Olaf Caroe, *The Pathans* (Oxford: Oxford University Press, 1958); Bernt Glatzer, "Being Pushtun-Being Muslim: Concepts of Person and War in Afghanistan," in Bernt Glatzer, ed., *Essays on South Asian Society, Culture and Politics II* (Berlin: Zentrum Moderner Orient, 1998, pp. 83–94).

40. The International Republican Institute, *Afghanistan Public Opinion Survey*, 3–16 May 2009, Lapis Communication Research, www.iri.org, p. 64.

41. On the rise, fall, rise, and fall of Dostum: Antonio Giustozzi, *The Ethnicization of an Afghan Function: Junbesh-i-Milli from its Origins to the Presidential Elections*. London: Crisis States Research Center, 2005.

42. For example, Alexander Klaits and Gulchin Gulmamdova-Klaits, *Love and War in Afghanistan* (New York: Seven Stories Press, 2005, pp. 276–78) described pro-Taliban Tajik Sunni mullahs operating against Uzbek militia forces in this time period.

43. Talk at American University, by Massoud Kharokhail, Kabul, 2 November 2009.

44. Hassan Abbas, "From FATA to the NWFP, the Taliban Spread Their Grip in Pakistan," *CTC Sentinel*, v. 1, n. 10, 17 September 2008, pp. 3–5.

45. Faisal Ali Khan, FIDA, interview, Washington, 3 February 2009.

46. Steve Coll, *Ghost Wars: The Secret History of the CIA, Afghanistan and Bin Ladin from the Soviet Invasion to September 10 2001*. New York: Penguin, 2005, p. 67.

47. Interview following talk at the Heritage Foundation, Washington, 26 March 2008.

48. Husain Haqqani, *Pakistan Between Mosque and Military*. Washington: CEIP, 2005, p. 3.

49. Ten to fifteen percent of the estimated 20,000 madrassas in Pakistan are estimated to be radical (Stephen Cohen, *The Idea of Pakistan*. Washington: Brookings Institution Press, 2004, p. 182). These are likely concentrated in the FATA.

50. The author, visiting Shia Touray Pushtuns in the Kurram Agency in 1987, saw great resentment at what they saw as the use of Sunni Islamist Afghans of HiH against them as a tool of Zia policies that they saw as anti-Shia.

51. Sources on Pakistani Islamic radical organizations include: Muhammed Amir Rana, *A to Z of Jehadi Organizations in Pakistan* (Lahore: Mashal, 2004).

52. Ahmed Rashid, "Musharraf, Stop Aiding the Taliban," *Daily Telegraph* (London), 6 October 2006.

53. David B. Edwards, *Heroes of the Age: Moral Fault Lines on the Afghan Frontier*. Berkeley: University of California, 1996.

54. Louis Dupree, *Afghanistan*, op. cit., details these changes.

55. Anthony Davis, "How the Taliban Became a Military Force," in William Maley, ed., *Fundamentalism Reborn* (London: Hurst & Co., 1998, pp. 43–44).

56. On the rise of the Taliban, see: Ahmed Rashid, *The Taliban: Militant Islam, Oil and Fundamentalism in Central Asia* (New Haven: Yale University Press, 2001).

57. On the post-2001 organization and how the Taliban evolved as an effective insurgent force, see: Thomas H. Johnson, "On the Edge of the Big Muddy: The Taliban Resurgence in Afghanistan" (*China and Eurasia Forum*, Quarterly, v. 5, n. 2, 2007, pp. 93–129); Emma Sky, "Increasing ISAF's Impact on Stability in Afghanistan" (*Defense & Security Analysis*, v. 23, n.1, March 2007, pp. 7–25); David Rohde and David E. Sanger, "How the 'Good War' in Afghanistan Went Bad" (*The New York Times*, 12 August 2007).

58. Interviews, Afghanistan, September 2009.

59. Interviews, Kabul, October–November 2008; Antonio Giustozzi, op. cit., pp. 43–46.

Chapter Three

60. Philip Jones provided this approach to examining Pakistani strategy.

61. "The Airlift of Evil." *MSNBC News Report*, 29 November 2001.

62. Husain Haqqani, "Pakistan is Playing a Cat and Mouse Game," *Gulf News* (Dubai), 19 October 2005.

63. Carlotta Gall, "Pakistan Lets Taliban Train, Prisoner Says," *The New York Times*, 4 August 2004, p. A1.

64. Arnaud de Borchegrave, "The Talibanization of Pakistan" (*The Washington Times*, 7 April 2007, p. A11); Carlotta Gall and David Rohde, "Militants Escape Control of Pakistan, Officials Say" (*The New York Times*, 15 January 2007, p. A1); Seth Jones, "Pakistan's Dangerous Game" (*Survival*, v. 49, n. 1, Spring 2007, pp. 15–32).

65. "ISI Protecting Obama" (*Dawn* [Karachi], 18 January 2007); "Musharraf Betting on Taliban" (*Daily Times*, 5 April 2007).

66. Talk at the Johns Hopkins University Asymmetric Conflict Symposium, Washington, 11 March 2008.

67. Gary Langer, *Public Opinion Trends in Afghanistan*, ABC News, 11 February 2009.

68. Interview, Washington, 6 June 2008.

69. Interview, Bagram Air Base, 14 October 2008.

70. Ben Rowswell, DCM Canadian embassy Kabul, Washington, 22 May 2009.

71. Doyle McManus, "US Drone Attacks in Pakistan Backfiring," *The Los Angeles Times*, 3 May 2009.

72. On the divisions within the Pakistani military, see Ahmad Faruqui, "Failure in Command, Lessons from Pakistan's Indian Wars, 1947–1999," *Defense Analysis*, v. 17, n. 1, 2001, pp. 31–40.

73. Interview following talk at the Heritage Foundation, Washington, 26 March 2008.

74. Interview, *60 Minutes*, 17 May 2009.

75. Interview, Kabul, 21 October 2008.

Chapter Four

76. Unclassified summary of the NIE. Office of the Director of National Intelligence, *The Terrorist Threat to the US Homeland*, Washington, DC, NIC, July 2007.

77. Katya Leney-Hall, *The Evolution of Franchise Terrorism: Al-Qaeda*, September 2008, Athens, Hellenic Foundation for European & Foreign Policy, Working Paper No. 1.

78. Kevin Johnson, "Weakened Al-Qaeda Is Still a Threat," *USA Today*, 8 September 2009.

79. Eli Lake, "Al Qaeda Bungles Arms Experiment. Biological or Chemical Weapons," *The Washington Times*, 19 January 2009.

80. Quoted in Alex Kingsbury, "Where the Terrorist Threat from Al Qaeda Is Headed," *US News & World Report*, 12 January 2009.

81. Rohan Gunaratna, *Inside Al Qaeda*. New York: Columbia University Press, 2002, p. 84.

82. Imtiaz Ali, "Extremists in Tribal Areas Use Gory DVDs to Celebrate and Exaggerate their Exploits," *The Washington Post*, 24 June 2008, p. A12.

83. Interview, Kabul, 21 October 2008.

84. On the shift to international vice Afghanistan-specific events as legitimation by the Taliban, see Thomas H. Johnson, "The Taliban Insurgency and an Analysis of Shab-namah (Night Letters)," *Small Wars and Insurgencies*, v. 18, n. 3, September 2007.

85. See generally Laura Mansfield, ed., *His Own Word, A Translation of the Writings of Dr. Ayman Al Zawahiri*. (No location given), TLG Publications, 2006. See generally Part 1, "Knights under the Prophet's Banner."

86. George Packer, "The Last Mission," *The New Yorker*, 28 September 2009, pp. 28–55, p. 44.

87. Interview, *NPR Fresh Air* radio program, 5 April 2007.

88. James Brandon, "The Pakistan Connection to the United Kingdom's Jihad Network," *Jamestown Terrorism Monitor*, v. 6, n. 4, 22 February 2008.

89. Tim Shipman, "CIA Warns Barack Obama that British Terrorists Are the Biggest Threat to the US," *The Daily Telegraph* (London), 7 February 2009.

90. Marc Sageman, *Understanding Terror Networks*. Philadelphia: University of Pennsylvania Press, 2004.

91. Drawn from Farhad Khosrokhavar, *Inside Jihadism, Understanding Jihadi Movements Worldwide*. Herndon, VA: Paradigm, 2008.

92. Nick Meo, "Disaffected Youth Seduced by the Notion of Holy War," *San Francisco Chronicle*, 17 July 2005.

93. "Leaked Plans Outline Government's Agenda to Tackle Roots of UK-Islamic Terrorism," *The Sunday Times* (London), 30 May 2004.

94. "Former Metropolitan Police Chief Says Britons Probably Planned London Attacks" (*The Sunday Times* [London], 10 July 2005); Ben Leapmen, "4,000 in UK Trained in Terror Camps" (*The Daily Telegraph*, 15 July 2007); Patrick Basham, "Many British Muslims Put Islam First" (*NRO Online*, 14 August 2006).

95. "Arrests Prevented Terrorist Bombing" (*The Copenhagen Post*, 4 September 2007); Nicholas Kulish, "New Terrorism Case Confirms that Denmark is a Target" (*The New York Times*, 17 September 2007).

96. "Germany Foils Massive Bomb Plot" (*BBC News*, 5 September 2007); Dirk Labs and Sebastian Rotella, "European Militants Now Get Training in Pakistan" (*Los Angeles Times*, 15 October 2007).

97. Mark Eeckhaut, "Extremists Trained in Afghanistan," *De Standard Online* (Brussels), 17 April 2009.

98. Cam Simpson and Evan Perez, "US Al Qaeda Cell Suspected," *The Wall Street Journal*, 24 September 2009.

99. "Home Grown Bombers," *The Economist*, 3 October 2009, p. 36.

100. Benjamin Haas and Daniel McGrory, "Al Qaida Seeking to Recruit African-American Muslims," *CTC Sentinel*, v. 1, n. 8, July 2008, pp. 13–14.

101. *Current and Projected National Security Threats to The United States*, Senate Armed Services Committee, 28 February 2006.

102. Daniel Markey, *Securing Pakistan's Tribal Belt*, CSR no. 36, August 2008, Council on Foreign Relations, p. 16.

103. Interview, Kabul, 29 October 2008.

104. P. G. Rajmohan, *Suicide Terrorism—South Asia 2006, New Delhi, 2007*. Institute of Peace and Conflict Studies paper. http://www.ipcs.org/article_details.php?article NoAfghanistan1942.

105. Craig Whitlock, "Al Qaeda's Growing Online Offensive," *The Washington Post*, 24 June 2008, pp. A1, A12.

106. Michael Scheuer, "Al Qaeda's Military Chief in Afghanistan Views the Ongoing Insurgency with Optimism," *Jamestown Terrorism Monitor*, v. 5, n. 28, 29 July 2008, pp. 7–8.

107. Anthony H. Cordesman, *The Afghan-Pakistan War: The Rising Threat: 2002–08*. Washington: CSIS, 11 February 2009, p. 10.

108. Yoran Schweitzer and Sari Goldstein Ferber, *Al-Qaeda and the Internationalization of Suicide Terrorism*. Tel Aviv University, November 2005, Jaffe Centre for Strategic Studies Memorandum no. 78, p. 33.

109. Paul Wideman, "Once Unknown, Suicide Blasts Soar in Afghanistan," *USA Today*, 10 September 2006.

110. Interview, Washington, 27 February 2009.

111. Hekmat Karzai and Seth Jones, "How to Curb Suicide Terrorism in Afghanistan," *Christian Science Monitor*, 18 July 2006.

112. 27 March 2009, White House press release. http://www.whitehouse.gov/the_press_office/Whats-New-in-the-Strategy-for-Afghanistan-and-Pakistan/.

113. Audrey Kurth Cronin, "Cyber-Mobilization: The New Levee en Masse," *Parameters*, v. 36, n. 2, Summer 2006, pp. 77–87.

114. See generally Laura Mansfield, ed., *His Own Word, A Translation of the Writings of Dr. Ayman Al Zawahiri*. TLG Publications, 2006. See generally Part 1, "Knights under the Prophet's Banner," p. 126.

115. Gail Sheehy, "A Wrong Must Be Righted," *Parade Magazine*, 27 December 2008.

116. Raffaelo Pantucci, "Transatlantic Airline Bombing Case Collapses in the United Kingdom," *Jamestown Terrorism Focus*, v. 5, n. 33, 18 September 2008.

117. Philip Sherwell, "Bhutto Blocked From Hiring US Bodyguards," *The Daily Telegraph* (London), 30 December 2007.

118. US Department of State, *Country Reports on Terrorism*, 2008, http://www.state.gov/s/ct/rls/crt/2008/122434.htm.

119. George Tenet, *At the Center of the Storm, My Years at the CIA.* New York: Harper Collins, 2007, pp. 352–54.

120. Michael Jacobsen, "Why Terrorists Quit: Gaining from Al Qaida's Losses," *CTC Sentinel*, v. 1, n. 8, July 2008, pp. 1–4.

121. Rhys Blakeley, "Darool-Uloom Deoband Issues Fatwa Against Terrorism," *The Times* (London), 2 June 2008.

122. On Al Qaeda targeting of Muslims, see: Zahir Jan Mohamed, "Radical Muslims Killing Muslims" (*The Washington Post*, 25 June 2003); Richard Hoagland, "Fighting for the Soul of Islam" (*The Washington Post*, 13 July 2003).

123. Audrey Kurth Cronin, *Ending Terrorism*, Adelphi Paper 394, 2008, p. 58.

124. Ibid., p. 69.

125. Ibid.

126. "Islamic Extremism in India. The Rise of Home-Grown Terrorism," *IISS Strategic Comments*, v. 15, n. 3, April 2009.

Chapter Five

127. On Taliban evolution and narcotics: Farhana Schmidt, "From Islamic Warriors to Drug Lords: The Evolution of the Taliban Insurgency" (*Mediterranean Quarterly*, v. 21, n. 2, Spring, 2010, pp. 61–77).

128. Thomas Ruttig, *The Other Side*, Afghan Analysis Network paper, July, 2009; Thomas Ruttig, *How Tribal are the Taliban*, Afghan Analysis Network paper, June, 2010.

129. Interview, Kabul, 19 October 2009.

130. Talk given at the Association of the US Army annual meeting, Washington, 6 October 2009.

131. Tom Shanker, "US Sees Makeshift Bombs Moving Beyond Iraq and Afghanistan," *The New York Times*, 29 October 2009.

132. Interview, Washington, 10 March 2008.

133. Eric Schmitt and Mark Mazetti, "Taliban Widen Afghanistan Attacks from Base in Pakistan," *The New York Times*, 24 September 2009.

134. GEN Stanley McChrystal, *COMISAF Initial Assessment* ("McChrystal Report"), Kabul, 20 August 2009, pp. 2–6.

135. Interview, Kabul, 20 October 2009.

136. Schmitt and Mazetti, op. cit.

137. "Report: Taliban appoint new regional chief in Afghanistan," *Xinhua*, October 21, 2007.

138. "Top Taliban Commander Held in Pakistan," *Xinhua*, 19 July 2005.

139. *Countering Afghanistan's Insurgency: No Quick Fixes*, Brussels, 2 November 2006, International Crisis Group Asia Report no. 126, pp. 9–11. http://www.crisisgroup.org/library/documents/south_asia/123_countering_Afghanistans_insurgency.pdf.

140. Interview, Bagram AB, 13 October 2008.

141. GEN Stanley McChrystal, *COMISAF Initial Assessment* ("McChrystal Report"), Kabul, 20 August 2009, pp. 2–7.

142. Griff White, "Taliban Shadow Officials Offer Concrete Alternative," *The Washington Post*, 8 December 2009, pp. A1, A15.

143. "Taliban Shadow Government Pervades Afghanistan," *CBS News* report, 27 December 2008. http://www.cbsnews.com/stories/2008/12/27/world/main4687823_page2.shtml.

144. Talk at the Atlantic Council, Washington, 15 October 2009.

145. Antonio Giustozzi, *Koran, Kalashnikov and Laptop: The Neo-Taliban Insurgency in Afghan*. New York: Columbia University Press, 2008, p. 47.

146. Interviews, Kabul, 21–29 October 2008.

147. "Tackling the Other Taliban," *The Economist*, 17 October 2009, pp. 34–36.

148. David Rohde, "Held by the Taliban," *The New York Times*, 21 October 2009.

149. Quoted in CJTF-82 News Release, 10 0ctober 2007, http:www.cjtf-82.com/Newsrelease/2007/October/039.

150. Interview, Kabul, 29 October 2008.

151. Interview, COL Patrick McNiece, Kabul, 29 October 2008.

152. Interview, Kabul, 20 October 2008.

153. Gary Langer, *Public Opinion Trends in Afghanistan*, ABC News, 11 February 2009.

154. Talk given at the Association of the US Army annual meeting, Washington, 6 October 2009.

155. Sean M. Maloney, "A Violent Impediment: The Evolution of Insurgent Operations in Kandahar Province 2003–07," *Small Wars & Insurgencies*, v. 19, n. 2, June 2008, p. 205.

156. UNODC, *Afghanistan Opium Survey 2008*, Executive Summary, August 2008, p. 4.

157. Carlotta Gall, "Taliban Open Up Northern Front in Afghanistan," *The New York Times*, 27 November 2009, pp. A1, A12.

158. GEN Stanley McChrystal, *COMISAF Initial Assessment* ("McChrystal Report"), Kabul, 20 August 2009, pp. 2–8.

159. Gary Langer, *Public Opinion Trends in Afghanistan*, ABC News, 11 February 2009.

160. Interview, Bagram AB, 12 October 2008.

161. Interview, Bagram AB, 13 October 2008.

162. Polling data from: Gary Langer, *Public Opinion Trends in Afghanistan*, ABC News, 11 February 2009.

163. Gary Langer, *Public Opinion Trends in Afghanistan*, ABC News, 11 February 2009.

164. Interview, Kabul, 3 November 2008.

165. Asia Foundation Surveys in 2007–08 and ABC Surveys in 2005–09 show these results.

166. Interview following talk at the Heritage Foundation, Washington, 26 March 2008.

167. Interview, Bagram AB, 14 October 2008.

168. Interview, Washington, 27 February 2009.

169. Jonathan S. Landay and Hal Bernton, "While U.S. Debates Afghanistan Policy, Taliban Beefs Up," *McClatchy Newspapers report*, 16 October 2009.

170. Talk at the Heritage Foundation, Washington, 26 March 2008.

171. Talk given at Carnegie Endowment for International Peace (CEIP), Washington, 25 February 2009.

172. Ruth Rennie, Sudhindra Sharma, and Pawan Sen, *Afghanistan in 2009: A Survey of the Afghan People*. Washington: The Asia Foundation, 2009, pp. 29–32.

173. Tom Coghlan, "Growing Afghan Kidnap Industry Mars Security Success in Kabul," *The Times* (London), 22 June 2009.

174. Hal Bernton and Hashim Shukoor, "Afghan Economy Stumbles Amid Election Uncertainty," *McClatchy Newspapers report*, 16 October 2009; Helena Malikyar and Tanya Goudzouzian, "Business Flees Afghan Instability," *Al Jazeera news report*, 18 November 2009.

175. Talk given at JHU Asymmetric Warfare Symposium, Washington, 11 March 2008.

176. "Musharraf Says Not All Taliban Terrorists," *The Daily Times* (Pakistan), 13 August 2007.

177. "Front Line Against the Taliban," *The Economist*, 28 November 2009, pp. 22–9. p. 28.

178. On messages to neighbors: "Taliban Seeks SCO Support in Resolving Afghan Crisis," *Xinhua News Agency Report*, 15 October 2009.

179. Greg Miller, "Questions About Al Qaeda's Next Move," *The Los Angeles Times*, 19 October 2009.

180. Ruth Rennie, Sudhindra Sharma, and Pawan Sen, *Afghanistan in 2009: A Survey of the Afghan People*. Washington: The Asia Foundation, 2009, pp. 102–105.

181. Briefing at the Association of the US Army annual meeting, Washington, 6 October 2009.

182. Talk at the Heritage Foundation, Washington, 26 March 2008.

183. Briefing at the Association of the US Army annual meeting, Washington, 6 October 2007.

184. Kabul, 23 October 2008.

185. On threats of terror attacks in Germany: Yassin Musharbash, Marcel Rosenbach, and Holger Stark, "New Video Message—Al Qaeda Threatens Terror Attacks in Germany After Elections," *Der Spiegel Online*, 19 September 2009. On targeting Italians: Gian Marco Chiocci, "Italians Still Targeted. Now the 007s Expect a Repeat," *Il Giornale.it* (Milan), September 22, 2009. Translated from Italian at World News Connection, NewsEdge Document Number: 20090 9221477.1_93f400b56b8996fc.

186. Talk given at the Heritage Foundation, Washington, 26 March 2008.

187. Bruce Riedel, "The Elections Are Coming. Is Al Qaeda?," *The Washington Post*, 10 August 2008, p. B03.

188. Briefing at the Association of the US Army annual meeting, Washington, 6 October 2007.

189. Interview, Kabul, 21 October 2008. Syed Saleem Shahzad, "Rough Justice and Blooming Poppies," *Asia Times Online*, 7 December 2006.

190. Interview, Kabul, 19 October 2008.

191. Antonio Giustozzi, *Koran, Kalashnikov and Laptop, The Neo-Taliban Insurgency in Afghanistan*. New York: Columbia University Press, 2008, pp. 15–21, 46–69.

192. GEN Stanley McChrystal, *COMISAF Initial Assessment* ("McChrystal Report"), Kabul, 20 August 2009, pp. 1–2.

193. Interview, Kabul, 21 October 2008.

194. Ibid.

195. Jason Staziuso, "Bush Ignores Afghan School Violence," *Seattle Times*, 30 January 2008.

196. "Over 360,000 Affected by Reduced Health Service," *IRIN*, 14 May 2008.

197. Interview, Massoud Kharokhail, Tribal Liaison Office, Kabul, 2 November 2008.

198. Afghan National Development Plan 6 figures, July 2008, quoted in Anthony H. Cordesman, *The Afghan-Pakistan War: The Rising Threat: 2002–08*, Washington, 11 February 2009, CSIS, p. 61.

199. Briefing at the Association of the US Army annual meeting, Washington, 6 October 2007.

200. Interview following talk at the Heritage Foundation, Washington, 26 March 2008.

201. Interview with Afghan source who had worked with UK forces, Kabul, 21 October 2008.

202. Interviews, multiple locations in Afghanistan, October–November 2008.

203. Briefing at the Association of the US Army annual meeting, Washington, 6 October 2007.

204. Talk given at the Carnegie Endowment for International Peace (CEIP), Washington, 27 October 2009.

205. Brian Bender, "Few Militants Driven by Religion, Reports Say," *The Boston Globe*, 9 October 2009.

206. *The Globe and Mail* (Canada) series, starting 21 March 2008, "Talking to the Taliban."

207. Graeme Smith, "Talking to the Taliban: A Poll from the Frontlines," *Globe and Mail*, 22 March 2008.

208. Interview, Kabul, 29 October 2008.

209. Briefing at the Association of the US Army annual meeting, Washington, 6 October 2007.

210. Tom Vandenbrook, "Afghan Roadside Bombs at Record Level," *USA Today*, 26 January 2009, p. 1.

211. Michelle Tan, "Use of IEDs Growing Rapidly in Afghanistan," *Defense News*, 14 September 2009, pp. 30–32.

212. Ibid.

213. Interview, COL Patrick McNiece, USA, ISAF deputy director of intelligence, Kabul, 29 October 2008.

214. Ibid.

215. Interview, Kabul, 20 October 2008.

216. Muhammad Amir Rana, *A to Z of Jehadi Organizations in Pakistan*. Lahore, Mashal, 2004, pp. 10–21.

217. Antonio Giustozzi, *Koran, Kalashnikov and Laptop. The Neo-Taliban Insurgency in Afghanistan*. New York: Columbia University Press, 2008, pp. 108–109.

218. "Fearful Asymmetry: A Shift in Taliban Tactics," *The Economist*, 1 May 2008.

219. Hekmat Karzai and Seth Jones, "How to Curb Suicide Terrorism in Afghanistan," *Christian Science Monitor*, 18 July 2006.

220. Interview in *Al-Sumud* magazine, issue 24, 14 August 2009, translated in FBIS, *Jihadist Websites—OSC Summary, 17 August 2008*.

221. Interview, Kabul, 29 October 2008.

222. Interview, Afghan source, Kabul, 21 October 2009.

223. C. J. Chivers. "Arms Sent by U.S. May Be Falling Into Taliban Hands," *The New York Times*, 19 May 2008, p. A1.

224. Talk given at the Association of the US Army annual meeting, Washington, 6 October 2009.

225. Talk at the Atlantic Council, Washington, 22 April 2009.

226. Interview, COL Patrick McNiece, ISAF deputy director of intelligence, Kabul, 29 October 2008.

227. Talk at the Atlantic Council, Washington, 20 May 2009.

228. Talk given at the Washington Institute for Near East Policy, Washington, 29 September 2009.

229. Talk given at the Association of the US Army annual meeting, Washington, 6 October 2009.

230. Eric Schmitt, "A Variety of Sources Feed Taliban's War Chest," *The New York Times*, 18 October 2009.

231. On the kidnapping threat in Afghanistan, examples of coverage of these widespread tactics are: "Gunmen Abduct Turkish National in Afghan West" (*Pajhwok Afghan New reports*, November 30, 2009); "Poland Develops Anti-Kidnapping Scheme for Afghan Mission" (*PAP News agency report*, 16 September 2009); "Armed Men Kidnap Two Doctors, Paramedics in Afghan North" (*Afghan Islamic Press report*, 13 October 2009); "Afghan Journalists Facing Threats from Taliban, Government–Media Watchdog" (*Pahjwok Afghan News report*, 2 May 2009); "Taliban Kidnap, Threaten School Teachers in Afghan South" (*Afghan Islamic Press report*, 20 April 2009).

232. Paul Collier and Anneke Hoeffler, "Greed and Grievance in Civil War," *Oxford Economic Papers*, v. 56, n. 4, October 2004, pp. 563–95.

233. Paul Collier, *Economic Causes of Civil Conflict and Their Implications for Policy*, World Bank paper, 15 June 2000.

234. James D. Fearon, "Economic Development, Insurgency and Civil War," in Elhanan Helpman, ed., *Institutions and Economic Performance*. Cambridge: Harvard University Press, 2008, pp. 292–328.

Chapter Six

235. United Nations Office on Drugs and Crime, *The Opium Economy in Afghanistan: An International Problem*. Vienna: United Nations Office on Drugs and Crime, 2003.

236. United Nations Office on Drugs and Crime, *Addiction, Crime and Insurgency, The Transnational Threat of Afghan Opium*. Vienna: United Nations Office on Drugs and Crime, October 2009, pp. 9–20.

237. United Nations Office on Drugs and Crime, *Afghanistan 2009 Opium Survey* (Vienna: August 2009); Eric Schmitt, "A Variety of Sources Feed Taliban's War Chest" (*The New York Times*, 18 October 2009).

238. United Nations Office on Drugs and Crime, *Addiction, Crime and Insurgency, The Transnational Threat of Afghan Opium*. Vienna: United Nations Office on Drugs and Crime, October 2009, pp. 9–20.

239. Scott Rennie, "Afghan Heroin Hitting Our Streets, Mounties Warn," *The Star* (Toronto), 6 August 2007, http://www.thestar.com/News/article/243554.

240. United Nations Office on Drugs and Crime, *Afghanistan Opium Survey, 2008*, Executive Summary. Vienna: United Nations Office on Drugs and Crime, August 2008, p. 5.

241. Dr. Barnett Rubin provided this insight.

242. United Nations Office of Drugs and Crime, *Afghanistan Opium Survey, Executive Summary*. Vienna: United Nations Office on Drugs and Crime, August 2008, p. viii.

243. On the importance of credit to opium, see: Adam Pain, *Opium Poppy and Informal Credit*. Kabul: Afghanistan Research and Evaluation Unit (AREU), 2008.

244. United Nations Office of Drugs and Crime, *Afghanistan Opium Survey, 2007*, August 2007, p. 15.

245. United Nations Office of Drugs and Crime, *The Dynamics of the Farmgate Opium Trade and the Coping Strategies of Opium Traders*, Strategic Study 2, Islamabad, 1998.

246. Talk given at the Atlantic Council, Washington, 20 May 2009.

247. Adam Pain, *Opium Trading Systems in Helmand and Ghor*. Kabul: Afghan Research and Evaluation Unit, January 2006, p. 4.

248. United Nations Office of Drugs and Crime, *Afghanistan Opium Survey, 2008, Executive Summary*. Vienna: United Nations Office on Drugs and Crime, August 2008, p. viii.

249. Interview with Ministry of Counter Narcotics official, Kabul, 26 October 2008.

250. Talk given at the Atlantic Council by Ashraf Ghani, Washington, 22 April 2009.

251. For example: Haytullah Gaheez, "Daughters Sold to Settle Debts," *Institute for War and Peace Reporting news report*, ARR n. 155, 30 December 2004.

252. David Mansfield and Adam Pain, *Counter-Narcotics in Afghanistan: The Failure of Success*. Kabul: Afghanistan Research and Evaluation Unit (AREU) briefing paper, December 2008, p. 2.

253. Jim Drummond, director of the South Asia division of the UK's DfID, talk given at CSIS, Washington, 28 May 2009.

254. Steve Kroft, "Afghanistan: Addicted to Heroin," *60 Minutes News Report*, 16 October 2005.

255. Talk given at the Atlantic Council, Washington, 20 May 2009.

256. Barnett R. Rubin and Jake Sherman, *Counter Narcotics to Stabilize Afghanistan, the False Promise of Crop Eradication*. New York: Center on International Cooperation, February 2008, p. 2.

257. Doris Buddenberg and William A. Byrd, eds., *Afghan's Drug Industry, Structure, Functioning Dynamics and Implications for Counter-Narcotics Policy*. United Nations Office of Drugs and Crime and World Bank, 2008, pp. 5–6.

258. Interview, Kabul, 26 October 2008.

259. Interview, Dr. Sayid Mohammed Amin Fatimi, Minister of Health, Washington, 23 July 2008.

260. Interview, Ministry of Counter Narcotics official, Kabul, 26 October 2008.

261. Kaveh L. Afrasiabi, "US, Iran Seek to Stop Afghan Narco-Traffic," *Asia Times*, 10 March 2009.

262. Interview, Kabul, 26 October 2008.

263. See: Doris Buddenberg & William A. Byrd, eds., *Afghan's Drug Industry, Structure, Functioning Dynamics and Implications for Counter-Narcotics Policy, 2008*, United Nations Office of Drugs and Crime and World Bank, pp. 1–22.

264. Eric Schmitt, "A Variety of Sources Feed Taliban's War Chest," *The New York Times*, 18 October 2009.

265. Tim Albone and Claire Billet, "Ruined Poppy Farmers Join Ranks with the Taliban," *The Times* (London), 28 January 2007.

266. Mohammad Ilyas Dayee, *Institute for War & Peace Reporting*, No. 290, 19 May 2008.

267. Interview, Kabul, 26 October 2008.

268. Christopher Blanchard, *Afghanistan, Narcotics and US Policy*, Report RL32696. Washington: Congressional Research Service, 2009, p. 1.

269. Interview, Kabul, 26 October 2008.

270. Ministry of Counter Narcotics official, Kabul, 26 October 2008.

271. Estimate taken from: Barnett R. Rubin, Jake Sherman *Counter-Narcotics to Stabilize Afghanistan, the False Promise of Crop Eradication*, New York: Center on International Cooperation, February 2008, p. 13.

272. Gary Langer, *Public Opinion Trends in Afghanistan*, ABC News, 11 February 2009.

273. Interview following talk at the Heritage Foundation by Ambassador Thomas Schweich, Washington, 16 May 2007.

274. Adam Pain, *Let Them Eat Poppies: Closing the Opium Poppy Fields in Balkh and its Consequences*. Kabul: Afghanistan Research and Evaluation Unit, December 2008, p. 2.

275. Rachel Donadio, "New Course for Antidrug Efforts in Afghanistan," *The New York Times*, 28 June 2009.

276. Talk given at the Association of the US Army annual meeting, Washington, 6 October 2009.

277. For example: Jon Lee Anderson, "Letter from Afghanistan: The Taliban's War," *The New Yorker*, 9 July 2007, http://www.newyorker.com/reporting/2007/07/09/070709fa_fact_anderson.

278. Doris Buddenberg and William A. Byrd, eds., *Afghan's Drug Industry, Structure, Functioning Dynamics and Implications for Counter-Narcotics Policy, 2008*, United Nations Office of Drugs and Crime and World Bank, p. 6.

279. Mohammed Hanif Atmar, Minister of Interior, Washington, talk given at the Brookings Institution, 27 February 2009.

280. Talk given at the Association of the US Army annual meeting, Washington, 6 October 2009.

281. The Senlis Council, *Feasibility of Opium Licensing in Afghanistan*. London: MF Publishing, 2005.

282. Vanda Feldab-Brown, *Opium Licensing in Afghanistan: Its Desirability and Feasibility*. Washington: Brookings Institution Policy Paper, August 2007.

283. Interview, Kabul, 26 October 2008.

284. Interviews, Kabul, October–November 2008.

285. David Mansfield and Adam Pain, *Counter-Narcotics in Afghanistan: The Failure of Success*. Kabul: Afghanistan Research and Evaluation Unit (AREU) briefing paper, December 2008, p. 3.

Chapter Seven

286. Interview, Kabul, 27 October 2008.

287. Talk given at the Atlantic Council, Washington, 15 October 2009.

288. The International Republican Institute, *Afghanistan Public Opinion Survey, May 3–16, 2009*, Lapis Communication Research, www.iri.org, p. 49.

289. John Lee Anderson, "The Man in the Palace," *The New Yorker*, 6 June 2005.

290. Gary Langer, *Public Opinion Trends in Afghanistan*, ABC News, 11 February 2009.

291. Antonio Giustozzi, *Koran, Kalashnikov and Laptop: The Neo-Taliban Insurgency in Afghan*. New York: Columbia University Press, 2008, p. 45.

292. Interview, Kabul, 26 October 2008.

293. Interviews, multiple locations, Afghanistan, October–November 2008.

294. Interviews, Afghanistan, September 2009.

295. Interviews, Kabul, October–November 2008; Giustozzi, op. cit., pp. 43–46.

296. Bashir Ahmad Nadem, "Religious Scholar Shot Dead in Kandahar" (*Pajhwok Afghan News*, 6 January 2009, http://www.pajhwok.com/viewstory.asp?lng Afghanistaneng&idAfghanistan67799 Bashir Ahmad Nazim); "Religious Scholar, Four Guards Killed in Kandahar" (*Pajhwok Afghan News*, 1 March 2009, http://www. pajhwok.com/viewstory.asp?lngAfghanistaneng&idAfghanistan70485); A. Jamali, "Taliban Forces Are Now Attacking Sunni Leaders in Afghanistan" (*Eurasia Daily Monitor*, v. 2 n. 107, 2 June 2005, http://www.jamestown.org/single/ ?no_cacheAfghanistan1&tx_ttnewsKabul5Btt_newsKabul5DAfghanistan30481).

297. Although ulema, especially sayids, did play an important mediative role. Sana Haroon, *Frontier of Faith: Islam in the Indo-Afghan Borderland*. London: C. Hurst and Co. Publishers, 2007, pp. 68, 78.

298. "Afghanistan: In Search of Justice," *National Public Radio*, 12–17 December 2008, http://www.npr.org/templates/story/story.php?storyIdAfghanistan98121740.

299. Carlotta Gall, "Afghan Lawmakers Review Court Nominees," *The New York Times*, 17 May 2006.

300. "Taliban Says Responsible for Pro-Karzai Cleric's Killing," *The News* (Islamabad), 30 May 2005.

301. Quoted in *The American Enterprise Institute Newsletter*, January 2009.

302. Sources on corruption include: USAID, *Assessment of Corruption in Afghanistan* (15 January 2009–15 March 2009); Yama Torabi and Lorenso Delesgues, *Bringing Accountability Back In* (Integrity Watch Afghanistan, June 2008); Manija Gardizi, *Afghan's Experience of Corruption: A Study Across Eight Provinces* (Afghan Integrity

Watch Afghanistan, December 2007); Yama Torabi and Lorenso Delesgues, *Afghan Perceptions of Corruption: A Survey Across Thirteen Provinces* (Integrity Watch Afghanistan, January 2007).

303. Interview, Kabul, 23 October 2008.

304. Talk given at Brookings Institution, Washington, 25 February 2009.

305. See, for example, Alissa J. Rubin, "Karzai Vows Corruption Fight, But Avoids Details," *The New York Times*, 3 November 2009.

306. *ABC Polling*, 6 December 2010.

307. Ruth Rennie, Sudhindra Sharma, and Pawan Sen, *Afghanistan in 2009, A Survey of the Afghan People*. Washington: The Asia Foundation, 2009, pp. 69–71.

308. Talk at CSIS, Washington, 5 August 2008.

309. Interview, Washington, 27 February 2007.

310. "Afghan Charged in New York with Financing the Taliban," *Reuters News Report*, 21 April 2009.

311. Benjamin Weiser, "Afghan Linked to Taliban Sentenced to Life in Drug Trafficking Case," *The New York Times*, 1 May 2009.

312. Dexter Filkins, Mark Mazetti, and James Risen, "Brother of Afghan Leader Said to Be on CIA Payroll," *The New York Times*, 28 October 2009.

313. Gaith Abdu-Ahad, "New Evidence of Widespread Fraud in Afghanistan Election Uncovered," *The Guardian*, 19 September 2009.

314. These results are at: http://www.transparency.org/.

315. Phyllis Korkki, "The Countries Most Known for Corruption," *The New York Times*, 6 December 2009, p. 2BU, http://www.transparency.org/policy_research/surveys_indices/cpi/2009/cpi_2009_table.

316. Interview, Washington, 27 February 2007.

317. Kenneth P. Vogel, "Afghanistan," *Politico*, v. 3, n. 85, 24 June 2009, p. 3.

318. Peter W. Galbraith, "What I Saw at the Afghan Elections," *The Washington Post*, 4 October 2009, pp. B1, B5.

319. Abubakar Siddique, "US Special Inspector: Afghan Corruption a 'Mix' of External, Internal Factors," *Radio Free Europe/Radio Liberty News Report*, 12 November 2009.

320. Interview, Kabul, 25 October 2008.

321. Interviews with former CLJ delegates, Kabul, October–November 2008.

322. Talk at the Atlantic Council, Washington, 15 October 2009.

323. One Afghan source in Kabul, October 2009, when he had exhausted the extensive substantive and personal complaints he had against Karzai, turned to his inability to compose decent Persian-language verse.

324. Talk at the Atlantic Council, Washington, 15 October 2009.

325. Dr. Najibullah Lafraie, *Resurgence of the Taliban insurgency in Afghanistan: How and Why?*, New York: paper delivered at the 50th Annual convention of the International Studies Association, 15–18 February 2009.

326. Gary Langer, *Afghanistan: Where Things Stand*, ABC News, 6 December 2010.

327. Talk at CSIS, Washington, 26 February 2009.

328. Gary Langer, *Afghanistan: Where Things Stand*, ABC News, 6 December 2010.

329. *Asia Foundation 2009 survey*, pp. 59–63.

330. On Ismail Khan, see: Dr. Antonio Giustozzi, *Genesis of a Prince: The Rise of Ismail Khan in Western Afghanistan 1979–92*. London: Crisis States Working Paper No. 4, September 2006.

331. On Afghan warlords, see: Antonio Giustozzi, *The Debate on Warlordism: The Importance of Military Legitimacy*. London: Crisis States Development Research Centre Discussion paper 13, October 2005.

332. Andrew Bushell, "Uzbek Warlord Remains Enigma to Outside World," *The Washington Times*, 23 February 2002.

333. Biden and Holbrooke have criticized Karzai for dealing with Dostum. "No Dream Team for Karzai," *The Economist*, 1 December 2008. Some participants in the meetings involving these individuals believed that Holbrooke, convinced he could "handle former Communist warlords" from his experience in the former Yugoslavia, was frustrated that he was unable to secure results from Dostum.

334. Brian Glyn Williams, "The Return of the Kingmaker. Afghanistan's General Dostum Ends his Exile," *Jamestown Terrorism Review*, 20 August 2009.

335. Interviews, multiple locations, October–November 2008. An example of pro-Ismail Khan Dari-language press is: Azhand, "Fragile Security in Heart," *Hasht-e Sobh* (Kabul), 30 September 2009. Translated from Dari at World News Connection, NewsEdge Document Number: 200910021477.1_f3e8017464e5617c.

336. Gary Langer, *Public Opinion Trends in Afghanistan*, ABC News, 11 February 2009.

337. On DDR: Simonetta Rossi and Antonio Giustozzi, *Disarmament, Demobilization and Reintegration (DDR) of Ex-Combatants in Afghanistan: Constraints and Capabilities*. London: Crisis States Research Centre Working Paper no. 2, series 2, June 2006.

338. Ron Synovitz, "Afghan Amnesty Law Draws Criticism, Praise," *Radio Free Europe/ Radio Liberty News Report*, 14 March 2007, http://www.rferl.org/content/article/1075272.html.

339. Interviews, multiple locations in Afghanistan, October–November 2008.

340. Interview, Kabul, 2 November 2008.

341. Interview, Bagram AB, 12 October 2008.

342. Atia Abawi, "Ignored by Society, Afghan Dancing Boys Suffer Centuries-Old Tradition," *CNN News Report*, 26 October 2009.

343. "Battle Lines Drawn over Contraception," *IRIN*, 15 March 2009, http://www.irinnews.org/Report.aspx?ReportIdAfghanistan83476.

344. Hama Yusuf, "Pakistan's Taliban Rising? Ask the Women," *Christian Science Monitor*, 26 May 2009.

345. The controversy is analyzed in: Laurun Oates, *A Closer Look: The Policy and Law-Making Behind the Shiite Personal Status Law* (Kabul: Afghanistan Research and Evaluation Unit (AREU), September 2009, http://www.areu.org.af/index); Jon Boone, "Afghanistan Passes 'Barbaric' Law Diminishing Women's Rights" (*The Guardian* [London], 14 August 2009).

346. Ruth Rennie, Sudhindra Sharma, and Pawan Sen, *Afghanistan in 2009, A Survey of the Afghan People*. Washington: The Asia Foundation, 2009, pp. 110–19.

347. Ibid., pp. 20, 124. Asked to identify the biggest problem facing women in their area, they responded: education/illiteracy (49 percent), lack of jobs/opportunities (28 percent), lack of rights/women's rights (21 percent). Nationwide figures for education are 15 percent and unemployment 26 percent.

348. World Bank, *Gender and ICTs in Fragile States: Afghanistan*, briefing, February 2008, http://siteresources.worldbank.org/EXTEDEVELOPMENT/Resources/ 20080225-Gender_and_ICT_in_Fragile_States-Afghanistan.pdf?resourceurlname Afghanistan20080225-Gender_and_ICT_in_Fragile_States-Afghanistan.pdf.

349. Ruth Rennie, Sudhindra Sharma, and Pawan Sen, *Afghanistan in 2009, A Survey of the Afghan People*. Washington: The Asia Foundation, 2009, p. 125. 92 percent of the women and 83 percent of the men surveyed supported equal opportunities in education.

350. Ibid., pp. 123–27.

351. Rahiem Taiez, "Ousted Female Afghan Lawmaker Fighting to Return to Parliament," *AP Worldstream News Report*, 5 April 2008.

352. Gary Langer, *Afghanistan: Where Things Stand*, ABC News, 6 December 2010.

353. Ruth Rennie, Sudhindra Sharma, and Pawan Sen, *Afghanistan in 2009, A Survey of the Afghan People*. Washington: The Asia Foundation, 2009, pp. 16–17.

354. An overview is Martin Walker, "The World's New Numbers," *The Wilson Quarterly*, v. 33, n. 2, Spring 2009, pp. 24–31.

355. Ruth Rennie, Sudhindra Sharma, and Pawan Sen, *Afghanistan in 2009, A Survey of the Afghan People*. Washington: The Asia Foundation, 2009, pp. 22–23.

356. Talk given at the Association of the US Army annual meeting, Washington, 6 October 2009.

357. Jack A. Goldstone, "Population and Security, How Demographic Change Can Lead to Violent Conflict," *Journal of International Affairs*, v. 56, n. 2, Fall 2002, pp. 3–23.

358. Telephone interview, M. Ashraf Haidari, Political Counselor, Embassy of Afghanistan, Washington, 29 June 2008.

359. Interview, Kabul, 20 October 2008.

360. Talk given at CSIS, Washington, 24 June 2009.

361. Talk given at CSIS, Washington, 28 May 2009.

362. Interview, Kabul, 27 October 2009.

363. Carlotta Gall, "Hunger and Food Prices Push Afghanistan to Brink," *The New York Times*, 18 May 2008.

364. Interview, Kabul, 2 November 2008.

365. Interview, Washington, 26 February 2009.

Chapter Eight

366. Steve Coll, *Ghost Wars The Secret History of the CIA, Afghanistan, and Bin Laden, from the Soviet Invasion to September 10, 2001*. New York: Penguin, 2004, p. 180.

367. The non-radicalized bulk of the madrassa system is potentially part of the solution:

Tahir Andrabi et al., "The Madrassa Myth" (*Foreign Policy Online*, June 2009, http://www.foreignpolicy.com); Barry Bearak, "Pakistan Battles its Tax Scofflaws," (*The New York Times*, 27 May 2000).

368. Rick Barton, "Bring People Power to Pakistan," *The Christian Science Monitor*, 19 May 2009.

369. See generally: Selig S. Harrison, *In Afghanistan's Shadow: Baluch Nationalism and Soviet Temptation*. Washington: Carnegie Endowment for International Peace (CEIP), 1981.

370. Frederic Grare, *Pakistan: The Resurgence of Baluch Nationalism* (Washington: CEIP, 2006); Shahzada Zulfiqar, "Endless War" (*The Herald*, April 2006, pp. 33, 36).

371. On claims of Afghan support: Shakeel Anjum, "Operation in Darra, Bara Soon: Malik," *The News Online* (Islamabad), 22 November 2009.

372. Nicholas Schmidle, "Waiting for the Worst: Baluchistan 2006," *Virginia Quarterly Review*, v. 82, n. 2, spring 2007, pp. 214–37.

373. Talk given at CSIS, Washington, 23 February 2007.

374. Ahmed Rashid, *The Taliban: Militant Islam, Oil and Fundamentalism in Central Asia* (New Haven: Yale University Press, 2001), p. 29; Steve Coll, *Ghost Wars The Secret History of the CIA, Afghanistan, and Bin Laden, from the Soviet Invasion to September 10, 2001* (New York: Penguin, 2004), p. 291.

375. Ahmad Rafay Alam, "The Beginning of the Talibanization of Lahore," *The News*, (Islamabad), 13 October 2008, http://www.thenews.com.pk/daily_detail.asp?idAfghanistan140667.

376. On the extent of pre-2004 Pakistani military operations in the FATA, see C. Christine Fair and Seth G. Jones, "Pakistan's War Within," *Survival*, v. 51, n.6, December 2009, pp. 167–79.

377. Hassan Abbas, *Police and Law Enforcement Reform in Pakistan: Crucial for Counterinsurgency and Counterterrorism Success*. Cambridge: Institute of Social Policy and Understanding, April 2009, http://belfercenter.ksg.harvard.edu/publication/18976/police_law_enforcement_reform_in_Pakistan_.html.

378. Hassan Abbas, "Transforming Pakistan's Frontier Corps," *Jamestown Terrorism Monitor*, v. 5, n. 6, 30 March 2007, pp. 1–4.

379. "US General Questions Frontier Corps' Loyalty," *Daily News* (Pakistan), 16 June 2008.

380. Peter Beaumont and Mark Townsend, "Pakistan Troops 'Aid Taliban': New Classified US Documents Reveal that Mass Infiltration of Frontier Corps by Afghan Insurgents is Helping Latest Offensive," *The Observer* (Pakistan), 22 June 2008.

381. Akram Gizabi, "Bajaur: Tribe and Custom Continue to Protect Al Qaeda," *Jamestown Terrorism Focus*, v. 3, n. 2, 18 January 2006, pp. 2–3.

382. "Car Bomb Kills Two Ansar-ul-Islam Men in Peshawar," *Dawn* (Karachi), 22 August 2009, http://www.dawn.com/wps/wcm/connect/dawn-content-library/dawn/news/pakistan/metropolitan/07-one-killed-three-injured-in-hayatabad-car-explosion-ha-06.

383. Ahmed Rashid, "Pakistan on the Brink," *The New York Review of Books*, v. 67, n. 10, 11 June 2009, pp. 12–16.

384. On more recent perceptions: Hilary Synnott, "After the Flood," *Survival*, v. 51, n.5, October 2010, pp. 249–56.

385. Ahmed Rashid, talk given at CSIS, Washington, 6 June 2008.

386. C. Christine Fair and Seth G. Jones, "Pakistan's War Within," *Survival*, v. 51, n. 6, December 2009, pp. 161–188.

387. Ahmed Rashid, talk given at CSIS, Washington, 6 June 2008.

388. Daniel Markey, *Hotbed of Terror*. Washington, Council on Foreign Relations, 11 August 2008, http://www.cfr.org/publication/16929/hotbed_of_terror.html.

389. C. Christine Fair and Seth G. Jones, "Pakistan's War Within," *Survival*, v. 51, n. 6, December 2009, pp. 161–188.

390. Makhdoom Babar, "Chinese Engineers Rescued Through Commando Action," *The Daily Mail* (London), 15 October 2004.

391. Carlotta Gall and Ismail Khan, "Taliban and Allies Tighten Grip in North of Pakistan," *The New York Times*, 11 December 2006.

392. Joby Warrick, "CIA Places Blame for Bhutto Assassination," *The Washington Post*, 18 January 2008, p. A1.

393. Hassan Abbas, "A Profile of Tehrik-i-Taliban Pakistan," *Counter Terrorism Center (CTC) Sentinel*, v. 1, n. 2, January 2008, pp. 1–4.

394. "Militants Overrun Pakistan Fort" (*BBC News report*, 17 January 2008); "Pakistani Troops Flee Border Post" (*Al Jazeera News Report*, 17 January 2008).

395. Zulfiqar Ali, "Over 4,000 Houses Destroyed in Waziristan Operation: Report" (*Dawn* [Pakistan], 8 November 2008); Iqbal Khattak, "Deserted Town Shows Human Cost of Operation Zalzala" (*The Daily Times* [Pakistan], 20 May 2008).

396. Mobarek A Virk, "Tehrik-e-Taleban Pakistan Banned," *The News* (Islamabad), 26 August 2008, http://www.thenews.com.pk/top_story_detail.asp?IdAfghanistan16831

397. Hassan Abbas, "Defining the Punjabi Taliban Network," *Counter Terrorism Center (CTC) Monitor*, v. 2, n. 4, April 2009, pp. 1–4.

398. Aoun Abbas Sahi, "The Punjab Connection," *Newsline* (Pakistan), October 2008.

399. Hassan Abbas, "Increasing Talibanization in Pakistan's Seven Tribal Agencies," *Jamestown Terrorism Focus*, v. 5, n. 18, 27 September 2007, pp. 1–5.

400. Graham Usher, "The Pakistani Taliban" (*Middle East Report Online*, 13 February 2007); Mukhtar A. Khan, "A Profile of the TTP's New Leader: Hakimullah Mehsud" (*CTC Sentinel*, v. 2, n. 10, October 2009, pp. 1–4).

401. Hassan Abbas, "The Road to Lal Masjid and Its Aftermath," *Jamestown Terrorism Monitor*, v. 5, n. 14, 19 July 2007.

402. Farhana Ali and Mohammed Shehzad, "Pakistan's Radical Red Mosque Returns," *Jamestown Terrorism Monitor*, v. 5, n. 20, 25 October 2007, pp. 3–6.

403. Jane Perlez, "Pakistan Finds Local Allies Against Ferocious Foe," *The New York Times*, 21 October 2009.

404. On Maulavi Nazir: Hassan Abbas, "South Waziristan's Maulavi Nazir: The New Face of the Taliban," *Jamestown Terrorism Monitor*, v. 5, n. 9, 10 May 2007.

405. "Taliban Bitten by a Snake in the Grass" *Asia Times Online*, 26 April 2008; "Taliban Claim Victory From a Defeat" *Asia Times Online*, 3 May 2008.

406. On the 2008 Pakistani military operations in Waziristan, see C. Christine Fair and Seth G. Jones, "Pakistan's War Within," *Survival*, v. 51, n. 6, December 2009, pp. 161–188.

407. Hassan Abbas, "Is the NWFP Slipping Out of Pakistan's Control?" *Jamestown Terrorism Monitor*, v. 5, n. 22, 26 November 2007, pp. 9–12.

408. Jane Perlez, "Pakistan Defies US on Curbing Attacks," *The New York Times*, 16 May 2008.

409. C. Christine Fair, "Pakistan Loses Swat to Local Taliban," *Jamestown Terrorism Monitor*, v. 4, n. 37, 26 November 2007, pp. 3–4.

410. Khalid Qayum and Khaleeq Ahmed, "Pakistan Deploys Troops in Swat to Curb Militants," *Bloomberg News report*, 25 October 2007, http://www.bloomberg.com/apps/news?pidAfghanistan20601102&sidAfghanistanakTcKrCtbmWE&referAfghanistanuk.

411. On the 2007 Pakistani military offensive in Swat, see C. Christine Fair and Seth G. Jones, "Pakistan's War Within," *Survival*, v. 51, n. 6, December 2009, pp. 161–188.

412. Jane Perlez, "Pakistan Defies US on Curbing Attacks," *The New York Times*, 18 May 2008.

413. Sabrina Tavernise and Pir Zubair Shah, "Tough Battle in Stronghold of Pakistan Insurgency," *The New York Times*, 16 June 2009.

414. Steven Munson and Walter Pincus, "Supplying Troops in Afghanistan With Fuel is Challenge for US," *The Washington Post*, 15 December 2009, p. A11.

415. On the 2008 Pakistani military operations in Swat, see C. Christine Fair and Seth G. Jones, "Pakistan's War Within," *Survival*, v. 51, n. 6, December 2009, pp. 161–188.

416. Ahmed Rashid, "Pakistan on the Brink," *The New York Review of Books*, v. 67, n. 10, 11 June 2009, pp. 12–16.

417. For example, see Abbas Memkari, "Extremism and All Kinds of Ups and Downs," *Jang* (Karachi), 1 April 2007.

418. Jane Perlez and Ismail Khan, "Militants Gain Despite Decree by Musharraf," *The New York Times*, 15 November 2007.

419. Paul Wiseman and Zafar M. Sheikh, "Pakistani Police Underfunded, Overwhelmed," *USA Today*, 5 May 2009.

420. Ahmed Rashid, "Hearts on the Line in Pakistan," *The Washington Post*, 12 June 2009.

421. "The Law in Whose Hands?" *The Economist*, 3 October 2009, pp. 49–50.

422. Sabrina Tavernise and Waqar Gillani, "70 Murders, Yet Close to Going Free in Pakistan," *The New York Times*, 5 August 2009.

423. Ismail Khan, "Mehsuds Hedge their Bets as Game On to Isolate Behtullah," *Dawn* (Karachi), 16 June 2009.

424. Sadia Sulaiman, "Haiz Gul Bahadur: A Profile of the Leader of the North Waziristan Taliban," *Jamestown Terrorism Monitor*, v. 7, n. 9, 10 April 2009.

425. Syed Saleem Shahzad, "Deal with Militants Emboldens Opposition," *Asia Times Online*, 24 February 2009.

426. Jane Perlez, "Pakistan Finds Local Allies Against Ferocious Foe," *The New York Times*, 21 October 2009.

427. "There They Go Again," *The Economist*, 24 October 2009, pp. 48–50.

428. "Tackling the Other Taliban," *The Economist*, 17 October 2009, pp. 26, 34.

429. Jane Perlez, "Pakistan Finds Local Allies Against Ferocious Foe," *The New York Times*, 21 October 2009.

430. Paul Alexander, "Taliban Commander Shot Dead in Northwest Pakistan," *AP Report*, 23 June 2009.

431. Kamran Khan: "After Baitullah, Battle On for Taliban Treasure," *The News Online* (Islamabad), 10 August 2009.

432. Mukhtar A. Khan, "A Profile of the TTP's New Leader: Hakimullah Mehsud," *CTC Sentinel*, v. 2, n. 10, October 2009, pp. 1–4.

433. Saeed Shah, "Is Pakistan's Taliban Movement on the Way Out?," *McClatchy Newspapers report*, 23 August 2009.

434. Quoted in *Dawn* (Karachi), 31 July 2008.

435. Julian E. Barnes and Greg Miller, "US Aiding Pakistani Military Offensive," *Los Angeles Times*, 23 October 2009.

436. Craig Cohen, "When 10 Billion is Not Enough," *The Washington Quarterly*, v. 30, n. 2, Spring 2007, pp. 7–19.

437. Interview, Kabul, 28 October 2008.

438. Talk given at the Association of the US Army annual meeting, Washington, 6 October 2009.

439. Hassan Abbas, *Police & Law Enforcement Reform in Pakistan: Crucial for Counterinsurgency and Counterterrorism Success*. Institute for Social Policy and Understanding, April 2009, p. 16.

440. Ashley J. Tellis, *Pakistan and the War on Terror. Conflicted Goals, Compromised Performance*. Washington: Carnegie Endowment for International Peace, 2008, p. 26.

441. Nasrullah Afridi, "Army Operation Likely in Khyber Agency" (*The News Online* [Islamabad], 23 November 2009); "New Front Possible in Anti-Taliban Fight" (*The Washington Post*, 13 December 2009, p. A22).

442. David E. Sanger and Eric Schmitt, "Administration Presses Pakistan to Fight Taliban," *The New York Times*, 8 December 2009, pp. A1, A12.

443. Jane Perlez, "Rebuffing US, Pakistan Balks at Crackdown," *The New York Times*, 15 December 2009, pp. A1, A8.

444. Robert Karniol, "Plugging the Gaps," *Jane's Defense Weekly*, 22 March 2006.

445. Mosharref Zaidi, "Politics, Not Extremism, Is to Blame for Pakistan's Plight," *The National Post* (Canada), 26 October 2009.

446. Talk at CSIS, Washington, 21 March 2008.

447. Ahmed Rashid, "Pakistan's Worrisome Pullback," *The Washington Post*, 6 June 2008, p. A19.

448. Jane Perlez and Ismail Khan, "Aid Package from US Jolts Army in Pakistan," *The New York Times*, 8 October 2009, p. A10.

449. Scott Shane, "CIA to Expand Use of Drones in Pakistan" *The New York Times*,

3 December 2009; Carol Grisanti and Musthtaq Yusufzai, "Pakistanis Outraged over Continued Drone Attacks" (*MSNBC News Report*, 26 January 2009, http://world blog.msnbc.msn.com/archive/2009/01/26/1761106.aspx); Jeremy Page, "Google Earth Reveals Secret History of US Base in Pakistan" (*The Times* (London), 19 February 2009, http://www.timesonline.co.uk/tol/news/world/asia/article5762371.ece).

450. Ahmed Rashid, "Waziristan or Bust," *The Times of India*, 26 October 2009.

451. Andrew Scheineson, *The Shanghai Cooperation Organization*. New York: Council of Foreign Relations Backgrounder Report, 24 March 2009, http://www.cfr.org/publication/10883/.

452. Geoff Dyer, "Obama to Press China, on Afghanistan," *The Financial Times* (London), 12 November 2009.

453. Interview with former Afghan cabinet minister, Kabul, 16 October 2009.

454. Krittivas Mukherjee, "India, China Russia Seek Role in Afghan Policy," *Reuters News Report*, 27 October 2009, http://www.reuters.com/article/idUSTRE59Q1TS20091027.

455. Eric Schmitt, "US Defense Secretary Issues Veiled Warning to China Not to Bully Neighbors Over Energy," *The New York Times*, 31 May 2008, p. A8.

456. Erik Eckholm, "China Muslim Group Planned Terror, U.S. Says," *The New York Times*, 31 August 2002.

457. Jim Yardley, "New Spasm of Violence in Western China as 11 Die in Wave of Bombings," *The New York Times*, 10 August 2008.

458. Tariq Niazi, *China, Pakistan and Terrorism*, Foreign Policy in Focus Commentary, 16 July 2007, http://www.fpif.org/fpiftxt/4384.

459. Jonathan Landay, "China's Thirst for Copper Could Hold Key to Afghanistan's Future," *McClatchy Papers News Report*, 8 March 2009.

460. Nicklas Norling, "The Emerging China-Afghanistan Relationship," Central Asia-Caucasus Institute Analyst, 14 May 2008, http://www.cacianalyst.org/?qAfghanistannode/4858.

461. See: Niamatullah Ibrahimi, *The Failure of a Clerical Proto-State: Hazarajat, 1979–84*. London: Crisis States Research Centre Working Paper No. 6, 2006.

462. Talk given at Heritage Foundation, Washington, 26 March 2008.

463. Interview, Kabul, 22 October 2008.

464. Matthew Levitt, talk given at the Washington Institute for Near East Policy, Washington, 10 March 2008.

465. GEN Stanley McChrystal, *COMISAF Initial Assessment* ("McChrystal Report"), Kabul, 20 August 2009, pp. 2–11.

466. Jason Motlagh, "Iran's Spending Spree in Afghanistan," *Time*, 27 May 2009.

467. Interview, Kabul, 28 October 2008.

468. Lionel Beehner, *Afghanistan's Role in Iran's Drug Problem*. New York: Council for Foreign Relations Backgrounder, 14 September 2006, http://www.cfr.org/publication/11457/.

469. Interview with Afghan government official, Kabul, 21 October 2008.

470. Ibid.

471. See: Rajmohan Gandhi, *Ghaddar Khan, Nonviolent Badshah of the Pakhtuns*. New Delhi: Penguin, 2004.

472. Sumit Ganguly and S. Paul Kaptur, "The End of the Affair: Washington's Cooling Passion for New Delhi," *Foreign Affairs Online*, 15 June 2009.

473. Paul Staniland, "Improving India's Counterterrorism After Mumbai," *CTC Sentinel*, v. 2, n. 4, April 2009, pp. 11–14.

474. *Pakistani Public Opinion on the Swat Conflict, Afghanistan and the US: Questionnaire*, 1 July 2009, WorldPublicOpinion.Org, http://www.worldpublicopinion.org/pipa/pdf/jul09/WPO_Pakistan_Jul09_quaire.pdf.

475. Some 80 to over 90 percent of Pakistanis polled in 2009 believe the US is trying to impose US culture on Muslim society or weaken and divide the Islamic world. Clay Ramsay, Steven Kull, Stephen Weber, and Evan Lewis, *Pakistani Public Opinion of the Swat Conflict, Afghanistan and the US*, 1 July 2009, World Public Opinion.Org, pp. 9–11, http://www.worldpublicopinion.org/pipa/pdf/jul09/WPO_Pakistan_Jul09_rpt.pdf.

476. Mosharref Zaidi, "Politics, Not Extremism, Is to Blame for Pakistan's Plight," *The National Post* (Canada), 26 October 2009.

477. Saeed Shah, "Pakistan's President Facing Military Anger Over His US Ties," *McClatchy Newspapers report*, 27 November 2009.

478. Talk given at the Republican National Lawyers' Association annual meeting, Washington, 22 April 2009.

479. Michael Scheuer, "India's Strategic Challenge in Pakistan's Afghan Hinterland," *Jamestown Terrorism Monitor*, v. 5, n. 32, 12 August 2008.

480. Sebastian Abbot, "US Looks for Saudi Help in Afghanistan, Pakistan," *Associated Press report*, 3 June 2009.

481. Andrew Scutro, "Surge to Strain Supply Lines," *Defense News*, 7 December 2009, pp. 1, 20.

482. Quoted in: Steven Munson and Walter Pincus, "Supplying Troops in Afghanistan With Fuel Is Challenge for US," *The Washington Post*, 15 December 2009, p. A11.

483. David Rhode, Carlotta Gall, Eric Schmitt, and David E. Sangar, "US Officials See Waste in Billions Sent to Pakistan," *The New York Times*, 24 December 2007.

484. Dan Balz, "Obama Says He Would Take Fight to Pakistan," *The Washington Post*, 2 August 2007.

485. On the potential for near-term collapse in Pakistan, see "Centcom Adviser Warns Pakistan In Danger; Says Pak Security Services a Rogue State Within a State" (*The News* [Islamabad], 24 March 2009); Pamela Constable, "In Pakistan, a Sense of Foreboding" *The Washington Post*, 27 April 2009, p. A6.

486. Ahmed Rashid, "Pakistan on the Brink," *The New York Review of Books*, v. 67, n. 10, 11 June 2009, pp. 12–16.

487. Interview following talk at the Brookings Institution, Washington, 25 February 2009.

Chapter Nine

488. Interview, Kabul, 19 October 2009. The minister was suggesting that this book be re-titled.

439. Yet the imperial—British or Soviet—experience can still provide valuable insights into Afghan realities. See, for example, Thomas H. Johnson and M. Chris Mason, "No Sign until the Burst of Fire: Understanding the Pakistani-Afghanistan Frontier," *International Security*, v. 32, n. 4, Spring 2008, pp. 41–77.

490. Sean M. Maloney, "The International Security Assistance Force: The Origins of a Stabilization Force," *Canadian Military Journal*, Summer 2003, pp. 3–11.

491. Carlotta Gall, "UN Official Raises Alarms Over Killings in Afghanistan," *The New York Times*, 16 May 2008.

492. Talk given at the Association of the US Army annual meeting, Washington, 6 October 2009.

493. NATO Deputy Secretary General Ambassador Claudio Bisogniero, *Assisting Afghanistan: The importance of a comprehensive approach*, Keynote address at the GLOBUS Conference, Bratislava, Slovakia, 17 January 2008, http://www.nato.int/docu/speech/2008/s080117a.html.

494. Rajiv Chandrasekaran, "Pentagon Worries Led to Command Change," *The Washington Post*, 17 August 2009.

495. "Afghanistan's NATO Force Needs Top Civilian: UN," *AFP News Report*, 4 January 2010.

496. Talk given at the Association of the US Army annual meeting, Washington, 6 October 2009.

497. GEN Stanley McChrystal, *COMISAF Initial Assessment* ("McChrystal Report"), Kabul, 20 August 2009, p. B–1.

498. Bill Gertz. "Inside the Ring," *The Washington Times*, 10 July 2008.

499. *Placemat*, 22 October 2009. http://www.nato.int/isaf/docu/epub/pdf/placemat.pdf.

500. Before an audience at the Atlantic Council in Washington, 11 May 2009. Craddock is the former Supreme Allied Commander Europe (SACEUR).

501. On national caveats in general, see: LTC Leah R. Sundquist, *NATO in Afghanistan: A Progress Report*, Carlisle Barracks, 25 March 2008, US Army War College Strategy Research Report; COL Michael L. Everett, *Merging the International Security and Assistance Force (ISAF) and Operation Enduring Freedom (OEF): A Strategic Imperative*, Carlisle Barracks, 8 February 2006, US Army War College Strategy Research Report; Susan Koelbl and Alexander Szander, "German Special Forces in Afghanistan Let Taliban Commander Escape," *Der Spiegel Online International*, 19 May 2008, http://www.spiegel.de/international/world/0,1518,554033,00.html.

502. Manfred Goetzke, "How the Rules of Afghanistan Have Changed for the Bundeswehr," *Deutsche Welte News Report*, 16 December 2009, http://www.dw-world.de/dw/article/0,,5019739,00.html. Jerome Starkey, "They Came, They Saw, Then Left the Afghan War Without a Single Mission," *The Scotsman* (Edinburgh), 9 October 2008, http://news.scotsman.com/world/They-came-they-saw-.4573584.jp.

503. Interview, Kabul, 12 October 2009.

504. Pentagon news conference, Washington, 18 May 2009, http://www.defense.gov/news/newsarticle.aspx?idAfghanistan53604.

505. Gary Langer, *Public Opinion Trends in Afghanistan*, ABC News, 11 February 2009.

506. Noor Rahman, "Afghans Dispute US Version of Raid Casualties," *Reuters News Report*, 20 May 2007.

507. Interview, Kabul, 20 October 2008.

508. Kirk Semple, "Official Calls for Sensitivity to Afghan Demands," *The New York Times*, 8 December 2008.

509. For an estimate of the scope of the problem, see: *Conflict-Related Civilian Deaths*, Kabul, 13 May 2009, NATO Briefing Chart. http://www.nato.int/nato_static/assets/pdf/pdf_2009_05/20090514_090513-Conflict-Related_Civilian_Deaths.pdf.

510. *ABC Polling*, 11 February 2009. These polling results likely also reflect that those in areas where indirect fire is being used probably are living in districts in south and east Afghanistan where the US presence is not popular for multiple reasons.

511. US Department of Defense, *Progress Toward Security and Stability in Afghanistan*, November 2010, p. 55.

512. For one example: Jessica Stern, *Terror in the Name of God*, New York: HarperCollins, 2004.

513. John R. Dyke and John R. Crisafulli, *Unconventional Counter-Insurgency in Afghanistan*, Monterey, CA, June 2006. Naval Postgraduate School thesis, p. 8, for example.

514. See: Sean Naylor, *Not a Good Day to Die: The Untold History of Operation Anaconda*. New York, 2005, Berkeley.

515. Wayne Washington, "Once Against Nation-Building, Bush Now Involved," *The Boston Globe*, 2 March 2004. http://www.boston.com/news/nation/articles/2004/03/02/once_against_nation_building_bush_now_involved/. Bush's State of the Union speech," *CNN News Report*, 29 January 2003, http://www.cnn.com/2003/ALLPOLITICS/01/28/sotu.transcript/.

516. Interviews, Kabul, October-November 2008. There are two highly diverging views of this situation. Karzai supporters and veterans of this stage of his administration report Karzai's concern about a cross-border insurgency. Northern Alliance figures believe he saw the Northern Alliance leadership (and increased political power of non-Pushtuns) as Afghanistan's major security threat.

517. Walter Pincus, "Growing Threat Seen in Afghan Insurgency: Defense Intelligence Agency Chief Cites Surging Violence," *The Washington Post*, 1 March 2006.

518. Talk at JHU Asymmetric Warfare Symposium, Washington, 10 March 2008.

519. COL Peter Mansoor, "How the Surge Worked," *The Washington Post* 10 August 2008, p. B–7.

520. On the background of this approach, see: MAJ Stephen C. Phillips, *Establishing a Suitable Tactical Design for Clear-Hold-Build Counterinsurgency Operations*, Ft. Leavenworth, 12 June 2009, Thesis at the US Army Command and General Staff College.

521. FM3-24, *Counterinsurgency*, Washington, December 2006, U.S. Army, paras 5-51–5-8. http://www.usgcoin.org/library/doctrine/COIN-FM3-24.pdf.

522. MAJ Quy H. Nguyen, Achieving Unity of Effort: *Leveraging Interagency Cooperation Between the Department of Defense (DoD) and the United States Agency for International Development (USAID)*, Ft. Leavenworth, 12 June 2009, Thesis at the U.S. Army Command and General Staff College.

523. Interview, Kabul, 20 October 2008.

524. *Security Summary*, Kabul, 13 May 2009, NATO briefing chart, http://www.nato. int/nato_static/assets/pdf/pdf_2009_05/20090514_090513-Security_Summary.pdf.

525. *IED Related Casualties*, Kabul, 13 May 2009, NATO briefing chart, http://www.nato. int/nato_static/assets/pdf/pdf_2009_05/20090514_090513-IED_Related_Casualties.pdf.

526. Joint Operations Intelligence Information System (JOIIS) 4 May 2009 figures quoted in Anthony Cordesman, *The Afghan War at End 2009: A Crisis and New Realism*, Washington, 4 January 2010, CSIS, p. 6. http://csis.org/files/publication/ 100104_afghan_war_at_end_09.pdf.

527. *ABC Polling*, 6 December 2010.

528. MG Mike Hindmarsh, "Special Forces Battle Against Terror," *Defence* (Australia), October 2006, http://www.defence.gov.au/defencemagazine/editions/ 200610/coverstory/coverstory.htm.

529. Interview, COL Patrick McNiece, ISAF deputy director of intelligence, Kabul, 29 October 2008.

530. Eric Schmitt, "Elite US Force Expanding Hunt in Afghanistan," *The New York Times*, 27 December 2009.

531. Interview, Bagram AB, 13 October 2008.

532. For example, see Dyke and Crisafulli, *ibid.*

533. Interview, Kabul, 23 October 2008.

534. Minister of the Interior Mohammed Hanif Atmar, talk at the Brookings Institution, Washington, 25 February 2009.

535. Syed Saleem Shahzad, "Afghanistan Strikes Back at Pakistan," *Asia Times*, 9 November 2006; "Afghans Among Seven Held Over Quetta Bomb Blast," *AFP Report*, 22 December 2006.

536. M. K. Bhadrakumar, "Spooks Spill Blood in the Hindu Kush," *Asia Times*, 23 September 2009.

537. Interview with Afghan government official, Kabul, 21 October 2008.

538. Rachel Morarjee, "What Has Afghans So Angry," *Time*, 30 May 2006. http://www. time.com/time/world/article/0,8599,1199254,00.html.

539. "Afghanistan: NGOs Worried About Security in the North," *IRIN News* report, 1 October 2009. http://www.unhcr.org/refworld/country,IRIN,AFG,4562d8cf2, 4acaea891e,0.html.

540. Sebastian Fischer, Matthias Gebauer and Severin Weiland, "Defense Minister Calls Kunduz Airstrike 'Inappropriate,'" *Der Spiegel Online International*, 4 December 2009 http://www.spiegel.de/international/germany/0,1518,665132,00.html.

541. Reza Shir Mohammedi, "Dozens of Afghan, Taliban Soldiers Killed," *Quqnoos News service report* (Kabul), 30 May 2009, http://quqnoos.com/index.php?option Afghanistancom_content&taskAfghanistanview&idAfghanistan3111&Itemid Afghanistan48.

542. Talk given at CSIS, Washington, 28 May 2009.

543. An example of US SOF working with Afghans is: John R. Dyke and John R. Crisafulli, *Unconventional Counter-Insurgency in Afghanistan*, Monterey, CA, June 2006, Naval Postgraduate School thesis.

544. Interview, Kabul, 27 October 2008.

545. Ibid.

546. Sources on Afghan Security Forces include: Anthony Davis, "Interview with Major General John McColl," *Jane's Defense Weekly*, v. 37, n. 22, 29 May 2002, p. 32; Anthony Davis, "Briefing: Afghan National Air Corps," *Jane's Defense Weekly*, v. 46, n. 1, 7 January 2009, pp. 28–31; Anthony Davis, "Briefing: Afghan National Army," *Jane's Defense Weekly*, v. 45, n. 1, 17 December 2008, pp. 24–29; Anthony Davis, "Interview with General Bismullah Khan Mohammedi, Chief of Staff, Afghan National Army," *Jane's Defense Weekly*, v. 45, n. 4, 23 January 2009, p. 24.

547. Historically, Tajiks have been overrepresented in Afghanistan's professional officers (at all but the highest levels) and soldiers since the 1870s, when British intelligence reported that uniformed Afghan regiments with European rifles were recruited from "Kohestanis." This also reflected the non-enforcement of conscription in several Pushtun provinces during the Golden Age.

548. Interview, Bagram AB, 13 October 2008.

549. Interview, Kabul, 23 October 2008.

550. US Department of Defense, *Progress Toward Security and Stability in Afghanistan*, January 2009, p. 35. http://www.defenselink.mil/pubs/Report_on_Progress_toward_Security_and_Stability_in_Afghanistan_1230.pdf.

551. Joint Operations Intelligence Information System (JOIIS) 4 May 2009 figures quoted in Anthony Cordesman, *The Afghan War at End 2009: A Crisis and New Realism*, Washington, 4 January 2010, CSIS, p.6. http://csis.org/files/publication/100104_afghan_war_at_end_09.pdf.

552. Talk given at the Association of the US Army annual meeting, Washington, 6 October 2009.

553. Telephone conversation, Washington, 23 November 2009.

554. Jonathan Burch, "NATO Takes Command of the Afghan Army, Police Training," *Reuters* News Report, 21 November 2009; "NATO Activates New Afghanistan Training Mission," *Army*, v. 60, n. 1, January 2010, p. 6.

555. Interview, Kabul, 26 October 2008.

556. Interview, Bagram AB, 13 October 2008.

557. Richard A. Oppel Jr. and Elisabeth A. Bumiller, "Afghanistan's President Says Army Will Need Allies' Help Until 2024 or Longer," *The New York Times*, 9 December 2009, p. A14.

558. Abubakar Siddique, "Difficult Prospects for Building a Viable Afghan Army," *Radio Free Europe/Radio Liberty Report*, 1 October 2009.

559. US Department of Defense, *Progress Toward Security and Stability in Afghanistan*, Washington, January 2009, p. 36.

560. Talk at the Heritage Foundation, Washington, 26 March 2008.

561. Interview, Bagram AB, 12 October 2008.

562. Talk at the Brookings Institution, Washington, 25 February 2009.

563. Ibid.

564. GEN Stanley McChrystal, *COMISAF Initial Assessment* ("McChrystal Report"), Kabul, 20 August 2009, pp. 2–15.

565. Talk given at CSIS, Washington, 22 May 2009.

566. Robert M. Perito, *Afghanistan's Police. Weak Link in Security Sector Reform*, Washington, August 2009, US Institute of Peace Special report 227. http://www.usip.org/files/afghanistan_police.pdf.

567. Talk at the Brookings Institution, Washington, 25 February 2009.

568. Judy Dempsey, "Training of Afghan Police by Europe Is Found Lacking," *The New York Times*, 18 November 2009, p. A16.

569. Interview, Bagram AB, 12 October 2008.

570. Ibid.

571. Interviews, multiple locations in Afghanistan, October–November 2008.

572. Sandra Jontz, "US Set to Boost Afghan Police Training," *The Stars and Stripes*, 3 October 2009. http://www.stripes.com/article.asp?sectionAfghanistan104&articleAfghanistan65151.

573. Interviews, multiple locations in Afghanistan, October–November 2008.

574. Mark Sappenfield, "Female Cops Test Traditional Gender Roles in Afghanistan," *Christian Science Monitor*, 19 January 2009, http://www.csmonitor.com/World/Asia-South-Central/2009/0107/p01s03-wosc.html; "Top Afghan Policewoman Shot Dead," *BBC News Report*, 28 September 2008, http://news.bbc.co.uk/2/hi/7640263.stm.

575. Joint Operations Intelligence Information System (JOIIS) 4 May 2009 figures quoted in Anthony Cordesman, *The Afghan War at End 2009: A Crisis and New Realism*, Washington, 4 January 2010, CSIS, p. 6. http://csis.org/files/publication/100104_afghan_war_at_end_09.pdf.

576. Talk at the Brookings Institution, Washington, 25 February 2009.

577. Ibid.

578. Talk at the Johns Hopkins University Asymmetric Warfare Symposium, Washington, 10 March 2008.

579. Talk at the Annual AUSA meeting, Washington, 6 October 2009.

580. Interviews, Kabul, October–November 2008.

581. Ibid.

582. Talk given at the Association of the US Army annual meeting, Washington, 6 October 2009.

583. Interview, Kabul, 2 November 2008.

584. Talk at the Brookings Institution, Washington, 25 February 2009.

585. Jon Boone, "Afghans Fear US Plan to Rearm Villages," *The Financial Times* (London), 12 January 2009.

586. Talk at the Brookings Institution, Washington, 25 February 2009.

587. Carlotta Gall, "Afghans Start Answering Call to Fight Taliban," *The New York Times*, 3 January 2010, p. 9.

588. Interview, Kabul, 27 October 2008.

589. Talk given at the Association of the US Army (AUSA) annual meeting, Washington, 6 October 2009.

590. Briefing given at the AUSA annual meeting, Washington, 12 October 2007.
591. Interview following talk at the Heritage Foundation, Washington, 26 March 2008.
592. Interview, Kabul, 26 October 2008.
593. Talk at the Heritage Foundation, Washington, 26 March 2008.
594. GEN Stanley McChrystal, *COMISAF Initial Assessment* ("McChrystal Report"), Kabul, 20 August 2009, pp. 1–2.
595. John F. Burns, "Karzai Sought Saudi Help with Taliban," *The New York Times*, 1 October 2008; Anand Gopal, "No Afghan-Taliban Peace Talks for Now," *The Christian Science Monitor*, 9 October 2009; Kim Sengupta, "Secret Saudi Dinner, Karzai's Brother and the Taliban," *The Independent* (London), 8 October 2008.
596. Interview, Afghan government official, Kabul, 21 October 2008.
597. GEN Stanley McChrystal, *COMISAF Initial Assessment* ("McChrystal Report"), Kabul, 20 August 2009, pp. 2–13.
598. Griff White, "Afghan Promises to Insurgents Often Empty," *The Washington Post*, 14 December 2009, pp. A1, A8.
599. Ali Jalali, former interior minister, at a talk at American University, Kabul, 27 October 2008.
600. Interview, Kabul, 27 October 2008.

Chapter Ten

601. Interview, Ashraf Ghani, Washington, 27 February 2007.
602. Matt Waldman, *Falling Short; Aid Effectiveness in Afghanistan*, ACBAR, Kabul, March 2008.
603. Interview, Washington, 12 February 2007.
604. Interview, Washington, 26 February 2008.
605. Simeon Djankov, Jose G. Montalvo, and Marta Reynal-Querol, *The Curse of Aid*, December 2007, paper, pp. 3–5, 24.
606. While Brahimi (and others) now regret Taliban non-participation at Bonn, this would have been physically difficult to realize and would have encouraged other players to act as spoilers. The Taliban had demonstrated their near-impossibility to engage diplomatically during the destruction of the Bamiyan Buddhas in 2001.
607. Emma Sky, "The Lead Nation Approach, The Case of Afghanistan," *The Journal of the Royal United Services Institution*, December 2006, pp. 20–26.
608. Gethin Chamberlain, "US Military: Afghan Leaders Steal Half of All Aid," *Sunday Telegraph* (London), 28 January 2007.
609. Interview, Washington, 27 February 2007.
610. Matt Waldman, *Falling Short; Aid Effectiveness in Afghanistan*, ACBAR, Kabul, March 2008.
611. Ann Jones, "How US Dollars Disappear in Afghanistan: Quickly and Thoroughly," *The San Francisco Chronicle*, 3 September 2006.
612. GEN Stanley McChrystal, *COMISAF Initial Assessment* ("McChrystal Report"), Kabul, 20 August 2009, pp. 2–18.
613. Talk at the Atlantic Council, Washington, 22 April 2009.

614. Among many sources critical of these efforts are: Ahmad Rashid, *Descent into Chaos* (New York: Viking, 2008, pp. 350–66); Rajiv Chandrasekhar, "US Pursues a New Way to Rebuild Afghanistan," *The Washington Post*, 19 June 2009.

615. Interview, Dr. Sayid Mohammed Amin Fatimi, Minister of Health, Washington, 23 July 2008.

616. Talk at CSIS, Washington, 28 May 2009.

617. Talk at CSIS, Washington, 28 September 2009.

618. Interview, Washington, 12 February 2007.

619. Interviews, Kabul, 16 October 2009.

620. Andrew Wilder, "A Weapons System Built on Wishful Thinking," *The Boston Globe*, 16 September 2009.

621. Interview, Kabul, 27 October 2008.

622. Interview, Bagram AB, 13 October 2008.

623. On Afghan perceptions of DDAs and Afghan governance and its interface with aid in general, see: Ruth Rennie, ed., *State Building, Security and Social Change in Afghanistan*, Washington, 2008, the Asia Foundation, http://asiafoundation.org/resources/pdfs/2008surveycompanionvolumefinal.pdf.

624. Talk given at CSIS, Washington, 28 May 2009.

625. COL Russell N. Wardle OBE, *The Search For Stability: Provincial Reconstruction Teams in Afghanistan*, Carlisle Barracks, May 2004, US Army War College.

626. On the importance of international support for the Hazaras, see: Richard A. Oppel Jr. and Abdul Waheed Wafa, "Hazara Minority Hustles to Head of Class in Afghanistan," *The New York Times*, 4 January 2010, p. A–4.

627. Interview, Massoud Kharokhail, Tribal Liaison Office, Kabul, 2 November 2009.

628. GEN Stanley McChrystal, *COMISAF Initial Assessment* ("McChrystal Report"), Kabul, 20 August 2009, pp. 2–12.

629. Talk given at the Washington Institute for Near East Policy, Washington, 29 September 2009.

630. "Afghan President Complains US, NATO Aren't Succeeding," *AP News Report*, 26 November 2008.

631. Talk given at CSIS, Washington, 28 May 2009.

632. Talk given at CEIP, Washington, 27 October 2009.

633. Talk given at AUSA annual meeting, Washington, 6 October 2009.

634. Interview, Bagram AB, 14 October 2008.

635. Sharon Pickup, US Government Accountability Office, talk given at the Afghan–American Chamber of Commerce Conference, Washington, 20 October 2009.

636. Interview, Kabul, 5 November 2008.

637. Interview, Bagram AB, 14 October 2008.

638. Sharon Pickup, US Government Accountability Office, talk given at the Afghan–American Chamber of Commerce Conference, Washington, 20 October 2009.

639. Talk given at CSIS, Washington, 28 May 2009.

640. Abubakar Siddique, "Afghan Hopes to Provide 'Land Bridge' Still Hampered," *Radio Free Europe, Radio Liberty Report*, 14 May 2009.

641. Talk given at the Washington Institute for Near East Policy, Washington, 29 September 2009.

642. Interview, Washington, 26 February 2008.

643. Talk given at CSIS, Washington, 28 May 2009.

644. Interview, Afghan diplomat, Ankara, 9 October 2008.

645. Jane Perlez, "US Fears That Increased Aid to Pakistan Will Feed Graft," *The New York Times*, 21 September 2009.

646. Ahmed Rashid, "Pakistan on the Brink," *The New York Review of Books*, v. 67, n. 10, 11 June 2009, p. 12.

647. An overview of the FATA security situation, its impact on Afghanistan, and its potential to be affected by US actions is: Thomas H. Johnson and M. Chris Mason, "No Sign until the Burst of Fire: Understanding the Pakistani-Afghanistan Frontier," *International Security*, v. 32, n. 4, Spring 2008, pp. 64–70.

648. Talk given at the AUSA annual meeting, Washington, 6 October 2009.

649. Ahmed Rashid, "The Pakistan Army's Political Gamble," *The Daily Beast*, 15 October 2009; Ahmed Rashid, "Pakistan Civilian-Military Ties Hit New Low," *BBC Online*, 16 October 2009.

650. Pamela Constable, "Senators Try to Reassure Pakistan About Relationship with US," *The Washington Post*, 9 January 2010, p. A–6.

Chapter Eleven

651. HQ ISAF Strategic Advisory Group "Unclassified Metrics" May 2009 figures quoted in Anthony Cordesman, *The Afghan War at End 2009: A Crisis and New Realism*, Washington, 4 January 2010, CSIS, p. 7. http://csis.org/files/publication/100104_afghan_war_at_end_09.pdf.

652. Joint Operations Intelligence Information System (JOIIS) 4 May 2009 figures quoted in Anthony Cordesman, *The Afghan War at End 2009*, ibid., p. 6.

653. James Appathurai, *NATO Weekly Press Briefing*, Kabul, 13 May 2009, http://www.nato.int/cps/en/SID-AFF94721-86524341/natolive/opinions_54724.htm.

654. Joint Operations Intelligence Information System (JOIIS) 4 May 2009 figures quoted in Anthony Cordesman, *The Afghan War at End 2009: A Crisis and New Realism*, Washington: CSIS, 4 January 2010, p. 6. http://csis.org/files/publication/100104_afghan_war_at_end_09.pdf.

655. Quoted by Ambassador Karl F. Inderfurth in testimony before the House Armed Services Committee, Washington, 23 January 2008. http://armedservices.house.gov/pdfs/FC012308/Inderfurth_Testimony012308.pdf.

656. Eric Schmitt, "Elite US Forces Expanding Hunt in Afghanistan," *The New York Times*, 27 December 2009.

657. Although, GEN McChrystal adds, neither is defeat. GEN Stanley McChrystal, *COMISAF Initial Assessment* ("McChrystal Report"), Kabul, 20 August 2009, p. 1.

658. President Barack Obama, Inaugural Address, 20 January 2009. http://www.whitehouse.gov/blog/read_the_inaugural_address.

659. Yochi J. Dreazen and August Cole, "Gates Says Taliban Has Momentum in Afghanistan," *The Wall Street Journal*, 26 May 2009.

660. Susan Page, "Approval of Obama on Afghanistan War Dives," *USA Today*, 25 November 2009.

661. Amy Belasco, *The Cost of Iraq, Afghanistan, and Other Global War on Terror Operations Since 9/11*, Washington, 28 September 2008, Congressional Research Service, Report RL 33110. http://www.fas.org/sgp/crs/natsec/RL33110.pdf; Todd Harrison, *Estimating Funding for Afghanistan*, Washington, 1 December 2009, Center for Strategic and Budgetary Analysis (CSBA), http://www.csbaonline.org/ 4Publications/PubLibrary/U.20091201.Estimating_Funding/U.20091201. Estimating_Funding.pdf.

662. Jonathan S. Landay, John Walcott and Nancy A. Youssef, "Are Obama Advisers Downplaying Afghanistan Dangers?," *McClatchy Newspapers report*, 11 October 2009.

663. Thomas H. Johnson and M. Chris Mason, "Refighting the Last War. Afghanistan and the Vietnam Template," *Military Review*, November–December 2009, pp. 2–14.

664. Scott Wilson, "Obama: US Security is Still at Stake," *The Washington Post*, 2 December 2009, pp. A1, A10.

665. GEN Stanley McChrystal, *COMISAF Initial Assessment* ("McChrystal Report"), Kabul, 20 August 2009, p. 1.

666. Tom LoBianco, "Clinton: Ousting Al Qaeda Only Goal in Afghanistan," *The Washington Times*, 16 November 2009.

667. Donna Miles, "Gates Lashes Out at Leakers," *American Forces Press Service news report*, 12 November 2009. http://www.defenselink.mil/news/newsarticle. aspx?idAfghanistan56659.

668. "NATO Chief: Leave Afghanistan and 'al-Qaeda Will Be Back in a Flash," *The Daily Telegraph* (London), 17 November 2009.

669. "Turkey Says No More Troops for Afghanistan," *Radio Free Europe/Radio Liberty News Report*, 6 December 2009, http://www.rferl.org/content/article/1896577.html; Delphine Strauss, "Turkey Rules Out Extra Troops for Afghanistan," *The Financial Times* (London), 7 December 2009, http://www.ft.com/cms/s/0/dd61c30e-e2d1-11de-b028-00144feab49a.html.

670. Interview, Kabul, 20 October 2009.

671. Mukhtar E. Khan, "The Return of Sharia Law to Pakistan's Swat Region," *Jamestown Terrorism Monitor*, v. 7, n. 4, 3 March 2009.

672. Gohar Ali Gohar and Hamidullah Khan, "TNSM, Taliban Reject Darul Qaza: Democracy, Sharia Incompatible: Sufi," *Dawn* (Karachi), 4 May 2009.

673. Rahim Wardak has impressed this fact on the author on several occasions.

674. Bill Roggio and Thomas Joscelyn, "Pakistan's Jihad. In the War on Terror, Islamabad is Both With Us and Against Us," *The Weekly Standard*, 15 December 2008.

INDEX

A

affinity groups, 25, 31, 35, 44–45, 50–52, 77, 218, 348, 370

Afghan conflicts, 187–243
  and center–periphery, 210–13
  and corruption, 199–208
  ethnolinguistic conflicts, 189–93
  and gender issues, 223–35
  and governance, 241–43
  internal conflicts, 187–243
  and land/water rights, 221–23
  and modernization, 208–10
  outcome of, 372–74, 395–97
  and political leadership, 213–15
  religious conflicts, 194–99
  and warlords, 215–19

Afghan insurgents, 130–69
  and collateral damages, 297–99
  countering, 291–332
  response to, 299–304
  and security forces, 309–23
  spread of, 307–9
  stopping, 328–32

Afghan narcotics, 170–86
  countering, 179–86
  impact of, 177–79
  and insurgency, 170–86
  and options, 181–83

Afghan Taliban
  post-2001, 86–88, 136–39
  pre-2001, 136–39
  rise of, 81–86

Afghanistan
  aid to, 333–67
  chronology of, xvii–xxii
  conflicts in, 187–243, 372–74, 395–97
  corruption in, 199–208, 358–59
  demographics of, 236–38
  economy in, 359–62
  future of, 368–97
  governance of, 241–43, 352–54
  influence on, 270–80, 374–81, 390–95
  insurgents in, 130–69, 291–332
  last chance for, 381–88
  map of, vi–vii
  modernization of, 208–10
  new Afghanistan, 362–64
  reconstruction of, 333–67
  security forces in, 309–23
  solutions for, 238–41
  threat to, 119–24

Afridi, Mangal Bagh, 251

Afzali, Zalmay, 178–80, 184

aid
  to Afghanistan, 267, 285, 333–67
  buying into, 346–52
  and conflict, 333–67
  and corruption, 358–59
  divided efforts for, 341–43
  and economy, 359–62
  Kerry-Lugar bill, 267, 285, 364–67
  to Pakistan, 364–67
  success of, 343–45

Akhund, Mullah Birader, 138

Al Qaeda resilience, 3–17

al Yazid, Mustafa Abu, 120

al-Libi, Abu Yahya, 120

Al-Zawahiri, Ayman, 120

Amanullah, King, 57

Anders, Dave, 142

Atmar, Mohammed Hanif, 43, 122–23, 148, 199, 306, 320–26

Atta, Ustad Mohammed, 182, 190
Aziz, Maulana Abdul, 257–58

B
Babur, Nasrullah, 34, 247
Bahadur, Hafiz Gul, 255, 264
Baluchistan insurgency, 245–47
Barrett, Richard, 168
Belcher, Chris, 142
Bhittani, Turkistan, 264
Bhutto, Benazir, 34, 124–25, 247, 268
Bhutto, Zulfiqar Ali, 77, 247
Biden, Joseph, 217
bin Laden, Osama, 13, 38, 86–87, 94, 100,
    102, 108, 115, 121–24, 131, 142,
    273
binabd-al-Hakim, Maulavi Abd-al-Hadi
    "Pash Wa'l," 166
Blanchette, Richard, 143, 165–66, 238, 303
Brahimi, Lakhdar, 337, 345
Bugti, Nawab Akbar Shabaz Khan, 245
Burke, Edmund, 187
Burt, Richard, 89
Bush administration, 95–98, 269, 274, 300,
    365, 392

C
Callwell, C. E., 291
Carter, Ashton, 284
Cavoli, Chris, 153–54, 162–64, 327
CENTCOM, 305–6
center–periphery, 210–13
change, pushing, 54–60
chronology of Afghanistan, xvii–xxii
Churchill, Winston, 187
client–patron relationships, 46–50, 55, 189,
    218
Clinton, Hilary, 379
collateral damages, 297–99
conflicts
    and aid, 333–67
    and center–periphery, 210–13
    and corruption, 199–208

defined by, 21–60
ethnolinguistic conflicts, 189–93
and frontiers, 10–13
and gender issues, 223–35
and governance, 241–43
internal conflicts, 187–243
and land/water rights, 221–23
and legitimacy, 36–39
losing, 13–17
and modernization, 208–10
multiple, 4–10
outcome of, 372–74, 395–97
and political leadership, 213–15
religious conflicts, 194–99
support for, 13–17
and warlords, 215–19
winning, 289–397
corruption, 199–208, 358–59
Cowper-Coles, Sherard, 6
Craddock, Bantz, 178, 295
Cronin, Audrey Kurth, 128

D
Daoud, Mohammed, 45, 140
demographics, 236–38
Dobbins, James, 73, 103, 275, 327
Dostum, Abdul Rashid, 66, 190, 194,
    216–17, 222
Drummond, Jim, 42, 240, 354, 363
Durand Line, 4, 11, 26, 39, 62–63, 68, 71,
    74, 85–86, 259–60, 278, 283–84,
    392, 396
Durand, Mortimer, 62
dwellers in vortex, 61–88

E
Eide, Kai, 345
Elphinstone, Mountstuart, 21, 54, 59, 65,
    191
Es'haq, Mohammed, 387
ethnolinguistic conflicts, 189–93
ethnolinguistic divisions, 25–30
exiles, returning, 220–21

INDEX

F

Fahim, Mohammed Qassam, 204, 219, 309–10

failure, 6–17

faith, 30–36

Farivar, Massoud, 147

Fazlullah, Mullah, 255–56

Ferdinand, Franz, 3

Fidai, Mohammed Halim, 325–26

Frontiers, 10–13, 61–63, 71–77, 89, 280–83

future of Afghanistan, 368–97

future of Pakistan, 388–90

G

Gailani, Pir Sayid Ahmed, 35

Galbraith, Peter, 207

Gates, Robert, 103, 272, 306, 375, 379

gender issues, 223–35

Gentilni, Fernando, 294

Ghani, Ashraf, 7–8, 139, 167, 189, 201, 205–6, 211–12, 219, 334, 339–42, 345

Ghani, Owari, 260

Ghazi, Mullah Abdul Rashid, 257–58

Gilani, Yousaf Raza, 72, 261–62, 268

Gingrich, Newt, 283

glossary, xi–xv

Goethe, 107

H

Hadiri, Mohammed Ashraf, 238

Hainse, Marquis, 148, 153, 160, 162, 320, 327

Hanif, Alim, 43, 122–23, 148, 199, 320, 323, 325

Haq, Qazi Mahbubul, 251

Haq, Zia ul, 73–74, 77, 79

Haqqani, Husain, 73

Haqqani, Jaluladin, 79, 133, 140–42, 144, 174, 264, 269, 328, 331

Haqqani, Sirajjuddin, 123, 133, 140–42, 144, 174, 264, 269, 328, 331

hard men, 1–4, 10, 15–17, 141, 382, 396

Hayden, Michael, 110

Haynes, Jeff, 314, 316

Hekmatyar, Gulbuddin, 2, 32–33, 53–54, 70, 74, 82, 92, 133, 140–42, 151, 328, 331

Hoffman, Bruce, 99, 149

Holbrooke, Richard, 180, 183, 200, 217, 270, 291, 375

I

infidels, 2–16, 56, 85, 114, 122–28, 156–61, 173–77, 228–29, 329–31, 351

institutions and power, 39–44

insurgents

in Afghanistan, 130–69, 291–332

in Baluchistan, 245–47

countering, 291–332

and development, 159–62

ethnicity of, 142–49

funding, 168–69

intimidation by, 162–63, 169

leaders of, 140–42

and legitimacy, 153–58

and narcotics, 170–86

in Pakistan, 244–87

recruiting, 163–64

response to, 299–304

and security forces, 309–23

spread of, 307–9

strategy of, 149–53, 164–67

intelligence surveillance and reconnaissance (ISR), 305–6

internal conflicts, 187–243

Ittehad-i-Islam, Abdurrab Rasul Sayyaf, 29

J

Jackson, Michael, 228

Jalali, Ali, 311, 332, 352

Jalil, Mullah Abdul, 138

Jawad, Sayid T., 206

Joya, Malalai, 234

INDEX

K

Kakar, Malalai, 323
Kalakani, Habibullah, 65
Karzai, Hamid, 30, 53, 56–58, 67–68, 97–
  99, 170, 190–201, 206–7, 211–12,
  221, 229, 277, 298–300, 356, 384
Karzai, Walid, 42, 201
Kennan, George, 333
Kerry-Lugar bill, 267, 285, 364–67
Khailzad, Zalmay, 68, 157
Khalis, Younis, 32, 63, 138–39
Khan, Haji Juma, 201
Khan, Ismail, 66, 157, 217, 2275
Kharokhail, Massoud, 67–68, 155, 229,
  242, 325, 356
Khattak, Afrasiab, 265
Kilcullen, David, 100
Ki-Moon, Ban, 294
Kipling, Rudyard, 130
Kiyani, Ashfaq Pervez, 267–68
Kukikhel, Ahmad Khan, 259

L

Lafraie, Najibullah, 212
Laghmani, Abdullah, 307
Lamb, Graham, 325
lands
  and ethnolinguistic divisions, 25–30
  land rights, 221–23
  and people, 21–25
  in vortex, 19–103
legitimacy of conflicts, 36–39
Lockhart, Clare, 333

M

Mahmoud, Sufi Shah, 262
Mahnken, Tom, 324
Malik, Rahman, 261–62
Manawi, Fazel Ahmad, 197
Manningham-Butler, Eliza, 117
Mansur, Maulavi Abdul Latif, 138
Maples, Michael D., 119
maps, vi–vii

Massoud, Ahmad Shah, 32, 51–54, 66–69,
  92–94, 120–22, 140–41, 194, 207,
  279, 387
Massoud, Behtullah, 269
Mazlumyar, Ali Shah, 179
McChrystal, Stanley, 146, 156, 294, 304,
  315, 320, 328, 330, 340, 356, 375–79
McGonville, James C., 315, 353, 357
McKiernan, David, 294, 375
McNiece, Patrick, 103, 119, 133, 137, 142,
  164, 166, 265, 276–77
Medley, Dominic, 315
Mehsud, Abdullah, 249
Mehsud, Behtullah, 63, 70, 79–80, 136,
  249, 254–59, 264–65, 269
Mehsud, Hakimullah, 265
Mehsud, Qari Hussein Raess, 265
Mehsud, Rehman, 265
Milley, Mark, 99, 139, 147–48, 305, 312,
  320, 322
Milovic, Zoran, 163, 357
Mir, Haroun, 194
modernity, 1–2, 32–33, 208–10, 241
Mohammed, Baz, 305
Mohammed, Maulana Sufi, 389
Mohammed, Nek, 248–49, 252
Mohammed, Sufi, 256
Mohammedi, Mohammed Nabi, 138
Mojadidi, Sayid Sibghatullah, 35, 331
Mujahid, Anwar-ul-Haq, 139–40
Mullen, Mike, 297
Musharraf government, 95, 98–99, 248,
  257, 281, 301, 365, 388
Musharraf, Pervez, 95–101, 125, 150, 248,
  252, 267–71, 280–86, 388
Mu'tasim, Mullah Agha Jan, 138

N

Najibullah regime, 57, 69–70, 216, 385
Namdar, Haji, 258–59
narcotics trafficking, 170–86
  countering, 179–86
  impact of, 177–79

and insurgency, 170–86
and options, 181–83
threats from, 172–79
Nazir, Maulavi, 258, 264
Negroponte, John, 302
Nikpai, Ruhollah, 188
Noorzai, Haji Bashir, 201
Novak, Michael, 199

O

Obama administration, 123, 133, 269–71,
    274, 304, 366, 375–81
Obama, Barack, 240, 285, 375–76, 386
Olson, Eric, 302
Omar, Maulavi, 257
Omar, Mullah, 2, 13, 38, 49, 69–70,
    85–86, 102, 136–41, 144, 150, 165,
    173, 273
outsiders, 235–36

P

Pakistan
    aid to, 364–67
    future of, 388–90
    influence on, 270–80
    insurgents in, 244–87
    map of, vi–vii
    policy of, 90–100
    strategy of, 100–103
    threat to, 124–26, 283–87
    in vortex, 71–76
Pakistani insurgency, 244–87
    countering, 263–68
    fights with, 261–63
    ongoing insurgency, 268–70
    responding to, 257–61
    rise of, 247–51
    spread of, 251–57
patron–client relationships, 46–50, 55, 189,
    218
people
    and ethnolinguistic divisions, 25–30
    faith of, 30–36

and land, 21–25
in vortex, 61–88
Peters, Gretchen, 168, 174, 177
Petraeus, David, 133, 143, 151, 167–68,
    183–84, 236, 240, 266, 294, 313,
    324–25, 327, 357, 366
political leadership, 213–15
Pound, Ezra, 1–5
power
    and institutions, 39–44
    state power, 44–47, 65–68
    and warlords, 215–19
Princip, Gavrilo, 3–4
Provincial Reconstruction Teams (PRTs),
    354–58
Pushtuns
    governance of, 76–81
    neighbors of, 68–71
    and state power, 65–68
    world of, 64–65

Q

Qabir, Abdul, 138
qawms, 25, 31, 35, 44–45, 50–52, 77, 218,
    348, 370

R

Rabbani, Burnhaddin, 32
Rahimi, Mohammed Asif, 306
Rahman, Abdur, 30, 40, 71, 146, 209, 211, 307
Rahman, Malik, 261–62
Rahman, Qazi Zia, 260
Rashid, Ahmed, 115, 253, 287
Rasmussen, Anders Fogh, 381
reconstruction projects, 333–67
Registani, Saleh, 189, 240, 311, 327
Rehman, Khalil, 264
religious conflicts, 194–99
Riedel, Bruce, 114
Rodriguez, David, 295
Rogers, Will, 368
Rohde, David, 142
Rowswell, Ben, 320

S

Said, Shaikh, 120
Saikal, Mahmoud, 54
Salam, Mullah, 151
Saleh, Amrullah, 306
Sandeman, Robert, 61
security forces, 309–23
self-defense, 323–28
Shaefer, Teresita, 246, 267
Sharif, Nawaz, 268, 270, 280
Sherzai, Gul Agha, 145
Shinwari, Faisal Ahmad, 196–97
Smith, Adam, 244
special operation forces (SOF), 304–6
Special Operations Command (SOCOM),
    305
Stanekzai, Mohamed Mahmud, 99
state power, 44–47, 65–68

T

takfir, 2, 85, 112, 114, 126–27, 331
Taliban in Afghanistan
    post-2001, 86–88, 136–39
    pre-2001, 136–39
    rise of, 81–86
technology, 16, 33, 111, 118, 135, 255,
    306, 343
terrorism
    networked terrorism, 108–11
    threat to Afghanistan, 119–24
    threat to Pakistan, 124–26
    threats from vortex, 105–287
    transnational terrorism, 107–29
timeline of Afghanistan, xvii–xxii
totalitarians, 1–2, 197, 225, 233, 329
transnational terrorism, 107–29

U

United States, role of, 270–80, 374–81,
    390–95

V

Varughese, George, 239
vortex. *See also* Afghanistan; Pakistan
    born in, 81–86
    creating, 76–81, 90–95
    dwellers in, 61–88
    lands in, 19–103
    out of, 1–17
    shaping, 86–88
    threats from, 105–287
    transnational terror from, 114–19

W

Wahid, Mullah Abdul, 222
war ideas, 111–14
Ward, Mark, 309, 344, 356–57, 359, 362
Wardak, Rahim, 153, 199, 291, 298, 306,
    310, 312, 327
warlords, 52–54, 215–19
water rights, 221–23
Waziristan insurgency, 263–68
Weber, Max, 11
Weinbaum, Marvin, 287
Winslet, Kate, 228

Z

Zahir, King, 209, 213, 278, 340, 347, 393
Zaihuddin, Qari, 264, 265
Zardari, Asif Ali, 262, 268, 271, 274, 281,
    364, 388
Zia, Eshan, 43, 46, 215, 242, 336, 363
Zia, ul Haq, 73–74, 77, 79